Edward Thring's Theory, Practice and Legacy

Reviews of the First Edition

'Salute the first gymnasium, the first full-time gymnastics master, the first swimming pool in any school, a philosophy of health education, a balanced view of team games, and an abhorrence of professionalism and publicity.'
—David Emms, *Conference & Common Room*

'Thring was a forceful figure, absorbed in his school, determined to make it great; he had the knack of knowing how to develop its physical life, as his introduction of a gym and swimming pool show.'
—Jeremy Harvey, *Times Educational Supplement*

'The chapters on the cult of athleticism and the ideal of manliness will be of particular interest to the serious student.'
—Nicholas Parry, *British Journal of Physical Education.*

'Tozer argues convincingly that Edward Thring's philosophy of physical education was essentially an Athenian one.'
—Professor Vincent McClelland, *Victorian Studies*

'This book is a must for anyone seriously interested in the Victorian public school. Its historical, objective approach must recommend it. The author is to be congratulated on his initiative.'
—Professor Brian Simon, *History of Education*

'The text is well written, in a scholarly style. The Thringian principles of true manliness expressed in this book remind us again of an inane cult of masculinity and esprit de corps.'
—D L Willey, *Bulletin of Physical Education*

'Malcolm Tozer certainly seems to have turned over every stone and looked in every corner; this book is the proverbial mine of information.'
—Roger Bottomley, *Sport & Recreation*

'Malcolm Tozer has made a commendable effort to explain the reasons for change and to categorise the many influences which bring it about. I commend the book to all serious students in the field.'
—David McNair, *Canadian Journal of Physical Education*

'Anyone who wants to know how we have got where we are in physical education will enjoy this book.'
—Professor Peter McIntosh, *New Zealand Journal of Health, Physical Education & Recreation*

'Malcolm Tozer combined a distinguished educational career with research on "Muscular Christianity", leading to the publication of one of the best books on the subject.'
—Professor Hugh McLeod, *Kyrkohistorisk årsskrift*

Edward Thring's Theory, Practice and Legacy:

Physical Education in Britain since 1800

By

Malcolm Tozer

Cambridge
Scholars
Publishing

Edward Thring's Theory, Practice and Legacy:
Physical Education in Britain since 1800

By Malcolm Tozer

This book first published 2019

Cambridge Scholars Publishing

Lady Stephenson Library, Newcastle upon Tyne, NE6 2PA, UK

British Library Cataloguing in Publication Data
A catalogue record for this book is available from the British Library

ISBN (10): 1-5275-2818-9
ISBN (13): 978-1-5275-2818-5

Front cover: Thring in the 1858 cricket XI.
Frontispiece: *The Uppingham Cricket and Fives Songs*, 1857,
by Christian Reimers.
All illustrations by courtesy of Uppingham Archives unless credited
otherwise.

Health of body, health of intellect, health of heart, all uniting to form the true man, and being the common object of teacher and taught.

Edward Thring, *Education and School* (London: Macmillan, 1864), 32.

TABLE OF CONTENTS

TABLE OF ILLUSTRATIONS

All illustrations © Uppingham Archives unless credited otherwise.

Cecil Reddie of Abbotsholme © Abbotsholme School

John Badley of Bedales © Bedales School

George Howson of Gresham's © Gresham's School

Charlotte Mason of the PNEU (public domain)

Maurice Jacks of Mill Hill © Mill Hill School

Thorold Coade of Bryanston © Bryanston School

Kurt Hahn of Gordonstoun © Gordonstoun

John Royds of Uppingham

Squash in the Uppingham School Sports Centre, 2010

Badminton in the Sports Hall, 2010

Cricket on The Upper, 2014

Hike in Iceland, 2014

Swimming in the Sports Centre, 2014

Rugby football on The Leicester, 2014

INTRODUCTION

Physical Education at Thring's Uppingham was published in 1976 as a case study of the development and role of physical education at a mid-Victorian English public school. Interest in the history of physical education in Britain had been stimulated thirty years earlier by Peter McIntosh, the deputy director of physical education at the University of Birmingham. At this period, 1946 to 1965, Birmingham was the only university in Britain to offer an undergraduate course in physical education. His *Physical Education in England since 1800*, published in 1952 with a new edition in 1968, quickly became the standard reference book for his students and for those at the numerous teacher training colleges that specialised in physical education.[1] This was followed in 1957 by *Landmarks in the History of Physical Education*, a collection of essays edited by McIntosh that examined examples of physical education from classical Greece to modern-day America.[2] Jonathan May's *Madame Bergman-Österberg*, 1969, extended the field by presenting the history of a leading women's physical education college within the biography of its founder;[3] and then David Smith re-examined the general provision of physical education in British schools in the nineteenth and twentieth centuries in *Stretching Their Bodies: History of Physical Education*, 1974.[4] Historical enquiry was also supported by a wave of unpublished theses, including those by George Knaggs, David McNair, John Mallea, Colin Crunden and Ida Webb.[5]

Interest in the history of physical education fell away in Britain during the 1980s with the demise of the specialist teacher training colleges, their absorption by polytechnics and universities, and the change of academic focus to the scientific and cultural disciplines associated with sport.[6] The

---

[1] Peter McIntosh, *Physical Education in England since 1800* (London: Bell, 1952/68).
[2] Peter McIntosh, *Landmarks in the History of Physical Education* (London: Routledge, 1957/65).
[3] Jonathan May, *Madame Bergman-Österberg* (London: Harrap, 1969).
[4] David Smith, *Stretching Their Bodies* (Newton Abbot: David & Charles, 1974).
[5] See the bibliography for details.
[6] The polytechnics became universities from 1992.

history of sport and of individual sports, sport's role in the history of
culture, and the history of sport's contribution to images of masculinity
and femininity, all these now took precedence in research and
publications, and they have continued to do so until the present day.[7]
    The new century brought a revival of interest in the recent history of
physical education when observers noticed the over-representation and
relative success in international sport of former pupils from the minority of
schools that were independent of state provision when compared with that
of their team-mates who had attended state schools.[8] This difference was
particularly noticeable at the five summer Olympic Games from 2000 to
2016 and it led to enquiries from sports administrators, educationalists,
politicians and the press about the high quality of physical education and
sports coaching at independent schools and the traditions on which they
were built. An introductory chapter in *Physical Education and Sport in
Independent Schools*, an essay in *The International Journal of the History
of Sport* and an additional online chapter to the book, published in 2012,
2013 and 2016 respectively, sought to provide some answers.[9]
    Physical education thrives in today's independent schools whereas it
struggles to maintain its place on the timetable in many state schools and
academies.[10] This situation matches that for other ingredients of the
broader curriculum, including art, design, drama and music. All these
subjects are valued in independent schools for their contribution to holistic
education and to foster the talents of every pupil, but they find it difficult
to survive in schools that are supported by the state. As Anthony Seldon

---

[7] Murray Phillips and Alexander Roper, "History of Physical Education" in *The
Handbook of Physical Education*, ed. David Kirk, Doune Macdonald and Mary
O'Sullivan (Thousand Oaks, CA: Sage, 2013), 127-128.
[8] See, for example, *The Daily Telegraph*, February 2, 2010 (Aislinn Laing); July 5,
2012 (David Cameron); and August 2, 2012 (Lord Moynihan).
[9] Malcolm Tozer, "In the Beginning" in *Physical Education and Sport in
Independent Schools,* ed. Malcolm Tozer (Woodbridge: John Catt, 2012), 31-37;
Malcolm Tozer, "'One of the worst statistics in British sport, and wholly
unacceptable': The contribution of privately-educated members of Team GB to the
summer Olympic Games, 2000-2012," *The International Journal of the History of
Sport* 30, no. 12 (August 2013): 1436-1454; and Malcolm Tozer, "Going the extra
mile: The contribution of privately educated members of Team GB to the summer
Olympic Games of 2016" in *Physical Education and Sport in Independent Schools,*
ed. Malcolm Tozer (Woodbridge: John Catt, 2016), 318-338.
[10] Academies have more freedom than other state schools over their finances, the
curriculum, and teachers' salaries and conditions. A key difference is that they are
funded directly by central government instead of receiving their funds via a local
authority.

wrote in his review of *The Ideal of Manliness: the Legacy of Thring's Uppingham*:

> The mission of independent schools is far more ambitious than that found in most state schools; in addition to often excellent academic education, they frequently devote a third or more of their time to holistic all-round development, including sports and the arts. Opportunities to discover and nurture whatever talents each pupil has are seen as an entitlement; they are readily available, well taught and generously resourced. This, Malcolm Tozer asserts, is the legacy of Edward Thring's Uppingham. Music, art, gymnastics, cricket, crafts and drama flourished alongside the academic curriculum at this mid-Victorian school well before they were adopted elsewhere. What Thring termed 'the ideal of manliness' is the forerunner of today's 'wholeness'. The education of the whole man and the attention to the individual pupil are now the norm in all good schools, but it was not always so.[11]

A re-evaluation of the role of physical education at Thring's Uppingham is therefore timely, as is an examination of its legacy to modern practice.

Physical education's place in the curriculum of state schools was more secure in the forty years immediately after the Second World War, and in this period most independent schools learnt from state school best practice. Optimism in the profession was high. Teachers' hopes for the subject's future were realised in 1991 when physical education was included as a compulsory subject within the new National Curriculum. This was also the period when the history of physical education was included in college and university courses for physical education teachers, and when research and publication on historical themes were strong. Teachers who entered the physical education profession after the 1980s, however, learnt nothing of the subject's history from their training: it is not on the syllabus for GCE A-level courses in physical education; almost all universities ignore it in their physical education undergraduate and teacher training courses (Leeds Beckett is an exception); and not one of the hundred-plus books recommended by the Association for Physical Education (afPE) for the professional development of its members is on the history of the subject.[12] David Kirk asserts that this has contributed to the sidelining of physical education in many schools:

---

[11] Malcolm Tozer, *The Ideal of Manliness: the Legacy of Thring's Uppingham* (Truro: Sunnyrest Books, 2015), front papers.

[12] Some A-level and degree courses do, however, have short modules on the history of sport. See also www.afpe.org.uk/physical-education/recommended-readings/, accessed April 25, 2018.

The absence of history from physical education teacher education courses and, indeed, from the field in higher education more broadly, is one telling sign that the physical education community will be unlikely to make a substantial contribution to radical reform, and perhaps why physical educators have been excluded, under-represented or ignored in policy debates.[13]

He argues that it is impossible to imagine a secure future for physical education if its advocates are trapped in the present, preoccupied with immediate concerns, heads down rather than heads up, and with no conception of the subject's past, nor of its place in the holistic big picture.[14] Universities and learned societies, he continues, are best placed to lead physical education, in part by securing the conditions that will encourage physical education teachers to fight for their subject's place on the timetable, to plot its future within the National Curriculum, and to encourage change so that it moves with the times.[15] One of Kirk's conditions is to reinstate the history of physical education in their training.

"If I have seen further than others," wrote Isaac Newton, "it is by standing upon the shoulders of giants." *Edward Thring's Theory, Practice and Legacy* will inform trainee teachers, practising teachers and teacher trainers of the men and women who, from 1800 to the present day, strove to secure a place for physical education in the curriculum for all pupils. Let them stand on these shoulders! Historians of education, gender, society and sport will find new material to illuminate their fields of study.

*****

Physical Education at Thring's Uppingham was a facsimile of the text of my master's thesis, "The Development and Role of Physical Education at Uppingham School: 1850-1914", that was submitted to the University of Leicester in 1974.

Much has been added to create the present book. The Uppingham Archives have increased enormously since the 1970s through donations and acquisitions, and material on the Thring years has also been discovered in many other archives, including in Bonn and Ottawa. New research by Timothy Halstead, James Mangan, Bryan Matthews, Nigel

---

[13] David Kirk, *Physical Education Futures* (London: Routledge, 2011), 143-145.
[14] Such preoccupation persuaded one advocate, Baroness Benjamin, co-chair of the All-Party Parliamentary Group on *A Fit and Healthy Childhood,* to announce in the House of Lords on December 5, 2016 that "the teaching of PE … has not changed since the 1940s".
[15] Email message to author, April 30, 2018.

Richardson, Cormac Rigby and the author has brought new insights as well as new information. In addition, the context of developments at Uppingham and for Thring's legacy has been expanded to take account of the social, political, educational, physical educational and sporting changes from 1800 to the present day.

It would have been impossible to contemplate this study without ease of access to the Uppingham Archives. I thank the Trustees and Headmasters of the school for granting it and for allowing me to publish what I found. The six Headmasters who span the forty years are John Royds (1965-74), Coll Macdonald (1975-82), Nick Bomford (1982-91), Stephen Winkley (1991-2006), Richard Harman (2006-16) and Richard Maloney, (2016+). I owe a huge debt of gratitude to Brian Belk and Jerry Rudman, successive archivists, for guiding me through their treasures.

I am grateful to past and present colleagues at Uppingham and to Old Uppinghamians who have helped me over the years: Jeff Abbott, David Ashworth, Peter Attenborough, James Barnett, Chris Dossett, Peter Flower, Geoff Frowde, Ben Goss, Timothy Halstead, Brian Ma Siy, Bryan Matthews, Casey O'Hanrahan, Simon Pattinson, Nigel Richardson, David Shipton, Sarah Singlehurst, Harry Spry-Leverton, Hedley Stroud, David Stewart, Neil Waddell and Garth Wheatley. Beyond Uppingham, I have benefited from the advice and help of Richard Aldrich, Harry Armytage, Charles Barr, Ian Beer, Lillian Beisiegel, Gerald Bernbaum, Paul Blackman, Karen Brazier, Mary Byatt, Tim Chandler, Tim Clough, Heather Edwards-Hedley, Peter Elliott, Camilla English, Robert Fisher, Ken Hardman, Jo Harris, Martin Holmes, John Honey, Ruan Jones, Sue Kalaugher, Jane Kirby, David Kirk, Liz Larby, Roy Lowe, James Mangan, David McNair, Dave Mills, Gerald Murray, David Newsome, Leslie Oakley, Alison Oliver, Harold Perkin, Elaine Phillips, Robin Proctor, Cormac Rigby, Rachel Roberts, Natalie Sanderson, Norbert Schloßmacher, Brian Simon, Barry Sterndale-Bennett, Roy Stephenson, Paul Stevens, Harold Tarraway, John Tosh, Dale Vargas, Bob Wight and Alexander Wolfshohl. I must also thank the staff at the Bodleian Library, the British Library, the Cambridge University Library, Cornwall Libraries and the London Library, and the support team at Cambridge Scholars Publishing.

My wife, Elizabeth, has lived with Thring for all those forty years. I thank her for her interest and support.

Malcolm Tozer
Portscatho, Cornwall; 1 January 2019

CHAPTER ONE

PROLOGUE

Generalisations are dangerous and often unfair. The traditional picture of the Victorian and Edwardian English public school assumes that all such schools were founded on Thomas Arnold, *Tom Brown's Schooldays* and Rugby football. A Rifle Corps, Blues on the teaching staff, and an ethos of *esprit de corps* were all part of the system. The cult of athleticism reigned supreme.

Exchanging generalisations for particulars, some published but unsupported statements about Edward Thring and his school peddle errors that range from casual reporting to deliberate misrepresentation. The school was never a College, nor did Thring wish to become a Doctor of Divinity: the mock dignity of the doctor's top hat he found abhorrent.[1] Thring would have been amused by the claim that he helped to create the Football Association, even though the school did not play that code, but he would not have taken kindly to the lyrics of his *Football Song* being included in an *Anthology of Rugby Football*; he loathed the game and never permitted its play.[2]

The erroneous claims made by well-respected historians are more damaging for they misrepresent Thring's principles and practice, and their inaccuracies have been spread abroad by subsequent authors who rely on secondary sources for their research. David Newsome came to regret labelling Thring as "clearly of the muscular school"; Peter McIntosh realised that he had overstated his case when he claimed that Uppingham "took the lead in developing games"; but Dominic Erdozain remains adamant that physical education at Thring's school was merely "an

---

[1] For example, Brian Simon and Ian Bradley, *The Victorian Public School* (Dublin: Gill and Macmillan, 1975), 185; and Robert Mackenzie, *Almond of Loretto* (London: Archibald Constable & Co, 1905), 123.

[2] Fred Leonard and George Affleck, *A Guide to the History of Physical Education* (Philadelphia: Lea and Febiger, 1947), 174; Morris Marples, *A History of Football* (London: Secker & Warburg, 1954), 142, 151 for Association football; and Kenneth Pelmear, *Rugby Football: an Anthology* (London: George Allen and Unwin, 1958), 122.

outsourced remedy for vice and temptation". Even James Mangan could casually ignore his own research when, in the introduction to a new edition of *Athleticism in the Victorian and Edwardian Public School*, he asserted that Thring's stand against the cult of games "was defeated by philistine old boys, housemasters, parents and pupils – and the *general* ethos of the system".[3] Readers of *Edward Thring's Theory, Practice and Legacy* will form their own conclusions.

It is true that physical education in schools invariably reflects the philosophy of the total educational environment but it is also possible, as with Athens and Sparta in ancient Greece, to have fundamentally opposed ideals and systems within the same contemporary society. Thring's Uppingham was an Athens surrounded by Spartan strongholds and after his death the Spartans closed in and even claimed Thring as one of their own.

Between 1853 and 1887 a balanced programme of physical education flourished at Uppingham School within a sane but revolutionary educational framework. The spirit survived after Thring's death but at other schools, its philosophy lived on through the first half of the twentieth century, and finally its practice became more readily acceptable in the years after the Second World War. The first National Curriculum for Physical Education owed much to Thring's legacy.

The spirit, philosophy and practice of this physical education are as valid and valuable today as they were at Thring's Uppingham.

---

[3] David Newsome, *Godliness and Good Learning* (London: John Murray, 1961), 220 and conversation with the author, April 1978; McIntosh, *Physical Education*, 47 and conversation with the author, April 1968; Dominic Erdozain *The Problem of Pleasure: Sport, Recreation and the Crisis of Victorian Religion* (Woodbridge: Boydell Press, 2010), 107-108; and James Mangan, *Athleticism in the Victorian and Edwardian Public School* (London: Routledge, 2000), xxxiii.

CHAPTER TWO

ENGLAND IN THE 1850S:
"THE AGE OF EQUIPOISE"

I

In 1853, when Edward Thring arrived as the newly appointed headmaster of the grammar school in the market town of Uppingham, ninety miles north of London, he inherited a boys' school with about twenty-five boarders and a few day pupils. By the time of his death in 1887, Uppingham School had risen from relative obscurity in England's smallest county to become a great public school. In the course of those thirty-five years Thring's reputation as an educational reformer grew in stature and his work both in and from Uppingham gained national and international attention. No man and no institution can exist in a social vacuum, for there is always a continuous interchange with the enveloping society and these environmental influences are especially strong during the formative years of a new enterprise. Thring arrived at Uppingham in a period unique in the century: "Of all the decades in our history," wrote G. M. Young, "a wise man would choose the eighteen-fifties to be young in."[1]

The first quarter of the nineteenth century saw the emergence of a new society. The traditional order was challenged as the middle classes developed wealth and gained in confidence, and their members began to demand a role in government. The traditional values were similarly challenged now that the social, political, intellectual and spiritual standpoints inherited from the previous century would no longer suffice. First and foremost, society was becoming more humane. Government and law began to operate with more justice and with a greater sense of compassion, and individuals and groups were inspired to condemn the unfair practices, corrupt administration, biased legislation and intolerant institutions of earlier centuries.

---

[1] George Young, *Victorian England: A Portrait of an Age* (London: Oxford University Press, 1936/69), 77.

Adjustments to permit greater freedom and to enhance the rights of the individual citizen were effected during the second quarter of the century as a succession of government reforms ensured a period of active liberalism. These ranged from major changes to the Criminal Law in the 1820s to the repeal of the Corn Law in 1846, and included the Representation of the People Act of 1832 for the reformation of parliament. This momentum for change was maintained in the years immediately after Victoria ascended the throne in 1837 but it slackened in the late 1840s as conservative forces regained power. England was still a traditional oligarchy and those classes who did not enjoy the hereditary privilege of government continued to be disgruntled and, despite the efforts of Radicalism and Chartism, many anachronistic institutions remained intact until the second half of the century. The ruling classes had given much away but they had retained the material and machinery of their power.

The Great Exhibition of 1851 in London's magnificent Crystal Palace was the blazing symbol of the middle years of the century and the material representation of the nation's progress in science, industry, commerce and the arts. The exhibition confidently demonstrated to the world the success of the British way of life and confirmed Britain's growing international influence: it was a huge success. There was great national pride at this time, a pride built on industrial innovation, commercial triumph, civic prosperity and military might. Britain was the centre of world manufacture, commerce and banking, with free trade as the dominant philosophy. Relative freedom from economic worries made it a prosperous time, not only for the owners of factories, mills, businesses and land but also, through tax reductions on food and a shortening of the working day, for their workers. Britain was also secure. No large-scale wars disturbed the middle years of the century and the country's supreme naval strength protected its trading routes abroad and its island fortress at home.

"The Age of Equipoise", to borrow William Burn's label for the period of mid-Victorian political and social calm, was built within the framework of traditional institutions and the balance was one of conservatism against progress.[2] Many of these institutions were found wanting during the previous half-century and they had gradually been reformed. Now there was need for an interlude of consolidation before further modernisation could be initiated, a plateau amidst an era of acceleration and adjustment. A balance between order and change was also evident in the moral code of the time. Great trust was put in all institutions from the family outwards,

---

[2] Burn dated it from 1852 to 1867. William Burn, *The Age of Equipoise* (London: Allen and Unwin, 1964), passim.

each emphasising duty and restraint, yet at the same time a strong belief in free discussion and free thought was widespread. This age, with the Great Exhibition at its centre, was the foundation of the next sixty years and of the remainder of Queen Victoria's reign.[3]

II

That Uppingham School could climb from an obscure country grammar school to a great public school in a few years illustrates the peculiar and fluid nature of English education in the nineteenth century. The public boarding schools are a highly distinctive English educational institution yet they were not dominant in the early years of that century, and were even perhaps at the lowest point in their history. All provision of schooling in the British Isles was independent of the state before the implementation of William Forster's Elementary Education Act in 1870 and Arthur Balfour's Secondary Education Act of 1902 but popular demand for efficient secondary education for children above the age of eleven had been growing much earlier. Sons and daughters of the aristocracy and the gentry were customarily taught at home by governesses when very young and by tutors when older, but this was inevitably an expensive process. Offspring of the professional and middle-class families received their education at small private schools. As portrayed in the novels of Charles Dickens and William Thackeray, these schools varied greatly in standard and reputation but supervision by teachers was much stricter than that in the public schools.

There were also around eight-hundred old grammar schools at the turn of the nineteenth century. These were usually endowed schools for boys that owed their foundation to the generosity and public spirit of merchants, yeomen or clergy in Tudor times. Their restrictive curriculum and traditional teaching were much the same as they had been at the time of their creation, consisting mainly of rote learning of Latin and Greek in preparation for the universities at Oxford and Cambridge or for entry to the professions, especially the Church. These schools were generally shunned by the artisan classes, who viewed their curriculum as irrelevant to their needs, and so most were small and many dormant. Some public schools, Shrewsbury School and Rugby School for example, were originally grammar schools but had grown in size, status and renown under powerful headmasters and through improvements in communication

---

[3] George Kitson Clark, *The Making of Victorian England* (London: Methuen, 1962), 43.

and travel. In this way it was possible for a small school with purely local connections to develop into a boarding school that drew its pupils from across the country. Other public schools were collegiate foundations linked to colleges at the two universities: Eton College with King's College, Cambridge and Winchester College with New College, Oxford are two famous examples. These schools were wholly boarding from their inception.

Seven schools were recognised as public boarding schools at the beginning of the nineteenth century, and two more as public day schools. Shrewsbury, Rugby, Eton and Winchester, together with Harrow School, Westminster School and Charterhouse, comprised the former; St Paul's School and Merchant Taylors' School, both in London, were the latter. The poor quality of teaching was broadly similar at the public schools and the grammar schools but, in addition, the public schools had their own particular problems. Boarding facilities were crude and discipline was harsh. It was customary for the headmaster to have sole responsibility for pupil management in a school for several hundred boys aged eleven to nineteen, and occasionally even older. Bullying, rebellion, and mass flogging were all part of the reaction, whilst drinking, gambling and other vices were rife amongst the boys. The social reforms of the second quarter of the century eventually reached the public schools and soon they came under concerted attack. Their classical curriculum did not meet the needs of the Utilitarians and the boys' vices did not satisfy the code of the Evangelicals. Reforms had to be made. The work of a small group of headmasters, notably Samuel Butler and Thomas Arnold, saved the public schools from near extinction and brought them to a position where their influence was to be far reaching and long lasting.

Butler was headmaster at Shrewsbury from 1796 to 1836. During that time he not only revised the curriculum and teaching methods, and in the process made his school the foremost for the two classical languages, but he also introduced delegated management of school organisation to the senior boys through the introduction of a prefectorial system. Arnold was headmaster at Rugby from 1828 to 1840. He altered the teaching of classics, favouring Greek above Latin, and made both more relevant to nineteenth-century needs by applying them to examine contemporary social issues. Arnold saw his school as a microcosm of the ideal Christian-Platonic society as he strove to instil manliness in his charges. Decisive leadership, strong pastoral care, a morally earnest curriculum, the prefectorial system, a chapel-centred school life, and his weekly sermon: these were his means, and his purpose was to convert evil children into saintly adults. Material conditions improved with smaller dormitories, individual studies, and stricter adult supervision.[4]

The work of Butler, Arnold and other headmasters lifted the public schools to a position of eminence that they had not enjoyed since the seventeenth century. As a result, the sons of the aristocracy were removed from their home-based tutors to join the throng at the leading schools and the rise of the middle classes made them affordable to an even larger clientele. By the end of the 1850s it was essential that the sons of respectable families should attend these schools, not least to learn from the aristocrats how to become gentlemen. The number of public schools increased three-fold by 1860 to meet this demand.[5]

Some of the new schools were founded as joint-stock companies and so were originally termed proprietary schools to distinguish them from the nine public schools that were above them in the social pecking order, and the numerous private schools below. Cheltenham College and Marlborough College are examples. As their fame grew so they would soon be grouped with the nine as public schools. A number of long-established grammar schools were now gaining national reputations for good teaching under forceful headmasters and the best were granting themselves public school status or were being raised to it by ambitious parents. The schools at Sherborne, Tonbridge and Uppingham were in this category. By the time of the Schools Inquiry Commission, set up under Lord Taunton's chairmanship in 1864, there were the nine original public schools, 122 proprietary schools (some with public school status), and about 800 grammar schools of which a few were well known.[6]

III

Uppingham Grammar School was founded in 1584. Like its sister foundation in the county town of Oakham, it was established by Robert Johnson, later Archdeacon of Leicester. Johnson provided each town with a school-room and a hospital; the latter gave lodging for the schoolmaster

---

[4] For more on Butler and Arnold see Tozer, *Manliness*, 33-43, 206.

[5] John Tosh, *A Man's Place: Masculinity and the Middle-class Home in Victorian England* (New Haven: Yale University Press, 1999), 117-118; John Tosh, *Manliness and Masculinities in Nineteenth-century Britain: Essays on Gender, Family and Empire* (Harlow: Pearson Longman, 2005), 85.

[6] The Taunton Commission examined all schools between the public school nine and the mass of private and elementary schools. It led to the Endowed Schools Act of 1869 which in turn created the Endowed Schools Commission which had extensive powers over the administration of individual schools.

and the usher, and the "fifteen poor people" over whom the two teachers also served as warden and sub-warden.[7] The two schools shared an endowment derived from rents and tithes totalling £266 – 13s – 4d.[8] Johnson ordained that the schoolmaster, "an honest and discreet man, master of arts, and diligent in his place", should teach freely all the "grammar scholars" born in the town.[9] Some exhibitions were provided to permit able boys to proceed to the universities. In 1587 both schools were granted their charters of foundation, and both were governed by these statutes until new schemes were formulated in 1874 in the wake of the Endowed Schools Act.

The hospital at Uppingham ceased to provide residential care in the early eighteenth century and the hospitalers then received their alms in their own homes. The hospital building was taken over by the school to provide boarding quarters for boys from distant homes and a few shed-like studies were built across the quadrangle against the school-yard wall. After this period of relative prosperity, pupil numbers fell in the remainder of the century, largely through increased rivalry from the school in Oakham. In this period Oakham boys won most of the Johnson exhibitions to Cambridge University. By the turn of the century, however, Uppingham was again attracting boarding pupils and twenty new studies were built to accommodate the swelling numbers. By 1811 another decline had set in and the number of boarders dropped to thirty.

Henry Holden was appointed headmaster in 1845 and under his leadership the school steadily grew in numbers and in reputation. He increased the teaching staff to include four masters, plus an assistant teacher to help with writing and arithmetic. The school had sixty-three boys in 1850 and the visiting examiner noted in his report to the governors of 1848 that "the high character of the School is becoming more known every day and in distant parts of England".[10] Despite this praise, the school remained an undistinguished market-town grammar school; even its reputation in the county was overshadowed by that of its neighbour and

---

[7] The usher was the assistant teacher. The term was still in use when Thring arrived at the school. Charles Bingham, *Our Founder* (Uppingham: Hawthorn, 1884), 41. Bingham was a boy at the school from 1865 to 1871. He won a scholarship to Trinity College, Cambridge, took Holy Orders, and became Rector at Boroughbridge in Kent.

[8] About £30,000 in 2018.

[9] Bingham, *Founder*, 42.

[10] Letter from William Sewell, October 6, 1848. In the Uppingham Archives (Hereafter UA). Sewell later served as Warden (or headmaster) of Radley College from 1853 to 1861.

rival in Oakham. When Holden was appointed headmaster of Durham School in 1853, taking eleven of the younger boys with him, Thring was left with twenty-five boarders and a few day boys. In the next twelve years he was to raise this figure to three-hundred.[11]

IV

At the beginning of the nineteenth century scant attention was paid to physical activity as an ingredient of education. Although there was undoubtedly an increase in such activity in schools by the middle of the century, it is hard to ascribe the changes to the intended or conscious efforts of educationalists, other than the introduction of prescribed exercises in some elementary schools from the 1830s.[12]

Well before 1800 games had been played in the public schools. Thomas Gray wrote in 1748 in his *Distant Prospect of Eton College* of the chase of the "rolling Circle's speed" and the urging of "the flying Ball". Cricket, boating and fives were popular there in the 1760s and instructors were on hand to teach boxing, fencing and dancing; all sports were organised by the boys for their own recreation.[13] Less formal but seemingly more popular pastimes included fighting, poaching and other forms of general lawlessness. In this same period Adam Smith travelled widely across continental Europe examining, among other things, the various educational systems. His experiences led him to plead in his *Wealth of Nations,* published in 1776, for physical exercises to be included in a projected state-provided education; their introduction was necessary to alleviate the cramping effects of the classroom.[14]

Continental influences were felt again in the 1820s when the work of the German gymnast Johann Guts Muths was approved for use in the British armed forces. One of his disciples, Per Heinrich Clias, was appointed in 1822 to organise courses for the Army and the Royal Navy, and in 1825 an English translation of Clias's work, *An Elementary Course of Gymnastic Exercises*, was published in London.[15] Thomas Arnold was

---

[11] For more on Holden's headmastership, see Bryan Matthews, *By God's Grace: A History of Uppingham School* (Maidstone: Whitehall Press, 1984), 62-72.

[12] George Knaggs, "A Study of the Historical Development of Physical Education in English Schools to 1945." (DEd diss., University of Houston, 1957), 188-194.

[13] Alicia Percival, *Very Superior Men* (London: Charles Knight, 1973), 21.

[14] Howard Barnard, *A History of English Education from 1760* (London: University of London Press, 1947/64), 45.

[15] McIntosh, *Physical Education*, 80. See also Per Clias, *An Elementary Course of Gymnastic Exercises* (London: Sherwood, 1825), passim. Clias was Swiss.

another early enthusiast for German gymnastics. Between 1819 and 1828, before going to Rugby, he ran a small private school at Laleham in the Thames Valley. A "gallows" and a "pole" were erected in the grounds to foster gymnastic exercises for both teacher and pupils.[16] In this same period Samuel Wilderspin, in his *On the importance of educating the infant children of the poor* (1823), advocated the provision of play areas in schools, together with equipment for games.[17]

Lord Byron talked his way in to the Harrow XI for the inaugural cricket match against Eton at Lord's in 1805, although he was keener to indulge in the post-match drunken festivities than to make his mark in the game.[18] Cricket, football and rowing were introduced at Westminster School in London from 1808 when the headmaster, William Carey, curtailed the boys' freedom to roam and restricted them to the school's grounds.[19] Boys arranged all their own games at Shrewsbury during the long headmastership of Samuel Butler from 1798 to 1836; Butler saw no educational value in them.[20]

The lawless recreations of the boys came under attack during the reforms of the public schools in the second quarter of the century. George Butler, headmaster of Harrow in Byron's time, was probably quickest off the mark; by the time of his retirement in 1829 games had effectively been compulsory for many years. The boys controlled everything but the licence to impose compulsion on a school of over 200 came from Butler.[21] One of the earliest actions of Benjamin Kennedy when he succeeded the other Butler at Shrewsbury was to provide a playing-field for cricket so that the boys might have "the means of innocent amusement and exercise in their leisure hours", but he allowed the boys' hunt to remain.[22] Thomas Arnold thought otherwise on his appointment to Rugby in 1828, for he banned hunting and poaching, and disbanded the boys' pack of hounds. The check on these pursuits led to an increase in other forms of recreation on the school site. Cricket had long been popular and football had an ancestry older than 1822 when William Webb Ellis "with a fine disregard

---

[16] Arthur Stanley, *The Life and Correspondence of Thomas Arnold* (London: Murray, 1844/52), 66.

[17] Barnard, *English Education,* 60.

[18] Christopher Tyerman, *A History of Harrow School* (Oxford: Oxford University Press, 2000), 159.

[19] Timothy Chandler, "Emergent Athleticism: Games in Two English Public Schools," *The International Journal of the History of Sport* 5, no. 3 (1988): 313.

[20] Chandler, "Emergent Athleticism," 321.

[21] Tyerman, *Harrow,* 192.

[22] George Fisher, *Annals of Shrewsbury School* (London: Methuen, 1899), 189.

for the rules" picked up the ball for the legendary birth of Rugby football. Organised games were firmly entrenched at Eton in the 1830s when the future Bishop Patteson, and Thring's contemporary, threatened to leave the field unless the use of bad language ceased.[23]

By 1850 cricket, football, rowing and various racket games were all common at public schools. Their development was not universally encouraged but, where it was, the role was purely recreational. The boys were responsible for the organisation of the games, though sometimes they had the aid of masters. Masters too would occasionally join the boys in play. In the same period, exercises based on the gymnastics of Guts Muths were being introduced in elementary schools.

---

[23] Charlotte Yonge, *Life of Patteson* (London: Macmillan, 1873), 40.

CHAPTER THREE

UPPINGHAM GRAMMAR SCHOOL, 1850-1857: "THE WICKETS ARE SET"

I

Geoffrey Hoyland's claim that Thring "made Uppingham" is not entirely true for in many small but important ways the transformation from country grammar school to well-known public school was initiated by his immediate predecessor, Henry Holden.[1] Holden, aged thirty-two on his appointment, was "Head-master and Warden" of "Uppingham Grammar-School" from 1846 to 1853. He was a sound scholar with a first in Greats from Balliol College, Oxford and in Holy Orders. His pupils remembered him as an eloquent preacher and a kindly pastor: he was on friendly terms with the boys, often visiting them in their studies during the evening.[2] Holden made many material improvements to the school, especially in the boys' boarding accommodation, and he introduced the prefectorial system to give senior boys some delegated authority for school discipline. Prefects were called praepostors, a term that is still used at the school today. He also founded the school library, started the school magazine, and encouraged its development with occasional contributions.[3] *The Hospitaler*, first published in January 1851, consisted largely of literary articles and contained little sporting intelligence when compared to school magazines of a generation later.

In Holden's time the boys rose at 6.30am, first school lasted from 7.00am to 8.30am, and was followed by breakfast. Second school ran from 10.00am to noon, with dinner at 1.00pm. On two days each week there was no afternoon school and on these half holidays the boys played

---

[1] Geoffrey Hoyland, *The Man Who Made a School* (London: S.C.M. Press, 1946), passim.
[2] *Uppingham School Magazine* (Hereafter *USM*), January 1888, 6 and June 1871, 140. (UA).
[3] *USM*, January 1888, 7.

games.[4] Recreational facilities at this time included two ball courts, a cricket field at the east end of the town, and the "Tectum".[5] The ball courts were used for bat-fives, a game played with a small hard ball and bats shaped liked battledores. The cricket field, later to be called The Upper, had been used by the school since 1827 when "Sir Gerald Noel, Bart." was

> requested to let the Governors on Rent, his Close of Grass Land in Uppingham Parish situate on the East side of Seaton Lane ... to be used as and for a Play Ground by the scholars of Uppingham School.[6]

This ground, which was enlarged in Holden's time, was used at various times for football and hockey as well as for cricket.[7]

The Tectum is first mentioned in the September 1852 edition of *The Hospitaler* in an editorial on building changes.[8] Here "it promises to be a tolerable play area in wet weather", and a few months later the editor reported that it was used for cricket and fives when "the melancholy days are come".[9] The same editorials mention the possibility of converting the Tectum "into a sort of gymnasium" for "amusement and healthful recreation", and the installation of simple apparatus was discussed:

> a ladder placed horizontally about seven feet from the ground throughout its length would afford an excellent opportunity of practising feats of strength in swinging and going forward by help of the hands alone, without interfering with any other games that might at other times be played.[10]

Nothing however was constructed and the Tectum remained solely an under-cover play area until Thring's time when an Eton fives court was built within it.

Cricket, hockey and football were the games played on the half holidays. The earliest reference to cricket in the school is in 1815 when

> a cricket match was played at Uppingham between eleven young gentlemen of that school and the same number of Oakham school, which

---

[4] Thomas Bonney, *Memories of a Long Life* (Cambridge: Metcalfe, 1921), 11.
[5] 'Memoranda of System, Discipline, etc' in the Henry Holden Collection. (UA).
[6] Henry Bothamley, *Some Notes on the History of Uppingham School*, 7. (UA). Bothamley was at Uppingham from 1897 to 1902.
[7] *USM,* January 1888, 3-4.
[8] The Tectum was also known as The Barn: *The Hospitaler*, September 1852, 97. (UA).
[9] *The Hospitaler*, November 1852, 129.
[10] *The Hospitaler*, November 1852, 129.

was won by the latter at one innings, the Oakham single innings being 89, and the Uppingham two innings being only 36.[11]

By the 1830s there was a "properly constituted Eleven" and matches were played against Uppingham Town, Rockingham Castle and Stamford.[12] A few years later a match was played with Oundle Grammar School and from 1841 the lists of all school XIs were recorded.[13] William Earle joined the teaching staff as "Usher and Sub-Warden" in 1850 and he quickly took an interest in the school's cricket. He played with the boys and in the School XI from that year and he presumably did some coaching.[14] During the early 1850s the games against the Town, Stamford and Rockingham Castle were maintained, and the first match against former pupils, known as Old Boys, was played in 1852; the school winning by 41 runs, Earle scoring 9.[15]

Cricket was certainly the most popular recreation in Holden's time, and this "most manly of games" was the subject of several editorials in *The Hospitaler* and also of some correspondence.[16] Occasional "field days" were made compulsory by the senior boys and fines were levied by them for non-attendance, although they were not always collected.[17] The more ardent players complained at the lukewarm response of "idle fellows", whereas the less talented complained at the monopolisation of the ground by the XI and the lack of "proper instruction and opportunity".[18]

A form of hockey had been played at the school in the seventeenth century and it may have persisted in the intervening years for it was the principal winter game in the 1850s.[19] It even transferred to the ice in severe winters.[20] Whether on ice or *terra firma*, play was much the same: any number of boys on each side employed inverted curved-handled walking-sticks to beat a small hard ball around a ground that had very few

---

[11] Robin Rome, Uppingham: The Story of a School – 1584-1948. Typescript, 1948, 38. (UA). Rome was at Uppingham from 1902 to 1906. He became a lieutenant-colonel in the Royal Artillery.

[12] Rockingham Castle was the home of the hereditary governor.

[13] William Patterson, *Sixty Years of Uppingham Cricket* (London: Longmans, 1909), 4.

[14] *The Hospitaler*, June 1853, 33.

[15] *The Hospitaler*, June 1852, 93.

[16] For example *The Hospitaler*, May 1852, 77.

[17] *The Hospitaler*, February 1851, 17.

[18] *The Hospitaler*, June 1852, 7 and 93.

[19] Bothamley, *Some Notes*, 4; *The Hospitaler*, October 1852, 14.

[20] *The Hospitaler*, February 1851, 27.

limits.[21] Football may have been played at Uppingham before 1850 and there were certainly attempts to introduce it in 1852.[22] The football advocates, who had played the game at their previous schools, pressed their case but they also conceded that hockey was better when the whole school formed the two sides for it allowed the younger boys to gain "some sport".[23] Their wish for the occasional game of football did not, however, meet with general approval.

Thomas Bonney, who was in the cricket XI in 1852, recalled that on half holidays there was a "calling-over" or roll-call but that the headmaster readily gave leave of absence to the older boys.[24] They were then free to roam the countryside and to swim in the Stockerston brook (two miles to the west) or in the river Welland at Thorpe (four miles to the south). Skating and sledging replaced swimming as the winter recreations.[25] "The result of our freedom", Bonney recalled

> was that several of us took an interest in natural history; some collected birds' eggs; a few, like myself, looked after fossils ... Churches or other buildings in neighbouring villages often had features of interest ..., and I still have sketches taken in these rambles. Our head was interested in these things, and some of us are indebted to him for a more liberal education than schools of that day generally provided.[26]

Bonney went on to become Professor of Geology at London University, President of the British Association and President of the Alpine Club.

Holden exchanged Uppingham for Durham School in August 1853. He left behind twenty-five boarders, "mostly old, waiting for Exhibitions", Earle, a "salaried undermaster", and an "inefficient writing master".[27] A month later, with the school "in full operation, if a small rebellion deserves this name", Edward Thring took up his office as headmaster of

---

[21] Bonney, *Memories*, 43; Matthews, *By God's Grace*, 68.

[22] Rome, Uppingham, 43.

[23] *The Hospitaler*, October 1852, 121.

[24] Bonney, *Memories*, 12. Bonney was Captain of School in 1851-1852.

[25] *The Hospitaler*, April 1853, 1.

[26] Bonney, *Memories*, 12.

[27] Edward Thring's Diary, 6 December 1858. (UA). (Hereafter Diary). All diary extracts from April 1862 to September 1886 are taken from George Parkin, *Life and Letters of Edward Thring* (London: Macmillan, 1898), the original diaries having been destroyed. A comparison of the contents of the surviving first and last diaries with the extracts quoted in Parkin indicates that the editor made frequent, but generally light, alterations.

Uppingham Grammar School.[28] When Holden eventually retired from Durham in 1881, he became the vicar at South Luffenham, only a few miles from Thring's Uppingham.[29]

II

Bonney's memories of relaxed school bounds and a freedom to roam the countryside are matched by those of John Skrine, one of Thring's early pupils from 1861 to 1867 and later a master. He recalled the "large liberty to ramble where we liked"; the only bounds were some of the back streets in the town with their pot-houses.[30] In the winter the boys skated and snowballed or perhaps followed the hounds.[31] Before the introduction of the athletic sports in 1859, cross-country runs involving much jumping of hedges, fences and streams were popular; one boy would lead, plotting his own course, and the rest would endeavour to follow.[32] Competitions at jumping the numerous toll-bars on the roads approaching the town were also common. Another early form of athletics was the paperchase, and this maintained its popularity right to the end of the century. Young boys took it in turn to provide the paper; the "foxes" were given an eight-minute start; and masters occasionally joined in the ten- or fifteen-mile journeys around the Rutland countryside.[33] These early runs involved the whole school and the virtues of their arduous nature were extolled with cries of "let us remember we are boys, aye, and English ones too, who ought not to be frightened at a cold or some slight ailment".[34]

Thring maintained friendly relationships with local farmers to ensure that his boys might roam without fear of punishment: the *School Rules* contained some related to the use of the countryside and an annual donation to the Rutland Agricultural Show undoubtedly helped. Boys who broke Thring's countryside rules were restricted to the main roads for their walks.[35] On one of the seemingly few occasions when a local farmer did complain, Thring was not particularly sympathetic: his diary recorded "I

---

[28] Diary, December 20, 1858.
[29] *USM,* January 1888, 4.
[30] John Skrine, *A Memory of Edward Thring* (London: Macmillan, 1890), 11, 33.
[31] The Cottesmore is the local hunt. *USM,* March 1924, 5.
[32] Willingham Rawnsley, *Early Days at Uppingham under Edward Thring* (London: Macmillan, 1904), 82.
[33] *USM,* November 1864, 377; February 1881, 34.
[34] *USM,* November 1864, 377.
[35] *USM,* November 1864, 377; *School Rules,* 1869. (UA).

don't think he can have been at a public school".[36] These friendships with land-owners and tenant-farmers were also essential if the boys were to get out into the meadows and woods to study nature at first hand. A journalist visiting the school once commented on the absence of "high fences and notices to trespassers", a feature he commonly found at other schools.[37] Thring was an ardent rambler and many half holiday excursions were taken in the company of boys or masters, accompanied by his Old English Sheepdog, Queer. Masters were also encouraged to roam the countryside with boys.[38]

Winter rural recreations also remained popular. Skating would be given public leave by Thring; snowballing was allowed but only on the cricket field; ice slides were common in the school quadrangles; and the construction of sledges had to meet the requirements of the *School Rules*.[39] The standing of all these rural pursuits was much the same throughout Thring's headmastership. The *Uppingham School Magazine* of the 1870s contained many articles reporting on "walks in the countryside", and John Graham's memories of the 1880s recall those of Bonney and Skrine.[40]

As at most schools of the period that were close to beaches, lakes and rivers, swimming was a popular summer recreation. Thring's first boys inherited the bathing places in the Stockerston brook and the Welland at Thorpe. The brook contained in its meandering stream a number of pits "so small, that when some dozen fellows are disporting themselves there, they more resemble herrings in a barrel than anything else".[41] These pits often silted up and subscriptions were occasionally levied to put this bathing place in "tolerable order". A better swim was to be had in the Welland even though that meant a four-mile walk each way.

III

"On the tenth of September 1853", Thring was later to record in his diary,

---

[36] Diary, June 22, 1860.

[37] W. Chas Sargent, "Uppingham School," *The Ludgate Illustrated Magazine,* May, 1894, 72.

[38] *USM*, March 1925, 5; Hoyland, *Man Who Made*, 53.

[39] *School Rules*, 1867. (UA); Rawnsley, *Early Days*, 99; *School Rules*, 1877. (UA).

[40] John Graham, *Forty Years of Uppingham* (London: Macmillan, 1932), 5. Graham was a boy at the school from 1888 to 1894. He returned as a master in 1900 on graduation from New College, Oxford.

[41] *The Hospitaler*, May 1852, 80.

> I entered on my headmastership with the very appropriate initiation of a whole holiday and a cricket match in which I recollect I got 15 by some good swinging hits to the delight of my few pupils.[42]

There were just enough boys and masters for the two teams. Both Thring and Earle played regularly for the school XI and the first recorded team photograph, of the 1858 XI, includes both masters; the boys wear their Sunday best.[43] Thring played in his clerical dress, having handed his large black wide-awake hat to the umpire. He bowled "a fast underhand ball, with some spin, and sometimes more than one bounce before reaching the wicket. Sometimes also … the ball would reach the wicket-keeper's hands without touching the ground at all."[44] Even when overarm bowling was legalised in 1864, he would continue to surprise the boys with his style. Willingham Rawnsley, a pupil from 1855 to 1864 and later a master at the school from 1871 to 1878, recalled that the headmaster's batting was decidedly "rustic" and that he usually fielded close to the batsman at second slip.[45] The early diary contains details of matches against Stamford, Rockingham, Market Harborough and the Old Boys.[46] The relaxed jollity of these matches is well recorded in Thring's two cricket songs, *The Uppingham Cricket Song* (1856) and *The Rockingham Match* (1858).[47]

Thring had been a keen fives player as a boy at Eton and also as an undergraduate at Cambridge, and he quickly introduced the Eton version of the game at Uppingham. A court was built to the Eton specifications (complete with buttress, step, ledge and dead man's hole) within the old Tectum, now with some glass in its roof to improve the light.[48] The new game soon proved to be a popular wet-weather recreation. Hockey was played on the cricket field during the winter months to occupy the gap between morning school and dinner at 1.00pm.[49] As in Holden's time,

---

[42] Diary, December 20, 1858.

[43] In UA.

[44] Bowling evolved from underarm to round-arm in 1835 and then to overarm in 1864. Patterson, *Uppingham Cricket*, 49.

[45] Rawnsley, *Early Days*, 88; Patterson, *Uppingham Cricket*, 49. Rawnsley entered Corpus Christi College, Oxford on leaving Uppingham.

[46] Diary, May 23, 1859; August 22, 1859; June 2, 1860; and June 10, 1860.

[47] See later in this chapter.

[48] For more on Eton fives, see Dale Vargas and Peter Knowles, *A History of Eton Fives* (London: Quiller Press, 2012), passim. The Tectum was demolished when the Chapel was built, and the fives court was installed across the quadrangle. *USM*, 1920, 24.

[49] Rawnsley, *Early Days*, 81.

there was no limit to the number of players and the rules were few; this meant that those who did not play right-handed could be "shinned".[50] Long spells of players dribbling with the ball were a feature of the game whereas team-play and tactics were negligible.[51]

Football was probably introduced to the school in Thring's first winter, 1853; it was certainly played the following year.[52] Robert Rice's prize Latin essay, "On Football", composed in December 1854 provides the earliest reference to the game. A match was described in the style of a classical epic: the scene was carefully set and several forbidding omens were exacted. Thring by implication played and an umpire was appointed. This new game, the author inferred, was devised by Thring to serve as a modern counterpart to the battles of Homeric times:

> And then they all snatched at the ball to move it forwards in various ways. (For recently the Master in Charge had taught them how the peoples of old had often had contests with races that were fierce.) In the same way now they all ran together in throngs: then again in flight they made different patterns as they ran, imitating the epic battles of old as they charged.[53]

Other sources refer to the game, soon to be called Uppingham Football, being "invented" by Thring but an examination of the first set of printed rules of 1857 shows that it was similar to the codes played at other schools.[54] Uppingham football owed most to the Eton Field Game with additions from the early Rugby game.[55]

The game was played on an oval pitch that tapered towards goals at each end; each goal was about twenty feet wide and seven feet high, the top marked by a rope; a large leather-covered oval ball was used. The object of the game was to kick the ball through the opponents' goal. A strict off-side rule demanded that all players had to be behind the ball, and the ball could only be handled if it had been caught cleanly or off its first bounce. The catcher could run with the ball or kick it but he was forbidden from passing it to a team-mate. Long fly-kicks, rather than lengthy dribbling of the ball along the ground, were a notable feature of the game.

---

[50] *USM*, November 1865, 270.

[51] Rawnsley, *Early Days*, 81.

[52] 'On Football' by Robert Rice (a pupil from 1852 to 1856) in Essays and Translations, a manuscript volume of work by boys, 1854-1864. (UA). Rice served as Warden (headmaster) of St Columba's College in Dublin, Ireland's premier school, from 1867 to 1891.

[53] Rice, 'On Football'. I thank Peter Attenborough for the translation.

[54] *USM*, April 1924, 67.

[55] Not the post-1871 Rugby Union version.

Prolonged "bullies" resulted when a player was tackled by the opposition; these were similar to the modern Rugby football scrum, with players stooping to drive the opposition towards their own goal, except that the ball could not be heeled backwards. A bully could result in a goal if the ball was forced under the rope.[56]

As *The Football Song* suggests (see the next section for the text) Thring intended the game to be a hearty "free fight"; "it was an opportunity devised by Providence to enable small boys to work off their original sin".[57] The rough and tumble of the game tested the boys to channel their pugnacity and it taught them to give and receive hard knocks in "good temper".[58] The whole school used to play at once as "two great opposing armies"; fifty each side by the late 1850s, distinguished by red and white bands tied around the waist. Thring and some assistant masters joined in.[59] In 1862, when he had "given up regular playing", Thring was asked to join in the match between the Sixth Form and the rest of the School. That evening he wrote in his diary:

> I could not help thinking with some pride, what Head Master of a great school ever played a match at football before. Would either dignity or shins suffer it? I think not.[60]

He played again the following week![61]

IV

In 1854 Thring appointed his first classics master, John Blakiston; a second, Robert Hodgkinson, arrived a year later together with Herr Schäfer.[62] The teaching team now numbered five. Schäfer taught music and German: he received the same salary and status as Hodgkinson in agreement with Thring's assessment that all masters were "equally superior men".[63] No more is known about Schäfer except that he may have come from Bonn.[64] Schäfer stayed at Uppingham for just one year and was

---

[56] *USM*, April 1924, 67.
[57] Hoyland, *Man Who Made*, 48-49; *USM*, September 1958, 119.
[58] Hoyland, *Man Who Made*, 49.
[59] *USM,* February 1888, 59.
[60] Diary, February 14, 1862.
[61] Diary, February 22, 1862.
[62] I have been unable to discover Schäfer's first name.
[63] Both received £120 per annum: Parkin, *Life*, 1:84, 329.
[64] The *Bonner Kalender* recorded a Herr Schäfer living at Saugaße 1, just north of Münsterplatz, from 1848 until 1855 but not thereafter.

succeeded by Christian Reimers, aged twenty-nine. Both Schäfer and Reimers were probably directed to Uppingham by Thring's brother-in-law, Dr Friedrich Breusing, who ran a boarding school for German and English pupils in that city. Thring looked to Prussia for men to teach subjects that were beyond the expertise of British graduates of the 1850s, including art, German, music and science. Reimers taught art and music. A gifted cellist, he had studied in Leipzig from 1846 and often played under Ferdinand David's leadership with Mendelssohn's Gewandhaus orchestra. His skill as a caricaturist has left a vivid record of musical life in the city when the composer was at his peak.[65] Reimers moved to live with Robert and Clara Schumann in Düsseldorf in 1850 when Schumann became conductor of the city's orchestra and he joined their circle of friends including Brahms and Liszt. When Schumann entered a mental asylum in Bonn in 1854, Reimers was one of the most regular visitors, giving daily reports to Clara: she had been advised by his doctors to stay away.[66] The Schumanns' two sons, Ludwig and Ferdinand, joined Breusing's school.[67]

The appointment of Schäfer and then Reimers at Uppingham was surprising in several ways. First, mid-Victorian England was notorious as "the land without music" with only William Sterndale Bennett (1816-1875) as a contemporary English composer known to foreigners. Secondly, as Robert Ensor noted, the upper classes "held music in Roman contempt as a field for foreigners and ill-bred underlings."[68] Thirdly, other than the provision of chapel choirs, the public schools had no musical tradition: indeed music was considered "rather unmanly" and more fitting as a feminine accomplishment.[69] And fourthly, and most remarkably, Thring was himself quite unmusical and tone deaf. "He did not know one tune from another", his daughter Margaret remembered, "except perhaps

---

[65] Several original portraits by Reimers are displayed in the Mendelssohn-Haus in Leipzig. Many reproductions are included in Paul Blackman, *Christian Reimers - A Spirited Performer* (Campbelltown, South Australia: Blackman, 2016).

[66] Reimers and Schumann played through the draft of the composer's cello concerto in March 1851, and in 1853 they played through the composer's last work, several romances for cello. Blackman, *Reimers,* 15.

[67] The registration booklet for Breusing's school requested by the Bürgermeister-Amtes (Mayor's Office) in Bonn, dated August 30, 1856, is held in the Stadtarchivs in Bonn. It lists the teachers and pupils. See also Nancy B. Reich, *Clara Schumann: The Artist and the Woman* (Ithaca: Cornell University Press, 2001), 146; and Dieter Kühn, *Clara Schumann, Klavier: Ein Lebensbuch* (Düsseldorf: Fischer, 1996).

[68] Robert Ensor, *England 1870-1914* (Oxford: Clarendon Press, 1964) 158.

[69] Paul David's notes in Parkin, *Life,* 2:307.

the National Anthem".[70] As Thring later explained to the Rev Edward White: "though I support music zealously from a sincere belief in it, I am an ignorant, careless savage, and know nothing about it".[71]

Uppingham music began with Sunday evening gatherings in the School House drawing room.[72] Schäfer and Reimers performed, and there was a small choir of six or so boys.[73] Thring contributed by writing lyrics for songs which were set to music by Reimers. Robert Sterndale Bennett, the grandson of William and a twentieth-century director of music at the school, believed that these were probably the first songs with English lyrics to be used at an English school;[74] they were certainly published some years before John Farmer went to Harrow and Joseph Barnby arrived at Eton.[75] Three songs stemmed from the partnership: *The Uppingham Chorus*, *The Cricket Song* and *The Fives Song*. The first, intended as the school song, was not particularly successful but the games songs were more attractive; their lyrics conveyed the pleasure of participating in sport. Christopher Cowan, one of Sterndale Bennett's successors, believed that it is a mistake to approach these songs with any solemnity for they were "real entertainment music" in the tradition of German student songs.[76]

THE CRICKET SONG (1856)

The wickets are set,
The field is met,
Oh the royal game and free,
The school shall win,

---

[70] *USM*, 1953, 5; Margaret Thring, *Memories*. Sue Kalaugher reports that "My own father, Edward's great nephew, was even more tone deaf – he couldn't tell the difference between the national anthem and three blind mice; however he used to accompany my very musical mother to concerts and patiently think deep professorial thoughts throughout." Professor Meredith Thring was an eminent inventor and engineer. Email message to author, July 31, 2018.
[71] Letter, May 20, 1873, quoted in Parkin, *Life*, 1:299.
[72] The gatherings lasted from 7.30pm until 10.00pm. The music was followed by plum cake and tea, and conversation; Marie Thring knew how to capture an audience. Rawnsley, *Early Days*, 74-75.
[73] William James, *Thring and Uppingham*, nd, 36. (UA); Diary, February 24, 1860, March 26, 1860 and November 5, 1863 (Parkin, *Life*, 1:138). James was at Uppingham from 1867 to 1874. He won a scholarship to University College, Oxford and became a barrister at the Inner Temple.
[74] All pre-1856 school songs in Robin Proctor's extensive collection have lyrics in Latin. Email message to author, February 9, 2018.
[75] *USM*, February 1934, 9.
[76] *USM*, 1953, 6.

Short out, long in,
'Tis a goodly companie.
Merry England, merry England,
Let foes say what they will,
Whilst Cricket we play
Each Summer day,
'Tis merry England still.

From field and hall,
Each yeoman tall,
And under the greenwood tree,
From tower and town,
White hand and brown,
Have won that name for me.
Merry England, merry England,
Our fathers' place we fill,
Whilst Cricket we play
Each Summer day,
'Tis merry England still.

The wickets are set,
The field is met,
Oh, who shall beat us? who?
Our champions stand,
Now good right hand,
And wary eye be true.
Merry England, merry England,
Our fathers' place we fill,
Whilst Cricket we play
Each Summer day,
'Tis merry England still.

Cricketers all,
If wickets fall,
As fall full well they may,
Give honour due,
Good hearts and true,
To those who win the day.
Merry England, merry England,
Fair field and win who will,
Whilst Cricket we play
Each Summer day,
'Tis merry England still

'Tis merry in hall
When beards wag all,

Let the game be lost or won,
For friend and foe
No difference know,
When the stubborn day is done.
Merry England, merry England,
Fair field and win who will,
Whilst Cricket we play
Each Summer day,
'Tis merry England still.

Our champions stand,
In many a land
They'll prove old England's fame,
In fight, each son,
Or lost, or won,
Bears high his father's name.
Merry England, merry England,
Let foes say what they will,
For gentle and brave,
On field and wave,
We will uphold thee still.[77]

THE FIVES SONG (1856)

Oh the spirit in the ball
Dancing round about the wall,
In your eye and out again
Ere there's time to feel the pain,
Hands and fingers all alive,
Doing duty each for five.
Oh the spirit in the ball,
Dancing round about the wall!

See again, now up it goes,
Whizzing by that startled nose,
Hands and feet are everywhere,
Twinkling in the middle air,
Bodies, bodies are no more,
All is hit, and spring, and score.
Oh the spirit in the ball,
Dancing round about the wall!

---

[77] Original in UA; Edward Thring, *Uppingham School Songs and Borth Lyrics* (London: T. Fisher Unwin, 1887), 21-25. Christopher Cowan made a recording of the song in 1953; in UA. *The Cricket Song* is also included in the CD *Songs of Cricket* by Cantabile, The London Quartet (Signum Classics, 2011).

Poets sung it long ago,
All the fight and all the woe,
Geryon and thundering Zeus,
Hundred-fisted Briareus,
Argus with his million eyes,
Oh, 'twas but a game of Fives.
Oh the lordly game of Fives.
Oh the spirit in the ball,
Dancing round about the wall![78]

The two games songs were published in sheet-music form in 1857 with a delightful title-page drawn by Reimers. It depicts numerous mortar-board clad boys, John and William Beevor playing cricket, and scenes of Uppingham that include the cricket field.[79]

Thring's lyrics for *The Football Song* were also written in this period, and appear to have drawn inspiration from the witches' scene in Shakespeare's *Macbeth*, but they were not set to music until a decade later.

THE FOOTBALL SONG (1866)

Cross-legged in a cave unblest,
Pitch-bedaubed, far in the West,
Wizards three themselves addrest
To a charm of wild unrest.
Wax from murd'red owners rive,
Sulphur-smothered all alive,
Strip of hide of maddened bull,
Breath of cobbler, fill it full,
Point of brad-awl, keen and fine,
Needles sharp, and hempen twine,
Stitch it well within, without,
Nimble be the charm and stout.
Lively be as prick of awl,
Quick as needle, round as ball,
Tight as hemp together pull,
Light as breath, and tough as bull.
Hide it close, then let it loose,
Led by quill of watchful goose,

---

[78] Original in UA; Thring, *Songs and Lyrics*, 28-29. Geryon and Argus were giants; Briarius had 50 heads as well as 100 arms.
[79] A copy is held in UA. The mortar-boards were soon replaced by caps, the uniform for German students. The Beevor brothers joined the school in 1857: John played in the XI and became a solicitor; William died young in 1873. Blackman, *Reimers*, 45.

On a day when on the plain
Toes twice sixty sport amain.
See the madness surge and rise,
Toes twice sixty kick the skies.
Shrieks of triumph, shrieks of woe,
Heads like nuts together go.
Cowards staring, cracking shins,
Rubbing hands, and no one wins.
Heels are flying into air,
Heads and shoulders anywhere.
Now the charm is working free,
Brad-awl point and mad-bull glee.
Potent as the golden ball
Ate cast amongst them all
Banqueting in Peleus' hall,
Many a god and goddess tall,
Kicking out in sudden brawl;
Went the ugly to the wall.
Stitch it well within, without,
Nimble be the charm and stout.
Lively be as prick of awl,
Quick as needle, round as ball,
Tight as hemp together pull,
Light as breath, and tough as bull.[80]

---

[80] Original in UA; Thring, *Songs and Lyrics*, 18-20. Robert Sterndale Bennett and Christopher Cowan made recordings of the song in 1929 and 1953 respectively; in UA. Ate was the goddess of mischief; Peleus was the father of Achilles.

CHAPTER FOUR

EDWARD THRING:
"I THINK I HAVE FOUND MY LIFE-WORK TODAY"

I

Edward Thring was born at Alford in the south-western county of Somerset on November 29, 1821. His father, John Gale Thring, was rector and squire of the parish; his mother, Sarah, was the daughter of the vicar of a neighbouring parish. Edward was the fifth of seven surviving children of the marriage.[1] His father, who had been educated at Winchester and St John's College, Cambridge was a sound scholar and all his sons were to receive their preliminary classical training from him. The rector also acted as a county magistrate and managed the considerable Alford estate. Sarah Thring, an intelligent and gentle woman, had scholarly connections in her own family but for Edward her strongest influence was as a steadfast Christian exemplar: "a more saintly woman in practice and in faith, I believe cannot be found."[2] George Parkin, Thring's official biographer, saw

> two chief factors from which Edward Thring derived his character and early impressions: on the one side a stern paternal authority grounded in a deep but sincere sense of Christian duty; on the other a singularly beautiful illustration of Christian life which was tender as well as strong.[3]

The Thring brothers shared a robust and boisterous boyhood on the Alford estate, in the pools of the River Brue at the bottom of the garden, and in the surrounding countryside. As a boy, Edward was remembered as

---

[1] Two of Thring's brothers were to find national fame: Henry (born 1818), later Baron Thring of Alderhurst, became an eminent lawyer and civil servant; Godfrey (born 1823) was a churchman and celebrated hymn-writer.
[2] Diary, undated entry (Parkin, *Life*, 1:9).
[3] Parkin, *Life*, 1:11.

always out of doors and his own memories recalled the freedom and the
luxury of life there. Nature was one of his first teachers and it maintained
its hold throughout his life: at Uppingham his diary was to note the
appearance of each year's first crocus, hyacinth, swallow, and so on.[4]
Whether rambling in the countryside, or visiting his "rural friends" in the
aviary, or holidaying in the Lake District, Thring always held a spiritual
regard for nature: "But what consoles me is the sight of life everywhere:
the rush of life in the tree and the grass. That is a wonderful comfort, that
thought."[5] Poetry was an extension of nature to Thring, even in childhood,
and his later jotting books contained much Wordsworth, Coleridge,
Tennyson as well as verses by other Romantics.[6] Wordsworth was his
greatest love and all his works were much read; the poet became a great
source of spiritual uplift to the schoolmaster. He would often talk on
Wordsworth to his boys and he would lend them some of his own volumes
to encourage their reading. One day he complained that he had
innumerable incomplete sets for the borrowed copies were not always
returned.[7]

Alford is situated in legendary countryside: Cadbury Hill is five miles
away and, after leaving Alford, the Brue flows along to Glastonbury. It is a
region rich in Arthurian myth and chivalric legend for Cadbury is believed
by many to be the site of King Arthur's castle, the nearby mere of
Somerset is where Arthur is reputed to have thrown his sword, Excalibur,
and the history of Glastonbury Abbey is finely interwoven with the search
for the Holy Grail. Thring knew the Arthurian tales well and when,
towards the end of his life, his friend Juliana Ewing visited Alford, he was
disappointed that he could not be there to conduct her to the Cadbury site.[8]
Sir Walter Scott was another early favourite and everything from the
beauty of the Waverley novels, the charm of the ballads, the music of the
lyric poetry to the glory of the romances, all brought pleasure and delight.
In 1885, when he addressed the Education Society as its President, Thring
told of his love of Scott;

> Here let me record my own deep obligations to Sir Walter Scott, the
> noblest of writers. Many of his novels I have read over and over again. The
> glorious lesson to honour, and paint with honour, antagonists and their

[4] For example, Diary, February 23, 1887.
[5] Skrine, *Edward Thring*, 126.
[6] Thring, White note book, begun 1847; Thring, Little jotting book. Both in UA.
[7] James, *Thring*, 22, 54; Skrine, *Edward Thring*, 128.
[8] Letter from Mrs Ewing to Thring, September 1884. In the wooden casket carved
by Thring. In UA.

beliefs, can be learnt nowhere so well as in him. Better be one of Sir Walter Scott's dislikes than the hero of many modern novels. … Health and honour flow forth from every word he wrote, an heir-loom to us all for ever. I rejoice in confessing my great debt to him, and others may get from similar reading the happy gains I got from him.[9]

II

Thring's childhood at Alford was a happy one and it was in the secure environment of the home that the contemporary Christian, Romantic and Chivalric foundations of his later life were laid. Life at school had its influence too but here the effects were to be negative rather than positive, and their result was seen in the realities of life at Uppingham rather than in moral precepts. Thring was eight when he went away to his first school, a private preparatory one in the nearby town of Ilminster. The school had a reputation for "ability and severity": Thring remembered the severity more than the ability and even in the last years of his life he could still contrast the freedom and the liberty of home with the prison-like nature of his preparatory school.[10] Thring told of his Ilminster years in his address to the Education Society:

> My first acquaintance with school began at eight years old, in an old-fashioned private school of the flog-flog, milk-and-water-at-breakfast type. All my life long the good and evil of that place has been on me. It is even now one of my strongest impressions, with its prim misery, the misery of a clipped hedge, with every clip through flesh, and blood and fresh young feelings; its snatches of joy, its painful but honest work, grim, but firmly in earnest, and its prison morality of discipline. The most lasting lesson of my life was the failure of suspicion and severity to get inside the boy-world, however much it troubled our outsides. Three long years were spent there.[11]

The harshness of Ilminster helped to produce Uppingham for, as Thring was to recall near the end of his life, "it was my memories of that school and its severities that first made me so long to try if I could not make the life of small boys at school happier and brighter."[12]

---

[9] Edward Thring, *Addresses* (London: T. Fisher Unwin, 1887), 18-19.
[10] Edward Thring, *Theory and Practice of Teaching* (Cambridge: Cambridge University Press, 1883), 68.
[11] Edward Thring, *An Address delivered before the Education Society*, 1885, 4. In UA.
[12] Parkin, *Life*, 1:13.

In 1832 Thring went up to Eton for nine years, first in Chapman's house and then as a Colleger: "Those nine years, with all their chequered feeling, did not leave me in ignorance of the good and evil of a great public school".[13] John Keate was Head Master at this time and the term before Thring's arrival witnessed the flogging of 80 randomly chosen boys in order that an incipient rebellion might be repressed. There were just nine masters to 570 boys in the upper school. Only the clever and the willing had opportunities to learn; the rest were left to fend for themselves. Thring was in Chapman's house for his first three years. James Chapman was a sensitive and kindly teacher who approached his work with evangelical and missionary zeal. Chapman's reports spoke well of Thring, the "little fellow" progressing steadily on all fronts.[14]

In 1835 Thring went into residence as a Colleger. At this time a Colleger's life was severe but the school authorities turned a blind eye. At eight o'clock each evening the 70 Collegers were locked in the Long Chamber, a large and bare room infested with rats, completely without supervision. Beds were in short supply so younger boys slept on the floor; older boys monopolised the few wash-basins.[15] Here boy government ruled, with the younger boys at the mercy of their elders. Thring was later to write:

> Who can ever forget that knew it, the wild, rough, rollicking freedom, the frolic and the fun of that land of misrule, with its strange code of traditional boy laws, which really worked rather well as long as the sixth form were well disposed or sober?[16]

In his late Victorian history of Eton, Henry Maxwell Lyte went further: "a boy who passed unscathed the ordeal of a Colleger's life must have been gifted in no common degree with purity of mind and strength of will".[17]

---

[13] Thring, *Education Society*, 4. There has always been a clear distinction at Eton between the 70 Collegers provided for by the original foundation of Henry VI and other fee-paying boys known as Oppidans who lived in boarding houses in the town.

[14] Parkin, *Life*, 1:16.

[15] Nigel Richardson, *Thring of Uppingham: Victorian Educator* (Buckingham: University of Buckingham Press, 2014), 8.

[16] Parkin, *Life*, 1:22.

[17] Henry Maxwell Lyte, *A History of Eton College* (London: Macmillan, 1899), 451. Parents vied for College places for their sons because the royal foundation paid the fees and a place at King's College at Cambridge University was the likely outcome.

Thring not only passed unscathed, he also triumphed: he left Eton as senior Colleger and Captain of School, and he was Captain of Montem on the last but one occasion on which this extravagant Eton festival was celebrated.[18] He was remembered as a "great runner long before the days of the 'athletic' sports", and ever keen to race with anyone who would take him on.[19] He played cricket and football, and was prominent for the Collegers in the match "at the Wall" with the Oppidans, but fives was his real love.[20] An Eton contemporary remembered Thring as "a capital fives player ... he used to make a good fight on the fives court with the captain of the cricket club who had more reach. ... His pluck and muscle were peerless."[21] On one occasion he had bagged a court before the arrival of a senior boy. Strong-arm methods were employed to remove him but the rightful player was not to be coerced. He flung himself to the floor to establish full occupation and defied kicks and blows with the cry "I'll die first". It was an appeal to the watching audience and it won him the nickname Little Die First.[22]

At Ilminster there had been no freedom, at Eton it was there in abundance. In between there must be a happy medium. In 1860 Thring contrasted Uppingham with his own schooldays: "Surely this leading the school in all their life, without destroying their freedom at all, must have a great effect."[23]

III

Thring went up to King's College, Cambridge in the autumn of 1841; he was in residence as scholar and fellow for five years. These "very quiet, powerful years" he later treasured as one of the best periods of his life.[24] At Cambridge he read much and worked hard, "now heavy with labour, now buoyant with hope, bringing great searching of heart, and much balancing of right and wrong, much anxious weighing of the value of

---

[18] For more on Montem, see Richardson, *Thring*, 11.

[19] Skrine, *Edward Thring*, 66.

[20] Boys who were not in College were Oppidans.

[21] *USM*, January 1889, 9; Parkin, *Life*, 1:27.

[22] Parkin, *Life*, 1:26; Cormac Rigby, *Edward Thring: The Teachers' Teacher* (Truro: Sunnyrest Books, 2017), 35. In UA and the Bodleian Library.

[23] Diary, February 28, 1860.

[24] Letter from Thring to Alfred Boucher, 1875 (Parkin, *Life,* 1:42.) Boucher joined Uppingham as a boy in October 1866, won a place at Trinity College, Cambridge and became a vicar in Leek, Staffordshire.

education and life, and their true use".[25] Under the system operating for
King's Scholars at that time, Thring took his degree without examination.
Proof of his scholarship comes in his winning of the University's Porson
Prize for Greek Iambics as well as various College prizes. He also won the
College Cooke Prize for scholarship and good behaviour, surely a
forerunner of the Uppingham medal "For good work and unblemished
character". In keeping with contemporary Cambridge opinion, Thring was
an enthusiastic Platonist, seeing the philosopher's *Republic* as the ideal
society that education should strive to create. In consequence, he was very
carping of Oxford's preference for Aristotle: "I am sick of Oxford men
with their flimsy pretty ways, like weedy racehorses at best".[26] During his
time as a fellow at King's, Thring agitated for the reform of the system by
which King's Scholars did not have to sit University examinations; later,
in 1851, the change was made.

That campaign took Thring into print with *A Few Remarks on the
Present System of Degrees at King's College Cambridge*. This was
published in 1846 by Macmillans and it was to be one of the early links in
a long chain of friendship with the publishing family. In 1868 Alexander
Macmillan recalled:

> It was nearly a quarter of century since I first knew you, and since my dear
> brother and I used to speculate on the line in which you were to become
> eminent, for you were among the first of Cambridge men whom his clear
> eye determined as fitted to do world work in one line or another.[27]

Daniel and Alexander Macmillan's publishing house in Trinity Street
became the meeting place for many undergraduates and fellows. It was
Daniel who in 1842 first drew Frederick Maurice's attention to the plight
of the poor and asked him to prepare some religious tracts for them. Later
the Macmillans were to introduce many undergraduates to the Christian
Socialist Movement. Thring was a regular visitor to Trinity Street and in
later life he remembered fondly "those early days, so vivid in my
memory", and he would speak of his good fortune in being "thrown in"
with the brothers at that time.[28] The Macmillans saw their publishing
business as a means of spreading God's word to the lower classes and it
was a cause that found a sympathetic admirer in Thring.

---

[25] Thring, *Education Society*, 4.
[26] Diary, January 8, 1863 (Parkin, *Life*, 1:128).
[27] Letter to Thring from Alexander Macmillan, 1868 (Parkin, *Life*, 1:42).
[28] Letter from Thring to Alexander Macmillan, July 28, 1882; British Library.

It was through the Macmillans that Thring saw the beauty and the quiet certainty of letting God plan his path. If the circumstances had been different Thring might have been a general or a bishop, and many believe that he could have been either, but he was content with his life's work as a teacher. When Thring informed Daniel Macmillan that he was taking the Uppingham appointment, Macmillan was delighted:

> It seems to me one of the surest ways of doing good. While a man is giving life and strength to his country in that way he does not proclaim himself either patriot or prophet, but merely seems to be working for wife and family. It has the great advantage of making no fuss.[29]

When Daniel died in 1857, Thring continued the friendship with his brother, Alexander. Macmillans published most of Thring's works, beginning with *The Elements of Grammar Taught in English* (1851) and *The Child's Grammar* (1852), both published before Thring went to Uppingham. The Thring and Macmillan families became very close: the Macmillans stayed at Uppingham and the Thrings returned the visits. The Macmillans recommended the school to their friends and several sets of boys came; then in 1861 Alexander asked if Thring could take his sons and the sons of Daniel.[30] They came: Daniel's eldest son Frederick entered Uppingham the following April and his younger brother Maurice, the father of Harold Macmillan, the future prime minister, followed in 1866.

The Macmillan friendship was not the only one to last well beyond the Cambridge days for in these years Thring cemented his relationship with William Witts and through him met Harvey Goodwin. Witts left Eton ahead of Thring and he was a fellow of King's College before Thring gained his degree. In his early years at Uppingham Thring twice asked Witts to join the staff, but without success. Then in 1861, quite out of the blue, Witts asked if he might still come. Thring was delighted and said yes at once. Witts and Goodwin were close friends at Cambridge: Goodwin was Vicar of St Giles where Witts served as his curate.[31] In 1847 they founded an institution in the town for "youthful offenders", their aim being to reform these boys rather than to punish them. Later, in 1853, this grew into a Cambridge branch of the Working Men's College and was run on the lines of the London original. Alexander Macmillan and some Trinity

---

[29] Thomas Hughes, *Memoir of Daniel Macmillan* (London: Macmillan, 1882), 214.
[30] Letters to Thring from Alexander Macmillan, April 10, 1858 and February 25, 1861; in casket, UA; letter from Thring to Alexander Macmillan, December 7, 1867; British Library.
[31] Hardwicke Rawnsley, *Harvey Goodwin* (London: Macmillan, 1896), 63, 121.

College men initiated this expansion and they invited Goodwin to be the college's first principal. When Witts moved to Uppingham, Goodwin entered his two boys for the school and, from that time until Thring's death in 1887, no Uppingham festival was complete without a sermon or a speech from him, first as Dean of Ely and later as Bishop of Carlisle. His "spirit of manly, practical Christianity for everyday life" was much in sympathy with the headmaster's: "Go and do" would be his message to the Uppingham boys.[32]

IV

Bernard Darwin regarded Thring as "the most Christian man of his generation".[33] Deep humility was the corner-stone of his faith: "the great secret of my own life has been the doing patiently and correctly the thing in hand, and waiting till God changed it, not striving to carve out my own way, but to watch and find what way He willed."[34] Christianity, life and education were equivalent to Thring and it was impossible to separate one from the others. Yet, though he was so ardent a Christian, it is not possible to chain Thring to any party of Christian thought and doctrine. At Cambridge he must have been exposed to much theological argument between the various Church parties but he dismissed their "controversial bickerings" as "gladiatorial shows".[35] From a review of Thring's sermons it is impossible to tell to which religious, philosophical or even political camp he belonged.

Thring was ordained deacon in 1846 and early in the following year he accepted the curacy at St James's Church in Gloucester. It was a new parish of mean houses on the eastern side of the city where most of the inhabitants were dockers or labourers on the nearby railway. It was a depressing area, an unhealthy one, and the infant mortality rate was high.[36] Thomas Hedley had been appointed vicar on the formation of the parish in 1842. Like many graduates of Trinity College, Cambridge he was a firm believer in such a mission to the poor yet, sadly, it eventually claimed his life at the early age of forty-two.[37] Thring was ever grateful to Hedley's

---

[32] Rawnsley, *Goodwin*, 66, 75-76, 80-82.

[33] Bernard Darwin, *The English Public School* (London: Longman, 1929), 126.

[34] Diary, October 8, 1859.

[35] Thring, Index Rerum. In UA.

[36] Geoffrey Hoyland found Thring's scholarly signature appended to many burial notices. Hoyland, *Man Who Made*, 22, 23.

[37] Cormac Rigby, "The Life and Influence of Edward Thring" (DPhil diss., University of Oxford, 1968), 66, 74.

influence and he related to his own biographer, George Parkin, how it was through Hedley's example that he experienced the intense religious conviction that he should consecrate all of his powers to God's service. Thring later told Hedley's daughter that her father "was the most single-minded Christian I ever met, and wise and intellectual withal. He stamped himself deep on me; much of my life here is indebted to him, how much I cannot tell."[38] On Hedley's death, two of his sons came to Uppingham as some of Thring's first pupils.

Hedley built a school alongside the church, and it was there that Thring gained his first insight into teaching. It was a rude shock:

> Never shall I forget those schools in the suburbs of Gloucester, and their little class-room with its solemn problem, no more difficult one in the world; how on earth the Cambridge Honour man, with his success and his brain-world, was to get at the minds of those little labourers' sons, with their unfurnished heads, and no time to give.[39]

It was this experience that laid the foundation of his methods at Uppingham for, as Geoffrey Hoyland asserted, "the dowdy National School of St James's is the true parent of Uppingham".[40] It was these children that inspired Thring.

> They gave me the great axiom, 'The worse the material, the greater the skill of the worker'.

> They called out the useful dictum with which I ever stepped silently over the threshold – 'If these fellows don't learn, it's my fault'.

> Nay, they taught me the more valuable lesson still, how different knowledge which can be produced to an Examiner is from knowledge which knows itself, and understands its own life and growth.[41]

It was glorious work at Gloucester, but it took its toll on Thring's health, and in the spring of 1848 he was forced to leave. For the next two years he convalesced at Great Marlow in the Thames Valley: during this period he read with private pupils and served as an Examiner for Eton, Rugby and Cambridge. In 1851 he took a curacy at nearby Cookham Dean, where he

---

[38] Parkin, *Life*, 1:46.
[39] Thring, *Education Society,* 5.
[40] Hoyland, *Man Who Made*, 24.
[41] Thring, *Education Society*, 6.

again taught in National Schools, and in this same period he prepared his
first two texts for the Macmillan brothers.

V

In the intervals between these occupations, Thring used his private income
to finance several long journeys across Europe: through France one year,
following the course of the Rhine on another occasion, and visiting cities
in Prussia on a third. Then, in the autumn of 1852, Thring embarked on the
traditional English gentleman's Grand Tour through Belgium, Prussia,
Bohemia, Austria and Italy, and then onwards through Greece and Turkey
to reach the Holy Land. His diary for this tour is largely a record of the
sites and galleries he visited: there is no reference to visits to schools and
universities, nor is there any contact with continental educationalists.
Towards the close of a meandering journey through the Italian art cities,
Thring was summoned early to Rome at his parents' bidding.[42] His
younger brother Godfrey, the future hymn-writer, was set to make a fool
of himself by proposing marriage to a young lady from Prussia, a match
that his parents thought unsuitable. Thring's diary of the trip petered out
and then went silent: he was in love.[43] He rescued Godfrey by making his
own proposal to Marie Koch, and she accepted.[44] All thoughts of the Holy
Land were forgotten. Thring rushed back to England to find employment.
He failed to land the headmastership of Durham School, which went to
Henry Holden, so he tried for Holden's post at Uppingham Grammar
School, and got it.

Carolina Marie Louise Koch, a year older than Thring and always
known as Marie, was the eldest of seven children of Carl Koch and
Conradina Terlinden. Both parents were born in Cleves, in 1783 and 1793
respectively, a duchy to the north-west of the Rhine that surrendered its
independence to Prussian control in 1815. Carl Koch was employed in the
Prussian Customs Service as a *Zoll und Steuer Inspektor* and was posted to
Hamm, across the Rhine in Westphalia, where he and Conradina married
in 1819, and then to Bonn, west of the river in Berg. Koch had now been
promoted to *Oberzoll und Steuer Inspektor* and from 1822, when Prussia
amalgamated all the territory west of the Rhine to form the Rhineland

---

[42] Venice, Verona, Padua, Ferrara, Bologna, Florence, Pisa, Lucca, Siena, Arezzo,
Perugia and Assisi.

[43] Diary of Thring's European tour, 1852. In UA.

[44] From a monograph about Godfrey Thring by his son, Arthur. Quoted in Sue
Kalaugher (née Thring), Victorian Grandmothers. Typescript, 2008, 12. (UA).
Godfrey was Edward's favourite brother and they continued to be close.

Province, his responsibilities increased. His office was in the heart of the city, a short walk from his home where Marie was born on November 24, 1820. By 1834 and six more children, the family had moved to a new home nearby.[45]

Marie and her siblings were raised within a cultured family in a cultured city. Bonn was the seat of the Elector of Cologne and the presence of his Court not only provided the 10,000 inhabitants with employment but also projected an aura of grandeur and a veneer of aristocracy. The small city was well-tended, pleasant and secure, and no industry and little commerce disturbed the cosy ambience. Carl Koch became a member of the city's *Lese- und Erholungsgesellschaft*, a gentlemen's "reading and recreation club", in 1822. With its close association to the Elector's Court and the newly founded University (1818), the *Lese* was the most sought-after club for the professional elite.[46] Facilities included a library, reading room and billiard room, together with space for concerts, balls, wine-tasting and general refreshment and recreation. The musical life at the *Lese* and throughout the city was strong.[47]

Research both in England and in Germany has uncovered no details of Marie Koch's life in Bonn from her birth in 1820 until her marriage to Edward Thring in 1853 but her father's profession, his membership of the *Lese*, the family's social position, the site of their successive homes, and the cultural atmosphere throughout the city all combine to suggest that she was socially adroit, well read, alive to music and probably proficient as a singer and pianist. These were the gifts that she brought to Uppingham.

The purpose of Thring's presence in Rome in November 1852 has been noted but there is no record of why Marie Koch was there. We can be certain, however, that an unmarried young lady of her social class would not have been there alone. The most likely explanation is that she was accompanying her ailing father on a journey in search of winter sunshine to restore him to good health. Koch was now aged sixty-five and had

---

[45] Koch's office was at Auf der Sandkaule 64; the family homes were at An der Windmühle 726 and Neustraße 735. *Bonner Kalender*, 1834, 1841, 1846, 1847, 1848, 1850.

[46] Koch's fellow members included the philosopher Karl von Schlegel, the author Ernst Arndt, the historian Barthold Niebuhr, the lawyer Bernhard von Gerolt, the musicians Heinrich Breidenstein, Nikolaus Simrock and Franz Ries, and Beethoven's patron, Graf Ferdinand von Waldstein und Wartenberg.

[47] In 1838 Breidenstein taught the Princes Ernst and Albert of Saxe-Coburg-Gotha, the latter becoming Queen Victoria's Prince Consort in 1840.

probably retired.[48] He did not long enjoy his new leisure, however, for he
had died by the time of his daughter's marriage on December 20, 1853.
Marie's mother travelled to England for the wedding; she had moved out
of the family home and settled into a small apartment close to the
Münsterplatz.[49] Marie's youngest sister, eighteen-year-old Anna, came to
Uppingham and lived with the Thrings. She served as the headmaster's
secretary until his death in 1887.[50]

Marie joined Edward in School House in January 1854 after their
marriage at Holdenhurst in Hampshire, and together they set about
constructing what Thring later called "the great educational experiment".
Five months earlier, on returning to Alford after his first look at the
school, Thring had told a friend: "I think I have found my life-work
today".[51]

VI

Edward and Marie maintained close contact with Bonn and the Koch
family in their first decade at Uppingham. They holidayed there for a
month in the summer until the costs involved with raising five children led
to a preference for the Lake District, and Prussian and Swiss governesses
were brought over for their daughters. The strongest professional link was
with Friedrich Breusing, the husband of Marie's third sister, Louise. Dr
Breusing was well-established within Bonn's professional, social and
cultural circles and his status enabled him to follow his father-in-law as a
member of the *Lese- und Erholungsgesellschaft,* joining in 1857. It is
likely that when Thring was in Bonn he would have accompanied
Breusing to lectures, concerts and the like but the unexplained absence of

---

[48] The *Bonner Kalender* of 1848 listed Carl Koch as the senior member of the *Zoll und Steuer* team but his name was absent the following year when the office moved and new inspectors were added to the team. The office moved to Weberstraße 25. Seven inspectors were present in both 1848 and 1849, three left in the interval, and two joined. *Bonner Kalender*, 1848 and 1849.

[49] The small apartment was at Fürstenstraße 38½. Information from the first *Bonner Bürger-Buch* of 1858 and the *Adressbuch der Universität-Stadt Bonn*, 1859/60.

[50] No reason for her leaving Bonn was recorded but her departure would have reduced the financial burden on her widowed mother and passed that responsibility to Thring. In later years Thring was called upon to give financial support to other members of the Koch family still living in Bonn. See, for example, Diary, November 16, 1860 and January 20, 1862.

[51] Parkin, *Life*, 1:55.

the *Lese*'s visitors' book for the period from the society's archives leaves the suggestion unproven.[52]

As with all contemporary grammar and public schools, lessons in Latin and Greek, English literature, mathematics and divinity dominated the timetable at Uppingham. These subjects were taught by Thring and the other housemasters, mostly Cambridge graduates and many in Holy Orders. But from the outset Thring wanted a broader and more rounded curriculum, one that suited boys of all abilities and not just the cleverest. This was alien to English practice but the norm in much of mainland Europe and in the German-speaking countries in particular. It is likely that Thring discovered this when in Bonn, and especially through conversations at the *Lese* with educationalists, philosophers, musicians and other like-minded intellectuals. It is there that he would have heard of the city's Humboldtian model of holistic schooling that aimed to motivate all children to realise their full potential. Wilhelm von Humboldt, the Prussian minister responsible for education from 1809 to 1810, used the term *Bildung* to describe this innovative curriculum that was now standard in all the state's schools and universities.[53] Philosophy, literature, science and the arts were taught alongside the traditional subjects, and pupils and students were encouraged to develop their own interests. Thring's adoption of *Bildung* theory and practice added music, art, gymnastics, modern languages and science to the Uppingham curriculum, and Breusing recruited men from schools in Bonn and other Rhineland towns to teach these new subjects in England.

---

[52] Alexander Wolfshohl, email messages to author, January 15 and March 14, 2017. Dr Wolfshohl is the archivist at the *Lese*.

[53] Wilfried Gruhn, "Germany: Educational goals, curricular structure, political principles", in *The Origins and Foundations of Music Education: Cross-Cultural Historical Studies of Music in Compulsory Schooling,* ed. Gordon Cox and Robin Stevens (London: Continuum, 2011), 50-52.

CHAPTER FIVE

MAKING A SCHOOL: "MACHINERY, MACHINERY, MACHINERY"

I

Thring did not have a blueprint for a school crackling in his pocket when he took up his headmastership in September 1853, not least because only a few months had elapsed since meeting Marie and needing an income to support her, but he did have an idea for a school based on all that he had experienced, good and bad, at Alford, Ilminster, Eton, Cambridge, Gloucester, Great Marlow and Bonn. His later career shows Thring to be a pragmatist: if a new idea suggested itself and was seen to contribute to the overall aims, then it was adopted and absorbed into the system. Uppingham Grammar School was, however, the sort of school that an ambitious young man would have looked for: it was small, modest, and ready for an enterprising headmaster. It was also isolated, a good quality for an experimental site, but accessible: railways were approaching Uppingham from several directions and these would be vital if the school were to grow beyond its local resources.[1]

Early in 1854 Thring began his reforms and then, at the end of 1858, he paused to take stock of what he had achieved and to look forward to what remained still to done. These expanded notes were logged in the front of his diary on December 20. They were later reorganised in a report to the school governors for Thring wished to expand the school further but he could not do so without their consent and financial backing; in fact the first was only grudgingly given and the second never came.[2] The introduction to *The Statement* sets the scene:

> The first necessities of schools are too often glaringly violated by those in best repute, and the public having had no true standard to refer to, have

---

[1] I owe this point to Bryan Matthews.
[2] The school's governors were retitled trustees in 1877 in accordance with the Endowed Schools Act.

learnt to look upon these blemishes as necessary conditions of great schools, whereas they are no more necessary than perpetual typhus fever is necessary.

There is a large percentage of temptation, criminality, and idleness in the great schools – a moral miasma – generated by known causes, and as certainly to be got rid of even by more mechanical improvements – a little moral drainage – as the average sickness of a squalid district. This is the task which the School at Uppingham has set itself to carry out.

The excellence of a School, over a series of years, depends, first, on its machinery for education; by which is meant appliances, whether material or otherwise, for conducting the work: the ship, and officers, and crew taken numerically. And, secondly, on the manner in which this machinery is worked: the discipline, knowledge and navigation of the vessel.[3]

"Machinery, machinery, machinery, should be the motto of every good school."[4] The first step, as we have seen, was to appoint a good staff. Men other than those appointed from Bonn needed a private income and to be prepared to sink their funds into the venture to build the boarding houses that would accommodate the new pupils. That Thring actually attracted such men gives some measure of his personal magnetism and dynamism, for at this stage there was no guarantee of success. By 1884, the tercentenary of Uppingham's foundation, the masters claimed to have invested £91,000 in the school and Thring had accumulated hefty overdrafts and mortgages.[5]

The school needed a team of masters with different strengths: "to teach an upper class requires more knowledge, a lower more skill as a teacher."[6] Boarding was arranged on a house basis but teaching was done in forms: a housemaster superintended his own house but taught a form of boys from all houses. In this way each master could he made responsible for a particular age group and his success or failure could be more easily judged. To ensure that each boy obtained individual attention, Thring limited the size of each class to 30. The masters were further expected to be with the boys in their out-of-school activities; the reminiscences of two,

---

[3] Edward Thring, *The Statement of the Rev Edward Thring, Head Master, respecting the Organisation of the School: and the Decree of the Governors,* 1859. In UA; hereafter *The Statement.*

[4] Diary, December 20, 1858 and Parkin, *Life,* 1:92.

[5] Parkin, *Life,* 2:150. That is about £8-10 million in today's terms.

[6] Diary, December 20, 1858.

Sam Haslam and Willingham Rawnsley, record much playing of football, cricket and fives with the boys.[7]

II

Once Thring had started to appoint masters, the next step was to see that the material appliances of the school were adequate. First priority was given to boarding houses: between 1856 and 1862 four new houses were built and others were converted from existing buildings. Three further houses were added between 1866 and 1872. Many schools had boarding houses before Uppingham but in general these were no more than hostels only marginally part of the educational system; at Uppingham they were central. As Canon Robinson noted to Thring's delight during the later Schools Inquiry Commission, "at Rugby the school made the houses, and at Uppingham the houses made the school."[8] Thring favoured free-standing boarding houses over dormitories grouped around quadrangles; the latter might look more impressive and make headmasterly control over discipline easier but they offered boys no difference between life in lessons and life out of school.[9] Each Uppingham house was "a little commonwealth" ruled by its housemaster as *paterfamilias*, housing his family and up to 30 boys. The influence of the housemaster, his wife and their children was vital for this added "home feeling".[10] Hardwicke Rawnsley certainly appreciated it:

> I had always felt strongly that we enjoyed a great advantage at Uppingham under Thring, where the home life of the masters was made to touch the whole school. The daughters of the masters moved like sisters among us, and one was never without a kind of sense that the atmosphere of home had followed one to school .... the presence of purity as one finds it in a good home affected the whole school.[11]

An examination of the town's census returns for 1861, 1871 and 1881 shows that only one of the twenty-two housemasters was a bachelor, and

---

[7] Mrs Haslam's diary is in UA; Rawnsley, *Early Days*, 95.
[8] Letter from Thring to W. T. Jacob, May 1873 (Parkin, *Life*, 1:193).
[9] Edward Thring, *Education and School* (London: Macmillan, 1864), 171-172. The walk from chapel to several houses took more than five minutes.
[10] Thring, *E&S*, 190-191.
[11] Eleanor Rawnsley, *Canon Rawnsley* (Glasgow: Maclehose, Jackson, 1923), 162.

he had married before the following census.[12] The homely feel would have been especially strong when newly married housemasters and their wives were bringing up large families of young children: in 1861, for example, there was an average of three under-sevens in each house.[13] This domesticity of boarding-school life was unusual, perhaps unique, and at odds with the arrangements in the schools described by John Tosh in his study, *A Man's Place*.[14] Sophia Haslam, the wife of the housemaster of The Lodge, kept a diary for the period 1870-73. Boys are named throughout as she records conversations in the dining hall, details of illnesses, triumphs in sports, and much more. Thring was an avid letter-writer and much of his correspondence was with the parents of his boys in School House; no doubt he insisted that each housemaster maintained similar contact *in loco parentis*.[15]

Each boy had a partitioned sleeping cubicle within a dormitory and his own study. Both were to be Uppingham hallmarks. Thring believed that "a large dormitory introduces far too great opportunity for undetected evil" and that "the single room cannot be so healthy."[16] These "tishes" gave the boys privacy at night for, as Thring wrote mockingly of Frederic Farrar's *Eric, or Little by Little*, "do not suppose, whatever words may assert, that little Christian confessors say their prayers, and kneel, and at last win respect of their more hardened companions in doing so."[17] A boy's study was his retreat and his sanctuary, and a place to decorate to his own taste. Thring awarded prizes for the best kept studies in his own house.[18] Ernest Hornung recalled them in the Uppingham novel, *Fathers of Men*:[19]

> They were undeniably cosy and attractive, as compact as a captain's cabin, as private as a friar's cell, but far more comfortable than either ... with a

---

[12] There were 7 houses for c160 boys in 1861, 12 for c330 in 1871, and 12 for c300 in 1881.

[13] There were 19 under-sevens in 1861, 22 in 1871 and 13 in 1881.

[14] John Tosh, *A Man's Place: Masculinity and the Middle-class Home in Victorian England* (New Haven: Yale University Press, 1999), 118.

[15] For example Parkin, *Life*, 1:19, 127, 256.

[16] Thring, *E&S*, 187.

[17] Tish is a shortening of partition. The quotation is in Thring, *E&S*, 151. Thring had another swipe at Farrar in his diary (October 27, 1860) when he wrote of the author's "unpractical dreams of humbug". *Eric* was an over-sentimental novel of life at school: Frederic Farrar, *Eric, or Little by Little* (London: A. & C. Black, 1858).

[18] Diary, December 13, 1887.

[19] Hornung was a boy in the school from 1880 to 1883. He left early for health reasons, sailing to Australia for its drier climate.

table and two chairs, a square of carpet as big as a bath sheet, a bookshelf and pictures, and photographs and ornaments to taste, fretwork and plush to heart's content, a flower box for the summer term, hot water pipes for the other two, and above all a door of (one's) own to shut at will against the world.[20]

III

The housemasters taught in their own house halls whilst the non-housemasters worked in makeshift classrooms or in some of the cottages about the town, so at first there was no pressure to build proper teaching accommodation. The numbers in the school, however, quickly swelled, doubling every two years in the 1850s; there were 38 boarders and 14 day boys in 1855, a total of 52.[21] The 100 mark was reached before the end of the decade; a whole day's holiday celebrated a school roll of 200 in May 1863; and then, two years later, Thring's self-imposed limit of 300 was reached. George Street was appointed in 1861 as architect for a new school-room and a chapel; they were opened in 1863 and 1865 respectively.[22] Other facilities also came in these early years: a gymnasium in 1859, a carpentry shop in the original school-room beside the church in 1863, and a cricket pavilion on The Upper the same year. Thring was gradually working towards his target that every school ought to provide "a School Library, Museum, Workshop, Gymnasiums, Swimming Baths, Fives Courts, or any other pursuits that conduce to a healthy life."[23] The purpose of the 1859 *Statement* had been to urge the governors to provide more facilities but in the end it was left to Thring and the masters to dig deeper into their own pockets.

IV

With "the ship, and officers, and crew" in place, Thring turned his attention to all the other ingredients of "machinery" that would promote

---

[20] Ernest Hornung, *Fathers of Men* (London: Smith, Elder & Co, 1912/19), 19. John Tosh reports that mid-Victorian public schools excluded women, family photographs, fabrics, fine china, and all talk of mothers and sisters. This was not true at Thring's Uppingham. Tosh, *Man's Place*, 18.
[21] *USM*, 1920, 23.
[22] G. E. Street was a leading architect of the day. He is best known for his ecclesiastical work, but he also built the Royal Courts of Justice in the Strand in London.
[23] Thring, *E&S*, 179.

excellence so that the system did not rest solely on the talented teacher: the school day, the curriculum, and the educational equipment.

> As little as possible should be left to the personal merit in the teacher or chance; as much as possible ought to rest on the system and appliances, on every side checking vice and fostering good, quietly and unostentatiously, under the commonest guidance.[24]

This is a veiled criticism of Thomas Arnold's methods at Rugby. Thring regarded *Tom Brown's Schooldays* as, in some ways, the "bitterest satire" ever written on education for it showed a school resting entirely on Arnold's personality and not on any concrete system that Arnold could pass on to his successors: "and my own experience more than supports its truth".[25] Thring noted in his diary:

> Dr. Arnold was a great man but a bad school master, and posterity will see this. What personal influence could do he did. What wise and thoughtful application of means should have done, he did not.[26]

Post-Arnoldian Rugby had been one of the schools where Thring served as an Examiner in the years after his Gloucester curacy.[27]

Before the introduction of the three-term year in 1877, Uppingham had two halves on the Eton model. They ran from early February to late June, and from mid-August to just before Christmas. The Eton practice of half holidays on Saints' Days was also adopted.[28] The pattern of the school day was first school from 7.00am to 8.30am (8.40am in winter); second school 10.00am to 12.00 noon; "Extra subjects" were taught from 12.00 noon to 1.30pm; afternoon school on whole school days ran from 2.30pm to 4.00pm (4.00pm to 5.25pm in winter); and private study was set each evening from 7.00pm to 8.45pm except on Saturday. There were no lessons on Sunday.[29] "Extra subjects", taught by the "Extra masters", was

[24] Diary, December 20, 1858.
[25] Edward Thring, *Three Letters and Axioms on Education*. 1866. In UA. The importance of *Tom Brown's Schooldays* will be discussed later.
[26] Diary, December 20, 1858. For more on Arnold see Tozer, *Manliness*, 33-43.
[27] Arnold's successors, Archibald Tait (1842-1848) and Meyrick Goulburn (1849-1857), let standards slip but they rose quickly when Frederick Temple was appointed (1858-1869).
[28] Patterson, *Uppingham Cricket*, 105; *Schools Inquiry Commission*. XVI, North Midlands Division. Special Reports of the Assistant Commissioners. 1869, 132-137.
[29] *Guide Book*, 1869. In UA.

the term used for the ingredients of the broader curriculum imported from Bonn. The members of the Schools Inquiry Commission commented on the unusual hours when they visited the school in 1865:

> Edward Baines, MP – 'are you bound by your charter of trust to begin at the very early hours mentioned in the morning?'

> Thring – 'I think not.'

> 'Do you approve of that; do you think it desirable on the whole to begin at those early hours?'

> 'I do very much; we have finished our main heavy work by 12 o'clock in the day, and it is a great boon to masters and boys.'

> 'I rather infer from that that you approve of and promote out of door amusements and exercises.'

> 'Very much indeed.'

> 'They form a conspicuous feature of your school?'

> 'A very conspicuous feature; I myself play a great deal.'[30]

V

All boys were taught classics, English, mathematics, history and geography by their form-masters, and one or more of singing, German, French, drawing and science (in order of popularity) by the extra masters. Within a few years gymnastics, carpentry and metalwork were added to the options, drawing became compulsory for the older boys, about a third of the school learnt to play a musical instrument, and a little drama was included.[31] Thring was convinced that the best education of the mind came through a classical, literary and mathematical training, and so these subjects were given greatest emphasis in the curriculum. These, he believed, made the mind "strong and ready" and did not confine it to "narrower ranges". Factual learning and mere "knowledge-power" played no part in the teaching of Latin and Greek; the purpose was to "exercise

---

[30] *Schools Inquiry Commission.* V, Minutes of Evidence taken before the Commissioners, part ii. 1868, 97.
[31] Parkin, *Life*, 2:201.

the mind" and the benefits gained were as much moral as intellectual.[32] In his Greek lessons, and following Arnold's example, Thring would link moral issues in Plato with passages in the Bible.

Literature and history were studied to present to the boys "the highest thought of the highest men in the most perfect shape."[33] Spenser's *Fairie Queene*, Shakespeare's *Macbeth* and *Hamlet*, Scott's novels, Chaucer, Milton and Johnson were all studied, with Keble's *The Christian Year* reserved for the younger boys.[34] History and geography themes were carefully chosen: an Old Boy recalled that "The Great Romans, The Great Dutchmen, the type of Englishman that built our Indian Empire, appealed to Thring."[35] Books studied included Mommsen's *Rome*, Motley's *Netherlands* and Kaye's *Indian Officers*.[36] The teaching of English grammar was fundamental, especially for the younger boys: "You might just as well feed and clothe an Indian like an Esquimaux as generalise rules for English, from the Latin or Greek languages."[37] Howard Candler, a Cambridge Wrangler, taught the senior mathematicians.[38]

Decorations in classrooms were important teaching aids: give "honour to lessons", Thring would say, with the addition of paintings of birds and animals; Livy should be read against a background of the Alps or modern Rome.[39] Thring aimed to have classrooms decorated to meet different educational needs (a Roman room, a Greek room, an English room, and so on) and, in the decorations of the School House hall, the photographs in his classroom, and the magnificent murals in the school-room, he gave ample evidence of his belief in the Platonic principle that a soul absorbs its

[32] Thring, *E&S*, 46.
[33] Thring, *Education Society*, 36.
[34] Diary, April 12, 1861; *Schools Inquiry Commission.* XVI, 149; and see the portraits in the Old School-room.
[35] James, *Thring*, 22.
[36] Theodor Mommsen's *The History of Rome* was published by Reimer & Hirsel in Leipzig as three volumes during 1854–1856; John Motley's *History of the United Netherlands* was published in London by Harper & Brothers as four volumes in 1867; and John Kaye's *Lives of Indian Officers* was published in London as two volumes by A. Strahan and Co. in 1867.
[37] Letter from Thring to Alexander Macmillan, June 6, 1857 – BL.
[38] A Wrangler had a first in mathematics. Candler taught at the school from 1861 to 1899. He was skilled teacher of the youngest and least able boys too, jollying them along with his unique methods, including counting '… nine, ten, onety-one, onety-two, onety-three …'.
[39] Thring, *Addresses*, 52, 138.

environment.[40] The school-room also contained 70 small portraits of famous painters from Polygnotus to J. M. W. Turner.[41]

VI

In 1872 the Clarendon Commissioners, who were examining the nine established public schools, instructed their Secretary to write to Thring to seek information on the organisation at Uppingham; this was a clear sign that the school had become well known. From Thring's replies we learn that the school had fourteen form-masters, including Thring, teaching the core of the curriculum; a mathematics specialist, Candler; three men teaching French and German; three teaching music; and one each for art, carpentry, gymnastics and metalwork: a total of twenty-five.[42] The school then numbered 300, making the pupil-teacher ratio 12:1.

In 1860 Thring secured agreement from his housemasters for each to take one boy free so that there could be a "stream of intellect" in the school: "No slight matter, judging by the average of the material we have hitherto had."[43] It was however the business of the school to teach and train every boy, and not just to offer knowledge to the clever and the hard-working: "everyone has to be dealt with; racing stables and a crack winner or two will not do."[44] Thring reaffirmed this belief in a speech on "Success in Life": "I don't want stars or rockets: I want every boy here to have a chance of showing his little light to help the world".[45] Thring's insistence that the school should take boys of all abilities led to the reputation that Uppingham was best suited to the average boy or the dullard rather than to the scholar.[46] This slight against the school's academic standing was undeserved, as James Mangan found when he examined the entrants for Jesus College, Cambridge for the period 1849-85: here the number of

---

[40] Diary, October 10, 1866; *Founder's Day*, 1882, 3, in UA; Hardwicke Rawnsley, *Edward Thring: Teacher and Poet* (London: T. F. Unwin, 1889), 41; Thring, *Addresses*, 162.

[41] Polygnotus was an ancient Greek painter from the middle of the 5th century BC.

[42] Parkin, *Life*, 2:191.

[43] Diary, April 2, 1860.

[44] Thring, *Education Society*, 12.

[45] *The Guardian*, November 2, 1887; quoted in Richardson, *Thring*, 99.

[46] Letter from Thring to the Rev Alfred Boucher, December 10, 1870: "I know one important private tutor where the delicate or stupid boys are sent to us, as the only place where real care is taken, and the clever and promising elsewhere. This is a compliment one could sometimes dispense with." Quoted in Parkin, *Life*, 1:297. Boucher had two boys in the school; both won places at Cambridge.

Uppinghamians ranked third behind boys from Eton and Harrow, both much larger schools with greater metropolitan and aristocratic intakes.[47]

We have seen already how professional connections and family friendships brought boys to Uppingham in Thring's first years (the Macmillan brothers and Goodwin in Cambridge, and Hedley at Gloucester) and there were many more. The Alford link brought four Cornish brothers and one Newbolt; the Thames Valley supplied six Powells, five Rawnsleys, and five Skrines. When the Rawnsley family moved to Lincolnshire they captured five Harman boys for the school. Many early staff attracted boys to the school through family connections, notably William Earle, William Witts, William Campbell and George Mullins. When Thring's second-eldest brother, Henry, worked as a successful lawyer on Merseyside, he proved to be a most effective recruiting sergeant for the school and the Liverpool-Manchester axis has remained strong to this day. Eton friendships brought still more boys. Soon a critical mass was reached and word of mouth brought further boys to the school "to be under Thring".[48]

---

[47] The Cambridge figures are taken from Mangan, *Athleticism*, 267.
[48] For more on the first boys see Richardson, *Thring*, 34-38; Rigby, *Teachers' Teacher*, 230-248.

CHAPTER SIX

EDWARD THRING'S UPPINGHAM, 1857-1863: "THE RACER'S SPIRIT"

I

In 1857 the first Committee of Games was formed, almost certainly on Thring's initiative. Its members were the Captain of School, the Captain of the XI, and three other senior boys, and it was to undertake "the management of all games" and to be "the arbiter in all disputes".[1] The first set of Committee of Games *Rules* was published the same year and included within them were the headmaster's rules for Uppingham Football. Two years later Thring introduced the Athletic Sports and "wrote out five rules for the racing for my Captain".[2] These were subsequently embodied in a later edition of the Committee of Games *Rules.* From 1862 the Committee also published result cards for the athletics.[3] Thring instructed the Committee on the subject of cricket as well, to the effect that all boys who played the game should help with the spring rolling of the pitch; the "all" is a reminder that attendance at games in this period was wholly voluntary, although all boys were encouraged to join in.[4] During these early years the Committee of Games was an extension of Thring's own authority, and trusted praepostors effected his policies.

Increased numbers in the school now brought a prolonged search for additional playing fields to supplement The Upper.[5] Van Diemen's Land, south of the town, was hired "temporarily" in 1860 and the Town's "late cricket ground" was now used by the younger boys.[6] The following year

---

[1] Rome, Uppingham, appendix.
[2] Diary, February 27, 1861.
[3] In UA.
[4] Diary, March 2, 1859.
[5] Diary, March and April 1860.
[6] Diary, April 4 and 8, 1860. The southern hemisphere island Van Diemen's Land was renamed Tasmania in 1856. The Uppingham use of the name suggests that this distant playing field seemed to be on the other side of the world. George

Thring was unsuccessful with his bid for eight acres of "Rectory Land", just to the south of the school on the opposite ridge, to supplement the distant Van Diemen's Land.[7] The school was now divided into two Hundreds for games; a third would be gained in due course.[8] The older boys in the Upper Hundred used the cricket ground to the east of the town with its rudimentary pavilion; both are depicted in Reimers's illustrated cover for *The Uppingham Cricket and Fives Songs.* Younger boys made up the Lower Hundred and used the field gained from the Town with its simple tent.[9] Within the Hundreds the various XIs for cricket were distinguished by different coloured caps and white jackets with matching coloured ribbons.[10]

The cricket matches with local sides were maintained throughout this period and a game against Oundle, sixteen miles to the south-east, was revived for a few years; "but they proved useless, and the match was dropped", Willingham Rawnsley recalled.[11] The boys tried to arrange a game with Rugby, then a much more prestigious school, but nothing materialised: "All in good time", Thring noted in his dairy.[12] For play within the school various pick-up matches were played: "Bells and Browns" (two prolific families) versus "The Rest", "Sixth Form" versus "The School", "Tall" versus "Short" and "Cambridge" versus "The World" are examples.[13] Attendance at all games was voluntary and on fine days many would choose to go off for a swim.[14]

Thring had inherited the Stockerston brook bathing place to the west of the town, and he had tried to improve it by paving the bottom at a cost of £25, but by the end of 1859 problems with the owner of the land adjacent to the brook forced him to look elsewhere for a new bathing place.[15] The earlier preference for the river at Thorpe, well to the south of Uppingham, fell out of favour because of the long trek and the time taken away from other school activities. The search for a new site occupied much of

Christian's house, Fircroft (originally Fir Croft), was built to the west of the field in 1871. The "temporary" lasted until at least 1889! *USM*, April 1885, 128.

[7] Diary, May 29, 1861.

[8] There were still three Hundreds for games when I joined the school in 1966, even though there were nearly 600 boys in the school.

[9] Diary, May 4, 1860.

[10] Patterson, *Uppingham Cricket*, 16.

[11] Rawnsley, *Early Days*, 99.

[12] Diary, May 4, 1860.

[13] *USM*, June 1863, 105.

[14] Rawnsley, *Early Days,* 88.

[15] About £3,000 in 2018. Diary, April 8 and December 27, 1859 and March 29, 1860.

Thring's diary but eventually a disused tar-pit just below The Upper was acquired. This was modified to create a suitable bathing place at a cost of £70, and it was opened to the boys on May 20, 1860.[16] Willingham Rawnsley, a boy at this time, recalled that

> though the water was anything but perfect, and always smelt somewhat of gas tar (it took its rise near the gas works), we all used it daily, and everyone learnt to swim. It was paved in the shallow part with rough flag-stones, and shelved from two to six or seven feet in depth.[17]

Thring gave public leave for bathing to begin at about the middle of May each year; thereafter boys had only to seek permission from their housemasters to go, although they could not go twice in one day.[18] Two periods were set aside in the day for swimming: 12.00 noon to 1.30pm for boys not involved in extra subjects, and 3.00pm to 6.30pm during the boys' free time.[19] Rawnsley remembered that "in summer cricket was the one game, but even that was not so rigidly attended but that one could at times go off with a friend before half-past four call-over … to bathe".[20] Special leave could also be given to a few senior boys to swim early on Sunday mornings.[21]

Fives continued to be a popular springtime recreation and a number of new Eton fives courts were built in the grounds of the boarding houses. An annual doubles competition was soon arranged, it was still going strong in the 1960s, and a small entrance fee was levied to swell the games fund.[22] The losing pair in each match paid for the ball.[23] Rawnsley remembered Thring playing regularly in his "grey flannels and black wide-awake"; he "played a fast game, and hit and volleyed with tremendous force".[24] When the Old Etonian William Witts joined the staff as housemaster and chaplain in 1861, he and Thring joined in the competition when the champions had been declared, challenging them to a game. Invariably experience triumphed over youth.[25]

---

[16] Over £8,000 today. Diary, May 10 1859 and May 20, 1860.

[17] Rawnsley, *Early Days*, 89.

[18] *USM*, June 1865, 178; *School Rules*.

[19] *Guide Book*.

[20] Rawnsley, *Early Days*, 88.

[21] *Guide Book*.

[22] *USM*, March 1864, 90.

[23] *USM*, March 1868, 25.

[24] Letter from Rawnsley, *USM*, March 1920, 25.

[25] *USM*, March 1864, 93. Perhaps the boys were exhausted from their earlier matches! Witts was housemaster of Highfield from 1863.

II

The 1857 edition of the Committee of Games *Rules* resolved that at least one game of football should be played each week in the winter and that non-attendance on declared "field days" should be punishable by a fine.[26] The *Rules* also contained the first printing of Thring's code for Uppingham Football:

I. The game is commenced by one side having a fair kick off at quarter distance.

II. Off-side. – A player is off his side immediately he is in front of the ball, and must return behind the ball as soon as possible. If the ball is kicked by his own side past a player when off-side, he <u>may not touch or kick it or advance</u>, until one of the other side has kicked it again when in front of him

III. If any player kicks off-side, the opposite side may claim a fair kick from the place where it was kicked off-side.

IV. No player being off his side may catch the ball and run, or touch the ball behind the goal-line or in touch.

V. If the ball is touched behind the line of goal by one of the side to which the goal belongs, there is a fresh kick-off at the quarter flag.

VI. When the ball is kicked into touch, the player who kicked it must go after it and bring it towards play, level with the spot on which it entered touch, and kick it straight into the middle of the game.

VII. The goal posts must be six paces apart.

VIII. A goal can be won in the open field by the ball being kicked under the cross bar and between the upright poles.

IX. If the ball is touched by an enemy behind the line of goal, a bully may be claimed five paces in front of goal.

X. Three bullies are equal to one goal; and if the ball is forced through goals from a bully, it counts as one goal.

XI. If whilst the ball is in the bully any one of the players fall down, the bully must be stopped at once, and begin again from the place where the ball is. No kicking is allowed in the bullies.

XII. The discretion of sending into goal, or giving any other orders, rests with the Heads of sides or the deputies appointed by them.

---

[26] Rome, Uppingham, appendix.

XIII. If any player kicks the ball behind his own goal and his own side touch it, the opposite side may claim a bully at the place where the ball was kicked, but if the opposite side touch it, it counts as an ordinary bully.

XIV. Any player who catches the ball in the air, or at first bound, may either kick it as best he can, or run with it towards the enemy's goal: provided that he is liable to be stopped by any means except tripping up; and if stopped or held, he must at once <u>kick</u> or <u>put down</u> the ball.

XV. A player may not, in any case, run with the ball in or through touch.

XVI. No player to be held unless he is himself holding the ball.

XVII. No use of hands or elbows to stop or otherwise impede players allowed. No tripping up ever allowed.

XVIII. No charging allowed, except when your adversary is running directly at the ball, or to catch one of your own side whilst running into the ball, according to Rule XIV. In this latter case you may not charge, unless you were behind the player when he caught the ball.

XIX. No charging allowed when a player is off-side; that is, <u>immediately the ball is behind him</u>.

XX. No ball is ever to be <u>struck</u> or <u>thrown</u> with the hand, or lifted from the ground. Stopping the ball alone allowed.

XXI. No ball ever to be kicked during play whilst in the air.

XXII. No player ever to kick except directly at the ball.

XXIII. No player may wear projecting nails or iron plates on the heels or soles of his boots or shoes. No padding allowed.

XXIV. No kicking with the heel or above the knee is fair.

XXV. No player to stand within six paces of the kicker when he is kicking out of touch, or kicking off.[27]

The rules ended with some "Advice to players": "The game is to carry the ball in a body across the field, and to try and force it through the goal". Fly-kicks were discouraged and the role of the "goal keeper" was explained: "no player should ever get in the way of the goal keeper or interfere with his kick", but each player was encouraged to "back up" his "goal keeper" when the ball neared his goal. The final advice was "do not

---

[27] The original copy of the rules is missing from the archives but a manuscript copy was made by Brian Belk in the 1960s. All underlining is in the original. The width of the goal at six paces is equivalent to about twenty feet.

be content with one kick at the ball but rush on and follow up your kick, and take the ball with you as far as you can".[28]

Masters continued to play football with the boys. Willingham Rawnsley remembered

> Dr. Benguerel, pronounced by us 'Bungarell,' and abbreviated into 'Old Bungy' ...played football most courageously.... Mr. Hodgkinson, who always played in full clerical costume – white choker, black trousers, and tall hat, though the latter would be flung aside when he warmed to his work – was a wonderfully speedy runner at football, but Dr. Benguerel was in the thick of the fight while his wind lasted. We played one side in white, the other in red jerseys, and I can hear now the Doctor's cry of encouragement or despair when he could run no more, 'Go it, vite vons!' or 'Oh, my vite vons, my vite vons!'[29]

Rawnsley is mistaken about jerseys, which were introduced in the mid-1860s after Benguerel had returned to Prussia.[30] Red and white caps had replaced the coloured waist-bands worn earlier; each boy needed one of each colour so that teams could be sorted out just before kick-off. This convention continued until the 1990s, but with red and white jerseys.

III

Thring instigated the athletics sports at Uppingham in 1859 at a time when many schools were adopting them. His diary for March that year relates the long search to find suitable routes for the steeplechases.[31] The heats and finals of the various races were spread over two or three weeks in March and seem designed to fill the interval between the end of the football season before Christmas and the start of the cricket season in April. When the boys returned to school in February, they were encouraged to use that month to train for the sports.

The 1859 sports contained eight events: "two steeple chases, two height and two width jumps, a hundred yard's race, under thirteen, and throwing the cricket ball".[32] The separate steeplechases and jumps were for boys over and under sixteen years of age. In 1860 this age divide was

---

[28] As above.
[29] Rawnsley, *Early Days*, 78-79.
[30] In 1861.
[31] Diary, March 8-10, 1859.
[32] *USM*, April 1864, 44.

moved down to fifteen, and the two groups of boys were soon labelled "Overs" and "Unders".[33] The two steeplechases in 1859 were held in a valley near Stoke Dry, a village two miles to the south of Uppingham; the other events were staged on The Upper.[34] Thring joined in some of the competitions, that year recording 4 feet 5 inches in the high jump and 16 feet 1 inch in the long jump. His diary records the boys' pleasure in the sports and his delight at his own performances.[35] The following year he noted that after the sports "one feels <u>one</u> with the boys".[36]

The following years saw the addition of more events. The mile and quarter-mile races were run on the roads around the town; a race over sheep hurdles was run on Van Diemen's Land; and a consolation race for boys who had not already won an event was introduced.[37] In 1860 a cup was presented for the overall champion; George Bigg was the first recipient.[38] Before the start of the 1863 sports there was much discussion and considerable difference of opinion on whether or not Thomas Poole, who had been the champion in 1861 and 1862, should be allowed to compete again. As a compromise, Poole stood down but was acknowledged as champion.[39] To prevent a repetition of this dilemma, handicapped races were considered but soon rejected.[40]

In the first years of the sports the steeplechases were the blue riband event; they moved from Stoke Dry to Ridlington, two miles north-west of Uppingham, in 1860. Thring appeased local farmers by the presentation of a silver medal with the school seal on one side and a cheque for £15 or £20 as the prize for the best beast at the annual Rutland Agricultural Show held in Oakham.[41] He hoped that this generosity would allow his boys to roam freely across the countryside throughout the year and, in general, it worked. The first steeplechases were long and difficult but an accident to a boy in 1860 persuaded Thring to shorten the distance to 600 yards for the "old set" and 400 yards for the young.[42] Even then he was always relieved when the races were over, "though we have reduced the chances of

---

[33] Rawnsley, *Early Days*, 85. The terms Overs and Unders are still in use in 2018.
[34] *USM*, July 1885, 225.
[35] Diary, March 19, 20 and 22, 1859.
[36] The stress is Thring's: Diary, March 14, 1860.
[37] Diary, March 13, 1860; *USM*, April 1863, 13, 26.
[38] Bigg won a place at Wadham College, Oxford and took Holy Orders.
[39] *USM*, April 1885, 127. Poole won a place at St John's College, Cambridge and took Holy Orders.
[40] *USM*, November 1863, 273.
[41] *USM*, March 1924, 5.
[42] *USM*, July 1865, 127; Diary, February 25, 1862.

accidents as much as possible".[43] These races brought out the "truly English qualities" of "trial to wind, pluck and endurance", or what Thring termed "the racer's spirit".[44] In 1864 thirteen-year-old Hardwicke Rawnsley, Willingham's younger brother, was one of the smallest boys to finish the steeplechase; he was nowhere near the front. Thring then offered another prize for a race between the two smallest boys; this time Rawnsley won.[45]

IV

In September 1859 two of Thring's masters, the Swiss-born Dr Gerold Benguerel and the Old Etonian George Mathias, proposed that a gymnasium be built. Thring readily agreed.[46] The construction of "a plain cheap building", situated below and just to the east of School House, began immediately and was opened on November 24 that year by Marie Thring on her birthday.[47] The boys "crowded in to great glee" and Thring noted that it was in great use on rainy days.[48] The wet-weather use would seem to have been the gymnasium's purpose for Mathias, who wanted to occupy the boys in his house when they could not play outdoors, whereas Benguerel was well acquainted with gymnastics.[49] He had previously taught at Dr Kortegarn's Institut in Bonn, a few doors away from Breusing's school; he taught German, French and science.[50] Matthew Arnold, one of Her Majesty's Inspector of Schools, had noted that the Prussians had cultivated gymnastics in their schools "with great care" since 1842 and in his later visits to schools there he recorded that the gymnastic teachers professed "to have adapted their exercises with precision to every age, and to all stages of a boy's growth and muscular

---

[43] Diary, March 2, 1861.
[44] *USM*, May 1863, 47 and January 1888, 38.
[45] Rawnsley, *Canon Rawnsley*, 11. Rawnsley went on to Balliol College, Oxford, took Holy Orders and co-founded the National Trust. See Tozer, *Manliness*, 182-192.
[46] Diary, September 2, 1859.
[47] Rawnsley, *Early Days*, 60.
[48] Diary, September 24 and December 1, 1859.
[49] Mathias is sometimes spelt Matthias. He later took private pupils on the Isle of Wight.
[50] Their schools were at Coblenzerstraße 39 and 100: *Bonner Kalender* 1855. Benguerel returned to the Rhineland in 1861 to work in the Prussian Education Department in Hanover. He became Director of the Kaiserliches Lyceum in Strasburg in 1871.

development".[51] Gymnastic exercises were practised in Bonn in the period when Benguerel taught in the city and a club, the Bonner Turnverein, was founded in 1860. The wet-and-cold weather provision for exercise would seem to have been Thring's initial reason for backing the project for he recorded in his diary that it will be "an excellent thing on rainy days and in winter".[52]

The list of teaching staff that accompanied the Christmas Examination results for 1859 includes "Serjeant Major Ellis, Drilling, etc." and in the same period Thring's diary notes an interview with an unnamed but "satisfactory" candidate for the "gymnastic place" and that he was "almost engaged".[53] The Crimean War of 1853-1856 that had exposed many defects in the physical fitness of men serving in the British Army, together with Lord Elcho's call for military drill to be introduced in the public schools in the wake of a French invasion scare of 1858, makes such a military appointment feasible but Ellis never arrived.[54] His printed name on that staff list is deleted in ink and replaced in Thring's handwriting by "Herr Beisiegel, Gymnastics and Fencing". Beisiegel later recalled that Thring had appointed him "about Christmas 1859"; thus he, and not Ellis, may have been the interviewee.[55] Beisiegel arrived at Uppingham at the start of the new Half on February 17, 1860 to take up this unique appointment at a British school.[56] It was not until 1910, when Edward Lyttelton appointed Reginald Roper at Eton, that a civilian was next

---

[51] Matthew Arnold, *Higher Schools and Universities in Germany* (London: Macmillan, 1874), 135. Matthew was Thomas Arnold's son; in 1851 he became one of Her Majesty's Inspectors of Schools.

[52] Diary, September 2, 1859.

[53] *Uppingham School – Christmas Examination*, 1859. In UA. Diary, December 3 and 6, 1859.

[54] The Crimean War was a conflict in which Russia lost to an alliance of France, the United Kingdom, the Ottoman Empire, and Sardinia. The United Kingdom and France were unwilling to allow Russia to gain territory and power at the expense of the declining Ottoman Empire.

In January 1858 an Italian nationalist failed in his attempt to assassinate Napoleon III. When the French authorities discovered that he had bought his explosives in England, French public opinion sensed a British-Italian conspiracy and clamoured for war. Nothing came of it.

Elcho's agitation resulted in a meeting in London early in 1860 to discuss the establishment of cadet corps in public schools; several schools formed contingents later that year. For more information see Tozer, *Manliness*, 285-286.

[55] Copy of a letter from Beisiegel to Edward Selwyn, May 22, 1902, Beisiegel papers, in UA.

[56] Thring's Diary, February 17, 1860.

appointed to teach physical education at a public school.[57] Most employed military or naval instructors who were not members of Common Room.

When, early in 1860, Thring realised that Beisiegel could also teach music, he was asked to give piano lessons and to assist with the choir; the music team now numbered two.[58] Beisiegel served the school loyally in music and gymnastics, a truly Platonic arrangement, until 1902; he was the first Prussian master to make Uppingham his permanent home. Twenty-three-year-old Georg Heinrich Carl Beisiegel was born on April 24, 1836 at Sankt Goar am Rhein, upstream from Bonn, where his father was the schoolmaster.[59] After schooling in Cleves, where he was captain of school, and training in gymnastics, probably at the Royal Central School of Gymnastics in Berlin, he began teaching in Coblenz where he heard of the Uppingham vacancy. Two years after his arrival in Uppingham he married a local girl, Sarah Susannah Jackson, and they made their home in the nearby village of Preston and raised three children. At some stage between the 1871 and 1881 censuses the family moved to Sunny Bank at the end of the Stockerston road out of Uppingham.[60] Beisiegel became a British subject in 1874.[61]

Beisiegel made a good impression on the other masters at the school and soon, at the suggestion of William Earle and William Campbell, he

---

[57] Eton College, *List of Masters,* 1911. Captain George Hodgson, late of the 44th Foot, was Instructor of Gymnastics at Cheltenham College from 1871. As an Old Boy of Marlborough College, and thus a gentleman as well as an officer, he would have been a member of Common Room but he may not have taught any gymnastics. He had served previously as Superintendent of the Military Gymnasium at Colchester, where sergeants would have done the actual instruction. This may have been the situation at Cheltenham, and it is what I met when I arrived at Uppingham in 1966. Brian Ware, a housemaster who taught geography, was Warden of the Gymnasium and Swimming Bath but Petty Officer John Hall did the actual teaching. See: Andrew Hunter, *Cheltenham College Register, 1841-1889* (London: George Bell, 1890), 49.

[58] Copy of a letter from Beisiegel to Edward Monckton (a trustee of the school), June, 1902, Beisiegel papers.

[59] Beisiegel was the eldest of eight children. When his father died in 1862, Beisiegel assumed financial responsibility for his mother and his siblings. One brother, Frederick, came to Uppingham and was in Thring's house from February 1864 to June 1865. Beisiegel to Monckton, as above; letter from Thring to Beisiegel, February 24, 1864. Beisiegel papers.

[60] The family was still at Sunny Bank in the 1901 census.

[61] Information from Miss Lillian Margarettte Beisiegel, his grand-daughter, 1972. She died in 1975. Camilla English recalls her aunt Lillian saying that Beisiegel was happy to settle in Britain because he did not feel comfortable with Prussian militarism: email message to author, June 10, 2018.

was welcomed to housemasters' meetings and granted a vote.[62] Old Boys remembered him as a popular master and a "real good old sport"; he regularly played with them at football.[63] He was equally well regarded in the town, serving over the course of his career as a Churchwarden, a Poor Law Guardian, a member of the Local Sanitary Authority, a governor of Oakham School, a founder of Uppingham High School for Girls, and as the representative for Uppingham South on the Rutland County Council.[64] From the early 1860s he was well acquainted with the leading British physical educationalists, including Archibald MacLaren at the Oxford Gymnasium, and from the 1890s he gained a national reputation. He was a founder member of the National Society of Physical Education in 1897 and three times its President, a member of the British College of Physical Education, and Vice-President of the National Physical Recreation Society.[65] The first and second organised examinations for students training to be teachers, including women at the first specialist physical education colleges; the third lobbied the government to make physical education compulsory in all elementary schools.[66]

V

The 1859 gymnasium was used throughout Thring's reign and was not replaced until 1904. The building was then converted into a buttery until it was demolished in 1981 to make way for an extension to the Music School and a new buttery. Honours boards on its walls that recorded the names of mid-Victorian gymnastic champions were visible until that time. The gymnasium had a rectangular plan and a simple "A" roof. The walls were panelled to a height of four feet, with white plastering above. Until gas lighting was added in 1860, the only illumination was by the windows high on the south wall.[67] The floor was originally covered with a dusty tan that "long annoyed" the gymnasts; in 1863 it was re-surfaced with dust-

---

[62] He also contributed to the masters' fund for school improvements. Beisiegel to Monckton, as above.

[63] George Turner, *Unorthodox Reminiscences* (London: Murray, 1931), 49.

[64] *USM*, June 1881, 185; November 1888, 335; and June 1956, 59. Beisiegel papers.

[65] Beisiegel papers; Malcolm Tozer, "Thring's 'favourite wish': Uppingham High School for Girls, 1888-1893," *Rutland Record* 38, (2018): 363-372.

[66] Ida Webb, *The Challenge of Change in Physical Education* (London: Routledge, 1999), 14, 17; Martin Polley, *The History of Sport in Britain, 1880-1914* (London: Routledge, 2003), 2:462.

[67] Diary, November 5, 1860.

free coral sand, six to twelve inches in depth.[68] The building was on two levels: the smaller part set ten feet above the main gymnasium was left clear of apparatus and was used for standing exercises and fencing.[69] The original apparatus in the lower part included parallel bars fixed into the ground (they were still there in 1904) and ropes hanging from the roof beams.[70] In 1863 a rope ladder and a slanting pole were installed.[71] A year later a slanting ladder, vertical poles, a cat-gallows and several pairs of clubs were added, and in 1866 there is mention of a horizontal bar.[72] An inclined plank, "well adapted for expanding the chest", was constructed in 1869.[73] Photographs taken in about 1885 show all this apparatus together with a vaulting horse, a set of low parallel bars, and a pair of rings. An undated memorandum in Beisiegel's handwriting lists the following apparatus, most made by local craftsmen:

2 strong Parallel Bars of oak, a higher and a lower one fixed into the ground

2 Horizontal Bars of different hights (sic) fixed into the ground and having iron Rods through the bars

1 Valting (sic) Bar with Sliding Ash Pole[74]

2 Pairs of Rings of different lengths.

1 slanting and 2 straight Climbing Poles of different thicknesses and fixed into the ground and screwed at the top (they are from 14 to 23 feet in length)

2 swinging Climbing Poles of equal thickness

2 stout Climbing Ropes each 22 feet long

---

[68] *USM*, May 1863, 71; extract from *The Gymnasium*, Beisiegel papers.
[69] Some manuscript notes on the gymnasium are in the Beisiegel papers.
[70] Bothamley, *Some Notes,* 19.
[71] *USM*, October 1863, 240.
[72] A cat-gallows is the equivalent of the high bar in modern Olympic gymnastics: William Dickinson, *A Glossary of the Words and Phrases of Cumberland: Supplement* (Whitehaven: Callander and Dixon, 1867), 7. *USM*, May 1864, 192 and May 1866, 90.
[73] *USM*, March 1870, 41.
[74] This would seem to be the cat-gallows.

1 Horizontal Ladder resting on a strong oak Frame, to be used at 3 different hights (sic) from the ground – it is 14 ft long, 2 ft 4 inch wide and has 12 spokes

1 Slanting Ladder 21 ft long 2 ft 2 wide, and has 19 spokes

1 Ladder Plank (by Maclaren) 17 ft 6 long, 1,5 wide and has 19 spokes[75]

1 Trapeze, jumping boards

There are 2 Cupboards containing a large quantity of Indian Clubs and Dumb Bells of many different weights – and Fencing Material

There is also one of the Griffiths patented pulling Machines.[76]

The last is presumably a forerunner of a modern multi-gym exercise machine.

In addition to class use, the boys had the run of the gymnasium for recreational activity during the winter in the half-hour before tea. When Robert Pitcairn published the first book about the school in 1870, he reported that the gymnasium was "well patronised".[77] An amusing picture of these afternoon sessions is recorded in the 1867 "Sketches from an Uppingham Scrapbook" published in the school magazine:

A noise of straining ropes and creaking timber; heavy panting, and thud of falling feet – what does it all mean? Such question a stranger asked himself, as he stood on the outside of a certain well-known door, and prepared with some curiosity and more trepidation to follow his cicerone into this home of mysterious sound. Then as the door opens, he that saw the sight relates, that there played before his eyes for one brief moment, like a waking dream, a vision of motion, a shifting panorama of human bodies twisting and straining in convolutions manifold, and swinging ropes freighted with life; in other words, Uppingham School Gymnasium at 4.33 p.m. on a wet day.[78]

---

[75] This was added at MacLaren's suggestion: extract from *The Gymnasium*, Beisiegel papers.

[76] Beisiegel papers.

[77] Robert Pitcairn, *Uppingham School* (London: Charles Drake, 1870), 14.

[78] And so on for another seven pages: *USM*, May 1867, 100-107. Cicerone is an old term for a guide who conducts visitors and sightseers to museums, galleries, etc.

VI

It was the innovation of the gymnastics and fencing classes as part of the curriculum that warranted Beisiegel's appointment. They were on the same footing as the other extra subjects and, together with his music teaching, provided his income. When questioned on the numbers attending these classes by the Schools Inquiry Commissioners in 1865, Thring replied that they were more popular than drawing, German and chemistry, and as popular as music, French and carpentry. The statistics collected by the visiting commissioners include those for all the extra subjects except gymnastics but, by applying Thring's equation, about 70 boys were receiving gymnastic tuition in 1865. The school at this time numbered 268. The annual fee for gymnastics was 2 guineas, compared with 8 guineas for drawing, chemistry, French and German, and 30 shillings for carpentry.[79] Thring agreed with a commissioner's suggestion that the popularity of gymnastics might be related to its favourable fee.[80] No information has been recorded for the numbers and fees for fencing.

The school library in the 1860s acquired three books on gymnastics soon after their dates of publication and these presumably give some indication of Beisiegel's gymnastics lessons. In 1864 the library received John Howard's *Gymnastic Exercises* (1860), followed a few years later by Archibald MacLaren's *Training in Theory and Practice* (1866) and *A System of Physical Education* (1869).[81] Howard described exercises to be performed on parallel bars, the horizontal bar, the suspended bar and the suspended ropes, together with routines using Indian clubs. The suspended bar matches Uppingham's cat-gallows, so everything that Howard lists could be undertaken in Beisiegel's gymnasium.[82]

MacLaren had built the University Gymnasium at Oxford in 1858 and there, with the support of the military authorities, he modified the educational gymnastic work of Guts Muths and Clias to meet British needs.[83] MacLaren divided exercise into "Recreative" and "Educational"

---

[79] *Schools Inquiry Commission.* V, 101. A guinea was one pound and one shilling, or 21 shillings. Beisiegel received about £250 a year for each pupil in today's terms, or £17,500 in total. His music teaching produced a second income. When he died in 1904, he left £7,157 in his estate, the equivalent of £800,000 in 2018. Teaching gymnastics and music at Thring's Uppingham was well paid.

[80] *Schools Inquiry Commission.* V, 101.

[81] *USM*, June 1864, 228; April 1876, 60; and June 1869, 168.

[82] John Howard, *Gymnastic Exercises* (London: Longman, Green, Longman and Roberts, 1860), passim.

[83] McIntosh, *Physical Education*, 92.

categories. The former included all the games played in schools which, although invaluable in terms of character-forming, did not as an object train the body. His educational exercise was a system of dynamic gymnastics designed to develop all parts of the body.[84] Beisiegel came to know MacLaren well so it is likely that the content and delivery of their gymnastic teaching were similar.

In *A System of Physical Education* MacLaren arranged his exercises into four sections depending on the nature of the movement.

> Section I embraces the moveable apparatus, which give light and uniform employment to the entire body. (For this reason they are made to constitute the preliminary course of the system.)

> Section II embraces all arrangements for the practice of Exercises of Progression, such as walking, running, leaping, and vaulting, which employ chiefly the lower limbs and lower regions of the trunk.

> Section III embraces all apparatus for exercises of rotation and oscillation, as the trapezium and parallel bars, giving employment to the whole of the trunk and upper limbs.

> Section IV embraces all climbing apparatus, as the ropes and poles, vertical and inclined, giving employment to the entire body, especially to the upper limbs and upper portion of the trunk.[85]

Four courses of exercise, ranging from "First Course, Simple Exercises" to "Fourth Course, Arduous Exercises", were devised, explained and illustrated, each course containing exercises from the four sections. The description of all the exercises occupies 335 pages.[86] Following the Prussian gymnastics tradition adopted by MacLaren at the Oxford Gymnasium, Beisiegel would have tailor-made exercises using fixed and portable apparatus (Indian clubs, vaulting horses, parallel bars, rings, and the like) to improve each boy's strength and agility. MacLaren acknowledged Beisiegel's pioneering work in his *Training in Theory and Practice*, and reported that his example had subsequently been copied at Radley College, Cheltenham, Clifton College, Marlborough and Rugby.[87] W. M. Vardon, who was appointed Uppingham's gymnasium assistant in

---

[84] Archibald MacLaren, *A System of Physical Education* (Oxford: Clarendon Press, 1869), 36, 105.

[85] MacLaren, *System*, 106.

[86] MacLaren, *System*, 116-130, 138-472.

[87] Archibald MacLaren, *Training in Theory and Practice* (London: Macmillan, 1866), 190.

the 1890s, reported that Beisiegel was alert to new methods in gymnastics and "wisely dipped into each".[88]

The climax of the year for the gymnastic pupils was the gymnastic competition, always held on the anniversary of the opening of the gymnasium, the first on November 24, 1860 with later ones needing several days and finishing on the anniversary.[89] Each class was examined in turn, beginning with the youngsters in the First Class, on to the senior boys, and finishing with the praepostors; Beisiegel judged the performances, occasionally assisted by Willingham Rawnsley. Rawnsley had been gymnastics champion in 1863 and he returned to the school as a master from 1871 to 1878.[90] Thring, Marie and her sister Anna always attended. It was part of Marie's birthday routine to present the gymnastic prizes to the winners, whose names were published alongside those for the academic subjects in the Christmas examination lists from 1863 onwards.[91] The prizes, in Thring's own words, were "rather a joke", a joke that was repeated year after year.[92] First prize was a goose, second a large pork pie, and third a pot of jam.[93] Occasionally a letter from a boy to the school magazine would suggest that "surely, a fellow who wins a Gymnastic prize, would like something more lasting than a pot of jam", but the goose and gymnastics became inseparable, an instant tradition.[94] Rawnsley, in a later memory of Thring, recalled that they were chosen "according to a fancy of the Head-Master's that prizes for Gymnastics should be things that perished in the using".[95] The goose was eaten with due ceremony in the victor's house.

---

[88] Extract from *The Gymnasium*, Beisiegel papers.
[89] Diary, November 24, 1860.
[90] *USM*, December 1871, 402.
[91] *Uppingham School – Christmas Examination*, 1863 and subsequent years. In UA.
[92] Diary, November 24, 1860.
[93] Rawnsley, *Early Days,* 109, 115.
[94] *USM*, May 1865, 120.
[95] Rawnsley, *Early Days*, 109.

Photographed by Sir Emery Walker; the negative is in the
National Portrait Gallery's collection

Uppingham Grammar School in 1853

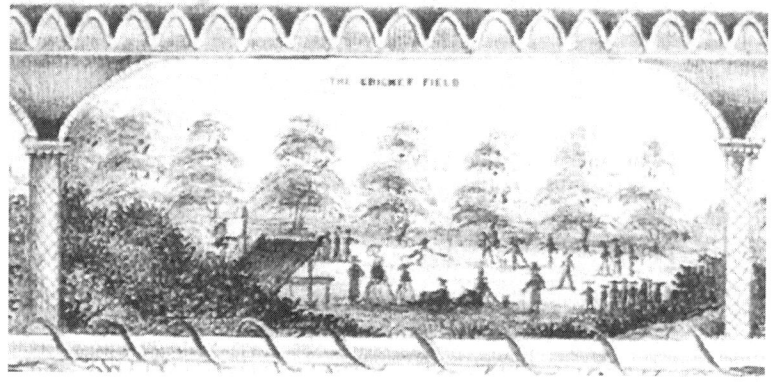

The Cricket Field (later The Upper) in 1857, by Christian Reimers

The 1859 Gymnasium, looking south

The 1859 Gymnasium, looking north

Anna Koch, Edward and Marie
Thring, c1854

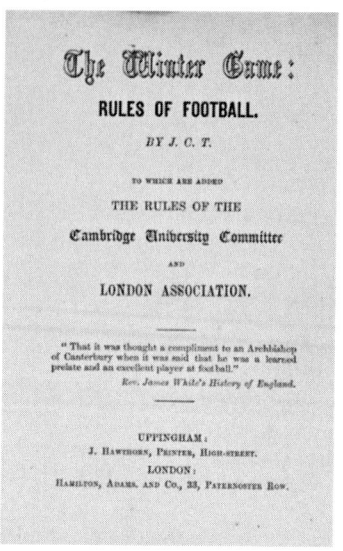

The Winter Game by Charles
Thring, 1862

Georg Beisiegel, c1870

Charles Thring, by his daughter
Annie, 1900 © Sue Kalaugher

Uppingham Football XV, 1862

Cricket Pavilion on The Upper, 1863

The Lower School in 1870, by William Witts

Uppingham from the south-west, 1870
(The Lower School, two boarding houses, the Chapel and the School-room)

Chapel from The Middle, 1881, by Charles Rossiter

School House, Chapel, School-room and studies, 1881, by Charles Rossiter

Swimming pool below The Upper, c1875

"Off to cricket", 1881, by Charles Rossiter

CHAPTER SEVEN

A PHYSICAL EDUCATION: "THE MASTER OF STRENGTH, AND TRAINED MOVEMENT"

I

Physical activity was always important to Thring. School holidays at Alford were spent in rambles about the Somerset countryside and at bathing in the Brue; he wrote of his attachment to the river in a poem composed in his Cambridge years:

> Companion of my boyhood
> my manhood's living friend
> I fain would know thy rising
> I fain would know thy end.[1]

Along with his brothers, Godfrey and Charles, he sent ferrets after rabbits, sailed in home-made coracles, and caught and stuffed birds.[2] It was a robust rural boyhood.

At Eton he played an energetic part in the school's embryonic sports. He did not win a place in any school team but, whether in cricket, football or fives, his bravery made up for any lack of inches or shortage of skill. The Long Chamber at night provided its own sporting challenges, long-jumping over mattresses spread across the floor or in battles hurling fireworks at one another.[3] At Cambridge he continued to play fives, in "the Eton version of hockey", and he rowed in the college boat; and when convalescing after Gloucester he played occasional games of cricket. In one match he was on the opposing team to his brother, Charles, who recalled:

> we made an unusually large score, and (Edward) was lying down after fielding, with a very bad headache. He went in and knocked up over 80

---

[1] Edward Thring, "To a River", Index Rerum.
[2] Richardson, *Thring*, 3.
[3] Rigby, *Teachers' Teacher*, 35; Richardson, *Thring*, 10.

runs very rapidly, beat our side and rid of his headache. Moral: when unwell, play cricket![4]

Thring never regained rude health after his Gloucester life and throughout his Uppingham years he was regularly afflicted with boils. The "when unwell; play cricket!" motto, although composed by Charles, might well have been adopted by Edward. In 1874 the headmaster went to console his Captain of School "who was broken down with overwork":

> I gave him sound advice through my own sufferings and weaknesses, but still more to make him feel, I think, quite differently when he found out how much I had had of the same kind. He said, 'I always thought you had an iron constitution.' I answered, 'Indeed no, for 17 years here I never had a day of perfect health, and I owe, under God, my sitting here alive by you to-day to the care in diet and exercise I have taken ever since I went to Cambridge.' I think I left him much comforted as well as wiser about self-training. I feel very thankful for being able to do it, and for all the painful experience that has opened my heart, and made me able to give comfort.[5]

Part of the care in diet and exercise was to play sports with the boys; cricket, football, fives and athletics. He had his own way of doing everything: "He would insist on some of us small boys learning to bat in his own style, planted on the wrong foot", John Skrine recalled. "He had his own theory of football tactics, and not a sound one; but he imposed it on us as the best possible, until defeat in foreign matches disenchanted us."[6] In cricket his bowling was "so old that it was new" and his style of batting was "peculiar to itself".[7] And he always played to win. Willingham Rawnsley as a boy witnessed Thring and Witts playing the school champions at fives:

---

[4] Quoted in Richardson, *Thring*, 20.

[5] Diary June 4, 1874 (Parkin, *Life*, 1:255). The Captain of School was George Irwin. He won a place at Christ Church, Oxford and joined the Bengal Civil Service.

[6] The only "foreign" matches in football at this period were with the Old Boys. Skrine, *Edward Thring*, 16. Skrine won a place at Corpus Christi College, Oxford, became a Fellow at Merton College, Oxford and took Holy Order before returning to Uppingham as a master. He became housemaster of Brooklands in 1881.

[7] Skrine, *Edward Thring*, 66; Letter from J. H. Green to *The Guardian* (November 2, 1887) in a 'Scrapbook of Memorials to Edward Thring' compiled by H. F. Wilson, 1887. In UA.

Once the ball took his partner a terrific blow on the head, and we paused to listen to a sympathetic apology, all we heard instead was: 'Why don't you keep your head out of the light?'[8]

Thring ceased to join in football and athletics early in the 1860s but he continued to play fives and cricket for another ten years, always dressed "in black trousers and braces", until rheumatism seized him in the leg.[9] After a game of fives on October 10, 1870 he noted in his diary:

I fear it is the last game I shall ever play … . It is hard to give up the last reminiscence of youth, but perhaps in one's forty-ninth year, and near the end of it, one may be well content to have a reminiscence of this kind.[10]

He played his last game of cricket the following summer, 1871.William Patterson, who also played in the match, recalled that Thring was allowed a runner but that the boy appointed inadvertently ran out his headmaster after a "short merry innings".[11] He continued to take "really good" walks until the last week of his life.[12]

Prowess in games gave Thring considerable personal satisfaction as well as keeping ill-health at bay. He was proud to feel that he was probably the first headmaster to play football with his boys; he was delighted when his "53 runs hit tremendously" astonished parents: but above all "having everything" with the boys made him feel "at <u>one</u>" with them.

II

One purpose of a physical education at Uppingham was, therefore, the maintenance of good health and the avoidance of illness. Thring's opinions on diet closely matched those expressed by Herbert Spencer in *Education: Intellectual, Moral and Physical* (1861). Spencer noted how "the raising of first-rate bullocks is an occupation on which educated men willingly bestow much time and thought," whilst "the bringing up of fine human beings is an occupation tacitly voted unworthy of their attention".[13]

---

[8] *USM*, March 1920, 25.
[9] Skrine, *Edward Thring*, 16, 25.
[10] Diary, October 10, 1870 (Parkin, *Life*, 1:223).
[11] Patterson, *Uppingham Cricket*, 49-50.
[12] Diary, October 12, 1887.
[13] Herbert Spencer *Education: Intellectual, Moral and Physical* (London: Williams & Norgate, 1861/91), 131-132. Thring did not, however, share Spencer's

Thring had been an enthusiast for the works of John Ruskin since the publication of the initial volume of *Modern Painters* in 1843 and he later wrote that he owed "to Mr Ruskin's Modern Painters more of thought and fruitful power than to any other book, or any other living man."[14] He shared his enthusiasm for Ruskin in his correspondence with his brother Godfrey.[15] Thring would have surely agreed with Ruskin that "The body must be made as beautiful and perfect in its youth as it can be, wholly irrespective of the ulterior purpose".[16]

All housemasters at Uppingham were required to match the diet in their own houses to that prescribed by Thring in School House, and "more especially in the matter of beer".[17] Further to that, sound health was to be derived from "gymnastics, games, pedestrianism and other forms of bodily exertion".[18]

> Dislodge it from lazing by the fire, or stuffing in the grub shop. Put it out of bed in the morning. Send it running down the road in the morning with the east wind. Kick it on the shins at football. Hit it on the knuckles at cricket. Pursue it into the classroom.[19]

Thring could not abide tobacco and his masters were forbidden to smoke in front of boys.[20] Housemasters were compelled to employ Thomas Bell, Thring's own doctor, for their boys and he had his own views on medicine:

> … doctors do lay the law down in a most one-sided way. They are accustomed to deal mainly with disease, and accordingly, in my opinion, are very often very bad judges of health and the healthy. We do not seek to avoid colds by wrapping boys up in furs, but by making them strong (doctors do wrap them up a great deal too much, and cure one cold by producing two), and so it is in all matters of health, there is a certain risk to be run; the question is, which is the most risky, the undue avoiding of risk, or the striving to make all the ordinary conditions sufficient?[21]

---

acceptance of the theory of evolution, dismissing him as "a most consummate donkey". James, *Thring*, 28.

[14] Thring, Index Rerum; Parkin, *Life*, 2:243.

[15] Letter from Edward to Godfrey, December 14, 1871 in Richardson, *Thring*, 268.

[16] John Ruskin, *Time and Tide* (London: George Allen, 1867/1905) letter 16, para. 95; Sara Atwood, *Ruskin's Educational Ideals* (Farnham: Ashgate, 2011), 99, 114.

[17] Parkin, *Life*, 1:329.

[18] Thring, *Theory and Practice*, 132.

[19] Thring, *Addresses*, 127.

[20] Rawnsley, *Early Days*, 38; Hornung, *Fathers*, 1.

[21] Parkin, *Life*, 1:329; Diary, June 4, 1879 (Parkin, *Life*, 2:90).

One parent was not convinced: in a letter to the local newspaper he objected to Bell's charges if his sons complained of "a headache or feeling out of sorts (and no wonder they should do so, when they are permitted to bathe under a midday sun, and are at cricket a good part of their time)."[22]

A scarlet fever outbreak in 1875 caused two fatalities in the school; not an unusual occurrence in mid-Victorian England and in a period when almost all families had experience of a life cut short by illness or accident. Thring opposed the "cowardly panic" of parents who wished to withdraw their boys from the school, and it was reported that boys who asked their parents to take them home were labelled "deserters".[23] To Thring the greater safety lay in courage, and it was a poor training in manliness to let boys quit school at the first hint of peril. A later outbreak of typhoid in the town caused Thring to modify his views and led to the appointment of Christopher Childs, an Old Boy and a doctor, as both sanitary officer and science master.[24] The memorial notice that was published in *The Athenaeum* on Thring's death noted that the school had "a reputation for healthy and vigorous life, physical and moral".[25] Thring would have approved.

III

Countryside pursuits, public school sports and Prussian gymnastics all contributed to the theory and practice of physical education at Thring's Uppingham. To the mixture was added Thring's unique stamp: physical education was not just for the talented and the few; it was for all boys.[26] The attention paid to the individual child was Thring's greatest contribution to life at school, and to physical education in particular.

Some of Thring's own words illustrate the theory behind the practice:

> The life builds the body. A bad life builds an ugly, unhealthy body; and a good life builds a good and healthy body, and in a short time prints the character on the body, as much as if a label was put round a man's neck, to ticket him as a scamp or an able man. (A lecture delivered at the University of Cambridge, March 5, 1887.)[27]

---

[22] Letter to the *Leicestershire and Rutland Mercury*, c1875, in Scrap-book of Archdeacon Johnson's School, Uppingham, 1874-1906. In UA.

[23] Parkin, *Life*, 2:6.

[24] Childs left Uppingham in 1882 and became a medical officer in Cornwall.

[25] Quoted in *USM*, January 1888, 38.

[26] George Parkin, "Uppingham," *The Century Magazine*, September 1888, 657.

[27] Thring, *Addresses*, 119.

If I wanted to train a soldier, I should not take a child and drill him every day and put him through the regimental movements; I should teach him to race, to climb, to swim, to be a gymnast, to play games, to make his body as strong, as active, as enduring as possible. It will be quite time enough to narrow this, and teach him the goose step, when he enlists. (A letter to George Parkin, written in response to questions about education at Uppingham, April 1880.)[28]

(All schools have cricket-grounds), but there is no principle on which the cricket-ground exists, which does not equally call for the existence of amusements and occupations for those who do not play cricket. (*Education and School*, Thring's first published book on education, 1864.)[29]

And more mundanely:

Plenty of exercise, mental and bodily, is the one practical secret of a good school. (As above.)[30]

There were four constituent parts to Thring's physical education programme: country pursuits (including swimming), gymnastics, athletics and games. Later, with the building of the indoor swimming pool in 1883, swimming would stand alone as the fifth.

The country pursuits of running with hounds, rambling, swimming, skating, sledging and so on are the timeless pursuits of the English countryside, and it was in this recreational light that they were encouraged by Thring. The country-born headmaster inevitably joined in. These activities were delightful, spontaneous and uninhibited; they allowed time for conversation and they led to studies in natural history and to a communion with nature. None of these recreations is itself of special merit but the whole produced a natural harmony between the boys and the countryside. What is of particular significance is that Thring continued to encourage them even when games, at Uppingham and elsewhere, began to play a more time-consuming role in the boys' lives.

Country pursuits were recreational but classes in gymnastics were on the timetable. To Thring

... the one pre-eminent mark of the highbred man is the simple play of the limbs that move with perfect ease, and, as they move, throw off a sense of liberty, and grace, and unconstrained command of strength, able at any

---

[28] Quoted in Parkin, *Life*, 2:201.
[29] Thring, *E&S*, 180.
[30] Thring, *E&S*, 130.

moment to do anything that courage may demand of activity, or duty impose on endurance.[31]

Uppingham had the first school gymnasium and the first gymnastics master. Much of the material that follows comes from rough notes compiled by Thring for a lecture that he was due to give to an unknown audience on the theme "The body: its life and teaching" in October 1887.[32] The notes were not completed and the lecture was never delivered because in the second week of that month he succumbed to his fatal illness. Some of the notes duplicate what he had written elsewhere.

The role of gymnastics was to ensure that "the body was exercised and trained" for its own sake, "irrespective of ulterior motive". The repertoire of skills learned in the gymnasium would ensure that the gymnast was "the master of strength, and trained movement".[33] Thring was sure that "it is also clear that as far as power goes, the less the training of the body was cramped by unduly exercising any one part, the better would be the result."

Athletics was essentially competitive, but always voluntary. The purpose of the sports was to push the individual boy to the limits of speed, endurance and strength. Numerous heats were arranged in the various events to provide measured competition for as many boys as possible, but to realise Thring's aim the sports had to be voluntary. The object was to inculcate the "racer's spirit":

> the world is so constituted that there is competition everywhere, and everywhere the weaker goes to the wall; all are certain at some time to be defeated, and if our Athletics teach us here at school to bear to be beaten with good grace and to look upon victory as by no means assuring us against future defeat, they will have been of real use to us in after life.[34]

Athletics thus gave boys experience of victory without pride and defeat without depression; indeed they were instituted to form "that manliness of character". The object had been gained when Thring heard that "E. H. Green, the winner of the first steeplechase, had been lately commended for distinguished gallantry in the battlefield."[35] The prizes awarded in the

---

[31] Thring, *E&S*, 132.
[32] In UA. There is no mention of the lecture in Thring's diary.
[33] Thring, *Theory and Practice*, 242.
[34] *USM*, April 1869, 34; Parkin, *Life*, 2:126.
[35] *USM*, June 1864, 232. No E. H. Green was in the school in Thring's early years, so this is probably J. H. Green who was at the school from 1851-58. Thring does

sports were to be looked upon "as motives to work instead of records of having worked", a Platonic rather than Homeric sentiment.[36] Ideally the prizes were modest, "things that perished in the using" as in gymnastics, but soon silver cups became the norm.[37]

"Games are wondrous vital powers", wrote Thring, "and a true school will deal with them as of the highest educational value". Games fulfilled a threefold role. First they presented a situation in which boys and their masters could mix:

> We mix much with the boys in games ... many a boy whom we must put at a low level in school redeems his self-respect by the praise bestowed on him as a games player, and the balance of manliness and intellect is more impartially kept.[38]

When the Schools Inquiry Commissioners interviewed Thring, they were surprised that he counted games as educational, and they were amazed that he and his colleagues joined the boys at their play.[39]

Secondly, games provided a healthy competitive environment: there was no choice between "manly games, or learning"; the choice was both. One could ...

> escape (from the classroom) to a thorough good game, and restore the balance of human nature by a hearty game on both sides (boys and masters), of both understanding a good drive or cut, of both admiring a stinging catch, which sends mutual respect into the tips of the fingers.[40]

Success in these games enabled the less intelligent boys to "attain some position among their fellows". Thirdly, character was trained in games; "Never cheat, never funk, never lose temper, never brag" were the unwritten rules that promoted manliness.

> For games represent the right actions of bodily life, and all right action is pleasure. But the very games they play are full of pain, possible

---

not name the battle, but it may be the Tauranga Campaign against the Maoris in New Zealand's Bay of Plenty in early 1864.
[36] Diary, December 16, 1870 (Parkin, *Life*, 1:227).
[37] Rawnsley, *Early Days*, 109.
[38] Parkin, *Life*, 1:90-91.
[39] The commissioners included Frederick Temple, Rugby's headmaster. Perhaps he felt embarrassed to confess that he too played games with the boys. Schools Inquiry Commission. V, 10,016-10,018; Tozer, *Manliness*, 78.
[40] Thring, *E&S*, 100, 248.

disagreeables, blows, defeat, disappointment, mortified pride, trials of temper, trials of courage, trials of honesty.[41]

It should be noted that team spirit, or what came to be called *esprit de corps*, was not listed as one of the qualities instilled by games. Thring had been reprimanded over this blind spot by John Mitchinson, the headmaster of King's School, Canterbury, in his review of *Education and School*, but to no effect.[42]

Physical education was an integral part of Thring's curriculum, and the boys were encouraged to approach it "on the same basis as our other school work". If a boy was good at athletics and games it did not necessitate that he be poor at Latin and Greek, and *vice versa*. Dominic Erdozain's superficial reading of Thring's theory and practice (in *The Problem of Pleasure: Sport, Recreation and the Crisis of Victorian Religion*) sees physical education as no more than "an out-sourced remedy for vice and temptation"; he is greatly mistaken.[43]

IV

Throughout this period the boys remained in charge of their games. In a manuscript on boarding schools, Thring wrote:

> I never played in any game excepting at the request of the boys ... I never play as a master; but leave control and management of the game in the hands of the boys. They are the judges of the rules and debated points. I take my place in the field as the Captains of the sides appoint; and though, naturally, experience in games has led to much consultation with me, yet it is on this ground alone that it takes place, and as they have improved becomes less necessary and less frequent. As for dignity I have none, and nobody wants any who is earnest and up to his place.[44]

The earlier comments of boys suggest that they saw his role in a rather different light, particularly when imposing his old-fashioned techniques

---

[41] Thring, *Addresses*, 121.

[42] *Contemporary Review*, 1864, l, 80-91.

[43] Erdozain, *Pleasure*, 107-108; emails, July 3 and 4, 2013 Erdozain writes: "I am willing to accept that my analysis of Thring was not the full picture! He was not a major figure for me. I think if you read the whole book you might have a more favourable view of the argument. On its own, some of it may sound a bit stark or critical. ... I am now overseas and working on something very different."

[44] Thring, *Three Letters*, 11.

and unsuccessful tactics. The masters not only played with the boys but also against them:

> Today the masters played the school. I got a 0, and 37 was our whole score, but we rather collared them after, and got them all out for 87. It was good fun. It is wonderful proof of our substantial unity that masters and boys can thus contend as two sides. It is something to be able to play with them, but far beyond that, to be able to play against them.[45]

The purpose of games was to arouse the quality of manliness and for this to work the games need not be treated as a "science". Thring was uneasy as the boys became more successful at cricket, and began to win more matches against foreign opposition, as he did not wish athletic prowess to be praised for its own sake. From his earliest days at Uppingham he was wary of "mock heroics" in games, for he knew full well that "strength is the school-boy's idol".[46] He held up to ridicule the professionalism of the athletes of ancient Greece.[47] Thring viewed any games coaching with suspicion as it might shift the emphasis from the average boy to the talented athlete. He watched school matches with mixed feelings: if the school won easily he was "sorry for it"; if they were surprisingly beaten it would "do them a great deal of good"; if they played without spirit he was annoyed. Nothing was to be done half-heartedly, and shirkers and slackers were rebuked: "The dilettante", Ernest Hornung recalled, "was the vilest of all types in his eyes, and the last to be encouraged at Uppingham."[48]

As games became more important to the boys, so Thring applied a number of vetoes to keep the movement in check. Although he regarded the spring rolling of the cricket pitch as a school duty, all other games fagging was forbidden; this included younger boys retrieving balls kicked off the pitch in football or fielding for practising batsmen in the days before the introduction of cricket nets. "If fagging enters into school-games, it taints them with a sort of curse of slavery for little boys."[49] The appointment of all games officers had to meet with Thring's approval and all were chosen from the sixth-form; muscle alone was not allowed to rule, it had to be accompanied by brain. In order to play in any school match, a

---

[45] Diary, September 5, 1865 (Parkin, *Life*, 1:148).
[46] Edward Thring, Little jotting book, entry dated June 1854; Thring, *E&S*, 127, 151.
[47] Euripedes Autoclyus, in UA: "These athletes are the veriest weeds of all ..."
[48] Diary, August 22, 1859, August 31, 1864 and May 28, 1872 (Parkin, *Life*, 1:141, 235); Hornung, *Fathers*, x.
[49] Thring, *E&S*, 243.

boy had to have "leave" from his form-master, his housemaster and the headmaster, and such permission could be withheld for poor work or bad behaviour.[50]

V

In March 1862 the school gave a concert for the townspeople of Uppingham. The reception was mixed, not least because this was the first experience of classical music for many in the audience. Indeed, a later concert had to be abandoned when it descended into chaos; singing in French struck some listeners as so comic that they burst into laughter.[51] But Thring persevered and gradually these concerts became regular events.

In the late 1870s Thring took a further step to develop good relations between town and school by forming the Mutual Improvement Society; "the name is important", Thring wrote to a friend.[52] He became president of the Uppingham Committee of Horticulture and Games, and masters including Charles Cobb, Alfred Tuck and Georg Beisiegel served on various sub-committees for "cricket", "games" and so on.[53] Marie Thring presented the town with embroidered banners and these were blessed at a ceremony in which "the good fellowship of English sport" was eulogised.[54] The school community of masters, their families and boys joined with their neighbours in Christmas jollities and Feast Week fun and games, provided a sports field and helped with the levelling of the ground, and formed clubs for cricket, football and tennis to encourage organised physical recreation.[55] A children's playground was constructed, athletic sports were arranged, and cricket and football clubs were formed for the younger boys.[56] The local girls were not to be forgotten, for the ladies of the school presided over the "Grasshoppers", a tennis club to complement the male "Locusts".[57] Oswald Powell, an Old Boy of the period, later recalled with glee watching Thring help with the instruction of this new-fangled game: "I love the picture of him with a Lawn Tennis racquet before a row of daughters of Upp: Tradesmen, showing the action and

---

[50] *USM*, November 1878, 229.
[51] Diary, March 18, 1862.
[52] Letter to E. F. Bennett, quoted in Parkin, *Life*, 2:81.
[53] Scrap-books of the Uppingham and District Cricket Club, 1857-1922. In UA.
[54] Skrine, *Edward Thring*, 200.
[55] Diary, November 19, 1878 (Parkin, *Life*, 2:93).
[56] Diary, July 9, 1879 (Parkin, *Life*, 2:93); Parkin, *Life*, 2:83.
[57] Skrine, *Edward Thring*, 200.

motions necessary for them to acquire".[58] All was in sympathy with Thring's maxim: "Merriment unlocks the heart and removes constraint."[59]

---

[58] Ann Donnelly *Bisham Abbey Village School; Uppingham School; Bedales School; A Family Connection* (privately published: 1974), 14. In UA. There are various claims for the origin of the modern game of tennis but all date to the early 1870s. Powell, at school 1881 to 1886, went up to Trinity College, Cambridge and became a schoolmaster.
[59] Thring, *Three Letters*, 12.

CHAPTER EIGHT

A PUBLIC SCHOOL, 1863-1870: "THE MANLY SPIRIT OF COMPETITION"

I

William Patterson, the author of *Sixty Years of Uppingham Cricket*, felt that a "new chapter" of Uppingham cricket began in 1863 but the changes influenced far more than just one game.[1] The *Uppingham School Magazine* made its first appearance in April: early editors included Walter Cornish, Lewis Nettleship and Willingham Rawnsley.[2] House matches were adopted for the various sports and games, the athletics championship was introduced, and silver cups were presented to the winners. House matches led to the call for inter-school matches and 1863 witnessed Uppingham's first "public school match". The cricketers gained a new pavilion on The Upper that year and soon clamoured for a professional player to coach them; the footballers were not to be outdone and tried to steer their game towards the newly accepted national code. An Old Boys' cricket club, the Uppingham Rovers, was founded in 1863 and the same year heard the first call for a school Rifle Corps. All these changes coincided with a gradual loosening of the reins by Thring and the emergence of greater government of school life by the senior boys. Up to 1863 all changes in the school can be directly linked to Thring but after this date certain powers connected with the day to day life of the boys were entrusted to the praepostors, although Thring always kept, and often used, a headmasterly veto. It is no chance coincidence that this period in the school's history sees the last use of the title Uppingham Grammar

---

[1] Patterson, *Uppingham Cricket*, 23. Patterson was a boy at Uppingham from 1868 to 1873 before entering Trinity College, Cambridge. On graduation he went into business in Liverpool. He was captain of cricket at both Uppingham and Cambridge.

[2] *USM*, April 1913, 45. Cornish proceeded to Exeter College, Oxford and took Holy Orders.

School and an increased use of the term "a public school".[3] Thring had made a school; the boys wished to create a public school.

The first financial accounts of the Upper and Lower Cricket Clubs were published in 1863. Income came from Thring, who paid the rent of The Upper, donations from masters, and subscriptions from the boys. A few years later the masters' voluntary donation became a compulsory subscription of £1 – 5s – 0d and they were also encouraged to donate to the athletics prize fund. The various subscriptions from the older boys (Middle 4th Form and above) and the younger boys (Lower 4th Form and below) were as follows:[4]

	Midsummer to Xmas		Xmas to Midsummer	
	Mid 4th up	Low 4th down	Mid 4th up	Low 4th down
Games	5/6d	4/6d	4/6d	3/6d
Library	2/-d	1/-d	2/-d	1/-d
Athletic Sports	-	-	2/6d	2/6d
Agric Prize to the Rutland Society	1/6d	1/6d	-	-
Total	9/-d	7/-d	9/-d	7/-d

The total income was £192 – 3s – 2d.[5] The bulk of this went on rent and maintenance of the grounds. In 1865 the masters met further expenditure with the eventual purchase of the Rectory Land on the ridge to the south of the school. With increased pupil numbers, this provided space for the new Middle Club as well as for the existing Lower Club.[6] It was soon called The Middle. Van Diemen's Land was now used less often.

The boys took a greater part in the organisation of their games from 1863. The power of the Committee of Games grew and the number of "resolutions" that its members decided increased enormously. Games were played every day except Sunday and compulsion to play operated once a

---

[3] Minute Book of the Uppingham Rovers C. C., 1864; *USM*, May 1863, 41.
[4] *Guide Book.*
[5] The masters' contribution equates to about £150 in 2018 and the boys' total to £23,000.
[6] *USM*, December 1865, 330.

week.[7] Fines were imposed on boys who failed to attend football games and on those who "cut" their turn to help with the rolling of the cricket field.[8] All boys were required to purchase a copy of the Committee of Games *Rules*.[9] These included sections on football, cricket and athletics in which laws of play, methods of team selection and codes of behaviour were described in detail. General laws referred to the constitution of the Committee. "Colours" were awarded to members of the top teams in cricket and football, a blue scarf or band being tied around the recipient's waist.[10] Cricketers generally wore white shirts and trousers, whereas red and white jerseys would soon be introduced for football and athletics.[11]

The individual Champion's Cup was introduced in 1864. Athletics, gymnastics, fives, swimming, and averages for batting and bowling in cricket all contributed marks on a weighted scale. House challenge cups in football and cricket were awarded for the first time that year and their results contributed with those of the individual sports to a house Athletics Championships.[12] This cumbersome arrangement was modified in 1871.[13] House matches were also proposed for hockey but in 1865 the game's place in the school was under review; they were, however, adopted for fives in 1869.[14] Thring published a set of rules for "House Matches and Sports": a copy had to hang "in every Boarding-House Hall, and in the Colonnade".[15]

1   In all cases, notice of the day and time of these must be posted by the proper authority, in the Colonnade, by 10 a.m. on the preceding day.

2   No House Match or Sports, when once posted, may be put off.

3   Music or other Pupils who wish, on account of playing in a House Match or competing in Sports, to change their Lesson or Practice Time, must apply to their Master before 5 p.m. on the day before the Match or Sports takes place. No application must be made on the day itself of the Match or Sports.

---

[7] *USM*, December 1864, 400 and April 1913, 54.
[8] *USM*, February 1867, 253 and April 1865, 80.
[9] *USM*, October 1863, 240.
[10] Rome, Uppingham, 133.
[11] *USM*, March 1866, 16.
[12] *USM*, September 1864, 282; October 1864, 336; and June 1865, 175-177.
[13] *USM*, October 1871, 182.
[14] *USM*, December 1865, 316 and November 1869, 325.
[15] The Colonnade was (and remains) a space underneath the School-room that was open on two sides and lined with notice-boards.

4   No Football Games, or Sports, to begin before 3.15 p.m. on whole
School days.[16]

The Committee of Games also produced rules for the various house
competitions, and Committee members officiated at the matches and the
sports.[17] Its members also kept spectators away from the edge of the pitch
and the racing grounds by means of hunting crops, their badge of office
and the Uppingham equivalent of a policeman's baton.[18]

II

The results of each November's Gymnastics Competition now contributed
marks for the Champion Cup. In the weighted scoring system that was
used, gymnastics earned 250 marks, equal to those for the steeplechase
and fives, and only below the 300 marks awarded for the mile race, the
current most prestigious event.[19] The high standing given to gymnastics
did not meet with the approval of all boys, however, as "everybody does
not learn gymnastics".[20] In the opinion of some, gymnastics did not rank
as a "public school game" and they would probably have agreed with
Matthew Arnold's observation after he had witnessed gymnastic displays
in Prussia:

> Nothing, however, will make an ex-school boy of one of the great English
> schools regard the gymnastics of a foreign school without a slight feeling
> of wonder and compassion, so much more animating and interesting do the
> games of his remembrance seem to him.[21]

The failure of several attempts to separate gymnastics from the other
athletic events making up the championships clearly indicates that its
favoured position was at the headmaster's insistence.[22]

During this period the boys examined all their games and sports to
check that they were of public school standing. The praepostors felt that
hop scotch, peg top and marbles were unsuitable activities, and so the
younger boys were discouraged from playing them. "Single-stick and

---

[16] In UA.
[17] *USM*, March 1870, 31 and April 1871, 86.
[18] *USM*, April 1871, 86. A hunting crop is a short whip without a lash. They were
still in use in the school a century later.
[19] *USM*, May 1864, 181-182.
[20] *USM*, April 1865, 78.
[21] Arnold, *Germany*, 136.
[22] *USM*, April 1886, 130.

boxing" were brought in to replace them but neither lasted long.[23] Other activities deemed to be "private school" games also suffered expulsion in this period, including rounders, quoits and bowls.[24] The "useful" art of fencing, taught by Beisiegel, was acceptable but it was never admitted to the championship.[25] A "Rifle Corps" was an institution common in "every other public school" wrote "A Volunteer" to the school magazine in 1863 and, as a result, a weekly "drilling class" was introduced for a short while in 1864.[26] An Old Boy, echoing Thring's own view, retorted: "Uppingham School took an honest pride in following its own course, irrespective, as far as possible, of other public schools". He questioned the need for a corps: "'deportment', 'exercise' and 'amusement' can be secured … from the good old games and the Gymnasium", and its introduction would "sap much of the interest in these true English-man-making games". He hoped to see Uppingham at Lord's one day, the home of English cricket, but this would never happen if a boy was "playing at soldiers in a fine uniform … when he ought to be learning to catch a ball".[27]

Hockey and fives also came under suspicion. By this period football was the well-established public school winter game and many felt that "despised" hockey belonged "to Private Schools and to street boys": hockey "ought not to rank as an established game in a school like this" argued one opponent.[28] He was content, however, to allow it as a recreational activity that was played between the end of morning school and dinner; it had the advantage that boys did not have to change their clothing to play. The Committee of Games debated hockey's future: the rules were modified; house matches were considered but never adopted; and a "North v South" game was maintained in 1864 for nearly two hours.[29] But by 1868 the game was moribund and two years later it had virtually disappeared, only retained by the boys in one house as a game played on their quadrangle.[30]

Fives, like gymnastics, had an exalted position in the scoring system for the Champion Cup. Increased play demanded the building of more courts in the grounds of boarding houses, and by 1869 nearly every house

---

[23] Rawnsley, *Early Days*, 57. Single-stick is sword-play with a wooden stick.

[24] *USM*, November 1868, 252; November 1869, 322; and December 1870, 354.

[25] *USM*, November 1866, 200.

[26] *USM*, May 1864, 192.

[27] *USM*, November 1863, 278.

[28] *USM*, December 1863, 332 and May 1866, 77.

[29] *USM,* November 1865, 270; December 1865, 316; and November 1864, 382.

[30] *USM*, October 1868, 191 and September 1870, 254.

had its own.[31] In 1867 fives was removed as a component of the house Athletics Championships and two years later it gained its own house challenge cup.[32] The introduction of the cup may have been to bring the game on par with cricket and football: certainly a defensive editorial in the school magazine lends support to that possibility.

> This really scientific game is sometimes apt to be looked down upon and slighted in comparison with the two more popular ones; but now the honour of representing one's House comes into question, Fives is likely to receive stimulus.[33]

Again, one suspects that Thring was giving support to his favourite game. When he and Witts gave up challenging the boys from 1872, younger masters took over the tradition.[34]

In 1863 suspicions of a different nature fell on the tar-pit bathing place below The Upper; its "ill-conditioned state" was persuading many boys to take the long hike to the Welland for a swim.[35] Inspection revealed that five drains ran into the pool, and so the search for yet another bathing place began.[36] In September the following year the editor of the school magazine was able to report that "a new Bathing Place has at last been obtained, and a want supplied, the pre-eminent, if not the only one, which marred the symmetry of the School arrangements".[37] A year later "Fenwicke's Basin", named after its donor, was opened with due ceremony and bathing had returned to the Stockerston brook, west of the town.[38] The Committee of Games now allowed for swimming competitions in its rules for the Champion Cup: 300 marks could be shared between the two branches of swimming: racing and "headers".[39] Fenwicke's Basin was, however, too narrow for the proposed races and the competition for the best "header" was abandoned after the first year. No reason was given but imagination easily conjures some comic events![40] Repeated requests for

---

[31] *USM*, May, 1864, 180-182; April 1864, 127; and September 1869, 241.
[32] *USM*, October, 1867, 203 and November 1869, 325.
[33] *USM*, November 1869, 303.
[34] *USM*, May 1873, 108.
[35] *USM*, May 1863, 42.
[36] *USM*, June 1863, 74.
[37] *USM*, September 1864, 242.
[38] *USM*, September 1865, 200.
[39] *USM*, May 1864, 180-182.
[40] *USM*, September 1867, 118.

swimming races were made in letters to the school magazine in subsequent years but it was not until 1875 that they were established.[41]

III

The programme for the athletics sports was expanded to twenty events in 1864 after the introduction of the Champion Cup; each event had its own prize. A new event, "the vault", seems to have been peculiar to Uppingham:

> W. F. Rawnsley obtained the first prize, C. E. Green being second, and S. R. Majendie third; best Vault, 5 ft. 10 in. This is also a new institution, and was voted by all a very pretty addition to the Athletic Sports.[42]

Willingham Rawnsley later recalled: "we ran to it, leapt into the air, seized the bar and by arm-work, learned in the gymnasium, raised our bodies over it. The hands alone being allowed to touch it."[43] Heights over six feet were recorded.[44] The Champion Cup marks now indicate that the mile race had replaced the steeplechase as the event gaining "the greatest reward and mead of glory".[45] In the fortnight prior to the sports the boys were encouraged to train daily in preparation for the various events, and a master published some "training hints" in the school magazine. These included "keep out of the 'grub-shop'".[46] The Committee of Games, however, reminded boys that "anyone deviating from the ordinary diet prescribed by his house shall be disqualified for any prize".[47] Rules for the conduct of the races, jumps and throws were published in 1865 and, in the same year, the sports became an inter-house competition with the inauguration of the Athletics Championship.[48]

Editorials in the *Uppingham School Magazine* explained the value of athletics to the boys of the school. These statements probably duplicated the text of Thring's own speeches at the annual sports prize-giving ceremony. On these occasions he would define the principles of athletics. "Now the object of all our games", the editor reported,

---

[41] *USM*, June 1869, 191; May 1870, 123; and October 1875, 268.
[42] *USM*, March 1864, 92.
[43] This is not to be confused with the pole vault. The author has mislaid this reference.
[44] 6 feet 2 inches in 1873. *USM*, May 1873.
[45] *USM*, April 1863, 13.
[46] *USM*, May 1863, 47 and March 1864, 65-67.
[47] Rome, Uppingham, 43.
[48] *USM*, April 1865, 80 and November 1865, 297.

but of the sports in particular, is to produce the manly spirit of competition, and the love of training the body, for training's sake; whilst the prizes won by the successful competitors are but a secondary, and, as it were, incidental result. For not only are 'all who do their best equally honoured', but the unsuccessful do in effect win a prize equally with their victors, since we cannot doubt that the lessons learnt on the racing-ground will have their practical application in any field of active life. Now whilst we readily admit that the actual competitors do certainly on the whole, compete in the aforesaid spirit, yet (if the comparatively small number of runners be any criterion) it is only too plain that the mass of the School has not yet appreciated the purpose in view, and so do not avail themselves of what they ought to consider their privilege.[49]

In answer to the critics of the sports, the editor added that "the object of the sports is something more than mere amusement of spectators", and that the sports were "not 'intentionally prolonged' for want of something better to do".[50] A month later, after a good entry for the sports, he continued:

If a reference to these statistics be our best way (and we know no other) of gauging the spirit of the School, we may with reason congratulate it on a marked improvement in this point. We may hope that runners are learning to compete, not for the chance of winning prizes merely, or even from the less venal desire of distinguishing themselves, nor again hanging back from the fear of being laughed at (for few laugh but those who dare not run); but doing their work well and honestly to the best of their power, and feeling the better for it (as they cannot fail to do under favourable conditions) in heart, mind and body.[51]

Only about a tenth of the school was convinced by these arguments. The rest either advocated a shorter period of sports so that they could quickly return to football or cricket, rather than stand as "shivering spectators" for the prolonged trial heats, or, as Thring suspected, like "blackguards" they "took the opportunity to go smoking or drinking".[52]

The arrangements remained unchanged, however, and the 1867 sports occupied most of March. The flat races were held on the Leicester Road, the steeplechases at Ridlington, the jumps on The Upper, and the hurdles and throws on Van Diemen's Land. This pattern was maintained until 1880, with the exception that the hurdles and throws at some stage transferred to The Middle.

---

[49] *USM*, March 1866, 2.
[50] *USM*, March 1866, 2.
[51] *USM*, April 1866, 34.
[52] *USM*, April 1866, 34; Diary, March 7, 1861.

The value of athletics came under scrutiny again in 1869. The current editor of the school magazine continued the defence, this time emphasising the character training brought about through competition.[53] But the period from the start of the Half in February until the beginning of the cricket season at Easter was still generally regarded as the "dullest" time of year, and only a "very small proportion of the School ever go in for a race at all, and still fewer take the trouble to train".[54] There were renewed calls for football in March.

IV

In 1859 Thring invited his younger brother, Charles, to join the teaching staff at Uppingham as a housemaster.[55] He had attended Shrewsbury School, where he played the school's own code of football known as "Dowling", and then went up to St John's College, Cambridge.[56] There, in 1846, he had been a founder member of the Cambridge University Football Club.[57] Two years later, Thring and Henry de Winton, another Old Salopian, called a meeting of footballers at Trinity College that was attended by Old Boys of Eton, Harrow, Rugby and Winchester, as well as from Shrewsbury, and over a period of eight hours they thrashed out a set of rules that blended the codes of the games played at their several schools. The results, known as the *Cambridge Rules*, became the basis of the rules of the Football Association on its foundation in 1863.[58]

Once at Uppingham, Charles Thring set about modifying his brother's rules for Uppingham Football to bring them more in line with the *Cambridge Rules*. These were published in 1862 as the *Simplest Game*, and were probably the most streamlined set of rules for football ever produced.

1. A goal is scored whenever the ball is forced through the goal and under the bar, except it be thrown by hand.

2. Hands may be used only to stop a ball and place it on the ground before the feet.

---

[53] *USM*, April 1869, 34.

[54] *USM*, December 1870, 347.

[55] John Charles Thring, but always known as Charles. He became housemaster of Red House in 1860.

[56] *The Times*, March 24, 1953. J. B. Lawson, the Librarian at Shrewsbury, drew my attention to this article.

[57] Basil Oldham, *History of Shrewsbury School* (Oxford: Blackwell, 1952), 232.

[58] Percy Young, *A History of British Football* (London: Paul, 1968), 93.

3. Kicks must be aimed only at the ball.

4. A player may not kick the ball whilst in the air.

5. No tripping up or heel kicking allowed.

6. Whenever a ball is kicked beyond the side flags, it must be returned by the player who kicked it, from the spot it passed the flag-line, in a straight line towards the middle of the ground.

7. When the ball is kicked behind the line of goal, it shall be kicked off from that line by one of the side whose goal it is.

8. No player may stand within six paces of the kicker when he is kicking off.

9. A player is out of play immediately he is in front of the ball, and must return behind the ball as soon as possible. If the ball is kicked by his own side past a player, he may not touch it, or advance, until one of the other side has first kicked it, or one of his own side, having followed it up, has been able, when in front of him, to kick.

10. No charging allowed when a player is out of play – i.e. immediately the ball is behind him.[59]

Running with the ball in the hands was now eliminated and, with the maintained absence of hacking, the game veered away from that played at Rugby School and by Old Rugbeians at the universities, and towards what in 1863 would become Association Football.[60] As Charles Thring wrote in the preface to his rules:

> I do not print these Rules with any desire of reconciling the games of football, as variously played at our old and great schools ... I admit at once that I put them forward as an antidote to the Rugby game, which has unhappily been lately adopted by many clubs ... But what I should more especially desire to effect, would be that our Universities should adopt this or some similar code of laws.[61]

---

[59] As with the original rules for Uppingham Football, the manuscript rules of the *Simplest Game* are missing from the Uppingham Archives. Charles Thring, *The Winter Game: Rules of Football* (Uppingham: Hawthorn, 1862).

[60] The Rugby code was to become Rugby Union Football in 1871.

[61] Thring, *Winter Game*, iii-iv. For more on Thring's involvement with the development of football, see Graham Curry, "Football: a Study in Diffusion" (PhD diss., University of Leicester, 2001), 39–78.

A satirical poem, "Football at R", that was published in the 1864 *Uppingham School Magazine* illustrates how civilised Uppinghamians felt their game had become when compared to the Rugby code:

> O – well for the schoolboy bold,
> Who will hack his best friend, but in play!
> But woe to the fallen boy,
> Who has a leg smashed in the fray![62]

From 1863 games were now played twice a week, on the Tuesday and Saturday half holidays, on the recently acquired field behind William Earle's house, Brooklands.[63] Every boy had to have a copy of the printed rules, "which may be obtained from the Captain of Games, at the small charge of 2d.", and was compelled to attend one game a week: a 6d. fine was imposed for non-attendance.[64] Two football clubs were formed: the Upper for boys in the top three forms, and the Lower for the remainder. After 1863 membership of the Upper Club was limited to boys taller than 5 foot 3 inches.[65] Red and white caps were introduced for the opposing sides (before this date boys often played wearing their mortar boards) and the teams began to change into "jerseys and flannel trousers" before play.[66] Almost all the masters played, including the foreigners Beisiegel, a "tower of strength", and Benguerel, "full of dash and enthusiasm".[67] Masters never changed out of their ordinary dress. Many pick-up games were played: Sixth v the School, Pickwick Club v Rest of the School, North v South (with the line drawn at Cambridge), and so on. A match against the Old Boys was proposed in 1863 but had to wait a few more years.[68] Early goal posts were not particularly rigid; the "inconvenience of the cross-bars coming down when the posts are violently pushed against" eventually led to the replacement of the wooden bar by a rope or tape.[69]

In 1864 football moved from the field behind Brooklands to Van Diemen's Land and this became the home of the Upper Club for football for the next fourteen years.[70] The same year witnessed the recording of the

[62] *USM*, April 1864, 119. There are seven more verses.
[63] *USM*, October 1866, 164 and April 1924, 67. I have not been able to identify this field; its use seems to have been short-lived.
[64] *USM*, October 1863, 240 and February 1867, 253.
[65] *USM*, November 1863, 276.
[66] *USM*, November 1863, 288; April 1913, 52; and December 1864, 400.
[67] *USM*, April 1913, 52.
[68] *USM*, November 1863, 277.
[69] *USM*, December 1863, 336 and March 1875, 17.
[70] *USM*, January 1864, 43.

names of football "XVs", the introduction of house matches, and a call for matches against "foreign" teams.[71] Charles Thring had previously applied to the Football Association for membership on behalf of the school, but without consulting his brother. The headmaster withdrew the application thus preventing Uppingham from becoming a soccer school and denying the possibility of foreign matches.[72] The boys were now grouped by the Captain of Football in to three Hundreds: Upper, Middle and Lower Clubs; each of about 100 boys.[73] Games with unlimited players were arranged in each club at the start of the season and then, after a few weeks' play, the captain of each club drew up the lists of the ranked XVs.[74] These XVs were created to give "increased interest and spirit to the game". The 1st XV on the Upper Club wore blue caps, the 2nd XV red or white ones, and the 3rd XV black.[75] From 1865 all matches, other than pick-up games, were played at fifteen a side.[76]

The introduction of house matches was also "to promote more spirit" by increasing "the rivalry among different houses".[77] "Rules for the Football House-Matches" were published in November 1864, and they included the introduction of "Umpires", one for each competing house. The rules stated:

1. That they be played in the Christmas Examination, and if not played out, be continued in the following half-year.

2. That each game last one hour and a half.

3. That unless some advantage be gained within that time, the game be continued some other day until some advantage be gained.

4. That each house nominate its own umpire, subject to the disapproval of the other house.

5. That the number playing for each side be left to the discretion of the captain of the side.

The last rule was amended to fifteen a side in the following year.[78]

---

[71] *USM*, November 1864, 378.
[72] Richardson, *Thring*, 166.
[73] *USM*, November 1865, 297 and December 1870, 350.
[74] *USM*, April 1924, 67.
[75] *USM*, December 1864, 428.
[76] *USM*, December 1865, 332.
[77] *USM*, December 1863, 329.
[78] *USM*, December 1864, 409. "Nominate" rather than "nominates" in Rule 4 is in the original.

No matches with "foreign" teams could be adopted but the Old Boys, who should have remembered the rules of the game, were persuaded to play. They supplied their first team to compete against the School in February 1865. The boys won the match against "an adverse fifteen ... picked up by hunting for representatives of the old school from all quarters".[79] The Old Boys did not, alas, take this innovation very seriously. The following year just eight travelled to Uppingham and had to be supplemented with recruits from the school's 2nd XV and, for the next match in 1870, only three Old Boys arrived.[80]

Between 1864 and 1868 there was a steady reform of the rules of Uppingham Football; the changes gradually eliminated the aspects from Rugby Football that were "thoroughly opposed to the general principles of our play".[81] The oval ball, which made the dribbling game so difficult, was the subject of much discussion but was retained for a few more years, and the goal was widened to forty feet.[82] Charging with the head lowered was prohibited in open play but allowed in the bullies, and "creeping" offside around the bullies was strongly condemned. Some penalty bullies for irregular play were also introduced.[83]

The same period saw more masters taking part in the games and their ladies beginning to watch them.[84] Masters played in cricket house matches but this did not happen in football; presumably these games were too physical and too competitive. Boys were still compelled to play just once a week but the pressure to join in began to increase. "Shirkers" were condemned and an article "Concerning Non-Football Players" was published in the school magazine in 1870. These were the "unfortunate few, who cannot, and a contemptible few, who will not join the game". The unfortunate few were those who suffered from ill-health; the contemptible included the "lazy" (for the most part), the "swells", the "glutton" and the "funk", the last who "hates Football, because he thinks he would get hurt".[85] The article was re-published almost verbatim in

---

[79] *USM*, March 1865, 35.
[80] *USM*, March 1867, 23 and March 1871, 16.
[81] *USM*, March 1867, 11-15.
[82] *USM*, March 1864, 64 and October 1867, 203. Charles Thring was a renowned kicker and dribbler: Curry, "Football", 74.
[83] *USM*, October 1866, 182; November 1865, 295; and November 1868, 250. This is a very early introduction of penalties in football. They were adopted in Rugby Union Football in the late 1880s and in Association Football by 1891.
[84] *USM*, November 1868, 265 and December 1867, 238.
[85] *USM*, December 1865, 312 and December 1870, 359-360.

1884.[86] Another author suggested that boys who repeatedly missed games should forfeit their colours.[87]

Despite the poor attendance of Old Boys at their matches with the school, there were proposals in the 1860s to form an Old Boys' Football Club. At this period Old Boys of Eton, Harrow, Winchester and Rugby had formed their own football clubs at the universities of Oxford and Cambridge.[88] Soon, in March 1868, the "Uppingham Football Club" was founded at Cambridge, with branches in Oxford and London.[89]

V

The different codes of football played at the public schools in this period made inter-school matches almost impossible. The telegraph and the railways made the organisation and travel arrangements straightforward, but they were the least of the worries. The first recorded public school match, between Marlborough and Clifton in 1864, quickly descended into an ill-tempered farce because of the code differences at the two schools and the match was not played again for many years.[90] No such problem existed for cricket, and it is at this game that Uppingham searched for a worthy opponent. An invitation sent to the near neighbours at Rugby was at first declined on the grounds that they did not play schools of Uppingham's "'standing', as they are pleased to designate us", but they later offered to send a house team.[91] Thring labelled the Rugby response "insolent" and the boys rejected the condescending offer of a house team. Two years later, Thring noted in his diary:

> A letter from C. E. Green to the Earles's in great glee; he had bowled out the Rugby eleven for twenty eight runs. He was the captain they sent the insolent message to, offering to send a house eleven to play us. This has stuck in his mind ever since, and now he has wiped it off.[92]

Uppinghamians were keenly aware of their social position as members of a new public school. Rugbeians clearly did not judge Uppingham to be a proper public school, not one of the Clarendon Nine, but Uppingham had

---

[86] *USM*, December 1884, 363.
[87] *USM*, March 1868, 24.
[88] Charles Alcock, *The Football Annual* (London: Lillywhite, 1870), 61.
[89] *USM*, April 1868, 42.
[90] McIntosh, *Physical Education*, 39.
[91] *USM*, May 1863, 41.
[92] Green was in William Earle's house, Brooklands. Diary, August 29, 1865.

been equally judgmental when it decided that the grammar schools at Oakham and Oundle were unworthy opposition. When, in the summer of 1863, Uppingham finally got "its uppermost desire for many years", it was against distant Rossall School on the Lancashire coast. Thring had arranged the match against this undoubted, if newly founded, public school through his friendship with the headmaster, the Rev William Osborne.[93] A four-day excursion was needed to accommodate the round trip of more than 300 miles and the two-day match. The score at the end of the first day's play was telegraphed back to an excited school: "Uppingham first innings, two hundred and forty-three; Rossall three wickets down for twenty-seven". The eventual result was a win for the visitors by ten wickets.[94] Great enthusiasm, by the townspeople as well as by the boys, greeted the visitors back at Uppingham and an eight-page account recorded every detail, including Green's heroic contribution, in the *Uppingham School Magazine*.[95] It was, however, to be the only Rossall match: the following year a measles outbreak kept the Rossall boys in quarantine and then the considerable separation of the schools produced headmasterly vetoes.[96] In 1865 geographically nearer Repton, a raised Elizabethan grammar school like Uppingham, issued a challenge that was accepted. This fixture between two East Midlands' schools has been maintained ever since.[97]

A match between "the School" and "Rev Earle's House" in June 1863 led to the introduction of house matches. Most housemasters played in their house teams.[98] Funds for a new pavilion on The Upper, nearly £400, were largely contributed by boys past and present, and by their parents. It was built by Foxton during the winter months after the 1863 season; he also built the School-room and the Chapel. The old pavilion was dismantled and re-erected on Van Diemen's Land to replace the tent.[99]

The employment of cricket professionals to coach the boys in the finer points of the game had made their first appearance at public schools in the 1850s. The Lillywhite brothers, William and John, began coaching at

---

[93] Rossall was founded as a proprietary school in 1844.

[94] *USM*, June 1863, 111-117.

[95] Patterson, *Uppingham Cricket*, 77.

[96] *USM*, June 1864, 194.

[97] Repton is in Derbyshire. Arthur Haygarth, *Cricket Scores and Biographies: 1855-1875* (London: Lillywhite, 1878), 103-104.

[98] *USM*, July 1863, 155 and October 1863, 237.

[99] About £11,000 in 2018. Patterson, *Uppingham Cricket*, 34; *USM*, November 1863, 288 and December 1863, 336.

Rugby in 1850 and at Winchester the following year.[100] Fred Silcock's appointment in that capacity, in November 1863 for the 1864 season, reflects the school's desire for accepted public school status.[101] The selection of Silcock was made by William Earle through his contacts with the Essex club; Silcock had played for the county side.[102] Later writings by Thring suggest that he was not altogether in favour of such an appointment but that he was sympathetic to the boys' ambitions. It was certainly preferable to bringing a cricket Blue on to the staff as an assistant master. The combination of Thring's doubts and a depleted games account after the building of the pavilion led to the compromise that a professional coach would be appointed only on alternate years.[103] The boys, not Thring nor the masters, would employ the professional, and the alternate years reduced the likelihood of a permanent appointment, one of Thring's fears. The professional's duties were also limited to two or three weeks at the beginning of the season; the remuneration was £5 a week plus expenses.[104] The early professionals (Silcock in 1864, Roger Iddison in 1866, and Edgar Wilsher in 1868 and 1870) had little opportunity to teach and no continuity from year to year but they nonetheless were successful in laying down the foundations of Uppingham's later cricket strength. All three men were well-known cricketers: Iddison had played for the United All-England XI and in 1861 had been a member of the first English team to tour Australia;[105] Wilsher was reckoned by W. G. Grace, who in 1871 organised Wilsher's benefit match, to be "one of the greatest bowlers we have had", and had been one of the original members of the United South of England XI.[106] The United All-England XI and the United South of England XI were two of several troupes of professional cricketers who toured England to play local teams, usually of twenty-two rather than eleven players. These matches drew large crowds, with the gate money going to the professionals.

Cricket, "like all good things", had become "something more than playing", declared an enthusiast in the school magazine, and the lessons

---

[100] Pelham Warner, *Cricket: Badminton Library* (London: Longmans, Green, and Co, 1920), 308.

[101] *USM*, November 1863, 288.

[102] Walter Bettesworth, *Chats on the Cricket Field* (London: Merritt & Hatcher, 1910), 172.

[103] *USM*, April 1864, 136 and May 1870, 257.

[104] Patterson, *Uppingham Cricket*, 54; *USM*, November 1864, 379.

[105] William Grace, *Cricket* (Bristol: J. W. Arrowsmith, 1891), 330; Harry Altham, *A History of Cricket* (London: George Allen & Unwin, 1926), 141.

[106] Grace, *Cricket*, 47, 134, 405.

learned in the previous season were to be "in the minds of the School in the winter months".[107] In 1864 William Earle resigned his place in the school XI, Thring had ceased to play in it some years earlier, and no master ever again played in the team.[108] Six XIs were established, four for the Upper Club and two for the Lower.[109] The lists of these teams and the batting and bowling averages for the season were recorded in the school magazine, and the averages counted weightily for the Champion Cup.[110] Cricket was now highly competitive and a challenge cup presented for the house matches enhanced this further.[111] Junior boys who failed to attend their cricket rolling duties on the "proper day" were fined by the Committee of Games.[112]

In 1865 a new cricket ground, the "Rectory Land" of Thring's diary, was acquired to reduce the number of occasions when the distant Van Diemen's Land was needed for play. A large eleven-acre area was levelled at the masters' expense, £300 plus an annual rent of £54.[113] The new ground, soon to be called The Middle, accommodated the existing Lower Club and, with the growing pupil numbers in the school, the new Middle Club. A "Thring XI" played a "Witts XI" in the opening match: Thring scored the first run and Witts took the first wicket, Thring's.[114] The new pavilion on The Upper now contained boards that listed the School XIs since 1848, and the club's 2nd XI gained its own match with the Old Boys in 1867.[115] Play on The Middle became keener, with the 1st XI players occasionally dropping in to give instruction; there was even a call for a professional to be hired for The Middle on the years alternate to The Upper; "a second-rate" man would do![116] In 1868 the whole school watched the two days of the match with the Old Boys and they witnessed the first win for the School.[117]

The question of the professional was raised again in 1870. Under the management of William Earle, and later two other masters, Alfred Tuck

---

[107] *USM*, October 1864, 291.
[108] *USM*, June 1864, 236.
[109] *USM*, June 1864, 239.
[110] *USM*, May 1864, 180-182 and December 1864, 442.
[111] *USM*, September 1864, 282.
[112] *USM*, April 1865, 80.
[113] £300 is equivalent to about £11,000 in 2018. *USM*, December 1865, 330; Patterson, *Uppingham Cricket*, 42.
[114] *USM*, May 1866, 100.
[115] *USM*, September 1866, 145 and October 1867, 170.
[116] *USM*, June 1868, 144.
[117] *USM*, October 1868, 194.

and Charles Cobb, the cricket club's finances were brought out of the red; this encouraged the boys to lobby for a professional every year.[118] There were even proposals to cut back on the prizes for athletics and to divert the savings to cricket, but Thring maintained his decision to allow a professional to be appointed on alternate years only on "the ground that Cricket ought not to be made a science".[119] A request for cricket fielding "fagging", a practice that was common at most public schools, also met a Thring veto.[120] Helping with the spring rolling of the pitches was of benefit to all boys, Thring termed it a "school λειτουρυα" or "school function", whereas fielding fagging deprived the fags of a game.[121]

VI

The Uppingham Rovers were formed in 1863 as one of the earliest clubs for public school Old Boys, only preceded by the Eton Ramblers (1862).[122] The club adopted the appropriate motto *Solvitur Ambulando*: we solve it by going on, or literally, it is loosed by walking. This was one of Thring's favourite Latin tags and it was the motto he gave to the Headmasters' Conference on its foundation in 1869.[123] The first page in the minute book of the new club announced:

This club was formed on the evening of – (no matter when) – during the year 1863: on the Rockingham road, as two Boys were returning to Brooklands from private work. It was then and there resolved that a cricket club, bearing the above title, be formed, whose object should be to play matches during the school Holidays, with XIs composed of Past and Present Uppinghamians.[124]

The founding members were Charles Green, the hero of the Rossall match, and two other members of the XI, Arthur Knowles and Richard

---

[118] The Rev Alfred Tuck joined the staff in 1871 and became housemaster of Constables in 1876; Charles Cobb, a layman, joined the staff in 1873 and became housemaster of Highfield in 1880. *Guide Book*; *USM*, March 1870, 11.

[119] *USM*, May 1870, 257 and November 1870, 293.

[120] *USM*, April 1870, 95.

[121] Diary, March 2, 1859; *USM*, April, 1873, 84-86.

[122] William Roe, *Public Schools Cricket 1901-1950* (London: Max Parrish, 1951), 192.

[123] Percival, *Superior Men*, 186.

[124] Minute Book of the Uppingham Rovers, 1864.

Fitz-Herbert.[125] At a meeting in Green's study, "sometime in February", summer holiday matches with the Rugby Club, The Cricket Company and West Essex were arranged. "Other matches in the 'Midland Counties' were to have been played but owing to the mismanagement of the promoter (A. Knowles) did not come off."[126] A formal announcement of the creation of the Rovers appeared in the *Uppingham School Magazine* in November that year.[127]

Green came from an Essex ship-owning family who had connections with William Earle, his housemaster at Brooklands. He joined Uppingham in April 1858, played in the XI for six of his seven years in the school, and he captained the side in his last season, 1864. His cricketing career continued to shine when he went up to Trinity College, Cambridge; gaining his Blue in his first summer, 1865, playing in the team in 1866 and 1867, and captaining the side in 1868. He also won a Blue in athletics as a high-jumper. The ship-owning business left him plenty of time for cricket, playing for the Sussex and Essex county sides, for the Gentlemen against the Players, and for I Zingari, an elite travelling club. He was elected President of the Marylebone Cricket Club, the ruling body of the game, in 1905.[128]

In the summer after its founding, the Uppingham Rovers held their first general meeting in the cricket pavilion; 48 members were present. The meeting drew up the "Rules of the Rover Club".

1. That members consist of those who have played in the Uppingham School Eleven. The committee however reserves the right of electing any Old Uppinghamian boy for special cricket merit.

2. That members, on being elected, pay an entrance fee of 5/- to the Secretary.

3. That the expenses of Umpires, Scorers, etc. at a match be defrayed by the Eleven playing.

4. That any member who, after having promised to play in a match, fails to put in an appearance, be subjected to a fine of 10/-, unless he give at

---

[125] Knowles was in the XI for three years, 1861-1863. He left just before the start of the 1864 season. Nothing more is known of him. Fitz-Herbert played in the 1863 XI. He went up to St John's College, Cambridge and in 1896 succeeded to the Tissington baronetcy in Derbyshire.

[126] Minute Book of the Uppingham Rovers, 1864.

[127] *USM*, November 1863, 244.

[128] Gentlemen v Players was an annual contest between the best of the amateur players and the professionals. I Zingari translates as The Gypsies.

least 10 days notice to the Secretary, and his reason for non-appearance
be most urgent.

5. That the Officers of the Club be appointed annually at the Old Boys'
    Match.[129]

Walter Earle (William's brother), an Old Boy and a new appointment
on Thring's staff, was elected secretary and the rules were published in the
school magazine.[130] Club membership had in one year changed from "<u>Past</u>
and <u>Present</u> Uppinghamians" to members elected from the School XI and
Old Boys with "special cricket merit". The club's exclusivity increased the
following year with the introduction of elections for membership by ballot,
with one vote in twelve keeping out the unwanted. A special Rovers' shirt
was made in the same period.[131]

---

[129] Minute Book of the Uppingham Rovers, 1864. 5/- is 5 shillings.

[130] Walter Earle was in the Uppingham XI from 1855 to 1857. He returned to the
school in 1864 after studying at St John's College, Cambridge and taking Holy
Orders. He became housemaster of Red House in 1866. He left Uppingham in
1873 to found Bilton Grange Preparatory School near Rugby. *USM,* September
1864, 266.

[131] Minute Book of the Uppingham Rovers, 1864.

CHAPTER NINE

GAMES MANIA: "THE TRAMP OF THE TWENTY-TWO MEN"

I

Cricket, football, rowing and various racket games were all common at public schools by the time Thring arrived at Uppingham in 1853. Senior boys were responsible for their organisation and financial arrangements; they set the rules of play and chose the distances to be raced; and they decided on the size of teams and how often boys should be compelled to play. Masters would occasionally join the boys in these activities; some used the opportunity to praise good sportsmanship and to correct unruly behaviour.

The first headmaster to realise that the boys' games could be used as an element of school management, James Mangan suggests, was probably Charles Vaughan at Harrow.[1] When this favourite pupil of Thomas Arnold was appointed in 1844 at the age of twenty-eight, with no experience as a schoolmaster, he had to deal with a school where ill-discipline was rife and pupil numbers were in free-fall.[2] His response was to introduce methods used by his own headmaster, including stricter supervision, a prefectorial system, and a chapel-centred school life, but with the addition of much encouragement for the boys to spend all their free time playing games. With disciplinary rather than educational aims, there was no need for masters to be involved. Vaughan worked through the senior boys and by early 1853 they had formed the Harrow Philathletic Club "with the view of promoting among the members of the school an increased interest in games and other manly exercises".[3]

---

[1] Mangan, *Athleticism*, 28-35.
[2] Down from 250 to 69. The Harrow vicar recommended that Vaughan should sack the lot and start again. Vaughan raised the roll to 438 by the time of his resignation in 1859. Tyerman, *Harrow*, 167, 245, 246, 247.
[3] Mangan, *Athleticism*, 28.

The first headmaster to go a step further and impose games on a school where the boys did not play them was George Cotton, reputedly the young master in *Tom Brown's Schooldays*. Cotton was appointed from Rugby to be Master of Marlborough in 1852, nine years after its founding. He inherited a chaotic, barbarian school in which fighting, bird-nesting and squirrel-hunting were the main recreations. "The sporting instinct of the school ... was so great that a boy who had been found with a partridge's or a pheasant's egg would ... have been thrashed within an inch of his life." In a speech to the assembled school Cotton outlined his policy:

> The Council informed me on my appointment that the school was in a bad state of discipline, and they hoped that I would allow no boy to go out except in pairs with a master. I told them that I could not accept office on such terms, that the school I hoped to govern was a public school, not a private one, and I would try and make it govern itself by means of prefects. The school now knows how matters stand. They must either submit to the prefects or be reduced to the level of a private school and have their freedom ignominiously curtailed.[4]

With the introduction of prefects, bounds were tightened, drinking and other forms of lawlessness diminished, and the school day became more organised. Cotton imported Rugby football and cricket to replace the country pursuits; these not only acted as an antidote to mischief and trouble but also enabled Cotton's influence to be diffused more effectively through the active participation of young men newly appointed to the staff.[5] Soon Cotton had introduced matches with other schools, including Cheltenham and Rugby, and by his retirement in 1858 (when until his death by drowning in 1866 he served as Bishop of Calcutta) he could look forward to the realisation of his three aims for Marlborough: the improvement and adornment of the chapel, a Balliol scholarship, and a victory over Rugby at Lord's.[6]

II

In 1860 a letter to the *Cornhill Magazine* from a parent, writing under the pseudonym "Paterfamilias", opened a controversy on the quality of education

---

[4] Arthur Bradley, Arthur Champneys and John Baines, *A History of Marlborough College* (London: John Murray, 1893), 138.

[5] James Mangan, "Athleticism: A Case Study of the Evolution of an Educational Ideology," in *The Victorian Public School*, ed. Brian Simon and Ian Bradley (Dublin: McGill, 1975), 150-152.

[6] Bradley, Champneys and Baines, *Marlborough*, 154.

at the public schools that led eventually to the creation of the Public Schools Commission under Lord Clarendon. Nine schools were inspected: seven boarding schools (Eton, Charterhouse, Harrow, Rugby, Shrewsbury, Westminster and Winchester) and two day schools (Merchant Taylors' and St Paul's). Paterfamilias complained that although the schools, and Eton in particular, provided a fair intellectual education, there was a complete absence of moral training. In the writer's view, gentlemen became gentlemen at Eton not through the education they received there, but because they were the sons of gentlemen.[7] By the time of the publication of the Clarendon report in 1864, a remedy had been found: games would provide the moral training. The commissioners recommended that much time should be given to these important activities, for not only did they aid health and provide exercise, but they also formed "some of the most valuable school qualities and manly virtues".[8] The report expressed worry at the poor teaching and philistine nature of the education at public schools, but it wholeheartedly rejected Paterfamilias's claim of moral laxity.[9]

> Boys from public schools have decidedly improved in point of moral training and character within the last twenty years. The old grossness and brutality have disappeared, and the use of coarse language is, at the larger schools, confined to a few ...[10]

> On the general results of public school education as an instrument for the training of character, we can speak with much confidence.[11]

Several reviewers of a few years earlier had welcomed *Tom Brown's Schooldays* for its athletic outlook and the games it advocated were even seen as "the most important branch" of education.[12] "It is in these sports that the character of the boys is formed. It is from them that the readiness,

---

[7] *Cornhill Magazine*, May 1860, 611.

[8] Lord Clarendon, *Public Schools Commission* (London: HMSO, 1864), I 41.

[9] *Dublin Review*, July 1865. 5. This records Lord Clarendon as saying that the average public school boy of 19 "has learnt to be manly and self-reliant, and has been imbued with the character of an English gentleman" ... but he "is unable to construe an easy sentence from the Latin or the Greek, is unacquainted with the literature of his own country, knows no modern language besides his own, is scarcely able to write that correctly, and knows nothing of physical laws" ... "after having passed the best years of his life in learning".

[10] Quoted in *Contemporary Review*, March 1867, 404.

[11] Quoted in *Dublin Review*, July 1865, 6.

[12] *Edinburgh Review*, January 1858, 174.

pluck, and self-dependence of the English gentleman are principally caught."[13] "They bind the different generations of the school together, they promote the attainment of skill in the game, and they prevent intellectual superiority from being the only one formally recognised in our education." The *Edinburgh Review* was not so sure:

> A boy might readily infer from 'Tom Brown' that he was only sent to school to play at football, and that lessons were quite a secondary consideration.[14]

The *National Review* agreed:

> Whatever novels may say to the contrary the mere athletic training produces a feeble, gregarious, helpless, cast of character, dependent for vigour that it has upon accidental circumstances, and unfit for the real work of life.[15]

But the warnings were generally ignored. Vaughan and Cotton had shown how games could be used to impose discipline in schools; the Public Schools Commissioners welcomed the role they played in moral training; Darwin's evolutionary ideas and Spencer's philosophical writings warned of the survival of the fittest; and the spirit of competition inherent in all games matched the feelings of the age. The floodgates opened: all schools would play games.

In this era of the most rapid expansion of the public school system, with many new schools founded and still more raised from old grammar schools, the basic formula for a public school was derived. Such a school should be a self-contained society, partly self-governing and partly ruled by an autocratic headmaster. The aim of its education was less in intellectual qualities and more in terms of leadership and the arts of social ascendancy: it was in this latter aspect that games would contribute their part. The end-product was the Christian gentleman personified in Tom Brown. As each new school came about, so the games ethos was more readily accepted and soon the older foundations followed suit. "Private school" games were summarily abolished, sometimes by the boys, sometimes by the headmaster. Marbles, peg-top, skipping, tip-cat, hopscotch and the like were quickly replaced by football, generally the Rugby variety, cricket and rowing. Even hockey became a "despised" game.

---

[13] *Saturday Review*, August 8, 1857, 128.

[14] *Edinburgh Review*, January, 1858, 193.

[15] *National Review*, November, 1864, 316.

Clifton under John Percival was typical of the newer schools which felt this distorted influence of Arnold: Rugby football was played on the "Close", and cricket "reflected the headmaster's influence quite as faithfully as the rest of school life".[16] At the mother-school, Rugby, the years after Frederick Temple witnessed the rise of the athletic "swell" to usurp the power of the prefects and saw a growing glorification of things muscular.[17]

Games however are essentially a boy-culture and, as Mangan noted, the emulation of Vaughan and Cotton by other headmasters had unforeseen results. Soon the tail was wagging the dog as boys at all schools clamoured for cups and colours, house competitions and school matches, resident professional coaches and better facilities. Within a few years games alone determined the status of a boy within his school, and the position of that school in the rank order of public schools.[18]

III

The publication in 1857 of Thomas Hughes's *Tom Brown's Schooldays* was partly responsible for the growing mania for games. If Hughes, "of childlike heart, of knightly loyalty, of the most humane generosity, and of the simplest Christian faith", had distorted the memory of Thomas Arnold's Rugby School, it was probably done in all innocence. He did not comprehend the headmaster's full ideal because only the physical aspect, with which he was most familiar, was within his understanding.[19] Hughes's own success at school came on the playing-fields. He captained "Bigside" at football and played in the game requested on Queen Adelaide's visit to the school. He was also captain of cricket and a

---

[16] Various authors, *Great Public Schools* (London: Edward Arnold, 1893), 214. Clifton was founded in 1862. Developments at two other new schools, Cheltenham (1841) and Bradfield (1850), can be followed in Timothy Chandler, "Games at Oxbridge and the Public Schools, 1830-80: The Diffusion of an Innovation," *The International Journal of the History of Sport* 8 no. 2 (1991):171-204.

[17] Various, *Great Public Schools*, 171-172.

[18] Mangan, "Case Study," 152; John Honey, *Tom Brown's Universe* (London: Millington, 1977), chapter 4.

[19] When a few years later Hughes saw that manliness was becoming muscularity and that the physical ingredients of Arnold's Platonic ideal had become the athletic ends, he tried to close the stable door. But it was too late; the horse had bolted and Tom Brown had run off with the ideal of manliness. For Hughes's change of heart, see Tozer, *Manliness*, 218-220.

member of the Rugby XI that in 1840 was the first to play at Lord's.[20] The 1841 MCC match, in which Hughes played a captain's innings, formed the substance of "Tom Brown's Last Match". It was in these games and through the pranks and escapades of this relatively unreformed Rugby that Hughes developed self-reliance, courage and sportsmanship: but this was hardly Arnold's ideal of manliness.[21]

The story of *Tom Brown's Schooldays* is simple and effective. Rugby is the setting in which Tom discovers himself and builds his character. There is nothing special about Tom, for he is an ordinary true-blooded English boy:

> It's very odd how almost all English boys love danger; you can get ten to join a game, or climb a tree, or swim a stream, when there's a chance of breaking their limbs or getting drowned, for one who'll stay on level ground, or in his depth, or play quoits or bowls.[22]

His father sends him to Rugby not to become a scholar ...

> Well, but he isn't sent to school for that – at any rate not for that mainly. I don't care a straw for Greek particles, or the diagamma, no more does his mother. What is he sent to school for? Well, partly because he wanted to go. If he'll only turn out a brave, helpful, truth-telling Englishman, and a gentleman, and a Christian, that's all I want ...[23]

To be "brave, helpful, truth-telling", these were almost the three Platonic virtues of manliness: courage, self-control and truth.

Tom is soon proud to be a Rugby boy and, after hearing his first Arnold sermon, he resolved "to stand by and follow the Doctor". The heart of the tale rests in the conflict between those boys who wished to maintain "the good old days" and those who have accepted the Doctor's morality. Tom is pulled back and forth between the two factions, but in the end of course good prevails over evil. Tom cemented his own manliness through his catalytic friendship with George Arthur, who is weak in physical power but leonine in moral courage.[24] Arthur's transformative effect on

---

[20] Norman Wymer, *Dr Arnold of Rugby* (London: Robert Hale, 1953), 174, 181.
[21] Edward Mack and Harry Armytage, *Thomas Hughes* (London: Benn, 1952), 19.
[22] Thomas Hughes, *Tom Brown's Schooldays* (London: Macmillan, 1857/1919), 79.
[23] Hughes, *Tom Brown*, 67.
[24] Dennis Allen, "Young England: Muscular Christianity and the Politics of the Body in Tom Brown's Schooldays," in *Muscular Christianity: Embodying the*

Tom persuaded many early readers to view him as the real hero of the story.[25] The message to be drawn from the actions of both Tom and Arthur was that a true Christian manfully co-operates with others in the fight for right. Hughes's manliness was defined as the fusion of high spirits, self-reliance, and courage in the service of all good works, and was the basic, and virtually sole, Christian virtue. This is an ideal drawn more from Charles Kingsley than Thomas Arnold: as Asa Briggs noted, "If Stanley [the headmaster's official biographer] saw what happened in Arnold's mind, Hughes saw what happened in many of his pupils' minds, in the minds of all the Tom Browns who made up the masses of the school".[26]

In accepting the Tom Brown stereotype, the new public schools also took on the love of physical activity that is explicit throughout the story. To fight with one's fists was seen as manly:

> Boys will quarrel, and when they quarrel will sometimes fight. Fighting with fists is the natural and English way for English boys to settle their quarrels.[27]

> After all, what would life be without fighting, I should like to know? From the cradle to the grave, fighting, rightly understood, is the business, the real, highest, honestest business of every son of man. Every one who is worth his salt has his enemies, who must be beaten, be they evil thoughts and habits in himself, or spiritual wickedness in high places, or Russians, or Border-ruffians, or Bill, Tom or Harry, who will not let him live in quiet till he has thrashed them.[28]

How Arnold would have shuddered at the prospect of Tom Brown taking on "Slogger" Williams in his name. Boxing and football, the Rugby variety of course, were encouraged as replacements for "private school" games that were now seen to be unmanly.

The novel was possibly the first writing to advocate team spirit at school as training in patriotism. After the "School-house" football victory Brooke, the captain, asks

---

Victorian Age, ed. Donald Hall (Cambridge: Cambridge University Press, 2006), 116.

[25] Maureen Martin, "'Boys who will be Men': Desire in 'Tom Brown's Schooldays'." *Victorian Literature and Culture* 30, no. 2 (2002): 485-486.

[26] Mack and Armytage, *Hughes*, 96-97; Asa Briggs, *Victorian People* (London: Odhams, 1954/70), 162.

[27] Hughes, *Tom Brown*, 257.

[28] Hughes, *Tom Brown*, 242.

... but why did we beat 'em? answer me that – (shouts of "your play").
Nonsense. 'Twasn't the wind and kick-off either, that wouldn't do it.
'Twasn't because we've half-a-dozen of the best players in the school. I
wouldn't change Warner, and Hedge, and Crab, and the young 'un, for any
six of their side – (violent cheers). But half-a-dozen fellows can't keep it
up for two hours against two hundred. Why is it then? I'll tell you what I
think. It's because we have more reliance upon one another, more of a
house feeling, more fellowship than the school can have. Each of us knows
and can depend on his next hand man better – that's why we beat 'em today. We've union, they've division – there's the secret – (cheer) ... I know
I'd sooner win two School-house matches running than get the Balliol
scholarship any day – (frantic cheers).[29]

Here then was ready-made team spirit; but not all games fostered it.
Cricket did:

".. What a noble game it is too." (said the master)
"Isn't it? But it's more than a game. It's an institution", said Tom.
"Yes", said Arthur, "the birthright of British boys old and young, as habeas
corpus and trial by jury are of British men."
"The discipline and reliance on one another which it teaches is so valuable
I think," went on the master, "it ought to be such an unselfish game. It
merges the individual in the eleven; he doesn't play that he may win, but
that his side may."
"That's very true," said Tom, "and that's why football and cricket, now
one comes to think of it, are such much better games than fives or hare-
and-hounds, or any others where the object is to come in first or win for
oneself, and not that one's side may win."
"And then the Captain of the eleven!" said the master, "what a post is his
in our School-world! almost as hard as the Doctor's; requiring skill and
gentleness and firmness, and I know not what other rare qualities."[30]

The carry-over into manhood was equally explicit. Harry East, Tom's
second friend, has now left the school:

"Bye-the-bye, have you heard from him?" (asked the master)
"Yes, I had a letter in February, just before he started for India to join his
regiment,"
"He will make a capital officer."
"Aye, won't he!" said Tom brightening; "no fellow could handle boys
better, and I suppose soldiers are very much like boys. And he'll never tell

them to go where he won't go himself. No mistake about that. A braver fellow never walked."[31]

Thus we have the Tom Brown formula; self-reliance came through fighting and boxing, and team games produced *esprit de corps*. It was a philosophy that could rule the Empire, but the distortion of Arnold's ideals was complete.

IV

Thomas Hughes's role in the conversion of moral manliness to hearty masculinity may have been unintentional but with William Cory and Leslie Stephen the consolidation of the philathletic ideal was deliberate. More importantly, Hughes was a Christian of simple faith whereas both Cory and Stephen became influential agnostics of the new age. It is to Cory and Stephen, and not to Hughes, that Edward Bowen at Harrow and "Mike" Mitchell and Edmond Warre at Eton owed their lineage.

Cory was an exact contemporary of Edward Thring at Eton and King's College, Cambridge.[32] On graduation he first thought of taking Holy Orders, then his attention turned to the Bar, finally, and with some relief, he accepted an invitation to return to Eton. London was near enough for Cory to be involved with the Christian Socialist Movement where he met Hughes. It is probably from him that Cory saw the latent potential of athleticism.[33] He was no sportsman at Eton and Cambridge, if only because of his very weak eyesight, but the mid-Victorian boost in games-playing at his old school owed much to Cory's influence. By 1860 he had instituted house matches for cricket and that year he presented a championship cup. One of his rules for the competition hinted at future developments: ordinary dress was not to be worn and all players had to wear white cricket shoes. His attentions were also felt on the river and reached their culmination in the now famous *Eton Boating Song*, written for the Fourth of June celebrations of 1863.[34]

---

[31] Hughes, *Tom Brown*, 307.

[32] Cory was known as Johnson during his Eton career. He changed his name in 1872.

[33] Francis Cornish, *Extracts from the Letters and Journals of William Cory* (Oxford: privately published, 1897), 58.

[34] The celebrations commemorate the birthday of George III, Eton's foremost patron. See also Faith Compton Mackenzie, *William Cory* (London: Constable, 1950), 40, 42.

Jolly boating weather,
And a hay harvest breeze,
Blade on the feather,
Shade off the trees,
Swing, swing together,
With your bodies between your knees,
Swing, swing together,
With your bodies between your knees.

Rugby may be more clever,
Harrow may make more row,
But we'll row for ever,
Steady from stroke to bow,
And nothing in life shall sever
The chain that is round us now,
And nothing in life shall sever
The chain that is round us now.

Others will fill our places,
Dressed in the old light blue;
We'll recollect our races,
We'll to the flag be true,
And youth will be still in our faces
When we cheer for an Eton crew,
And youth will be still in our faces
When we cheer for an Eton crew.

Twenty years hence this weather
May tempt us from office stools,
We may be slow on the feather,
And seem to the boys old fools,
But we'll still swing together,
And swear by the best of schools,
But we'll still swing together,
And swear by the best of schools.[35]

Cory was an effective and influential teacher but he also displayed a partiality for good-looking boys and a weakness for pupils from aristocratic families. He "adored" athletes as long as they had a mind, and

---

[35] Jim Wortley, www.etoncollege.com/UserFiles/Files/BoatingSongsheet.pdf. The music was composed by Captain Algernon Drummond whilst serving with his regiment (The Rifle Brigade) in Lahore in India.

he thought bookish scholars "incomplete people".[36] Cory found an ample supply of handsome boys ready to relish his intellectual Hellenism in the eight sporting and intelligent sons of Lord Lyttelton, one of the Public Schools Commissioners.[37]

Cory's lasting influence beyond Eton came through his poetry; *Ionica* was published in stages between 1858 and 1877. Whether on the romance of the river and the cricket field, or on the glory of battle and the hopes of the patriot, the poems always reflected a Platonic agnosticism with never a gleam of Christian hope. His 1863 *A Retrospect of School Life* gives perhaps the fullest intimation of his philosophy:

> There courteous strivings with my peers,
> And duties not bound up in books,
> And courage fanned by stormy cheers
> And wisdom writ in pleasant looks,
> And hardship buoyed with hope, and pain
> Encountered for the common weal,
> And glories void of vulgar gain,
> Were mine to take, were mine to feel.
> And to myself in games I said,
> 'What mean the books? Can I win fame?
> I would be like the faithful dead
> A fearless man, and pure of blame.
> I may have failed, my School may fail;
> I tremble, but this much I dare;
> I love her. Let the critics rail,
> My brethren and my home are there.'[38]

The immense popularity of *Tom Brown's Schooldays* had inspired admiration, even adoration, of Arnold's Rugby; other public schools were quick to be associated with the collective glory; now Cory expressed through *Ionica* and the *Eton Boating Song* the sentiment that no earlier generation had felt. The cult of "the old school" was born.

---

[36] Tyerman labels him "a sort of high priest of intellectual pederasty": Tyerman, *Harrow*, 275; Compton Mackenzie, *Cory*, 42; Arthur Benson, Introduction in William Cory, *Ionica* (London: George Allen & Unwin, 1905), xx; Cornish, *Cory*, 33.

[37] Cory was forced to resign from Eton in 1872 after an indiscreet letter to a pupil was intercepted by the boy's parents and brought to the notice of the headmaster.

[38] Cory, *Ionica*, 126-128.

V

Mid-Victorian technology helped to promote the cult of the old school, especially the railway and the telegraph that ran alongside. Old Boys could communicate swiftly with each other and with their schools; reunions and sports matches against the boys were arranged at short notice; frequent trains made weekend travelling from Oxford, Cambridge and London to the schools both cheap and swift; Old Boy cricket and football tours might fill the long university vacations; and London would play host to Old Boys' dinners. All these exploits were then lovingly recorded in school magazines.

The universities of Oxford and Cambridge followed the lead of the schools and took on their love of games. Boys who had enjoyed sport at their public schools generally wished to continue their participation once at university; some on graduation three or four years later became the schoolmasters of the next generation, taking their cricket, football and fives with them to complete the circle.[39] In this way Charles Thring (Shrewsbury and St John's), William Witts (Eton and King's) and Sam Haslam (Rugby and St John's) moved from public school to Cambridge and on to Uppingham; many more young men made similar journeys to other schools. The universities were also the cradles for the organisation of competition and the codification of rules. Distances for athletic sports and rowing races had to be agreed; numbers playing in matches at football and other team sports had to be settled; and rules for the different versions of football played at the schools had to be blended. The last, no easy task, led to the creation of two national codes: that played by the Football Association from 1863 and its rival, the Rugby Football Union, in 1871.

Until the following decade, dons at the universities who wished to marry had to relinquish their fellowships so there was a steady turn-over of young men; nearly half of all dons were in their twenties and many were athletic.[40] Matthew Arnold complained that "the real studies of Oxford are its games" as these men took a leading role in university sport; the Rev Leslie Stephen, a tutor at Trinity Hall, Cambridge from 1854, was one. It is after his rejection by the Apostles, a society of intellectuals, that Stephen's response was to become leader of the university's athletic set. He encouraged long-distance walking to guard against "idleness and effeminacy" and became president of its club, the Boa Constrictors. He was known to have walked to London and back merely to attend a

---

[39] For more on this circle, see Chandler, "Oxbridge", 171-204.
[40] Paul Deslandes, *Oxbridge Men: British Masculinity and the Undergraduate Experience, 1850-1920* (Bloomington: Indiana University Press, 2005), 58.

dinner.[41] The Athletics Sports, founded in 1860, and the first University Athletics Match with Oxford in 1864, both owed their inception to Stephen. He competed against Oxford too, winning the mile and the two miles in 1860, and the latter again in 1861.[42] He coached the college's rowing VIII, prizing the sport as the epitome of team spirit, and he led Trinity Hall to head of the river in 1859 and again in 1862.[43] Undergraduates delighted in his company because he shared their pursuits; it was Stephen who presided at sporting dinners and wrote the college's boating song. Composed in haste after the 1862 triumph, it contained too many jokes on the names of the crew to stand comparison with Cory's Eton anthem. The chorus went:

> Then here's a health to old Trinity Hall!
> A health to the captain, a health to us all!
> To the men who have row'd us up head of the river!
> We have got there at last; – may we stay there for ever.[44]

Stephen became the very personification of a muscular Christian and his approval of boys being flogged at school as "a sacred initiatory rite" and "a sort of strange chivalry" went down well with many schoolmasters.[45] According to his biographer, Noel Annan, it is he and not Kingsley who ought to be regarded as the founder of that movement.[46] Soon, however, Stephen lost his own Christian faith; he resigned his fellowship and veered towards agnosticism. Only the Spartan masculinity of the muscular Christian ideal remained.

VI

The playing of games at Harrow received a boost when Edward Bowen, a graduate of Trinity College, Cambridge, joined the teaching staff in 1860; he remained there until his death in 1901. When the Modern Side was

---

[41] Frederic Maitland, *The Life and Letters of Leslie Stephen* (London: Duckworth, 1906), 64-65; Noel Annan, *Leslie Stephen: The Godless Victorian* (London: Weidenfeld & Nicholson, 1984), 29.

[42] Maitland, *Stephen*, 61.

[43] Annan, *Stephen*, 29.

[44] Maitland, *Stephen*, 61.

[45] Tyerman, *Harrow*, 336.

[46] Stephen's humorous definition of a muscular Christian in his *Sketches from Cambridge* (1863), "he should fear God and walk a thousand miles in a thousand hours", should not be taken seriously. Leslie Stephen, *Sketches from Cambridge* (London: Smith Elder, 1863), 22; Annan, *Stephen*, 26; Maitland, *Stephen*, 138.

created in 1869 to provide an alternative to the traditional classical curriculum, Bowen became its first Master. In addition, Bowen was for thirty-seven years a well-respected bachelor housemaster, first in a small house, Grove Hill with eight or so boarders, then in a large one, The Grove, with 30.[47]

Games became compulsory for all boys from the 1860s. They occupied as much time in the school's week as formal lessons, and absentees were caned by the monitors.[48] Spencer Gore, an Old Harrovian, reckoned that the "object of every boy" was to get into the cricket XI, and the moment when he was "given his flannels" would be "the supreme moment of his life".[49] The government of the boys was dominated by the athletes from 1869, the year when Montagu Butler, Vaughan's successor as Head Master, permitted boys other than the intellectual elite of the sixth-form to become monitors. Arthur Holt, a Harrow master, applauded:

> [the] brilliant cricketer and the sturdy footballer will always have authority. Make that authority constitutional and responsible, and you will at least escape a good deal of friction; while such boys, if they know that they are trusted, will often be found to exert an influence for good which does not always belong to brains ... But it is a familiar experience that the athlete who might have become a source of trouble as an irresponsible force is found to add strength to the government, on the principle that an old poacher often makes the best gamekeeper.[50]

Others were not so sure for by 1874 the rule of the athletic "bloods" had bred bullying and crushed individualism. Leaning out of a study window or walking down the middle of the road could earn a boy a beating by a monitor; almost all boys were caned at some time in their school careers; and public fights between boys were common, often with masters looking on. Boys were made to conform to the consensual type and replicate the approved image of "good form". The wearing of spectacles, for example, was seen as unmanly; perversely, this prevented some boys from excelling at sport.[51]

---

[47] Grove Hill, 1864-81, and The Grove, 1881-1901: census information from 1871-1901. He was known as The Sleuth, for obvious reasons. Tyerman, *Harrow*, 314.

[48] Tyerman, *Harrow*, 257, 288, 338. Prefects are called monitors at Harrow.

[49] Various, *Public Schools*, 24; Spencer Gore, 'Harrow Cricket', *National Review*, July 1894, 680.

[50] Holt in Schoolmasters, *The Public Schools from Within* (London: Leopold, 1906), 148; Tyerman, *Harrow*, 317.

[51] The age of the motor-car put an end to the monitors' road privilege. Tyerman, *Harrow*, 317, 323, 336, 337.

To his contemporaries Bowen was the walking embodiment of *mens sana in corpore sano,* a tag that suited him "to a T". He was always an avid rambler. When an undergraduate he had walked the ninety miles from Cambridge to Oxford in less than twenty-four hours, and in later life he claimed to have walked all England's coastline and a goodly portion of the Alps.[52] At Cambridge he had been a keen footballer and there he played a small role in the formation of the Association rules. His fame at Harrow as a games player was legendary, his enthusiasm was boundless and his caution negligible. Racquets, gymnastics ("mere Greek iambics of physical training") and swimming were all present at Harrow in the 1860s but they were of little account in the boys' eyes and none at all in Bowen's. They failed to inspire a sense of comradeship. Cricket and, above all else, football were second to none in "fostering a healthy, manly, unselfish corporate life".[53] To Bowen:

> It is not only the gain of doing in a manly way what others do, and sharing the common life, nor the health that comes to body and mind from mingled activity and sport, but on the football field the character is more revealed, for imitation or for blame, than at any other moment of the day.[54]

To enable games to do their work most effectively, Bowen believed that boys and masters should be of equal rank when on the playing-fields, and that due attention should be given to younger boys; he created teams for boys under fifteen and under sixteen, the Infants and Colts.[55] Masters were encouraged to play, indeed Bowen was still playing football until shortly before his death at the age of sixty-five, but they should take no part in the organisation or coaching. This attitude had the benefit of keeping professional attitudes at bay but, in passing all authority to senior boys, the masters effectively sanctified the rule of the bloods.[56] The dominance of games in the life of boys and many masters also retarded the intellectual and social development of both. Talk of games rather than intellectual pursuits was the staple of school conversation, school-work was seen as of secondary value, boys were kept as boys when they should

---

[52] James Cotton Minchin, *Old Harrow Days* (London: Methuen, 1898), 73; James Bryce, *Studies in Contemporary Literature* (London: Macmillan, 1903/20), 355.
[53] William Bowen, *Edward Bowen* (London: Longmans, 1902), 146, 147, 187, 225, 231.
[54] Edward Bowen in Edmund Howson and George Warner, *Harrow School* (London: Arnold, 1898), 251.
[55] James Mangan, *'Manufactured' Masculinity: Making Imperial Manliness, Morality and Militarism* (Abingdon: Routledge, 2012), 109.
[56] Tyerman, *Harrow*, 339.

have been becoming men, and the worship of the athlete slipped easily to the aesthetic delight in the beautiful body.[57]

Bowen is best remembered today for his words to *Forty Years On*, that anthem for Harrovians. John Farmer, who joined the Harrow staff as music master in 1862, formed a memorable partnership with Bowen from 1867 to 1877 that produced over thirty songs, mainly on games.[58] *Forty Years On* cemented love of the old school to the cult of games, Harrow football in particular:

Forty years on, when afar and asunder
Parted are those who are singing today,
When you look back, and forgetfully wonder
What you were like in your work and your play,
Then, it may be, there will often come o'er you,
Glimpses of notes like the catch of a song –
Visions of boyhood shall float them before you,
Echoes of dreamland shall bear them along,
Follow up! Follow up! Follow up
Follow up! Follow up
Till the field ring again and again,
With the tramp of the twenty-two men.
Follow up! Follow up!

Routs and discomfitures, rushes and rallies,
Bases attempted, and rescued, and won,
Strife without anger and art without malice, –
How will it seem to you, forty years on?
Then, you will say, not a feverish minute
Strained the weak heart and the wavering knee,
Never the battle raged hottest, but in it.
Neither the last nor the faintest, were we!
Follow up! etc....

Forty years on, growing older and older,
Shorter in wind, as in memory long,
Feeble of foot, and rheumatic of shoulder,
What will it help you that once you were strong?
God give us bases to guard or beleaguer,
Games to play out, whether earnest or fun;
Fights for the fearless, and goals for the eager,

---

[57] Dale Vargas, a former Second Master of Harrow, has written to me: "It is wrong to tar Bowen with the same brush as the games maniacs". I hope that I have not done so.
[58] Tyerman, *Harrow,* 347, 349.

Twenty, and thirty, and forty years on!
Follow up etc.[59]

Edgar Castle, in his *Moral Education in Christian Times*, argued that Bowen had no illusions about athleticism.[60] Certainly the superficial frivolity of his essay on "Games", published in the *Journal of Education* in 1884, lends support to Castle's view. Here games are extolled for their aesthetic pleasure, male companionship, and general social influence for good. There are even some passing shots at the over-zealous games master. However, underlying that frivolity is the thesis that games are the most important and most valuable of all factors in the educational process. Games induced respect for command, obedience, dignity and courtesy; in addition they corrected "laziness, foppery and man-of-the-worldness". Bowen had no doubt that "the best boys are, on the whole, the players of games".[61] If he had no illusions about athleticism, he certainly did little to stem its tide. Bowen's philosophy was Spartanism, for the muscularity of muscular Christianity had smothered the Christian foundations. "There lies more soul in honest play, believe me", wrote Bowen, "than in half the hymn-books." His favourite maxim was "Always play the game".[62]

---

[59] A base is the Harrow name for a goal. Note that school-work is mentioned just once, in the fourth line of the first verse.

[60] Edgar Castle, *Moral Education in Christian Times* (London: Allen & Unwin, 1958), 321.

[61] Edward Bowen (U.U.), "Games", *Journal of Education*, 1 February 1884; Bowen, *Bowen*, 222-225.

[62] Bryce, *Studies*, 350; Bowen, *Bowen*, 224, 260.

CHAPTER TEN

CHANNELS OF COMMUNICATION: "THE JOY OF STRENGTH AND MOVEMENT"

I

Thring regularly explained his "great educational experiment" to the boys. In his sermons and speeches he spoke directly to them; in his songs, through the school magazine and by his choice of books for the library his message was less direct but equally pervasive. The masters, Old Boys, the boys themselves and occasionally their parents all contributed their part. In physical education these channels of communication of Thring's philosophy were vital, for it was all too easy to concentrate on the means and lose sight of the end.

Henry Holden's magazine, *The Hospitaler*, ceased publication on Thring's appointment as headmaster and it was not until ten years later that its successor, the *Uppingham School Magazine*, appeared. The appointment of successive schoolboy editors seems to have been made by Thring, and the post was always given to a loyal praepostor. The earliest editors were Walter Cornish, Lewis Nettleship and Willingham Rawnsley. The magazine in the first years had a high literary content but gradually sporting intelligence came to dominate the pages. Detailed reviews of all school sporting, athletic and gymnastic events were supported with news of activities by Old Boys in the same spheres. Even some of the literary contributions were on sporting themes: "The Paperchase", "Football at R", and "Cricket – Pro and Con" are three early examples. "Accounts of the Doings of the Uppingham Rovers" nearly filled an autumn edition each year. Much of the correspondence from boys, Old Boys and masters was on sporting matters, and "*nomination* in the Magazine" seems to have proved a useful way of deterring "foxes" in the paperchase from cutting corners.[1] Naming and shaming of those who cheated in the 2018 London Marathon had a mid-Victorian Uppingham precedent.

---

[1] *USM*, November 1864, 382.

Most editorials from 1865 onwards previewed the season's prospects in the various games. They also commented on fielding deficiencies in cricket, absenteeism in football, and lack of "pluck" in athletics. The editorials also served to extend Thring's influence: if reprimanding boys for "slackness" possibly came from the headmaster, the explanation of the "value" of physical activity certainly did.

Letters from "our correspondent" at Oxford or Cambridge were common in the 1870s. These recorded the sporting successes of Old Boys and announced the creation of various Old Boy clubs. They also served to keep the school well informed of national sporting developments at a time when codes of play and rules for competition were being decided for many sports, and they were instrumental in bringing the Uppingham football rules closer to those of the two national codes, Association and Rugby. These letters, together with other contributions from Old Boys, became so numerous that at one stage a reviewer from another school wondered if the magazine had become the journal for Old Uppinghamians.[2]

By the 1870s literary articles, even on sporting themes, hardly ever appeared in the school magazine and the mass of correspondence on sporting matters was so great that much had to be diverted to the Committee of Games.[3] The relationship between the magazine and games, or between its editors and the Committee of Games, came under strain in 1874. An editorial commented that the inundation of the magazine with the accounts "from the never-failing fountain-head, of cricket and its brother games, has for some years been an increasing evil". There was a "danger of over-estimating and turning into main objects matters whose real place is subordinate". The editor decided that in future the magazine would only admit accounts of school matches and final house matches; other results would be "merely given in a tabulated form". One presumes that the "advice from those competent to give it" included Thring's.[4] An attempt to condense the "Accounts" of the Uppingham Rovers the following year did not meet with the same success.

The exchange of magazines with other schools became common after 1875 and the *Uppingham School Magazine* now contained much sporting news about its rivals that had been extracted from its "contemporaries". Comparison of performances became inevitable and included the

---

[2] It was customary for copies of school magazines to be sent to the libraries of schools already friendly to Uppingham and to others where association was an aspiration.
[3] *USM*, March 1872, 3.
[4] *USM*, March 1874, 2-3.

tabulation of results from athletics championships.[5] A "letter to the Editor" in 1879 from H. H. Stephenson, the school's cricket professional since 1872, became the first of a unique series of coaching texts that broadened his influence with the boys.

This same period witnessed the establishment of matches in several sports between teams representing England, Ireland, Scotland and Wales, and the creation of highly exclusive invitation teams. The school magazine was quick to report on Old Boys who had won international "caps" and the like. The earliest entries were for Charles Green's selection for the annual cricket match between the Gentlemen and the Players and Edward Turner's inclusion in the England Rugby Union XX to play Ireland, both in 1875.[6] Between 1875 and 1887, the last third of Thring's headmastership, Uppingham's international tally was three for cricket (Alfred Lucas, Sandford Schultz and Stanley Christopherson), eight for Rugby Union football (Edward Turner, his brother George Turner, Ellis Markendale, John Schofield, Charles Wilson and Alan Rotherham for England; Robert Mackenzie and George Robb for Scotland), and one for Association football (Charles Wilson for England, unusually winning caps in both codes). In addition, 27 Oxford and Cambridge Blues were won: sixteen in cricket, six in Rugby Union football, two in Association football, and three in rowing.[7] The last is remarkable, for Uppingham was never a rowing school.

II

Christian Reimers left Uppingham in 1857 to concentrate on his career as a performer. He joined Charles Hallé's Manchester's Gentleman's Society Orchestra, soon to be known as the Hallé Orchestra, and played as a senior member of the cello section for twenty-one years.[8] He was succeeded at Uppingham by another string player, the violinist Heinrich Riccius, aged 25.[9] He had studied at Mendelssohn's Conservatorium in Leipzig under

---

[5] *USM*, July 1882, 238.

[6] *USM*, September 1875, 226 and December 1875, 375. Turner was at Uppingham from 1868 to 1872. He played for England in 1875, 1877 and 1878. He became a surgeon at St George's Hospital in London.

[7] *USM*, April 1913, 87.

[8] Blackman, *Reimers*, 46-50.

[9] He came from a musical family: his uncle, August Riccius, was conductor and chorus-master at the Stadttheater in both Hamburg and Leipzig; his brother, Karl, was conductor of the Königlich Sächsischer Opernchor and chorus-master at the

Ferdinand David and in 1854 he was one of the founder members of the Dresdner Tonkünstler-Verein before moving to Cologne to become the city's chorus-master.[10] He was now close to the Breusing circle in Bonn, the likely source of the news of a vacancy at Uppingham.

In addition to his lessons with individual pupils, Riccius was given an hour one evening each week to work with the choir.[11] Marie Thring's musical evenings had now evolved to become regular concerts with an audience of 200 boys, masters and their families. Many were noted in Thring's diary: "Concert … went off very well. The boys encored loudly for the first time, before they only clapped."[12] Then, in March 1862, the school gave its first concert for the townspeople of Uppingham.[13] Two more Thring songs were set to music by Riccius and, with the three from Reimers, were published in 1858 as a volume of *School Songs*. Thring added a preface:

> There is a tendency in schools to stereotype the forms of life. Any genial solvent is valuable. Games do much; but games do not penetrate to domestic life, and are much limited by age. Music supplies the want …[14]

Thring's *Echoes of Uppingham* now displaced the unsuccessful *The Uppingham Chorus* as the official school song whilst *The Rockingham Match* described the annual visit to a nearby castle for a game of cricket.

> Blue caps, where are my blue caps?
> They marshal fair
> On yon green hill
> Fearing and catching, stopping there,
> Batting and hoping, winning there, wandering free,
> Near stream and tree,
> By two and by three,
> Or stretched at length on the grass,
> Their full plates pass.[15]

Königlichen Hoftheater in Dresden. "Karl August Gustav Riccius", accessed May 18, 2017, http://www.stadtwikidd.de/wiki/Karl_August_Gustav_Riccius.
[10] "Briefdatenbank der Schumann", accessed May 18, 2017, https://sbd. schumann-portal.de/Person.html?ID=2773; "Staatskapelle Dresden", accessed May 18, 2017, http://www.staatskapelledresden.de/en/staatskapelle/kapellehistorisch/tonkuenstler verein/; "Niederrheinische Musik-Zeitung", accessed May 18, 2017, https://de.wikisource.org/wiki/ Niederrheinische_Musik-Zeitung.
[11] Diary, November 5, 1860.
[12] Diary, May 19, 1861.
[13] Diary, March 18, 1862.
[14] Edward Thring, *School Songs* (Cambridge: Macmillan, 1858).

Thring's lyrics for the *Old Boys' Match* were composed in 1862 but were not set to music until 1881 when W. Richter joined the staff.[16] The jollity of the premier cricket match of the season was well captured:

> Summer, ho! we sought him, found him,
> Made the jolly traitor yield,
> June, he caught him, caught him, bound him,
> All his posies tumbled round him,
> Flung him on the cricket field.
>
> Jolly sun, we do implore thee,
> Stay with us the whole year round,
> Young boys almost do adore thee,
> Old boys come to bask before thee,
> Lie still on the cricket ground.
>
> Sunshine for the match of matches,
> All the ground a sunny shield,
> Sunny hours in sunny snatches,
> Sunny hits, and sunny catches,
> Sunshine on the cricket field.
>
> Sunshine for the old who meet us,
> Old and young, a sunny game;
> Sunny game, they shall not beat us,
> Sunny game, though they defeat us,
> Sunny life for Uppingham.[17]

Riccius left Uppingham in 1862 shortly after the concert for the townspeople. He departed in haste and he may have been seriously ill.[18] Thring had to fill the gap quickly with an English appointment because his brother-in-law and recruiter in Bonn was busily engaged in trying to save his school from financial collapse.[19] The Rev Ogle Wintle joined Uppingham from a curacy in Bridgwater in Somerset; his sole qualification to teach music was five years' service as a boy chorister at Christ Church,

---

[15] In UA.

[16] I have been unable to discover Richter's first name.

[17] Edward Thring, *Songs of Uppingham School* (London: E. Stanford, 1881) no. 8.

[18] "Briefdatenbank der Schumann", accessed May 18, 2017, https://sbd. schumann-portal.de/Person.html?ID=2773.

[19] He failed to save the school and it closed in 1862. Thring bore a heavy loss on money that he had lent Breusing. Breusing later took private pupils at his home. Diary, February 7 and March 3, 1862.

Oxford.[20] Wintle muddled through for three years: reviews of his concerts in the school magazine contained many complaints, and he even confessed his inadequacy to Thring.[21]

School concerts of the period of Reimers, Riccius and Wintle comprised two halves with a short interval in between. The first was devoted to sacred music (including anthems, airs from oratorios, and motets); the second to secular (opera arias, glees and ending with one of the school songs).

III

The early music teachers worked wonders with the boys but their frequent replacement as they moved on to further their careers or to return to Prussia proved frustrating, and the Wintle hiatus had allowed standards to slip. Thus in 1865 Thring consulted England's foremost musician, William Sterndale Bennett, and asked him to find a suitable man for a permanent appointment when he next travelled to Leipzig. Sterndale Bennett had regularly attended Mendelssohn's Conservatorium in the city since he was first acclaimed by its academy in 1837 and where he had enjoyed "billiards and daily lunches" with Mendelssohn, Schumann and Ferdinand David.[22] He asked David, the principal violin teacher, if he could recommend anyone for the Uppingham position, and David suggested his own son Paul, aged 25.

How Sterndale Bennett persuaded Paul David, a talented member of the Mendelssohn and Schumann circle, to accept Thring's invitation is not known; what is certain is that David sacrificed personal renown in his own country to give Uppingham a distinction and excellence in music above any other English school in the nineteenth century.[23] On the conclusion of his studies, David had joined the violin section of the Karlsruhe orchestra, a post he held for two years. There he developed a warm friendship with Johannes Brahms, singing through early versions of his songs and playing in the A-major quartet prior to its publication, and also with Josef Joachim,

---

[20] He may have been approached by one of the Thring family living at nearby Alford. Joseph Foster, *Alumni Oxonienses: the Members of the University of Oxford, 1715-1886* (Oxford: James Parker & Co, 1891), IV 1591.

[21] Matthews, *By God's Grace*, 218.

[22] Larry Todd, *Mendelssohn: A Life in Music* (Oxford: Oxford University Press, 2005), 327.

[23] For more see: Malcolm Tozer, "From Prussia with love: music at Uppingham School, 1853-1908," *Journal of Historical Research in Music Education*, forthcoming.

the foremost violinist of the age.[24] David travelled to Uppingham accompanied by Joachim, no doubt at his father's suggestion for he also asked Sterndale Bennett to help his son settle in to life in England. Thring was obviously pleased with his catch for he declared March 13, 1865 "a half holiday in honour of Herr David's arrival".[25]

Under David's direction music was soon "an essential part of school life": it became a timetabled subject in the 1870s and more than a third of the 300-strong school was learning an instrument.[26] David and Beisiegel did all the teaching for the first three years but by 1875 they had assistance from one and then two colleagues. All boys had two lessons a week and those who learned an instrument had two more: woodwind teaching was added to piano and strings in 1872. David set two of Thring's earlier songs to music, *The Football Song* in 1866 and *Echoes of Uppingham* in 1873, and they collaborated that same year on a new school song, *Ho! Boys, Ho!*. "What may not come of School Songs", Thring wrote enthusiastically in his diary. May that year witnessed the first concert with every item an Uppingham composition:

> The whole concert Uppingham. What an epoch! The boys encored the school song again and again, and all rose and stood whilst it was being sung. It was a grand time … Never before in England has such a thing happened as a great school having its own music in this way and rising with it. The zeal of the boys was wonderful.[27]

The last years of Thring's life witnessed David and Skrine presenting him with hymns for use at the start and end of each term; on their receipt he noted in his diary:

> I trust very much to our literature in days to come keeping the school true to high principles, and giving them esprit de corps.[28]

David, to Thring's "great delight", also collected together all the school songs and arranged them for publication and, at some time in this period, Thring composed a second version of *The Old Boys' Match*.[29] It was never set to music but it was published posthumously by his daughter, Sarah:

---

[24] *The Musical Times*, July 1, 1906, 455.
[25] *USM*, April 1865, 81.
[26] *USM*, March 1876, 4; James, *Thring*, 35, 38; *The Musical Times*, 453.
[27] Diary, May 13, 1873 (Parkin, *Life*, 1:246).
[28] Diary, November 29, 1884 (Parkin, *Life*, 2:167).
[29] Diary, October 8, 1887.

Crabbed age and youth
Cannot live together.
Poet, tell the truth
In the summer weather.

Youngest welcome rung
Out of grey old gables,
Old Boys all were young,
Whispered old young fables.

So we met, and played,
Young and old together;
Merry work we made.
Poet, keep your tether.[30]

IV

Thring spoke to the boys often on the importance and value of physical activity; the time of the athletic sports was a favourite occasion. The sports were inaugurated in 1859 and prizes were first presented in 1861. The prize-giving was held in the school-room after the sports and was always followed by a speech from the headmaster. Thring regarded this occasion as "of wonderful importance for communicating and exemplifying our life".[31] The speech, a correspondent to the school magazine recalled, "though addressed on the same subject and to the same audience year by year, was yet new and old at once to all present".[32]

Thring would speak

> On pluck and fair play and the value of wide sympathies, and the difference between a strong body and a plucky heart, that the one is as dead without the other.[33]

The school's system of physical education was founded on the principle of "the sound mind in the sound body". All work done with one's whole powers, whether intellectual or physical, was good work. Excellence was an important Thring virtue; the "dilettante", the "amateur" school inspector, all forms of "half-heartedness", met with his scorn. The lessons of good

---

[30] Edward Thring, *Poems and Translations* (London: T. Fisher Unwin, 1887), 84.
[31] Diary, May 2, 1862 (Parkin, *Life*, 1:120).
[32] *USM*, September 1866, 136.
[33] Diary, March 23, 1861.

temper and fairness taught in athletics and games were of incalculable benefit to the boys.[34]

Young boys were encouraged to approach physical activity "on the same basis as our other school work". If a boy was good at his studies it did not mean that he had to be poor at games, and *vice versa*.[35] Prizes, coloured bands, and names of honours boards were incentives to work hard: "those who run should not do so because they can get so much money if first and so much if second, but because it is a noble thing to endure and train the body".[36]

The role of gymnastics was also explained. This was "the only representative we have of pure exercise of the natural body, combining strength and skill, and stands quite apart in its character from either the races or the games". Many of the best readers in the school, Thring asserted, were to be found among the gymnastic pupils, thus illustrating the link between "Bodily" and "Intellectual" work.[37] In addition, Thring noted

Of the 43 [athletics] prizes, 33 had been won by the gymnastic pupils, showing not only was the thing [the sports] physically good, but that the same spirit which makes a boy delight in, or at least endure the training of the gymnasium, makes him also winner in the race.[38]

Thring realised that bodily strength, along with the pastry cook, could become a "divinity" in the boys' eyes, and warnings against both were regularly issued.[39] So too were warnings against hero-worship:

Made a speech, expressing my conviction of the progress of true principles in the school, that they get wider and deep, and that though I suppose we must have fools and beasts sometimes, that they are less and less worshipped, that there is less 'donkey worship'. I gradually got my speech round to this phrase, and I think I have settled for a season the mock heroes …[40]

[34] *USM*, June 1868, 166-167.
[35] *USM*, June 1864, 232.
[36] *USM*, March 1865, 2.
[37] *USM*, June 1864, 195.
[38] *USM*, June 1864, 232.
[39] Thring, *E&S*, 127.
[40] Diary, November 26, 1865 (Parkin, *Life*, 1:151).

Thring also chose his visiting speakers carefully. Harvey Goodwin, Bishop of Carlisle from 1869, was a frequent guest. In his Founder's Day sermon of 1882, he noted:

> … that it is quite certain that a boy's character is formed quite as much out of school as in it, that it is the free and honourable intercourse with his peers quite as much as the direct teaching which he receives from his masters, that makes the boy what he ultimately becomes. Nay, even in the case of the master himself, it is not mere scholarship or technical skill that will make a man successful in his profession, unless he also possesses and cultivates other qualities which boys respect, and which give a tone to the school, and affect in a hundred indefinable ways a boy's conduct and heart.[41]

Two years later, at the Tercentenary Celebrations for the school's foundation, he commented on the "grand feeling of competition" and the "grand ardour for athletic sports."[42]

V

"I see Thring plainest in the pulpit" recalled Ernest Hornung, "no longer a little old man, but majestic noble and austere".[43] It was in his sermons, "the true organ of his thought", that Thring would most often explain to the boys the purpose of life and the role that Uppingham was to play.[44] For the first few years of his headmastership the boys attended services in the parish church and Thring was denied access to the pulpit, yet on each Sunday evening he would deliver his sermon in the School House hall. Looking back in 1886, Christian Reimers recalled the "gentle force" of Thring's words.[45] In September 1860 Thring moved the services to the school-room adjacent to the parish church and now made his sermon an

---

[41] *Founder's Day 1882*, 37. In UA.

[42] *Uppingham Tercentenary*, 1884, 13. In UA.

[43] Hornung, *Fathers*, vii. Hornung was at Uppingham in the 1880s when Thring was in his sixties.

[44] Skrine, *Edward Thring*, 79.

[45] "I was compelled to attend Sunday Services, which wise regulation caused some struggle for my independent mind, but I soon thoroughly enjoyed the chants and psalms led by sweet boys' voices and learned the grand lesson that the masses of mankind must be educated for the influence of divine worship by gentle force and cunning devices to court that mighty lever of progress – *habit*." Quoted in Blackman, *Reimers*, 151.

integral part of the pattern of worship.[46] Thring long felt the need of a chapel of his own, free from "party opinions", and in 1865, after Witts had set the chapel-building fund off to a good start with a donation of £1000, his wish was realised.[47]

In 1858 Thring published a volume of the School House sermons to serve as a prospectus for the school and to assure prospective parents that he was trustworthy on religious matters. It was dedicated to the masters, "true fellow-workers and friends", and prefaced in characteristic style:

> These sermons are sent into the world as part of a system, and as exponents, in some degree of the experience of working men, that it is possible to have a free and manly school life, complete in all its parts, neither lost in a crowd, nor shut up in a prison, nor reared in a hot-bed.[48]

Nearly 400 manuscripts of other Thring sermons are held in the Uppingham Archives, and of these about a third were published in 1886 in the two-volume *Sermons Preached at Uppingham School*.[49] Reading these sermons more than a century later, one is struck by the simple sincerity: they read as parables. They were neither intellectual nor theological, nor did Thring speak down to the boys. Each sermon would seem to have been written out at one attempt; Thring might make a few amendments on reading over the manuscript, but here the main purpose was to insert the pause marks needed for his delivery. That delivery contained "no art, no dexterity of phrase or of articulation"; he merely would speak straight from the heart, with rarely a movement except to turn the leaves. Each sermon had a biblical text and most a title: the length, in an era notorious for prolixity, was no more than ten minutes. Thring stood as a "prophet" of God, and in his sermons he spoke as Moses to a "chosen people".[50]

Many of the sermons dealt with "character": "Character not thieving", "Fierce idlers, weak characters", "Half-heartedness", "Honour and loyalty, or the tempter's power", and "The School, its rank" are titles of sermons that were in this vein. To Thring the supreme virtues were "Truth", "Bravery" or "Courage", and "Self-mastery"; together they made "Manliness". These terms occurred in many sermons. Truth

---

[46] Diary, September 29, 1860.

[47] Diary, March 6, 1859; Thring, *E&S*, 195.

[48] Edward Thring, *Sermons Delivered at Uppingham School* (Cambridge: Macmillan, 1858), vii. Hereafter *Sermons Delivered*.

[49] Edward Thring, *Sermons Preached at Uppingham School* (London: Deighton, Bell and Co, 1886). Hereafter *Sermons Preached*.

[50] All quotations are from Oswald Powell, *USM*, 1953, 32.

… is the knowledge of ourselves, and the humility springing from such knowledge.[51]

Truth is the doing what we know to be right each moment that a thing we know to be right has to be done.[52]

Bravery:

True bravery wants no strength but its own life.[53]

… the lowest kind of bravery is animal bravery.[54]

The truly brave strong man will face any danger that ought to be faced; the truly brave strong man will master any fear, fear of shame, and fear of ruin, as well as fear of danger; the truly brave strong man will not give way to mean temptations and fearful lusts.[55]

Self-mastery:

If we train ourselves to be perfectly ready, to bear hunger and cold then we have got rid of the main temptation. If we are able to have the hardy elastic feeling of not caring for hardship then is our own spirit strong within us, then are we beginning to be free indeed. Food and warmth and vanity soon pass into laziness and lust and a hatred of active life.[56]

Manliness blended truth, bravery and self-control to complete the Platonic ideal. "Manliness means the cheerful bearing heat and cold, hunger and thirst, work and hardship, pain and weariness."[57]

You are called upon to war against the flesh; that is, to learn not to care for any mere bodily feeling in comparison with higher things. If you bear hunger without ill-temper, that is being Christ's soldier; if you give up dainties and nice things to eat or drink, that is learning to be Christ's soldier; if you can work on when tired, or begin work when tempted to indulge the body in rest or play, that is learning to subdue the flesh. See, then, how well adapted our life here is to give this self-command, and how much that may perhaps have seemed tiresome, or want of freedom even, is

---

[51] Thring, *Sermons Delivered*, 13.
[52] Thring, Sermon 203. In the box of manuscript sermons. In UA.
[53] Thring, Sermon 64.
[54] Thring, Sermon 155.
[55] Thring, Sermon, 157.
[56] Thring, Sermon 134c.
[57] Thring, *Sermons Preached*, 2:362.

in reality Christ's service and perfect freedom. For which is free, he who gives way to his own love of ease or impatience of control, or he who learnt thoroughly to master himself, and in obeying, to be lord of his own heart? Our set times, then, are most valuable assistances to freedom, training you not to care for your own fancies, but at any moment, whatever you are about, to be able to turn to what is right. Just as a war-horse is trained to turn, to charge, to stop, to wheel, to back, so that in the battle he and his rider may conquer, so we are trained never to think of self when there is a call to duty. And again, in their proper degree, how our very games and exercises strengthen the body and will do it right, and make the mere sitting idling by the fire, or lounging in the sun, childish and contemptible; or again, furnish opportunities for self-denial, by being given up readily at the calls of higher duties. All these things, then, are to make you free – and are freedom – breaking off from your necks, if rightly done, the slavery of selfish fleshy appetites.[58]

The "joy of strength and movement" is evident in many sermons and "the blessing of health" that came from games was often praised; but always games were regarded as of secondary importance compared to the ideal of manliness, and warnings against making games a "science" span Thring's whole life at Uppingham:[59]

> Another making excellence in games his object and being put out by anything which interferes with that, because he is working for himself and not for Christ. (1853)

> What a field there is for life. What scope for tenderness to the weak, for not putting difficulties in the way of the young. And in yourselves, what scope for doing the right and giving up hand and foot and eye, the love of power in games, the love of skill in lessons, for the sake of just doing at the time the distasteful task with friendly welcome. (1875)

> I must think that to be known through England for true manliness is a better thing than to have a name for cricket. (1884)[60]

William Patterson reported that Thring preached in 1868 on the text "For He hath no pleasure in the strength of a horse, neither delighteth He in any man's legs", but no other record of this sermon has been found.[61]

Thring's purpose was to send out true, brave, resolute, manly Christians:

---

[58] Thring, *Sermons Preached*, 2:191-192.
[59] Thring, Sermons 32, 70 and 373.
[60] Thring, Sermons 68 and 124; *Sermons Preached*, 2:362.
[61] Psalm 147, verse 10. Patterson, *Uppingham Cricket*, 50.

Your daily life here is just planned out on such a plan as to try your
courage in little things every day; to try your courage in good whether you
have the life in you that can readily resist temptation in this way and be
brave; to try your courage in body, in games and outdoor life whether you
have the life in you to overcome weariness, laziness and pain and be brave
in body; to try your courage in your main work, whether you have the life
in you which can overcome the dislike of tasks, resist idleness, feel the
brave spirit that hour after hour can do its work lovingly in spite of the pain
of hard reading and the allurements of amusement, and be brave
intellectually.[62]

Truth claims that your amusements shall be manly, and hearty, and
honourable, that there shall be no cheating; neither the cheating which
steals time and cheats God's working day of works nor the cheating which
in the game itself takes more than is right.[63]

Thring's last sermon was never preached for he was taken with a fatal
illness on the day it was to have been delivered. His text was "knowing
good from evil" (Genesis III, 4-5).

I need not point out how completely God's plan is carried out in the plan of
a School like this. What opportunities for manliness and self-denial there
are in the work and the games, in the in-door life and the out-door life.
How much of the joy of manliness is here as well as its trials. What room
there is for obedience. How your life together calls for gentleness and
forbearance with one another.[64]

After writing these words Thring turned to his diary, and closed the
day's entry almost in prophecy: "And now to bed, Sermon finished, and a
blessed feeling of Sunday coming"[65]

VI

Thring received considerable support from his colleagues for his vision of
the role that physical education could play in the boys' lives. Many staff
shared his love of the countryside and would ramble with the boys to
collect natural history specimens. Willingham Rawnsley echoed Thring's
own opinion with his statement that "a good walk in the country can do

---

[62] Thring, Sermon 63.
[63] Thring, Sermon 122.
[64] Thring, Sermon 360. It was not delivered.
[65] Diary, October 15, 1887. The last entry. There is no full-stop at the end, as if the
sentence had been left unfinished.

more in some ways for a boy with eyes than twenty games of cricket or football".[66] An expedition to Norway was organised by Gerold Benguerel in the 1850s, and in 1872 Sam Haslam and Rawnsley formed a Natural History Society.[67]

As we have seen, the gymnasium was the idea of two masters and the costs were borne by the whole staff. The acquisition of playing-fields and the building of fives courts similarly owed much to the generosity of Thring's colleagues. All masters subscribed to the boys' games and athletics funds, and three looked after the finances for the various physical activities: William Earle, Alfred Tuck and Charles Cobb. Much of the athletics equipment was donated by Thring's son, Gale.[68]

Thring believed that one of the most important roles that games could play was to provide an out-of-school opportunity when boys and masters could associate and compete on equal terms. Here Thring received enormous support from his masters. The diary of Sophia Haslam, Sam's wife, reveals how often he was playing fives, cricket or football, or watching house matches or the sports.[69] Throughout Thring's headmastership his staff enthusiastically joined in the boys' games: their *valete* on leaving the school often included the phrase, "will be greatly missed by us in our games". Masters also helped with the formation of sports clubs in the town and played in teams of cricket and football.[70] In addition, many masters could preach what Thring would term "a manly sermon".[71]

Thring's Old Boys were very loyal to the school. Many who wrote letters to the *Uppingham School Magazine* wished the school to preserve all the customs that they remembered from their youth, and commissioned reminiscences generally recalled the past nostalgically. Published biographies and memories were generally sympathetic to Thring's principles and practice. A contemporary published memorial to Ernest Blyth, who died in 1865 shortly after leaving school, supported the games-playing principles of Thring's early years.[72]

---

[66] Rawnsley, *Early Days*, 114.

[67] *USM*, March 1872, 40.

[68] Gale Thring joined the staff in 1881.

[69] Diary of S. L. E. Haslam, 1870-1873. In UA. The Haslams ran The Lodge from 1871 to 1892 and then transferred to Brooklands until 1908; thirty-seven years of housemastering.

[70] Scrap-books of the Uppingham and District Cricket Club.

[71] Diary, July 3, 1881 (Parkin, *Life*, 2:110).

[72] He was at school from 1856 to 1862, and in the cricket XI for his last two years. He won a scholarship to Christ's College, Cambridge.

The masters at Uppingham, generally speaking, take part with the boys in
their games; thus indicating much good sense as well as kindly feeling.
Many are the important results of such a coming together out of school, as
admirably adapted to develop character and increase knowledge, as to
invigorate health. They will find there many illustrations of the rules of
science, and opportunities of directing conduct; the boys will learn to
appreciate their companions, to recognise general cultivation, noble traits,
manly feelings, and the evidences of generous dispositions, as well as of
gentlemanlike deportment.[73]

Rawnsley, a contemporary of Blyth, was sure that "skill or pluck" in
games was "a real help to a boy who had never been able to win any
positive commendations in class". Games helped to develop character; "to
endure defeat bravely was itself a victory".[74]

Some correspondence by Old Boys to the magazine was hostile to
change. Gymnastics was defended against the possible intrusion of
military drill; poor standards of sportsmanship by spectators at matches
was rebuked; the awarding of cups for school competitions was seen to
"degrade" the amateur spirit; the fall-off in cricket prowess was condemned;
and the purity of untainted sport was supported with a quotation from
Bishop Selwyn: "It is part of the moral training, through physical
processes, which is necessary that the man may be thoroughly furnished
for good works".[75] Other Old Boys positively yearned for change, seeking
the employment of a cricket professional to coach the boys, urging the
conversion from Uppingham football to one or other of the national codes,
and advocating more matches with other schools and tours to take on
London clubs.

A picture of life at Uppingham in the 1880s may be found in Ernest
Hornung's *Fathers of Men*. This school story by the brother-in-law of
Arthur Conan Doyle, the creator of Sherlock Holmes, was a great success
in the years either side of the Great War. It tells how a stable boy is sent by
his dead father's former employer to a school modelled on Thring's
Uppingham. After a series of conventional episodes, including cricketing
glory, he leaves to work on a sheep station in Australia. The impression
conveyed in the first half of the tale is especially realistic; the second lacks
some validity, not least because the author left for Australia for health

[73] Blyth, *In Memoriam*, 19.
[74] Willingham Rawnsley, *Edward Thring: Maker of Uppingham School* (London:
Kegan Paul, Trench, Trubner & Co, 1926), 48.
[75] *USM*, November 1863, 279; June 1883, 170; September 1867, 157-158; March
1885, 85; and April 1872, 81. The Selwyn quotation is from *The Colonial Church
Chronicle, and Missionary Journal*, 1872.

reasons before he reached the sixth-form. Although very myopic, Hornung "loved cricket as a game and recognised it as a great training for life".[76] Raffles, the hero of his more famous stories about a gentleman-burglar, played for the Gentleman of England; Jan Rutter, the hero of the Uppingham story, had to make do with captaining the School against the Old Boys.

VII

The attitude of boys of the early Thring years to their physical education is hard to assess because there is a ten-year interlude between the demise of *The Hospitaler* in 1853 and the birth of the *Uppingham School Magazine* in 1863. The only writings by boys that have survived are some prize essays and translations that were kept by Thring, and some published sixth-form essays. Little of use can be found in the prize essays other than a Latin ode "On Football" but the essays published in 1860 in *School Delusions* tell the modern reader more. Thring regarded the collection as "valuable not only as explaining much of our life here, but as a genuine expression of feeling from amongst yourselves".[77] Extracts from the essays, not surprisingly, reflect Thring's own views:

> … a moderate use of games will conduce more than anything towards clearing the minds from sluggishness and awakening it well for renewed labours. (Marmaduke Athorpe)

> But what is manliness? Living free and fearless so long as one is on the side of right, scorning a base action, ever keeping the heart pure and chaste, conquering the passions, always upholding right and law, … helping the helpless. (Oswald Holden)

> Much can be learnt from games where honourable rivalry is excited, and in which, if we would excel, we require perseverance and patience in a great degree … The hard-worker and hard-player is almost certain to be the best man. (Norton Roupell)

A fourth essay by James Cartmell expanded on the Platonic ideal of music and gymnastics. Plato's contrasting illustrations of mind and muscle were

---

[76] Shane Chichester, *E. W. Hornung and His Young Guard* (Wellington: College Press, 1941), 8.
[77] *School Delusions*, 1860, preface. In UA.

given nineteenth-century portrayals: a "well trained pugilist" was of "low mental power" whereas a "book-worm" was "weak in animal life."[78]

An article in an 1864 issue of the school magazine proclaimed the value of games as an integral part of school life and a rejection of the lawlessness of earlier recreation.

> The old idea that the present School are not, and never will be, equal to their predecessors in feats of strength, endurance, or skill, ought surely to become exploded as year by year our Athletic Sports come round.
>
> Reverence for Antiquity has its good side, but when it tries to persuade us that the old days of bullying and fights produced pluckier fellows than our own, it goes a little too far.[79]

The former "delightful recreations" were now giving way to organised games in the search for public school status. A dialogue on "Chapters in School Life" compared the character training given by various games. Cricket: "Pray what greater mortification, what greater opposite to pleasure, can there be, than missing a catch, when a whole field is looking at you?" Football: "Or of being in goal, alone, some dozen biggish fellows charging down on you?" Fives: "Or missing half a dozen easy balls running, and your partner getting sulky?" And Cross Country: "Or having a stitch half the way in a paperchase?"[80]

The "value" of the various games was hotly contested in correspondence to the magazine: one game was always seen to be more "scientific" than another. "Private school" games like hockey were victimised and were soon to disappear. Football and cricket became the most prestigious activities whereas gymnastics and athletics needed Thring's support. "Loafers" and "shirkers" were continually rebuked; "perhaps they would enjoy 'hide-and-seek' and such sports".[81] The status of the talented games player began to increase: members of the cricket XI gained silk scarves, worn not just on the cricket field, and the football XV wanted their own emblem.[82] Privileges awarded to the most talented players increased and

---

[78] *School Delusions*, 10, 43, 47, 85. Athorpe was Captain of School and of the XI before proceeding to Corpus Christi College, Oxford (he died young); Holden also went to Corpus Christi College, Oxford and took Holy Orders; Roupell won a scholarship to Trinity Hall, Cambridge and joined the Indian Civil Service; and Cartmell won a scholarship to Christ's College, Cambridge and later became one of its tutors.
[79] *USM*, April 1864, 98.
[80] *USM*, December 1863, 299.
[81] *USM*, February 1867, 253.
[82] *USM*, October 1869, 275.

the XI, in an era of formal surnames, went by their Christian names amongst their peers.[83] The hero as a games player now made his appearance. In the 1870s "a good and earnest spirit", but of conformity, was at work:

> This spirit is of late growth, but it pervades everything the School does, Athletics, Cricket and Football, and to it must be mainly attributed the excellence attained by the School in such pursuits.[84]

> [It would] win for Uppingham and Uppinghamians a character for hard-working and successful perseverance, above all persevering Englishmen.[85]

To boys, games were now an "important science".[86] In the 1880s, however, the "professionalism" of games was somewhat checked and a "fairer and better spirit" was again displayed in games.[87]

---

[83] Hornung, *Fathers*, 181.

[84] *USM*, March 1873, 4.

[85] *USM*, March 1874, 14.

[86] *USM*, March 1875, 5.

[87] *USM*, June 1878, 28-129; February 1884, 36.

CHAPTER ELEVEN

PHILATHLETICISM, 1870-1876: "ACTS OF TREASON AND MOCK MANLY MEANNESS"

I

Uppingham was not immune to the mania for games. John Skrine had been a boy at the school for six years from 1861, serving as captain of school and playing in the football XV for his last two years. In 1873, after graduating from Merton College, Oxford and taking Holy Orders, he returned to the school as a master. He noticed that Uppingham had changed in the intervening years; it was larger, more prosperous, better provided and more confident. But, in Skrine's eyes, all was not well: "Prosperity is the trial time of ideals, and it was so for ours." The boys were no longer proud of the school's distinctiveness and a "spirit of conventionalism" was evident; the title Uppingham Grammar School had fallen out of favour and now the words "public school" were in common usage. Discipline was less than perfect and the standard of morality lower. Along with this relaxation of the school's character went some weakening of Thring's own magnetism. There was even a fancy that Thring was dispensable and it was rumoured that he would soon retire.[1]

Skrine's Oxford years had seen Thring fighting for the economic and political survival of the school as it faced the Schools Inquiry Commissioners, and he had devoted much time and energy to its agency of response, the Headmasters' Conference. This had its first meeting at Uppingham in December 1869. In addition, throughout this period Thring was engaged in a prolonged running battle with his own governors over their financial support for the school. Nothing was forthcoming, leaving Thring and the masters to dig deeper in their own pockets. With his energies drawn to these external matters, changes occurred at the school without his real attention and the public school lobby of boys and Old Boys gained momentum. The Old Boys at Oxford and Cambridge wished

---

[1] Skrine, *Edward Thring*, 95-98.

to place their school alongside the "great" schools of the Clarendon Nine, and a nationwide reputation in cricket and football was regarded as the quickest and surest way to achieve this end. To a large extent, the Old Boys succeeded, for it is arguable that Uppingham's fame came first, not as Edward Thring's school, but as a nursery for great cricketers.

In 1863 the total expenditure on games was £192 – 3s – 2d; in 1873 this had risen steeply to £500 – 7s – 5d.[2] The school roll had increased by a half (200 to 300) but games expenditure had more than doubled. There were now separate games and athletics accounts and cricketers in the Upper Club had to pay an extra levy of up to £1.[3] The Committee of Games had gained more power and the management of games underwent considerable reform. The Committee now comprised the Captain of Games, the Captain of School, the Captains of Cricket and Football, and five other members.[4] The ex-officio members were at first chosen to represent different age groups in the school; later nominations from the whole school were elected by ballot.[5] Canvassing for election was regarded as "ungentlemanly behaviour".[6] The captains of cricket and football were elected by the "colours" in each team but were subject to Committee of Games approval.[7] Notices of appointment of games officers needed Thring's approval and signature but, with his external pre-occupations and frequent absences from school, this was unlikely to prevent the formation of a powerful new sphere of government in the school to rival the authority of the praepostors. The Committee of Games *Rules* had now expanded to 31 pages, were soon to include rules for fives, and also rules relating to who might be admitted to the cricket pavilion and what privileges they could enjoy there.[8] Attendance at games was compulsory on the three days each week when there was no afternoon school.[9] A "School Shop" was established by the Committee in 1876 to supply sports equipment to the boys, and its profits were paid into the games account.[10] The number of house matches played increased with the introduction of challenge cups for under-sixteen teams, and the regularity

---

[2] £23,000 to £53,000 in 2018 prices.
[3] *USM*, April 1874, 69; *Committee of Games Rules*, 1877, 7. In UA.
[4] *Committee of Games Rules*, 1877, 2.
[5] *USM*, June 1874, 147 and March 1874, 38.
[6] *USM*, November 1887, 349.
[7] *USM*, December 1872, 359.
[8] *USM*, March 1875, 13 and December 1871, 385.
[9] *USM*, May 1873, 119.
[10] *USM*, October 1876, 283.

of matches played by school teams in cricket and football also rose.[11] At the request of Old Boys, the results of school matches were sent for publication in *The Field*, *The Sportsman* and *The Football Annual*.[12] These three journals were founded in 1853, 1865 and 1875 respectively as part of the games mania to satisfy the increasing demand amongst men and boys for news, opinion and gossip about sport.

II

By 1871 the temporary appointment of cricket professionals at the beginning of the summer season had given way at most public schools to the innovation of the resident coach. Gentlemen, too, were turning their attentions to the coaching of cricket. Two Old Harrovians, the Hon. Frederick Ponsonby and the Hon. Robert Grimston, had helped with the Harrow XIs since 1850 and an Old Etonian, George Dupuis, coached at his old school when he joined the teaching staff in 1858: Dupuis became the first "games master" to be appointed at a public school.[13] John Galpin, of the Hampshire club, had already been appointed at Uppingham as professional for the first weeks of the 1872 season when Charles Green, one of the founders of the Uppingham Rovers, financed the additional appointment of a resident coach for the whole summer.[14]

Heathfield Stephenson began his work on April 15 and immediately offered to present a prize bat to the player who gained the highest batting average in "foreign" matches that summer.[15] Stephenson's work brought immediate results: the *Cricket Annual*'s report on the school noted:

> Cricket is in a flourishing condition at Uppingham, where H. H. Stephenson has taken up his quarters, and is teaching the boys some of that straight play for which he is so famous. [The Uppingham XI was] not far removed from the first rank of Public School Elevens in 1872.[16]

The success troubled Thring. After the Haileybury match, which had been added to the Repton one in 1868, had resulted in a victory on The Upper for Uppingham by an innings and 250 runs, he confided to his diary:

---

[11] *USM*, May 1871, 132.
[12] *USM*, May 1870, 183.
[13] Warner, *Cricket*, 308; *The Times*, February 2, 1912, 9.
[14] *USM*, March 1872, 38.
[15] *USM*, May 1872, 134.
[16] Quoted in *USM*, March 1873, 6.

I am sorry for it. They are a nice set of fellows, and it will spoil their
outing. Moreover, I don't want the cricket to get too powerful in the
school, and to be worshipped and made the end of life for a considerable
section of the school.[17]

The next day there were additional worries.

This afternoon (I cannot help connecting the fact with the cricket) Heald
came to ask leave to hold a meeting of the praepostors at 7 pm, and about
eight came to my study to ask counsel, as six of the eleven, the leading six,
met in one of their studies (a praepostor's) about a week ago, and sent forth
for wine and made claret cup. This is one of the most utter acts of treason
and mock manly meanness I have ever had to deal with considering the
circumstances. The deliberate, quiet, lying betrayal of trust by leaders in
the school. I greatly feel it belongs to the professional and cricket as a
science, and the setting up of rival power in the School by having so much
made of things not taught by a master. It is very grievous in any case, and I
really don't know what to do. I should dismiss Wright at once, if the thing
had come before me as found out by me and not through the praepostors. It
is good finding the praepostors acting against the school heroes in this
way.[18]

During this period Green was pressing Thring to accept Stephenson as
a full-time resident professional. Green was now captain of the Cambridge
XI and the supreme hero of the school; when he appeared in his I Zingari
colours at each year's Old Boys' match, all the boys "adored from a
distance".[19] Thring clearly liked Green and so agreed to have a meeting to
discuss the matter of the professional just before that year's Old Boys'
match. Green, either innocently or deliberately, knew how to flatter the
headmaster, as the conversation recorded in Thring's diary illustrates:

I do not know that I ever in my life heard anything more inspiriting and
touching than C. E. Green's statements in talking with me before this, 'that
the stupidest boy who went out of Uppingham knew and felt he had a
mission in life' and much more to the same purpose. It is a glorious work
of the Spirit of the living God when this living feeling of true life catches

---

[17] Diary, May 28, 1872 (Parkin, *Life*, 1:235).
[18] Diary, May 29, 1872 (Parkin, *Life*, 1:235). John Heald was Captain of School,
1871-1872. He won a scholarship to Trinity College, Cambridge and took Holy
Orders. Henry Wright survived, leaving the school in October to take up a place a
New College, Oxford. He became a solicitor and Under Sheriff for Lancaster.
[19] James, *Thring*, 40. I Zingari was the most prestigious of the travelling clubs.

fast hold of men like him, – a feeling, a life, not a knowledge power, or a school of thought, but a spirit of holy effort. Thank God for it.[20]

Green's "mission in life" was cricket and he had long earmarked H. H. Stephenson as the man best fitted to bring cricketing glory to the school. They had met and talked during the match at Rossall in 1863 when Green was captaining the Uppingham XI and Stephenson was the Rossall professional. The dilemma remained as the Old Boys' match approached:

> Great effort being made to me to pardon the six of the eleven who played the traitor last half, and admit them to the old boys' supper, but I will not. A great principle is at stake … It is very painful to me punishing these fellows, and it spoils the match and supper for me besides exposing me to all sorts of arguments; but I do not see any way by which the school can be reached but by executing them, and at this crisis, when I am going to give way to the demand for a resident professional, I must show that both the school honour and the school government are above cricket. I must give way on the professional. It is better to make and control a movement than to be dragged by it. And not to have one has become equivalent to losing rank as a school, which would damage my rank with the boys immensely. So I mean to give way, and take it into our regular routine.[21]

"And not to have one has become equivalent to losing rank as a school, which would damage my rank with the boys immensely." Here was Thring's predicament.

III

Between 1871 and 1876 Thring appointed several men to the teaching staff who had sporting interests: Willingham Rawnsley and Christopher Childs, like Skrine, were Old Boys of the school and all had played in the XI, the XV or both. Walter Perry had captained the Sherborne School XI and represented the Gentlemen of Dorset; Alfred Tuck continued to play for the MCC; Wyatt Barnard and Charles Cobb joined the town's cricket club; and Sam Haslam was a keen player.[22] None of these were Blues or games masters in the mould of Dupuis but their commitment to cricket must have raised its importance in the boys' eyes.

---

[20] Diary, August 22, 1872 (Parkin, *Life*, 1:238-239).

[21] Diary, August 15, 1872 (Parkin, *Life*, 1:237).

[22] Perry left Uppingham in 1890 to become Headmaster of Hillside School, West Malvern; Barnard became housemaster of the School Lane House in 1881.

Stephenson's advice to the boys was that cricket was to "be *played*, and not *played with*", and that each aspect of the game was to be "worked at in a scholarly way".[23] Tips on batting, bowling and above all fielding filled many pages of the school magazine. Practice nets were erected on The Upper and The Middle to increase the effectiveness of the coaching sessions, and a professional "bowler" was appointed to assist Stephenson's work.[24] Thring's ban on "fielding fags" was circumvented by the Captain of Cricket, now resplendent in blue cap and jacket, when he "encouraged" younger boys to act as fielders during coaching sessions on The Upper.[25] The 1873 season ended with a published analysis of the performance of each member of the XI, an initiative that was maintained annually.[26]

Over the course of the next few years cricket continued "its gradual but steady development from a pastime to an important science", reported the *Uppingham School Magazine*.[27] Two masters took over the "arrangements for all matches, and Thring ruled that a master should always accompany the XI on away matches, and that the boys should attend chapel at the host school.[28] The 1873 *Cricketer's Companion* contained a gushing report on the standard of play of the Uppingham XI. Glamorous matches had been added to the fixture list: the MCC sent a strong team, and an elated school won by two runs in a two-day match; the Free Foresters were also entertained; and an invitation to play Surrey Club and Ground, Stephenson's old club, at The Oval was accepted. This last soon developed into a three-match London tour. After successive victories against Haileybury by over an innings, the members of the XI found laurel leaves in their plates at the Haileybury headmaster's farewell breakfast. Thring's thoughts, predictably, were devoted to fears of hero-worship and the spirits of the vanquished.[29] The same year, at Green's instigation, a return match to play the MCC brought the school's first visit to Lord's.[30] Uppingham cricket had arrived!

IV

Stephenson settled in Uppingham at the end of the 1873 cricket season. He opened a sports shop in the High Street, one minute's walk from the

[23] *USM*, April 1873, 42.
[24] Patterson, *Uppingham Cricket*, 66.
[25] *USM*, June 1872, 184 and April, 1873, 84-86.
[26] *USM*, September 1873, 300-301.
[27] *USM*, March 1875, 5.
[28] *Guide Book*, 25.
[29] *USM*, September 1875, 208.
[30] *USM*, September 1875, 210.

school-room and chapel. Green had chosen his man well for he was to become the "first of the great school coaches" and was rated by W. G. Grace, the foremost cricketer of his generation, as "one of the best coaches of young players". Hugh Rotherham, Uppingham's captain in 1879, agreed: "I don't suppose a better school coach ever existed than H. H. Stephenson – at any rate I never met one."[31]

He was born in Esher in Surrey on May 3, 1833; he and his sister were brought up by their mother after his father, a surgeon, died when Stephenson was aged six.[32] His first employment was as a huntsman for the Duc d'Aumale, an *émigré* member of the French royal family who had been granted permission by Queen Victoria to live on the Claremont estate near Esher.[33] As his cricketing career flourished, Stephenson continued to work for the family during the winter months, at times on their other estate at Wood Norton in Worcestershire.[34] He made his debut for the Surrey county side against Kent in August 1853 and continued to play for the club until 1871. He represented the Players in their annual match with the Gentlemen from 1857 to 1869.[35] His first claim to fame came whilst playing in a match in Sheffield in 1858; he took three wickets with three consecutive deliveries, the first recorded hat-trick. The feat was rewarded with a collection and he was presented with a hat bought with the proceeds.[36] In 1859 he was a member of the first English team to tour abroad, winning all its matches in Eastern America and in Canada, and in 1862 he led a party of twelve English professionals to Australia where they played twelve matches against area XVIIIs and XXIIs. This was the first visit of an English team to the colony and was the forerunner of the modern cricket Tests.[37]

---

[31] Ernest Swanton, "Great Schools in Sport – No 35, Uppingham," *Illustrated Sporting and Dramatic News*, November 15, 1935, 376. Rotherham, who joined the family watch manufacturing company in Coventry on leaving school, went on the play for Warwickshire from 1884 to 1903, and he played for the Gentlemen v the Players on several occasions between 1880 and 1885. *Golf Illustrated*, 22 December 1899.

[32] Patterson, *Uppingham Cricket*, 70; Roy Stephenson, *H. H. Stephenson: A Cricketing Journey*. (Uppingham: Uppingham Local History Study Group, 2009), 5.

[33] Louis Philippe, King of France from 1830 to 1848, and his extended family were forced into exile and took residences in the Esher area.

[34] Stephenson papers. In UA; Stephenson, *Stephenson*, 33.

[35] Patterson, *Uppingham Cricket*, 70; Stephenson, *Stephenson*, 58-59.

[36] Stephenson, *Stephenson*, 15-17.

[37] Eric Parker, *The History of Cricket* (London: Seeley, Service and Co, 1949), 448; Warner, *Cricket*, 181. Stephenson's role in this episode of cricketing history is commemorated in a tapestry at the Melbourne Cricket Ground. "The tapestry

A contemporary memory of Stephenson comes from William Caffyn, a fellow Surrey professional:

> He was a tall man, and possessed a long reach when batting, which he always made good use of. He was a fine leg-hitter, generally hitting square, and had also a splendid on-drive. His off-play for so great a player was undoubtedly weak; nor can I call to mind a batsman who scored so heavily as he did, who was so little noted for his cutting.

At bowling he was "a genius":

> He bowled very fast, with a tremendous break from the off. Indeed we may almost look upon Stephenson as the pioneer of break-back round-arm bowling. As a bowler he had good days and bad. Sometimes he would bowl in a manner that was almost unplayable, while at another he would seem to lose his command over the pitch of the ball. For a few seasons he was in my opinion, about the most difficult bowler in England.[38]

He was also a "really first-class" wicket-keeper and had stumped the sixteen-year-old Grace for a duck in the opening first-class innings of his legendary career.[39] Seven years later in 1871, Grace and Stephenson met again in the North versus South match at The Oval, on this occasion Stephenson's benefit match. In the first innings Grace was out leg-before-wicket for the first ball of the match. Stephenson's face obviously registered dismay, for the size of the benefit would depend largely on the drawing power of Grace. Grace later recalled that as he walked past Stephenson he said; "Keep up your heart H. H. … I shall take care that it

---

was commissioned by the Melbourne Cricket Club to commemorate the 150th anniversary of the current site of the Melbourne Cricket Ground in 2003. The individual scenes on the tapestry were developed in watercolour by Australian artist Robert Ingpen, and the tapestry was then woven based on these designs by the Victorian Tapestry Workshop. The tapestry is approximately 7 meters long, and is one of the highlights of our stadium tours. The tapestry is also a chronological timeline of events at the MCG, which means that HHS is one of the very first figures depicted on the tapestry - he appears at the top left. He is effectively tied with Tom Wills in order of appearance, and is depicted on the tapestry standing next to William Caffyn." Email from Greg Hunter (Collections Registrar at the Melbourne Cricket Ground), November 21, 2018. Tom Wills was Australia's first cricketer of significance and the founder of Australian football. He was born in Australia but educated at Rugby School and Magdalene College, Cambridge.
[38] Parker, *Cricket*, 260.
[39] Frederick Bamford, *W. G. Grace - Cricketer.* (London: Wisden, 1916), 1.

does not occur in the second innings". Grace took care and scored a masterful 268 for one of his best innings of the season. Stephenson's benefit was secure and he presented a gold ring to Grace as a token of his gratitude.[40]

Stephenson had visited Uppingham before his appointment in 1872. In July 1854, Thring's first summer, he had played on Van Diemen's Land for an All-England XI against an Uppingham and District XXII, the home side winning.[41] It is unlikely that Thring and Stephenson could have met on this occasion for the school was on its summer holiday and Thring was probably in Bonn. Green had kept in touch with Stephenson in the years after the 1863 Rossall match; he played for Cambridge and then Essex against Stephenson's Surrey, and both played in several Gentlemen versus Players matches. Stephenson's reputation for "good manners, a high sense of honour and a generous heart", in part a legacy of Claremont and Wood Norton, would have gone down well with Thring. Boys saw him more as "a tyrant, but a benevolent tyrant", whose word was always law, and his position in the school community had the "status of a recognised master".[42] John Graham, who knew him as a boy and was later a master at the school, reckoned that "wise masters made him their friend and confidant".[43]

Stephenson's shop in the High Street soon became a favourite place for boys to congregate and to talk cricket with a "Member of the All-England Eleven".[44] Stephenson had plenty to tell. The walls were lined with cricketing souvenirs: photographs of Stephenson in the teams that toured America and Australia, signed portraits of Grace and Lillywhite, photographs of School and Rovers XIs, and old score-cards. The last would later include England versus Australia at The Oval in 1880 with an Old Uppinghamian, Alfred Lucas, opening the innings with Grace, and Stephenson officiating as an umpire.[45] No piece of later public school sporting journalism was complete without mention of "H. H.", and the authoritative cricketing text from the *Badminton Library* opened its chapter on "The Art of Training Young Cricketers" with Stephenson's maxim:

[40] Grace, *Cricket*, 135; Ashley-Cooper, *Grace*, 11.
[41] Scrap-books of the Uppingham and District Cricket Club; Stephenson, *Stephenson*, 12. It was his second match for the touring side.
[42] Patterson, *Uppingham Cricket*, 70; Roe, *Cricket*, 64; Rawnsley, *Maker*, 49.
[43] Graham, *Uppingham*, 49.
[44] Advertisement in *Hawthorn's Almanac*, 1890. Beisiegel papers.
[45] Stephenson papers. Lucas was at school 1869 to 1874; he played successively for Cambridge University, Surrey, Middlesex and Essex; and in five Test matches.

To the batsman, the straight bat.
To the bowler, the good length.
To all cricketers, enthusiasm.[46]

V

Old Uppinghamian cricketers were beginning to find fame as Stephenson was setting to work at the school. Charles Green had been a school hero since 1863; now he was regarded as the "Father" of Uppingham cricket. Profits from the family-owned Orient Line enabled him to pay a third of Stephenson's salary each year as well as make other donations for the development of the game. The gratitude of the Uppingham Rovers to Green was expressed in an illustrated testimonial that was presented to him in 1871 and the boys followed suit with an address "signed by about half the school" in 1873. Green accepted both as "proof of genuineness of old school boy friendships".[47]

The exclusivity and clubbishness of the Rovers increased during the 1870s as "the object of the Club" became the "promotion of good cricket and good fellowship".[48] The entrance fee quadrupled from five shillings to a guinea and the election of members was "left in the hands of the committee".[49] Ernest Hornung, a keen cricketer, recalled in *Fathers of Men* "the famous and exclusive Old Boys' Club for which few indeed were chosen out of each year's Eleven".[50] It was no longer simply a club for Old Boy cricketers, or even the school's best cricketers. Rover "flannel and ribbons, also coats and caps" could be obtained from Stephenson's shop in Uppingham and a Rover sash had to be worn at all formal dinners, including the supper after the Old Boys' match. Wives, fiancées and other ladies could be presented with the club ribbon.[51] The portraits of elegantly dressed ladies in the "Doings of the Uppingham Rovers" show that many chose to follow the team on its summer tours.

The first London Rovers' Reunion was held at Lord's in 1871 during, surprisingly, the Eton versus Harrow match.[52] A Rovers' Dinner followed in the evening. A feature of these dinners from 1874 to 1884 was the

---

[46] Warner, *Cricket*, 307.
[47] *USM*, November 1871, 325 and June 1873, 176.
[48] "Doings of the Uppingham Rovers", I, 1875. Electronic copies of all five volumes are held in UA.
[49] About £100 in 2018. Minute Book of the Uppingham Rovers, 1874 and 1878.
[50] Hornung, *Fathers*, 209.
[51] *USM*, May 1873, 136; Minute Book of the Uppingham Rovers, 1871 and 1876.
[52] *USM*, May 1871, 116.

"Rovers' Dinner Song". These were always composed by a Rover, usually under the pseudonym of the Rhyming Rover or the Irish Warbler, and sung to popular tunes of the day.[53] The lyrics included the names of eminent Rovers, fond memories of Uppingham ("the dear old place, God bless it"), and of H. H. ("While she sends recruits to our camp / With the Stephenson stamp / Our club need never fear to lose its fame.")[54] Stephenson, however, was never elected a Rover even though honorary membership was permitted in the club's constitution: Gentlemen and Players, of course.

The songs exude the heartiness of sporting gatherings of the period:

> They'll play to win, whether out or in,
> As the world they go travelling through,
> And stick together through thick and thin
> As Rovers alone can do.[55]

And,

> The young ones play the cricket
> And the old ones jaw and dine.[56]

The 1876 Dinner was held shortly after the University match when it had been "Uppingham's year" at Cambridge.[57] Rovers had played commandingly for the light blues in the nine-wicket win: Alfred Lucas contributed 67 and 23 not out, Douglas Steel 24, William Patterson 105 not out and six wickets, and Henry Luddington 6 and ten wickets.[58] The Rhyming Rover recorded the historic event:

> O Cricket, the pride of the nation,
> The sport of the brave and the free;
> On many a festive occasion
> We've offered our homage to thee.
> And now at this cricketing dinner,
> When a toast I'm called on to choose,
> I charge you to drink in a brimmer
> To the health of our Uppingham Blues.

---

[53] The lyrics of songs for 1874, 1876 to 1880, and 1882 to 1884 are in UA.
[54] Songs of 1874 and 1877.
[55] Song of 1879.
[56] Song of 1880.
[57] Altham, *Cricket*, 156.
[58] 'Doings of the Uppingham Rovers', I, 1876. Steel, at school 1870 to 1875, was a four-year cricket Blue and a two-year soccer one; Luddington, at school 1868 to 1873, was a two-year Blue but he never played for the school XI.

'Ere the 'Varsity Match many wondered
What would happen to the poor Cambridge men,
When the scorers of over six hundred
Would be certain to do it again.
But Oxford's backers soon grew sadder;
They found it quite another pair of shoes.
And their whole team collapsed like a bladder
When opposed to the Uppingham Blues.

For LUDDINGTON, swift, sure and steady,
Sends his trimmers in true to the bails;
And PATTERSON, cunning and ready,
Soon finds where the batsman fails.
The crack was snuffed out in a minute,
And his downfall the side did confuse:
And Oxford in short were not in it,
When opposed to the Uppingham Blues.

The LUCAS's play was perfection,
And STEEL kept the game well alive,
And "the old girl" silenced detraction
With her *"not out, a hundred and five"*.
It was plain as day from the beginning,
That the Cambridge side could not lose;
But they owe the whole merit of winning
To the play of the Uppingham Blues.

Who taught them this excellent cricket?
Was the question of many that day,
Who taught them to keep up their wicket,
And to hit just as well as they play?
Oh, who did these cricketers nourish?
Who trained their eyes, nerves and thews?
'Twas STEPHENSON: Long may he flourish!
The coach of the Uppingham Blues!

The wine-cup, the wine-cup bring hither,
And fill, fill up true to the brim.
May Uppingham's fame never wither!
Nor her cricketing glory grow dim!
Tho' banish'd by sewers, stinks and fever,
Her heart and her pluck she won't lose.
May the old school flourish for ever!
And three cheers for the Uppingham Blues![59]

---

[59] In UA. "Tho' banish'd by sewers, stinks and fever" will be explained shortly.

Five Uppinghamians played for Cambridge the following year, a record for one school, but Oxford was victorious on this occasion.[60] This crop of "Uppingham Blues" had been in the School XI in 1872 and 1873, and their number also included the "naturally gifted" Thomas Fleming who did not go on to university but emigrated to America.[61] All had received one or two years of Stephenson's coaching but their earliest years were without his influence. Some credit, therefore, must be given to Edgar Wilsher who coached them at the start of the 1868 and 1870 seasons. Harry Altham, the cricket historian, termed the 1870s as the "palmy days" of Uppingham cricket.[62]

From 1864 to 1874 the "Accounts of the Doings of the Uppingham Rovers" were reported at length in the school magazine but in 1875 the current editor, Samuel Jeyes, wished to condense the accounts in the magazine proper and issue the full text as a supplement.[63] Jeyes reported that he had received many complaints from readers on "the inordinate amount of space" given to the Rovers: "Writing so boisterously hilarious could not fail to grieve the melancholic among us". Green sharply withdrew that year's Accounts and the Rovers published the full text at their own, probably Green's, expense. Copies were sold in Uppingham from Stephenson's shop and the Rovers noted with delight that demand from the boys outran the supply. The next year the Accounts, unabridged and still "boisterously hilarious", took their accustomed place in the *Uppingham School Magazine*.[64]

Ernest Hornung married Arthur Conan Doyle's sister, Constance, in 1893 and this brought the creator of Holmes and Watson within the Uppingham orbit. Conan Doyle enjoyed the hospitality of the Rovers on their tour of Sussex in August 1896 and recorded his impressions in "The U R's."

> You Rovers have the name,
>   I have heard it near and far,
> That you are a merry family
>   U R, U R, U R.[65]

---

[60] Patterson, *Uppingham Cricket*, 106.

[61] James, *Thring*, 38. Fleming was at Uppingham from 1870 to 1873, playing in the XI for two years and the XV for one.

[62] Altham, *Cricket,* 214.

[63] Jeyes was at the school from 1869 to 1875. He won a scholarship to Trinity College, Oxford; secured a first and became a barrister; and later completed the circle by becoming editor of *The Standard,* a London morning newspaper.

[64] *USM*, September 1875, 230, October 1875, 277, November 1876, 320 and April 1913, 57.

[65] "Doings of the Uppingham Rovers", II, 1896.

VI

With the formation of the Rugby Football Union in 1871 as a rival to the well-established Football Association, most schools adopted one code or the other. Almost all the Clarendon Nine maintained the dribbling game of the Association (including Eton, Harrow, Shrewsbury, Westminster and Winchester) whereas most of the newer schools followed the lead of Rugby. These national changes were reported to Uppingham by an Old Boy, Edward Turner, who had played both codes. He and his brother, George, gained the school's first international football caps, in the Rugby code, in the mid-1870s. Edward always maintained that they had introduced the stooped position in the Rugby scrum from the Uppingham bullies of their schooldays when the general trend was for a more upright stance.[66] After an expanded commentary of the two codes, Turner reported that the Uppingham game was "the most happy combination of the two rules", that it enables school leavers to adapt easily to "soccer" or to "rugger" at the universities or with clubs, and he pressed for the retention of the local code.[67] Other Old Boys were more impressed by the Association game; they advocated exchanging the oval ball for the round and eliminating the "fruitless" bullies of the Uppingham game.[68] These suggestions were well received in the school for both the oval ball and the bullies were soon to go to encourage "open play" and "much dribbling".[69] But the game, though much changed from Thring's original and now a near cousin of the Association code, was still "Uppingham Football".

The combination of national developments and the achievements by Old Boys helped to increase interest in football amongst the boys and to raise the status of the game closer to that of cricket. House matches became more competitive: members of the Committee of Games had to make more frequent use of their hunting crops to keep the touch-lines clear of spectators, and umpires were directed to ignore "appeals except from those playing in the match".[70] Appealing to the umpire was clearly acceptable in both cricket and football; public school play a century later would still allow it for cricket but frowned upon its use in the two football codes and in hockey. Specially made shorts, jerseys, stockings and boots (all sold from Stephenson's shop) were worn by all players; results of house matches and those against the Old Boys were sent to *The Sportsman*

---

[66] Rome, Uppingham, 157.
[67] *USM*, April 1872, 54-60.
[68] *USM*, December, 1872, 338-341.
[69] *USM*, November 1873, 316 and March 1875, 34.
[70] *USM*, March 1870, 31.

and the *Football Annual*; personality sketches of the members of the XV were published in the school magazine; and lists of the XVs were painted on boards in the gymnasium.[71] There were rumours of an imminent game with Repton, a cricket opponent since 1865, but it never materialised.[72] Boys did however play some matches in London during the 1871 Christmas holidays, but under the Rugby code.[73] A few "foreign" teams, usually led by an Old Boy, made their first visits to the school in 1873; they found the local rules "a great trial to their patience".[74]

A contemporary reporter believed that the years 1875-1876 were a "turning point" in the development in the Uppingham game. The reforms of this period were later embodied in the Committee of Games *Rules* of 1877.[75] Old Boys playing Association football at Oxford welcomed the changes as preparing "the school for the Association rules, to which they must all come".[76] Changes included the adoption of a rectangular pitch to replace the former oval; the substitution of a throw-in from touch for the former kick-in; and the prohibition of handling the ball, except when on the run. The "full back", formerly termed the goal-keeper, was allowed to handle and to catch the ball.[77] The 1877 season included two matches where the school played the Association rules, and at eleven-a-side; both visiting teams were led by Gale Thring, Edward's elder son, at that time an undergraduate at Trinity College, Cambridge. He had been a boy at the school from 1865 to 1874, playing in both the XI and the XV. Boys reported that they enjoyed being able to adapt their play to the Association game but its rules were "naturally not considered as good as our own".[78]

VII

Cricket and football were now the two most important games in the school; all other physical activities carried little or no status in the boys' eyes. The numbers attending Beisiegel's gymnastic classes had fallen but he did gain new classes with the boys of the Lower School; they had their

---

[71] *USM*, October, 1871, 297; March 1873, 24; and September 1874, 231; *Football Annual*, 1870.
[72] *USM*, October 1871, 297.
[73] *USM*, April 1913, 61.
[74] *USM*, March 1875, 16.
[75] *USM*, February 1877, 27.
[76] *USM*, December 1876, 365.
[77] Committee of Games *Rules*, 1877.
[78] *USM*, November 1877, 344.

own competitions and prizes.[79] Pressure on places for boys aged thirteen and above had persuaded Thring to move all junior boys to Springfield on the Stockerston Road, thus allowing the combined rolls to go above 300. Robert Hodgkinson built this fine mansion, the junior boys transferred to it in 1868, and Hodgkinson became Master of the Lower School.

Athletics alone now scored for the Athletics Championships. Interest grew in the standard of performance achieved by the competitors, and the Uppingham results were compared in the school magazine to those at other schools, but the number of actual competitors was small. Winning replaced taking part as the object of the sports. The one event seemingly peculiar to Uppingham, the vault, gradually lost favour and was dropped from the programme in 1874.[80] Fives continued as a springtime recreation and in 1875 the Committee of Games resolved to record its rules "which before were only known by tradition". These twelve rules were posted on school notice-boards and published in the school magazine.[81] The following year the Committee tried to revive hockey as a "School Game", and the captain of football was asked to "superintend" it; but the "Hockey XVs" never appeared and the game died out altogether until its re-introduction by Charles Cobb in 1896.[82]

The idea of a Rifle Corps was revived in 1876 when the editor of the school magazine asserted that there was "much material that should form excellent subject for the sergeant's function and the sergeant's severity":

> We are not in a position to compare the condition of our physique with that of similar societies; but if, on such comparison, it should be discovered that Uppingham shews off badly by the side of her contemporaries, we may find excuse for the defect in the peculiar nature of the country, consisting as it does of small hills and valleys; and in the fact that it is hard to stir from Uppingham or its vicinity without very soon sinking or rising; and that in point of fact a large fraction of the School do sink and rise across a particular valley about half-a-score of times a day; - which operates largely to cause the peculiar slight stoop to be noticed frequently among Uppingham boys.[83]

But the drilling that was introduced seems only to have been for the boys of the Lower School. 1875 did, however, see the appointment of a

---

[79] "Uppingham School – Christmas Examination, 1878". In UA.
[80] *USM*, April 1874, 74.
[81] *USM*, March 1875, 17 and April 1875, 64-65.
[82] *USM*, March 1876, 27 and April 1876, 70.
[83] *USM*, March 1876, 4-5. The four "hill houses" were situated to the south of the town and on the ridge on the other side of a valley.

"professional swimming-master". Swimming had now moved from Fenwicke's Basin in the Stockerston Brook to a new pool constructed in the brook below The Upper. On taking up this new appointment, William Ellingworth immediately received the names of 150 boys who wished to learn to swim. The first swimming races were for the 70 to 80 boys who had learnt to swim that year, and were over "100 yards, to be swum in two laps, up and down the bathing place, and to be got over in any way the swimmers might find most to their taste".[84] More than half the school thronged the banks to watch the competition for the Ellingworth cups.[85] Recreational swimming, however, was curtailed through the demands of cricket, and there were proposals to limit it to whole school days and to forbid it on half holidays. The days of wandering off for a swim were over.[86]

---

[84] *USM*, October 1875, 268; photographs in UA.
[85] Scrap-book of Archdeacon Johnson's School, Uppingham, 1874-1906. W. C. Ellingworth also worked as a confectioner in the town: 1881 Census.
[86] *USM*, May 1873, 119.

CHAPTER TWELVE

UPPINGHAM-BY-THE-SEA, 1876-1877: "FLY SWALLOW TO THE WEST"

I

In 1875 an outbreak of scarlet fever caused two fatalities in the town of Uppingham. The drainage system was found to be primitive but, despite Thring's pleadings, the local Board of Guardians did nothing. Typhoid fever soon followed and five boys of the school died. A local sanitary inspector pronounced the town's wells pure; Thring was not convinced and, with the town persisting in its lethargy, he sent off a sample of water to London. Inspectors soon arrived and condemned the Uppingham drainage system. The recommended repairs and improvements were, however, not implemented for many months and the parents of Thring's boys were becoming anxious. On November 2 Thring disbanded the school, ending the term a month early. The boys re-assembled on January 28 but a further outbreak of disease enforced a second dispersal on March 11. The future of the school was now at stake. Thring was strongly condemned in the national press for keeping the school open and a mass withdrawal of boys was imminent. Thring looked for suggestions at a meeting of housemasters: William Campbell of Lorne House offered, "Don't you think we ought to flit?"[1]

Thring agreed and immediately made plans to travel west to find a safe haven. He never claimed that what followed was divine intervention but on March 12, 1876 he came close:

> One thing I feel more than I ever have felt, that a great shaping power is round about me, guiding, and ruling, and making, and moulding this fierce crucible work and fiery rush of evil and danger, and friendship, and help to

---

[1] For more on the typhoid epidemic and the evacuation to Borth see: John Skrine, *Uppingham-by-the-Sea* (London: Macmillan, 1878), passim; Nigel Richardson, *Typhoid in Uppingham: Analysis of a Victorian Town and School in Crisis* (London: Routledge, 2008), passim; and Richardson, *Thring*, 179-212.

all about one, and that some strange birth of strange good and marvellous divine purpose is to come out of it all. Tomorrow I start for Liverpool, and on Tuesday for Borth and other places in North Wales.[2]

Borth, a coastal village situated seven miles north of Aberystwyth in mid-Wales, proved ideal. The railway to Shrewsbury had opened in 1863, thus linking the village to all major towns in Britain, and the owner of the Cambrian Hotel was willing to exchange the fickle summer-season influx of holiday-makers for the chance of a long-term let. Residents of nearby cottages were happy to accommodate any overflow as paying guests. The hotel had opened seven years after the arrival of the railway and was surprisingly spacious: "10 Private Sitting Rooms, 42 Bed Rooms, extensive Cellaring, detached Laundry, Stabling, Coach-houses and other requisite Out-buildings, and also a large Bowling Green and Croquet Lawn".[3] On April 4 the boys reassembled at Borth and spent a whole year at "Uppingham-by-the-Sea".[4] The school returned to a healthier Uppingham on May 4, 1877.[5]

..… fly swallow to the west:
Before thee, life and liberty; behind a ruined nest.[6]

Beisiegel's gymnasium was installed in one of the hotel's coach-houses and the locally-hired swimming instructor had four miles of good beach to teach from.[7] John Skrine recalled that "Grounds for football were found … the best was a meadow just below Old Borth, of excellent turf, which dries quickly after rain; though the peaty soil, lately reclaimed from

---

[2] Diary, March 12, 1876 (Parkin, *Life*, 2:44).

[3] *Aberystwyth Observer*, October 14, 1871. The hotel received another exodus during the Second World War: London's Chelsea College of Physical Training. The building was demolished in 1976 in order to make way for luxury flats and maisonettes.

[4] "Uppingham-by-the-Sea" was the heading used for two reports about the school at Borth by John Skrine that were published in *The Times* on April 14, 1876 and April 23, 1877. It was also the title of Skrine's memoir of the year's exodus.

[5] There were occasions when Thring doubted that the school would ever go back. In 1902 Beisiegel, a housemaster at Borth, recalled: "When affairs looked black and Mr Thring was fearing that the School might never as such return to Uppingham, I was one of those selected by him to be on the Staff of a new School he meant to start." Beisiegel to Monckton, Beisiegel papers.

[6] "The Prologue" in Edward Thring, *Borth Lyrics* (Uppingham: Hawthorn, 1881), 9.

[7] Skrine, *Uppingham-by-the-Sea*, 15, 41.

the marsh, would quake under the outset of the players."[8] The last of the football house matches left over from Uppingham were played soon after arrival; then, much as usual, the athletic sports were held on the roads around Borth. The village boys, fired by a novel example, invented their own athletics.[9] The heavy roller from The Upper was one of the first pieces of school equipment to arrive at Borth and some cricket nets were quickly set up among the sand-dunes in front of the hotel.[10] A local landowner, Sir Pryse Pryse, lent the school a meadow on his estate at nearby Gogerddan and a cricket square was prepared.[11] On each half holiday that summer a "panting cricket train" was provided by the Cambrian Railway to transport boys the four-mile journey to and fro. In a volume of *Borth Lyrics*, composed on his return to Uppingham, Thring waxed romantically:

> Open on the level sward
> Slid Gogerddan's hills between,
> When Gogerddan's genial lord
> Looked upon the starry green,
> Lady-bright with summer stars,
> Heard the schoolboys' loud hurrahs.
>
> Lo! the panting cricket train
> Up the valley slowly creeps,
> Lo! a boyish hurricane
> E'en o'er Cader Idris sweeps.
> Never in the good greenwood
> Lived more gaily Robin Hood.[12]

Cricket matches against other schools continued as before, except those with the longest journeys were replaced by Welsh opposition. An innovation of the year at Borth was away matches at cricket and football with Shrewsbury School: Uppingham won the former, the latter was drawn.[13] Shrewsbury played Association football and the changes made to the Uppingham rules in 1875-1876 allowed for the eleven-a-side match to proceed with minimal confusion. The draw was an appropriate result.

---

[8] Skrine, *Uppingham-by-the-Sea*, 53.
[9] Skrine, *Uppingham-by-the-Sea*, 27, 52, 53.
[10] There is a watercolour of "The School's Practising Ground at Borth" in "Doings of the Uppingham Rovers", II, 1876.
[11] Skrine, *Uppingham-by-the-Sea*, 17.
[12] Thring, *Borth Lyrics*, 16.
[13] Skrine, *Uppingham-by-the-Sea*, 52.

The year at Borth not only saved the school from "the Valley of the Shadow of Death" but it also rescued it from the cult of athleticism.[14] Team games could no longer dominate school life when 300 boys shared one proper cricket pitch, and that four miles away. Artificial recreations lost their attraction among the cliffs and beaches, mountains and rolling surf on the Cardigan coast:

> Playgrounds – leagues on leagues of shore;
> Classrooms – all the sea-king's caves;
> We are touched by Ariel's power,
> Free of air, and earth, and waves.[15]

The reality of hare-hunting replaced the make-believe of the paper-chase; fishing in the Lery occupied both boys and masters; rambles were made to collect shells, seaweed and flora; and the exploration of ancient British camps provided hours of fun. Masters organised expeditions following rivers or up in to the mountains.[16]

> Presto! – woods, and mountains, shells,
> Rocks and sea-anemones;
> Thrice turn round and shut your eyes,
> Open to a fresh surprise.
>
> Little bits of fairy world,
> Fairy streamlets, dropping rills,
> And the Lery softly curled
> In amongst the dreaming hills.[17]

Skrine particularly enjoyed "the pleasant moments ... spent on the beach at sunset, whither the School flocked down after tea for half-an-hour's leisure in the after-glow". The boys played ducks and drakes or else chatted in small groups: it was Thring's favourite time of day.[18]

---

[14] Diary, November 4, 1880 (Parkin, *Life*, 2:86).
[15] Thring, *Borth Lyrics*, 15. Ariel is Prospero's eyes and ears in Shakepeare's *The Tempest*, using his magical powers to foil other characters' plots to bring down his master.
[16] Beisiegel led the expeditions for School House boys to free Thring to catch up with correspondence and other administrative tasks. Letter from Thring to Beisiegel, July 27, 1876. Beisiegel papers.
[17] Thring, *Borth Lyrics*, 15.
[18] Skrine, *Uppingham-by-the-Sea*, 28.

II

These are the raw facts of a remarkable flight; the spirit is logged in the three much-annotated volumes of Thring's Bible.[19] The bookmark for the first volume still rests at Genesis XXVIII, verses 11-22, the text for Thring's last Borth Commemoration service on St Barnabas Day 1887. This chapter had a special connection with the Borth exodus: it was used for a sermon soon after the return and in several other commemoration sermons. Genesis XXVIII tells part of the life of Jacob, and Thring's interpretation gave him both meaning for the adventure and purpose for the school's return to Uppingham. Thring had already started in the years before Borth to identify his own life with that of Jacob. In May 1873 a visiting bishop took Jacob as the theme for his sermon to the school, and Thring felt that the choice was prophetic: "I had been pondering on that chapter, and taking Jacob's vow this very season."[20] Jacob was seen as "the father of all the toiling, striving men, who have to make their own way; the men who through many mistakes, and much suffering purge out the meaner views and mixed motives, and come out at last into the full Light of God, princes of God, no more Jacob, but Israel."[21]

Jacob had lived all his life in a wealthy and peaceful home where religion played an important part. In this secure atmosphere he had experienced all the usual minor vexations of life but he was spared the real worries. Nothing in terms of religious doubt or personal trial came to test him. Jacob's life was simply too comfortable, everything was taken for granted. One day God called to Jacob and asked that he should relinquish all this security and follow Him. Without any clear motive Jacob made his decision and chose to follow the call to foreign lands. That decision saw the end of wealth and security, and in their place came all the fears and deprivations that are part of the life of an outcast. Jacob bemoaned his plight, bitterly contrasting his former life as a rich man with his present state as one of the poorest of the poor. One night, as Jacob slept in some strange land, he experienced his now well-known dream, of a ladder stretching up to heaven, and at the top seeing not only angels but also God Himself. In this dream God revealed to Jacob that he was one of the chosen people and that his descendants would be forever blessed. On

---

[19] In UA.
[20] Diary, May 5, 1873 (Parkin, *Life*, 1:246).
[21] Thring, *Sermons Preached*, 2:364.

awakening, Jacob returned to his former home, forsaking his life as an outcast and for the rest of his years led a truly godly life.[22]

After the year at Borth, the school, like Jacob, returned home. Jacob had a mission, so too did Thring:

> Those, who have been saved by a great deliverance, have been saved for a great purpose: to give witness before Caesar, to stand out boldly, and fearlessly in the world, and maintain truth, and purity, and obedience, self-government, and honour, in the face of the prevailing powers of the day, if need be, and fashionable idolatries. The being saved means this. I am sure, if you will quietly think over the fact, that for one whole year this school was in exile, and at any moment might have come to an end in that grim struggle for life, when more than once all seemed lost to those who really knew what was going on, a strong feeling will take possession of you, that a great debt is owed by the school to God, Who opened the way, when there seemed no way, and saved it through all. The school has a work to do in the world, or it would not have been saved.[23]

Thring was now revitalised to deal with "the prevailing powers of the day" and the "fashionable idolatries". Old Boys bemoaned the fall in sporting interest and prowess, and blamed the unsettling move to Borth and the new timetable that Thring put into operation on return, but the reins were now back in Thring's hands. In his last Borth sermon, Thring reminded the school that the whole episode was far more than a pleasure excursion; indeed, the Borth year is a great divide in the history of the school. Thring saw the typhoid epidemic as an act of God sent to point out that the school had strayed from its true path and had taken the easier road of conventionalism. His identification with Jacob gave him the will to rediscover those earlier ideals and the energy to put them into practice, and once back at Uppingham this is indeed what Thring did.

Thring often said that Borth provided the happiest time in his long career and, as Nigel Richardson judged, it confirmed much of his educational thinking and practice, and restored his belief in the essential goodness of human nature and the importance of trust. The repercussions of that year were as powerful and far-reaching as those of a deep geological fault that strikes across the face of the countryside, and they restored Thring's ideals and practices. Never again in his lifetime were they seriously challenged.[24]

---

[22] This is the essence of Thring's telling of the story in the 1879 Borth sermon: *Sermons Preached*, 2:18.

[23] 1882 Borth Commemorative sermon (UA).

[24] Richardson, *Thring*, 207-208.

Georg Beisiegel and his assistant in the Gymnasium, after 1877

H. H. Stephenson, back row seated, in the first English team to tour abroad, 1859, winning all its matches in Eastern America and in Canada (public domain)

H. H. Stephenson in 1862 (public domain)

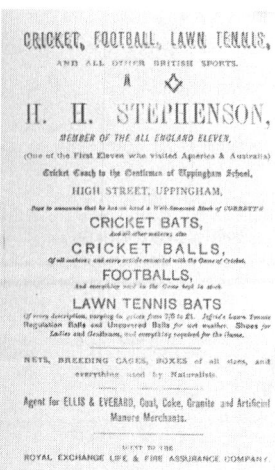

H. H. S's Sports Shop

H. H. Stephenson in the 1880s

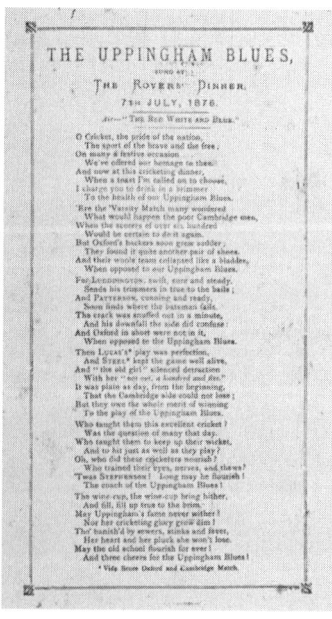

The Uppingham Blues, 1876

Cambrian Hotel and beach at Borth, 1877 (published 1881), by Charles Rossiter

The "Practising Ground" at Borth © Uppingham Rovers

Uppingham Cricket XI at Borth, 1876

Uppingham Football XV at Borth, 1876

Swimming Bath exterior, 1883

Swimming Bath interior, 1883

Swimming Bath, 1883, by Charles Rossiter

Old Uppinghamian footballers with Thring, 1880s
(Note the water tower that supplied the Swimming Bath)

Britannia and John Bull congratulate the Uppingham Rovers on their twenty-first birthday, 1884. © Uppingham Rovers

Thring with the visiting headmistresses, 1887

"Dreaming of cricket", 1880s, by Charles Rossiter
("Gradus ad Parnassum")

CHAPTER THIRTEEN

THE RELIGION OF ATHLETICS:
"FASHIONABLE IDOLATRIES"

I

Edward Mack, the distinguished American historian of British public schools, saw the years between 1870 and 1890 witnessing "the greatest upsurge of passionate adoration to which the schools had ever been subjected". Much of the adoration was centred on games:

> The passion for games, checked somewhat in the sixties, blossomed more fully under the influence of the increased competitive spirit of the age, encouragement by the new plutocracy, and the more widespread interest in imperialism, until it assumed proportions undreamed of in the sixties.[1]

Inter-school matches steadily increased from the 1860s and school magazines logged the records of their rivals as well as their own. In 1875 The *Public School Magazine* was founded to distribute news of public school sport and to raise "a spirit of healthful rivalry between young Athletes of our several Schools": Uppingham was noticeably omitted from the first issue.[2] When *The Public Schools Year Book* was published in the following decade, nearly a third of it was given over to games at the various schools.[3]

The 1870s saw "the height of the craze for games". They were now commonly compulsory on three days a week; a youngster asked in *The Cliftonian*: "I want to know why everything here is compulsory. I like football well enough, but when I am forced to play whether I feel inclined

---

[1] Edward Mack, *Public Schools and British Opinion since 1860* (New York: Columbia University Press, 1941), 123, 134.

[2] *Public Schools Magazine*, March 1875, 2. The magazine did not live long, nor did its successor, *Public School Magazine*, 1898-1902.

[3] *The Public Schools Yearbook*, 1889. This later became *The Public and Preparatory Schools Yearbook* (to include prep schools) and then *The Independent Schools Yearbook* (to include girls' schools).

to or no it is not pleasant."[4] Inter-school matches gained considerable status and large crowds would go to Lord's in London on the day of a public school match. In the 1850s the Eton and Harrow match there attracted hardly any spectators; by 1864 it was necessary to rope off the playing area; in 1880 the match became so important that it affected the duration of the London social season.[5] The same period saw the large-scale publication of books on sport, including the renowned *Badminton Library*, and the expansion of the communications media. Edward Lyttelton, formerly a member of William Cory's coterie at Eton and now an assistant master at Wellington, observed:

> Nowadays, the (Boat Race) crowd assembled to see the practice of the crews equals the number of those who used to watch the actual race; moreover, the minutest facts connected with the play of each oarsman's muscles are anxiously picked up on the spot, form a paragraph in the daily papers, and are telegraphed to the Antipodes.[6]

Games were now generally accepted for their moral training. Clement Dukes was the school doctor at Rugby; in his view they taught self-reliance and self-control. Games also kept sexual temptations at bay for they taught a boy to respect his own body as "the casket of his soul" and, as such, "the thought even of defilement will not enter his mind, or if it enter will be indignantly repelled". The morning cold bath, now the attendant of compulsory games, was advocated for the same reasons: "the hot bath at bedtime, so commonly resorted to compulsorily, and so strongly advocated by many, is capable of serious harm to many a boy by suggesting ideas and feelings which lead to practices that otherwise might never have been originated". Together games and the cold bath would produce a manliness with "the utter absence of effeminacy".

> If all boys were encouraged to be manly, energetic, and enthusiastic at their games, they would be trained to become healthy and ingenuous throughout their whole school life; failing this course, there will arise an unmanly precocity in self-indulgence and betting, smoking, and drinking; boys will

[4] Quoted in Octavius Christie, *A History of Clifton College, 1860-1934* (Bristol: Arrowsmith, 1935), 74; Mack, *Public Schools*, 163; Charles Cotterill, *Suggested Reforms in Public Schools* (Edinburgh: Blackwood, 1889), 27.
[5] Edward Lyttelton, "Athletics in Public Schools," *Nineteenth Century*, January 1880, 45.
[6] Lyttelton, "Athletics," 45.

naturally develop into premature "men of the world", and schools become tainted with an atmosphere of "society" which no master can purify.[7]

It was not necessary for games to be played well or skilfully for the moral effects to be experienced: the knocks and bruises, bumped balls and dropped catches would nonetheless still come. This was one of the reasons why both Edward Thring and Edward Bowen opposed coaching by masters. The Public Schools Commissioners in the 1860s had suspected that the attentions of games masters and professional coaches would soon turn games into a "science", and by the late 1870s this was the case. The athletic means to a moral end were becoming the end.[8] In addition, the "deification of success" and the "worship of the athlete" brought problems in their wake, for the effects of games lasted far beyond the hours of play. Boys day-dreaming of their matches damaged the intellectual interests of the school, and the athletic hero and his worshippers seriously undermined the prefectorial system of government. Many schools now followed Harrow's example, choosing their prefects from the games players rather than from the scholars. At Rugby, where they did not officially rule, the bloods began to do so unofficially as the prefectorial system started to decay.[9]

To counteract this damaging individualistic trend, but to keep the important moral advantages of games, *esprit de corps* was raised as the supporting creed. Thomas Hughes in 1857 had suggested the alliance of team games and *esprit de corps* in *Tom Brown's Schooldays*; Leslie Stephen, William Cory and Edward Bowen in the 1860s had claimed it as the new secular manliness; now this ideal received general acclaim. Edward Lyttelton was one spokesman:

> A boy is disciplined (by games) in two ways: by being forced to put the welfare of the common cause before selfish interests, to obey implicitly the word of command, and act in concert with the heterogeneous demands of the company he belongs to; and secondly, should it so turn out, he is disciplined by being raised to a post of command, where he feels the gravity of responsible office and the difficulty of making prompt decisions and securing a willing obedience.[10]

Now team spirit and training in leadership were added to the manly qualities instilled by games. The change involved other increases in the

---

[7] Clement Dukes, *Health at School* (London: Cassell, 1884), 79, 138, 301.
[8] *Public Schools Commission*, 1:41.
[9] Lyttelton, "Athletics," 45, 48; Mack, *Public Schools*, 123, 124, 126.
[10] Lyttelton, "Athletics," 44.

regimentation of school life: bounds and regulations proliferated; more time was given to studies and games and less to leisure; the freedom that every early Victorian headmaster thought vital, for personal recreation or to roam the countryside, was abolished.[11]

II

Bowen's Spartanism gained more followers at a school that revelled in Scotland's brisker climate. Hely Hutchinson Almond, a Scot, was a product of Glasgow University and Balliol College, Oxford. On his return to Scotland he served as an assistant master at Merchiston Castle near Edinburgh. Rugby football and cricket had been newly imported to Scottish schools at this time and Almond became keenly involved in their development at Merchiston. In 1862 a nearby private school came up for sale and Almond sank his funds in the venture. The development of Loretto School mirrors Thring's Uppingham: on arrival Almond found 12 boys; by 1876 this had risen to 88; the 100 mark was reached two years later; and in 1882 Almond's self-imposed limit of 120 was attained. The foundation on which Almond built Loretto was physical education: to keep the body in the best possible condition became a point of conscience and a matter of religion. Scholarship, music and the arts, crafts and hobbies, and even the chapel, all played minor roles when compared to physical education.

The equation of life at Loretto was simple. Fresh air, personal cleanliness, careful diet, regular hours of sleep and study, physical exercise and sensible dress, combined to produce hardy men.[12] Almond's campaign began with the introduction of open-necked shirts, wide-opened windows in the dormitories at night, and the rejection of suits and stiff collars. Flannel shirts, tweed shorts and the morning cold bath were introduced in 1864, soon followed by working in shirtsleeves in classrooms, the banning of waistcoats, and forbidding "tuck" between meals. The 1870s witnessed the end of school caps, playing golf without coats, the introduction of sensible "anatomical" boots, changing into flannels for games, and the replacement of tweed by flannel for everyday wear.[13] Many of the innovations may now seem commonplace but at the time they were all regarded by many observers as foolhardy. One of Almond's more permanent legacies to British education is the hardy dress of open-necked

---

[11] Mack, *Public Schools*, 214; Simon and Bradley, *Victorian*, 65.
[12] Robert Mackenzie, *Almond of Loretto* (London: Archibald Constable & Co, 1905), 230.
[13] Mackenzie, *Almond*, 68, 78, 79, 86.

shirt, tweed shorts and woolly jumper, an attire still to be seen at many public and preparatory schools in the decades after the Second World War.[14]

The playing of games was so important that Almond invented "Loretto time", fifteen minutes ahead of Greenwich, so that more daylight was available to accommodate the two and a half hours allocated to them in the daily routine.[15] All games were "moral agents" that helped in the formation of character, and in this respect football had the edge over cricket.[16] If it was too wet for games then cross-country runs, conducted on a basis of personal trust, were undertaken. No matter what the weather, no matter how deep the snow, boys would still be off on their "grinds".[17] If games were to be moral agents, they had to be played by all, and not just by a few and watched by many. If a boy did watch a school match, he would have to take his own exercise afterwards.[18] Matches with other schools were important in that they imbued the spirit of chivalry, fairness and good temper; they tested "the manly prowess of teams of schools". Almond also devised the team play of the passing game in Rugby football. This did not at first please the boys for they felt that the opposition would think that passing the ball to a team-mate just before a tackle was mere "funking".[19] But it won matches.

Success in games was a means of demonstrating the value of Almond's system:

> As for the collective success of the School, it is natural that I should be keen. It is natural that I should desire to prove by results the soundness of the system of physical training I am trying to work out. How else but by success against larger numbers could I teach boys to believe that many things which are irksome to them at the time are tending to turn them out into the world stronger, more active, and more high-spirited men than they would otherwise be?[20]

Athletic successes indeed brought both Almond and the methods he applied at Loretto to the nation's attention. In 1873 the first Loretto boys entered Oxford; in 1878 some were in the Rugby football XV; in 1880

---

[14] When Bryanston School became co-educational in 1972, many senior boys chose to go back into shorts. Information from Harold Tarraway.

[15] Mangan, *Manufactured Masculinity*, 300.

[16] Henry Tristram, *Loretto School* (London: T. Fisher Unwin, 1911), 90.

[17] Mackenzie, *Almond*, 171.

[18] Mackenzie, *Almond*, 237.

[19] Tristram, *Loretto*, 123.

[20] Quoted in Mackenzie, *Almond*, 124.

Loretto fielded five Oxford Blues; in 1881 eight former pupils played for the university and ultimately won Blues; and in 1884 11 of 12 were Blues, with seven in Rugby football. From this period until the end of the century there were generally three or so Old Lorettonians in the Oxford and Cambridge XVs.[21] Then in 1900, as the *Public School Magazine* reported, came "The Triumph of Loretto": both captains had been at Loretto together.[22] This success had its roots at school: in 1883 a Loretto cricket XI travelled to Uppingham, a school three times as large, and humbled the home side on its own wicket.

Almond combined the physical qualities of muscular Christianity with the scientific and rational spirit of the age as embodied in the philosophies of Herbert Spencer. To be manly meant to be physically able, and through physical activity the virtues of courage and temperance could be fostered and the sense of *esprit de corps* felt. Courage was the root virtue, the one "most closely allied to purity". "Surely, whatever tends to quicken the circulation, to raise the spirits, and to purify the blood is, *ipso facto*, a moral agent".[23] This was a Sparto-Christian ideal of manliness.

III

When the Public Schools Commissioners visited Eton in 1864, they noted:

> The cult of cricket playing has now reached a pitch of perfection which demands of those who are ambitious of success in it, professional instruction and long and constant practice. Five hours a day, at least on half holidays (or twice a week), and two hours at least on the whole school days are considered by the boys necessary to get into the Eleven.[24]

Richard Mitchell joined the school two years later and, with George Dupuis, brought Eton cricket to a high plateau of success that was to last until his retirement in 1901. He became Eton's equivalent to Harrow's Bowen.[25] Harrow had stolen a march in the pursuit of athletic success, winning all but two of the matches at Lord's in the period 1850 to 1869,

---

[21] Mackenzie, *Almond*, 122.

[22] Noted in Mangan, *Manufactured Masculinity*, 303.

[23] Hely Almond, "Football as a Moral Agent," *Nineteenth Century*, December 1893, 902.

[24] Quoted in FitzJames Stephen, *National Review*, November 1864, 315.

[25] But in different sports: football for Bowen; cricket for Mitchell.

but now Mitchell would restore the balance.[26] His cricketing pedigree was
faultless: he had played with distinction in the Eton XI for four years,
captaining it in 1861, and the brilliance continued at Balliol where he was
a four-year Blue and captain of the side in all but his first year.

Back at Eton, Mitchell at first only offered coaching tips at the request
of boys, and then just to the Upper Club, but by the following decade he
had taken overall control of the game. He imposed his own style of play
throughout the school, and he began directing school matches from the
boundary. Matches at Lord's against Harrow gained such importance that
Mitchell was not averse to spying on the opposition in the weeks before
the game, nor to providing the opening batsmen with Dutch courage
during the actual contests.[27] Mitchell's appointment, rather than Bowen's,
set a trend that most schools would soon follow. Gilbert Coleridge recalled
that "He did not impress us in school as a profound scholar", but added
that he was very popular with the boys, and known as Mike.[28] Percy
Lubbock was more specific: though Mitchell was both a form-master and
later a housemaster, he was never a master in the conventional sense; "he
held a position that was other and peculiar; he guarded and guided the
cricket of the school, at least at its more exalted levels, and of the Eleven
he was known to be the genius, the friend and critic ever at their right
hands".[29] Mitchell became the best-known of the games masters, Oxford
and Cambridge Blues or those who had played sport for their country, who
were appointed at public schools primarily to coach games. Certainly
Etonians knew which of studies or games ranked higher in Mike's eyes:
"Never talk to Mr. Mitchell on extraneous subjects, such as a General
Election, during the progress of a Public School match when Eton is
playing".[30]

The developments in other school games matched those of cricket.
Football, with the Wall and Field games peculiar to Eton, was purely an
internal game and so it did not rank as highly as cricket. Rowing, as the
Public Schools Commissioners found, did: "The Captain of the Boats is
the greatest man in the school, and next to him ranks the Captain of the
Eleven".[31] Other games might develop in the individual player "an

[26] 1850-1869, Harrow 12, Eton 3, unknown 4; 1870-1899, Harrow 10, Eton 8,
unknown 9. Information received from Dale Vargas.
[27] Howson and Warner, *Harrow School*, 232 (note – this is a Harrow book).
[28] Gilbert Coleridge, *Eton in the 'Seventies* (London: Smith, Elder, 1912), 171, 172,
177.
[29] Percy Lubbock, *Shades of Eton* (London: Jonathan Cape, 1929), 161.
[30] Robert Lyttelton, "Eton Cricket", *National Review*, May 1894, 432.
[31] Quoted in FitzJames Stephen, *National Review*, November 1864, 315.

element of selfishness and consequent conceit" but rowing, with its "let's all pull together" philosophy, could not. Competition on the river not only taught neatness of wrist, a sense of rhythm, acute feeling for balance, subtle variation of power, judgement, pluck, and gallant effort to a stroke's command, but also gave "the glorious sense of brotherhood which animates a crew in their united struggle for a common end, the unselfishness of the result, and, above all, the long, hard weeks of hopeful training. Good for the body and good for the soul".[32]

The man behind the developments in rowing was another Old Etonian, Edmond Warre. Also a Balliol man, Warre returned to Eton in 1860 after a distinguished academic career: he gained a double first. Poor eyesight had prevented his participation in ball games so it was to the river that Warre had turned for sport. In his final year he was president of the University Boat Club, and on arrival at Eton he immediately took the rowing VIIIs under his charge.[33] Like Mitchell, Warre was not regarded by the boys as an inspiring teacher but, as the best rowing coach in England, his position in the school was supreme. Two decades later, and to the surprise of many, Warre succeeded James Hornby as headmaster. A critical letter in *The Times* greeted the news with dismay: he lacked scholarship, he was a poor preacher, he had written nothing of note, but he was known throughout England as an expert rowing coach and an able field officer in the cadet corps.[34] Percy Lubbock, a boy in Warre's time, saw him as a dignified, conventional, but boring teacher; he was not at all a proper schoolmaster, but more a leader or a statesman. He assumed the role of Eton's "head of state", for it was the responsibility of others to educate his subjects. Even in his dress of straw hat, striped blazer and flannels, the sportsman generally overcame the don, and only when a lesson could be twisted towards Odysseus and the raft or the construction of an Athenian galley would Warre teach enthusiastically.[35] Athleticism flourished as Warre imposed an ideal of manliness that was boyish in conception: he was, in Lubbock's view, a great schoolboy wanting to produce everlasting schoolboys.[36] Edward Mack's assessment of his twenty-one-year reign at

---

[32] Coleridge, *Eton*, 146-147.
[33] Charles Fletcher, *Edmond Warre* (London: John Murray, 1922), 27, 34, 58, 79, 92.
[34] Despite Warre's double first! *The Times*, July 26, 1884. Also quoted in Fletcher, *Warre*, 106.
[35] Lubbock, *Eton*, 13-14, 27; Eric Parker, *Eton in the 'Eighties* (London: Smith, Elder, 1914), 280; Eric Parker, *Playing Fields* (London: Philip Allan & Co, 1922), 257; Coleridge, *Eton*, 173.
[36] Lubbock, *Eton*, 27.

Eton was apposite: "he was eminently fitted to create a model school for turning out athletic philistines, and that was, indeed, exactly the sort of school that he developed so effectively."[37]

IV

The cult of athleticism made steady progress over the sixty years from 1830, beginning with the decision of public school headmasters to clamp down on lawless recreations off the school site, to provide fields and facilities for play, and to insist that boys stayed within bounds in their leisure time. The boys responded by adopting and adapting a range of activities to match their surroundings and the different seasons: cricket and rowing were already popular pastimes with established rules and codes of behaviour; football and fives, however, had to be modified to meet local needs. Most headmasters took no further interest and left the organisation to the boys until George Butler at Harrow saw that it was easier to impose discipline if senior boys were given authority to compel their juniors to play. Games occupied free time.

Masters joined in the boys' games as the reformed schools accepted Thomas Arnold's lead that pastoral welfare was as important as classroom teaching; some like Charles Wordsworth at Winchester used the opportunity to encourage good behaviour. As Arnold's methods gained wider acceptance from the 1840s, so men who had worked under him at Rugby became the headmasters of the next generation, some at newly founded schools and others at revived ancient ones. Charles Vaughan at Harrow and George Cotton at Marlborough needed to impose the new discipline on unwilling pupils, and both used games as one of the means. Vaughan gave senior boys authority to rule in the boarding houses and power to compel on the playing-fields; Cotton appointed young and athletic masters to do the job.

The Clarendon Commission of the 1860s had doubts about the quality of the teaching in public schools but only praise for the role that games played to improve boys' health, provide exercise and serve as moral trainers. As the public school system expanded to meet the expectations of the increasingly ambitious middle classes, with even more new foundations and raised grammar schools, so the playing of games by boys and their masters was universally accepted as a standard component of school life. Headmasters and parents were sure of the benefits they would reap and were happy to accept what the boys wanted in return: status and

---

[37] Mack, *Public Schools*, 129.

symbols, cups and colours, professional coaches and foreign matches, more time for play and better facilities.

The muscular Christian message of Thomas Hughes's *Tom Brown's Schooldays* was eagerly bought and happily transmitted by the new public school parents; each hoped that every son would "turn out a brave, helpful, truth-telling Englishman, and a gentleman, and a Christian." Affection for schools and regard for their ability to inspire group loyalty reached levels never experienced before and soon, through the efforts of William Cory at Eton and nameless versifiers at other schools, love of school was extended to include love of the old school. Improved mail services and new-fangled telegrams, rapid trains and the invention of the weekend, all combined to encourage Old Boys to meet more often, dine together in London, enjoy reunions at school, and show the boys that they had not forgotten how to play their games.

Many of these Old Boys had taken their love of sport to the universities and there became instrumental in the codification of rules and the etiquette of competition. Young dons joined them at play and, despite the disapproval of senior fellows, endeavoured to give sport respectability and moral authority. Some, like Leslie Stephen, separated the muscular from the Christian. Now as graduates, many Old Boys worked to improve the sporting provision at their old schools, in part to raise each school's status, in part to boost their own social standing. Some returned as masters, others gave freely of their time as coaches, more made generous financial support. The period witnessed a massive expansion of inter-school sporting contests.

Loretto's whole-hearted commitment to character training and Spartan hardiness led the schools even further into the athletic sector, and two of Hely Almond's legacies found special favour in English schools: the passing game in Rugby football and the cold bath. Edward Bowen also advocated Spartan living at Harrow and games were extolled as the best moral trainers. Bowen's insistence that senior boys, and not masters, should have all authority over games unwittingly passed much school management to the heroes of the XI and XV and the reign of bloods and hearties began in earnest.

The 1870s saw games become the most obvious feature of public school life. Results of school matches filled the back pages of newspapers and journals, thus enabling proud fathers and loyal Old Boys to cheer their team from afar. Sport rather than religion defined and bound each school community and team spirit, or *esprit de corps*, was praised as the new manliness. Rugby football, rowing and, to a lesser extent, cricket were the vehicles for its inculcation. Eton had appointed the first games masters in George Dupuis and Richard Mitchell, but they were not the last. No ambitious public school could afford to be without several Blues and international players on their teaching staff. Some schools relinquished their city-centre sites and moved to the countryside to gain a healthier environment and to provide more room for playing-fields; these included Charterhouse, Christ's Hospital and Shrewsbury. Sport's hold over the public schools was confirmed, even sanctified, in 1884 when Edmond Warre was appointed Head Master of Eton. What was right for England's premier school must be right for all.

V

Thring was present at the fourth annual meeting of the Headmasters' Conference, held at Winchester in 1873, when the increased importance of games warranted their first appearance as a topic for discussion. John Percival of Clifton complained that too much attention was given to games:

> It is not so much the amount of time ordinarily given to school games, as the amount of talk which follows upon the time and the impression the games make upon the boys' minds, which are absolutely ruinous, so far as many boys are concerned, to intellectual development.

Robert Henniker of Rossall responded:

> I contend that athletic exercise is good not only for the bodily but also the moral strength of a boy. I like every boy in my school to have so much exercise and fresh air that, when bedtime comes, he may soundly sleep till next morning without even dreaming.

Montagu Butler of Harrow argued that the cost of prizes for some games was becoming excessive, and he blamed the subscriptions from parents and "injudicious friends" for bringing this about. George Blore of King's, Canterbury criticised the increased publicity given to school matches and vehemently condemned the self-advertisement of present society. Then, almost gingerly, William West from Epsom College volunteered a suggestion: "I think we might judiciously introduce something like the German system of gymnastics, where every muscle is regularly brought into use and strengthened." Thring could keep quiet no longer:

> It seems to me it is useless to talk, or to trust to personal influence unless you can find for every boy a place for the sole of his foot where he can distinctly feel that whatever he may be in other subjects, he has self-respect

and is respected. I have in mind sundry boys, which in my judgement, the gymnasium has absolutely saved, and others who in the carpentry have found the place they wanted.

Perhaps they had heard before all about the "great educational experiment"; perhaps, like Thring's own boys, they waited for the phrase "True Life"; whatever the reasons, the words fell on deaf ears. Frederick Fanshawe of Bedford School got the meeting back to the real business in hand; "I do not suppose that without games we should have any means at all of fostering esprit de corps amongst boys." The discussion carried on in this vein, whilst Thring remained silent.[38]

Most public school headmasters found it impossible to resist the march of games. Some, like Vaughan and Cotton, needed to impose discipline on a reluctant school. Most saw games as the one area of school life where boys and masters could congenially mix. Health was seen to improve, and the discomforts and hard knocks that are always part of games were believed to be good character training. Teaching was in general dull and the classrooms cramped, so games brought some light relief, especially if little other amusement was provided. The adulation of the successful athlete might be unwanted, but then boys always did worship physical strength; besides if games sent the boys to bed dog-tired, there were no worries about immorality. In addition, sport was an aspect of school life that could be left to the boys as a training ground in management and the group loyalty inherent in team games was useful in the smooth running of boarding houses. Games also provided an area of the curriculum where competition was definitely acceptable, and even the dullard could play his part without embarrassment. As time went by, boys, Old Boys, masters, headmasters, governors and parents came to believe that all must be well in "the religion of athletics".[39]

For it was a religion. The original message of muscular Christianity had been sincere and its ethos came as a breath of fresh air after the mawkishness of Evangelicalism and the piety of the Tractarians. Sadly, as we have seen, the Christianity gradually became servant of the muscularity, and soon disappeared altogether. This was the pattern of the times. The erosion of belief had begun under the influence of the Utilitarians and then accelerated in the era of Darwinism. Distinguished churchmen found themselves on opposing sides in the battle of biblical truth against scientific evidence; much of the poetry of Alfred Tennyson and Matthew

---

[38] *Report of the Meeting of Head Masters of Schools*, Winchester, 1873, 56-60. (In UA)
[39] Mack, *Public Schools*, 338.

Arnold epitomised the mingled doubt and hope of mid-Victorian society. Science brought a chill to the very belief in orthodox religion, especially from 1862 to 1877 when the conflict was at its most bitter. By the 1880s church attendance was markedly down and the trend was accentuated by the increasing tendency of the Church to split into extremes of denomination. Then, with the Forster Act of 1870, came the inevitable separation of religion and education. As the century ended, so headmasters found it progressively more difficult to appoint avowed Christian masters, and then too came the lay headmaster.[40]

As the belief in true Christianity declined, so the ideal of *esprit de corps* rose in its stead as a secular sentiment. *Esprit de corps* had its good points. Some saw that it put down bullying, and it cannot be denied that to put the side before the individual can be a good thing, but in the forced concealment of all emotion and the suppression of individual character in order to create a uniform type, the effects were not attractive. Platonic Athens had given way to Sparta. At its worst this fostered a violent partisanship, and positive hatred was sown between groups of people artificially selected in the same world of schools. The Eton and Harrow matches, with up to 15,000 spectators crowded into Lord's, became a feud, almost a vendetta, and it was impossible to include the two teams in the same luncheon room. Corporate spirit was identified with athletic warfare.[41]

---

[40] Peter Jones, *The Christian Socialist Revival, 1877-1914* (Princeton: Princeton University Press, 1968), 5; Schoolmasters. *Public Schools*, 135; Geoffrey Best, *Mid-Victorian Britain* (London: Weidenfeld & Nicolson, 1971), 163-165.
[41] Edward Lyttelton, *Memories and Hopes* (London: Murray, 1925), 43.

CHAPTER FOURTEEN

IDEALS REGAINED, 1877-1887: "I DON'T MEAN TO MEDDLE AUTHORITATIVELY"

I

George Parkin, Thring's choice as his biographer, caught the headmaster's post-Borth mood well.

> The year at Borth had been to Thring a period of acute anxiety, but his cares were mingled with keen enjoyment and deep satisfaction. His school machinery had stood admirably the extraordinary strain put upon it. The system established by years of painful endeavour had proved adequate to meet a great and unexpected crisis. Besides this, the year of exile had appealed to all his soldierly qualities – to those sides of his character which often made his friends regret that he had not chosen a military career. On the whole, it may be doubted if he ever passed a happier year of school life than that spent at Borth, though he had gone forth from Uppingham holding as it were his life in his hand; and though the issue of the enterprise long hung in doubtful balance. The freedom of the long line of coast in front of Borth, and of the splendid hill country behind, the bracing air of sea and mountain, the more bracing atmosphere of daring enterprise in which he moved, all gave him a health and buoyancy which he had not known for years before.[1]

He was ready to take on the "prevailing powers of the day".[2]

At Borth Thring re-founded a school, Uppingham-by-the-Sea, that was true to his original principles, whilst in Rutland the typhoid continued to rage. A repentant town put its drainage system in order and at Easter 1877 cheeringly welcomed the school back. The streets of Uppingham were festooned with streamers, bunting and evergreen arches, together with banners bearing messages: "Welcome Home" and "Flourish School: Flourish Town". Several evenings were given over to processions, bands

---

[1] Parkin, *Life*, 2:75.
[2] See Chapter 12 Part II.

and speeches; the church bells were rung in the school's honour; and Thring was presented with an illuminated address.[3]

The school that reassembled for the summer term was more or less at full strength.[4] The trials of the Schools Inquiry Commissioners, the founding of the Headmasters' Conference, and the evacuation to Borth had all sorely tried Thring; but he had survived and he had triumphed. Thring and Uppingham were now household names, and Thring's educational philosophies gained wide acceptance. He was called upon to deliver speeches, preach sermons and present prizes at Cambridge University, Harrow School and Cheltenham Ladies' College, to name just three. He was elected President of the newly founded Education Society and he was asked to send an address to teachers in America. Numerous requests for books were satisfied with the publication of *Theory and Practice of Teaching*, soon followed by two volumes of sermons. Unlike the earlier *Education and School*, which sold badly, *Theory and Practice of Teaching* ran to several editions and sales of 25,000 copies, many to college libraries. His principles and methods were adopted in other schools, and he was to correspond with teachers and educationalists world-wide. Thring's new-found fame and relative peace of mind stiffened his determination to fight against the influx of conventionalism at Uppingham.

That Thring was successful is vividly recorded in the daily entries in the diaries of a boy, Reginald Grove, who was at Uppingham from October 1883 to July 1887. The son of a Huntingdonshire doctor, he joined George Christian's house at Redgate from King's College Choir School, Cambridge where he had served as a chorister. Once at Uppingham he threw himself into everything with great enthusiasm: lessons, music, theatricals, sport, hobbies and the chapel. He was by no means just an average boy but his enthusiasm was greater than his abilities: he did not win a scholarship; he never reached the XV or the XI; he did not win at the championships for athletics or swimming; he never performed as a soloist at a concert, nor did he take a major part in a theatrical; and he won just one prize, for chemistry in his final term. He was house captain for just a few days when the holder had an interview at Cambridge University. But as an all-rounder, a great trier, a regular communicant and a loyal supporter of his house and school, he represents the Thringian ideal. It comes as no surprise that he left the school as the proud holder of the

---

[3] Richardson, *Thring*, 209.
[4] The school moved from an academic year of two halves to one of three terms from this date.

medal "For good work and unblemished character", and that on his last morning every member of Redgate came to his dormitory to say farewell.[5]

II

During the 1880s overall expenditure on games was lower than in the previous decade: the 1882 total was £346 – 10s – 2d compared to £500 – 7s – 5d in 1873.[6] The main saving came in rents, for the school now owned most of its playing fields: subscriptions from boys and masters were thus reduced. In 1877 the school had gained access to a new playing field to the west of the town between the Stockerston and Leicester roads. It had been bought by Howard Candler, the housemaster of West Bank, and let to the school. A few years later, in 1881, Candler sold the land to the school's trustees. First called the "New Ground" but soon renamed "The Leicester", it became the Upper Club's football ground.[7]

All games were still largely controlled by the boys, with masters only showing close interest when their houses were playing.[8] The house leagues of the previous decade were abandoned, to be replaced by knock-out competitions requiring fewer matches.[9] Uppingham had resisted the appointment of games masters; one wonders if such men would have permitted the praepostors of Christian's house to stage a game of cricket between older and younger boys in which the seniors batted with broomstick handles whilst the juniors had proper bats.[10] Housemasters were now forbidden by Thring from playing in house matches, although it is likely that they had only done so in cricket. They were also instructed not to direct play from the boundary, and a similar ruling was applied to house captains for junior matches.[11] No doubt reluctant sportsmen felt under pressure to make up the numbers for house teams but, apart from

---

[5] The diaries are in the possession of Peter Flower, Reginald's grandson. Typed copies are held in the Uppingham Archives.

[6] *USM*, February 1883, 36.

[7] *USM*, November 1878, 231; March 1880, 69; and May 1900, 65. Grove diaries, February 9, 1885.

[8] Graham, *Uppingham*, 10. Grove made the lists of XIs for The Middle in his penultimate summer term, a task he found as demanding as his school work. Grove diaries, June 25, 1886.

[9] Only knock-out competitions are mentioned in the Grove diaries.

[10] Grove diaries, June 12, 1885.

[11] *USM*, October 1884, 284 and July 1885, 22.

those occasions, compulsion to play games was minimal.[12] Grove seems to have decided for himself whether or not to play cricket and football, to enter the swimming and athletics sports, or to join in 8-mile paperchases, particularly when he reached the Sixth Form.[13] Grove wore spectacles, and at times a pince-nez, throughout his school years but, unlike at Harrow in the 1870s, it was never suggested to him that this was unmanly.[14]

To play in house and school teams, or to enter the sports, was regarded as a privilege and not a right; Thring's punishments for serious offences, such as the possession of a catapult or an air pistol, could include the removal of that privilege.[15] Senior boys who sought to ape the habits of the bloods and hearties at other schools were swiftly reminded that these were not Uppingham's ways. In the autumn of 1886 two seventeen-year-olds, Joseph Whitwell (captain of the XI, a three-year cricket colour, and in his second year in the XV) and Ernest Drabble (also in his second year in the XV), set off for football practice but never reached The Leicester. Instead they changed out of their flannels, donned civilian garb, and wandered down to the Uppingham Flower Show in the Market Square. It is likely that the ready availability of liquid refreshment or the presence of village girls was the attraction rather than the horticultural produce on display. Both boys were spotted and reported to Thring. Grove, their contemporary, recorded what happened next:

> Drabble and Whitwell both in XV and Whitwell captain of the XI had their colours taken away and 10 each for going to the Flower Show yesterday; … is awful shame, especially the licking part.[16]

No doubt the "licking part" made as deep an impression on Grove and the rest of the school as it did on the culprits' behinds.[17] But Thring could

---

[12] With a maximum of 30 boys in a house, all would be needed to field the Overs and Unders 15-a-side football teams.

[13] The 8-mile paperchase was in 1886. Grove ran; some boys cut corners. Grove diaries, November 20, 1886.

[14] See Chapter 9 Part VI. Grove diaries, February 21, 1883. Quoted in Smith, *Stretching*, 29.

[15] One of the new stain-glass windows in the School-room was broken in 1887. Thring suspected that a catapult or pistol had been used. Grove diaries, April 4, 1887.

[16] Grove diaries, November 24, 1886. Also quoted in Smith, *Stretching*, 49-50.

[17] Whitwell and Drabble were soon back in Thring's good books and they regained their colours. Whitwell played in the 1887 XI and Drabble in the 1887 XV. Whitwell served with the British Red Cross Society's Motor Ambulance Corps in the Great War; he was awarded the Croix de Guerre in 1915.

match severity with tolerance. In a situation similar to the previous decade's worrying over whether or not to appoint a cricket professional, Thring allowed the praepostors to exchange their German-style caps for straw boaters, the fashionable headgear worn at most public schools, and to cane junior boys for insolence.[18] No doubt Thring applied his earlier argument: "And not to have [done so] has become equivalent to losing rank as a school, which would damage my rank with the boys immensely."[19] He did not, however, agree to the request from the Committee of Games to exchange flannels for knickerbockers and stockings, the dress for football at most schools.[20]

The question of the Rifle Corps was raised in the "troubled" times of 1885. British pride has been dented by the death of General Gordon at the siege of Khartoum and, nearer home, by the Fenian Dynamite Campaign that had caused havoc in London.[21] "Of what importance are games", asked "Martial Spirit" in the school magazine, "when compared with the glorious occupation of learning how to fight for one's home, country, and freedom?"[22] That Uppingham, almost alone amongst public schools, did not form a Volunteer Movement or a Rifle Corps throughout this period must have been at Thring's insistence.

Activities other than football and cricket continued to gain considerable support from Thring. Recreations in the countryside matched those of the early Thring years and the headmaster's favourite Eton fives steadily gained new courts.[23] The boys had ample time at the weekends to roam freely: Grove, for example, followed the hounds, made brass rubbings in local churches, and walked to both Rockingham Castle and Kirby Hall, round trips of 12 and 16 miles.[24] He also collected primroses from

---

[18] Grove diaries, October 16, 1886 and February 19, 1887. Seniors boys could not be beaten by the praepostors on grounds of dignity. Just two boys are recorded as being "licked" in Grove's year as a praepostor. Six praepostors shared the 24 "cuts"; Grove declined the honour.

[19] Diary, August 15, 1872 (Parkin, *Life*, 1:237).

[20] Smith, S*tretching*, 49.

[21] The Fenians fought for Home Rule in Ireland. They set off bombs in several sites across the city on three dates in January. Thring held a memorial service for General Gordon; Grove diaries, March 13, 1885.

[22] *USM*, December 1885, 372.

[23] Graham, *Uppingham*, 5; *USM*, November 1883, 316.

[24] He also walked the 36 miles home at the end of one term, accompanied by a friend. His grandsons repeated the feat in the 1960s; email from Peter Flower, June 15, 2018. Grove diaries, March 8, 1884 (hounds), February 13, 1886 (Rockingham Castle), February 12, 1887 (Kirby Hall), March 10, 1887 (brass rubbing), April 14, 1887 (walks home) and more. Grove won an Exhibition to Sidney Sussex College,

Wardley Wood to decorate his study.[25] What would Edward Bowen have made of that? Gymnastics still needed Thring's support but Grove was a regular pupil at the weekly class throughout his school career.[26] Numbers attending Beisiegel's lessons had dwindled to such an extent that the seven or eight competitions for different age-groups of earlier years, each consisting of about eight boys, were replaced in 1878 by streamlined competitions: six competitors in the oldest group, five in the under-fifteens, and five in the under-thirteens. The seventy competing gymnasts of the 1860s had fallen to sixteen.[27] Athletics too needed support from Thring and the masters. In 1880 the sports moved off the roads on to The Leicester. The steeplechase remained at Ridlington until 1885 when a water jump was constructed on The Leicester to accommodate the race there. It provided great amusement to the spectators, if not to the runners.[28] Gale Thring generally looked after athletics, and he presented a set of "skeleton hurdles", but the Captain of Games arranged the heats, fixed the programme, and acted as starter: the races were started at the drop of a flag.[29] Thring and masters judged the events whilst Stephenson superintended the timekeeping.[30] The attitude of the boys to the sports had changed little. Editorials in the school magazine continued to ask for athletics to be looked upon "in the light of a School game", but only a small fraction of the boys actually entered. Grove was one, training for and competing in

---

Cambridge. After qualifying at Guy's Hospital in London, he took over his father's practice and was a GP until his death in 1948.

[25] Grove diaries, March 30, 1884; February 25, 1885; and June 7, 1885. On other occasions he had snowdrops and violets sent from home; Mrs Christian gave him some lily of the valley; and he bought cut flowers in the town.

[26] Smith's assertion that Grove "had the English schoolboy's traditional apathy towards gymnastics, finding a wide variety of reasons to justify his absence" is pure fiction. Grove reported that he "cut" three of Beisiegel's lessons in four years, but no reasons were listed. And he was not averse to cutting Thring's Aristotle construe to do editing work on the school magazine. Grove diaries, February 19, 1886; June 4, 1886 (to do Homer); June 25, 1886 (to do magazine editing); January 24, 1887 (Aristotle); Smith, *Stretching*, 29.

[27] *USM*, June 1878, 92. Grove never mentioned that he entered the gymnastics competitions, so the number of actual gymnastics pupils would have been higher, perhaps much higher.

[28] *USM*, March 1880, 69. Grove diaries, April 11, 1885 and April 12, 1886.

[29] *USM*, April 1882, 107 and June 1882, 174; Hornung, *Fathers*, 192; Graham, *Uppingham*, 20.

[30] "Athletics Card", 1884. In UA.

the 100 yards and 250 yards every year.[31] Others who entered only trained half-heartedly, and many did not even bother to change out of the normal clothing.[32] Thring maintained the extended format of the original 1859 sports, and he continued to extol the virtues of athletics at the annual prize-giving ceremony.[33]

III

Thring had long appreciated the recreational, life-preservation, and educational benefits to be gained from swimming and an indoor swimming pool had been on his wish-list of school buildings ever since 1863.[34] One happy result of the typhoid epidemic and the evacuation to Borth was the creation of a new waterworks company in the town. Wells were sunk just to the east of The Leicester playing field.[35] In 1883 an indoor swimming pool was constructed between the wells and the Stockerston road: it was the first such pool at an English school.[36] Built at a cost of £1350, the pool also gained its steam heating from the waterworks.[37] The water surface measured 90 feet by 25 feet and ranged in depth from 3 feet to 6 feet. The deep end was rounded, and at the shallow end there were broad steps for the non-swimmers. Equipment included a springboard, a high stand (nicknamed "The Pulpit"), and a projecting board from which beginners were taught. The heating system only warmed the deep end so the bathers had to stir the water to pass the heat on to the shallow end.[38] A more efficient heating system was installed a few years later, and the certainty of sufficient water was increased when a water-tower was built.[39] Until its construction …

---

[31] *USM*, March 1882, 45; Grove diaries, February 29, 1884; February 10, 1885; March 22, 1886; February 24, 1887; and more.

[32] *USM*, July 1884, 239.

[33] *USM*, June 1884, 188.

[34] *USM*, June 1863, 88; Thring, *E&S*, 179.

[35] For more on the difficulties finding an adequate water supply, see Richardson, *Typhoid*, 165.

[36] The waterworks' shareholders and the school's masters asked Beisiegel to oversee the construction and to appoint "a Bather", the swimming instructor. Beisiegel to Monckton, Beisiegel papers.

[37] Equivalent to £155,000 in 2018. Marie Thring mentioned "the huge Swimming Bath, heated by steam" in a letter to Parkin, December 1, 1883. (In UA).

[38] *USM*, June 1883, 144.

[39] *USM*, November 1887, 329.

the perennial jest retailed to newcomers that the water in the school bath got so thick by half-term that once an adventurous fag, adept at diving and of name unknown, had in some past era, also unspecified, dislocated his neck by diving into the mud.[40]

A passage built parallel to the pool on one side provided a changing area and a room in which William Ellingworth, who continued as the school's swimming instructor, stored towels and curtains. The north face of the building contained buttresses that were designed to house fives courts; they were not constructed until after Thring's death. The south side accommodated an area large enough to include tennis courts. These may have been grass courts at first but in 1886 the level surface was covered with asphalt.[41] A rim several inches deep was added, allowing the area to be flooded with water in winter to provide an ice-skating rink.[42]

The new bath proved most popular and Thring was able to congratulate the school at the end of its first term of use on "upwards of four thousand washings in the ten weeks during which it was open". Grove was a regular bather, taking his first dip on June 14, 1884.[43] The total of "washings" reached 13,240 by the end of 1883, and in each succeeding year Ellingworth's statistics were logged in the school magazine.[44] That the bath was used for "washings" as well as for swimming is borne out by a commemorative poem that was published in the *Uppingham School Magazine* in November 1883.[45] When one remembers that the weekly bath in every boarding house was shared by up to six boys, used in order of descending age, the joys of cleaner water on an oceanic scale can be appreciated.[46]

---

[40] Graham, *Uppingham*, 7.

[41] It was later known as Bath Parade.

[42] *USM*, June 1883, 144; letter from Grace Thring to Parkin, February 6, 1886. (In UA). In 1969 the swimming pool and the asphalt area were incorporated within the new Sports Centre. This building and the accompanying fives courts were demolished in 2010 when a new Sports Centre was built on the southern edge of The Leicester. A new Science School was built on the Stockerston Road site in 2014.

[43] He also watched the swimming and diving competitions but he did not compete. Grove diaries, February 25, 1884 and more.

[44] *USM*, June 1883, 144 and March 1884, 88.

[45] See *USM*, November 1883, 284.

[46] I owe this point to Brian Belk (at school 1913 to 1917).

All boys, "except those who claim exemption under medical advice", were taught to swim and dive by Ellingworth.[47] Occasionally he gave demonstrations of his skills, "accomplishing many aquatic feats, and winding up ... with a high dive, cigar in mouth, reappearing after some seconds imperturbably smoking".[48] On one occasion "Professor Beckwith and some other professional swimmers" gave an exhibition. Frederick Beckwith claimed to be Champion of the World, and it is likely that he was accompanied by his son and daughter, Willie and Agnes, both accomplished swimmers.[49] John Graham, a boy at the school from 1888 to 1894, remembered Ellingworth as "a good instructor and a popular little man ... very short and round like an india-rubber figure".[50]

Recreational swimming was organised on a house basis. Each boy was limited to two or three swims each week during the nine or ten months of the year when the pool was open. It was usually closed at the request of the waterworks company from December to February, and in the occasional drought.[51] The beginners' races that had been introduced by Ellingworth in 1875 were now enlarged to form a swimming sports, twenty years after the Committee of Games first planned for them. The 1884 Committee devised 4-length and 14-length races for "all ages" and a 2-length race for boys under fifteen. In addition, there were competitions in both age groups for "running headers" and "distance diving", swimming under water for distance. In 1885 a boy sank to the bottom in the latter competition and had to be rescued by Ellingworth.[52] The various competitions were held in March each year, and Thring judged the headers.[53] The Ellingworth prizes for beginners were maintained.

Courses of instruction were also given in life-saving and an annual examination for the Royal Humane Society's medal was inaugurated in November 1883.[54] The following year witnessed 55 boys entering the examinations.[55] The introduction of swimming lessons and life-saving

---

[47] Archibald Sinclair and William Henry, *Swimming: Badminton Library* (London: Longmans Green and Co, 1903), 348.

[48] Graham, *Uppingham*, 89.

[49] *USM*, July 1883, 222.

[50] Graham, *Uppingham*, 89. Graham proceeded to New College, Oxford before returning to Uppingham in 1900 as a master. He was housemaster of Highfield from 1909 to 1911; he retired in 1927.

[51] *USM*, February 1887, 3.

[52] Grove diaries, March 20, 1885.

[53] *USM*, March 1884, 48; "Athletics Card", 1884; Diary, March 1, 1887.

[54] The Society was founded in 1774 by two doctors, William Hawes and Thomas Cogan, who were keen to promote techniques of resuscitation.

[55] *USM*, December 1883, 342 and February 1885, 29.

instruction may have been prompted by the deaths through drowning of several boys and Old Boys of the school during the 1860s and 1870s. The instruction gained tangible reward in 1886 when a boy was awarded the Certificate of the Royal Humane Society for saving his sister from drowning.[56]

IV

The standard of cricket at Uppingham after Borth never reached the heights of the previous decade. The enthusiasts blamed the unsettling move to Wales and the inconvenience of the new daily timetable that Thring had put into operation in the wake of the recommendations of the Schools Inquiry Commissioners. William Patterson, the historian of Uppingham cricket, noted "a falling off in the amount of practice; and growing dislike in the game".[57] Cricket was still Uppingham's major game, but the surge in athleticism had passed. "XRX", writing in the *Uppingham School Magazine*, found other causes for the decline in interest. "Seldom or never are more than six games put up on each day" and "the composition of these is practically the same day after day". There was also "the increasing tendency to make Cricket a profession, and every Cricketer a specialist". No room was made for those wishing for "simple enjoyment of a delightful game".[58] The cricket cult was killing its own roots. In response to this criticism, the number of XIs on The Upper and The Middle was increased so that "a game would be provided every half holiday for nearly every boy who was really ambitious for one".[59] The game also witnessed "dissension and unpleasantness" in a conflict over team selection. Was the captain to consult the old colours or Stephenson? The Committee of Games applied a compromise: the captain should consult his old colours, but "when there is a professional his advice shall be taken in the making up of the first four elevens".[60]

Patterson also judged that "cricket spirit in the school" fell away during the 1880s. Ernest Hornung, at school from 1880 to 1883, recalled in his Uppingham novel, *Fathers of Men*, that even the Old Boys' Match failed to produce high quality cricket:

---

[56] *USM*, February, 1886, 37.
[57] Patterson, *Uppingham Cricket*, 106.
[58] *USM*, June 1878, 128-129.
[59] Patterson, *Uppingham Cricket*, 110.
[60] *Committee of Games Rules*, 1877, 6.

It had other qualities less dependent on the glorious uncertainty of the game. It was the most popular feature of the prime festival of the year. It afforded the rising generation an inspiring glimpse of famous forerunners, and it enabled those judges of the game to gauge the prowess of posterity.[61]

Stephenson, now nearly fifty, complained at the "great slackness at practising at the nets":

> Several days from 12 to 1 o'clock, myself and Brown had no one to bowl to, and it was not because they had not been told to go, or invited to come. I have myself asked players to come to my net on the following day at twelve, and they have readily promised to be there, but have failed to keep their promises. When I have asked them in the afternoon why they disappointed me in the morning, the answer I met with is, that they "had some other work to do." I quite agree with them for attending work before "play", but I am rather disappointed on the next occasion, when the same players fail to keep their promise at twelve, and give the same reason for being away, to find on going through the town – these "gluttons" for work hanging about, or inside, a "grub shop".[62]

Matters were not as they were in "Mr W. S. Patterson's" time when players "would just as soon think of cutting second school, as failing to go to the Professional's net when told to do so, or invited there".[63] A few years before, the nets on The Upper were crowded from noon onwards but they were now largely deserted. If the legend that the "cricket master" could

> enter any classroom and point at a member of the division and say, "Mr. Blank, I want you" thereby summoning from his studies, whether it was Nebuchadnessar or the Peace of Nucias to a much more rigorous examination of his own net,[64]

was unlikely in the 1870s, it was certainly impossible now. Old Boys came to Stephenson's support: "If fellows will only do what he *knows* is right, and not what they *think* is right, the school Eleven would be much better".[65] Hornung pictured Stephenson of the 1880s as "a maker of history whose fame … sat sadly on the failing giant".[66]

---

[61] Hornung, *Fathers*, 179.

[62] *USM*, April 1883, 110-111.

[63] *USM*, April 1883, 110-111.

[64] *USM*, April 1885, 104; "Doings of the Uppingham Rovers", IV, 1963.

[65] *USM*, March 1885, 85.

[66] Hornung, *Fathers*, 21.

Cricket was now just one part of the whole Uppingham curriculum; no more powerful, and certainly no less powerful, than music, the classics or the chapel. Thring maintained his interest in the game right up to his death. His diary contains reference to almost every school match played and he followed developments beyond the school. In a letter to Parkin from the post-Borth years, Thring wrote:

> I have been greatly interested and pleased at the success of the Australian cricketers. Mark me, cricket is the greatest bond of the English-speaking race, and is no mere game.[67]

But there were few regrets when in 1882 the school's annual cricket tours to London were quietly abandoned.[68] The results of the only inter-school matches from 1877 to 1887, against Haileybury and Repton, were generally in Uppingham's favour so perhaps Stephenson and the Old Boys protested too much.[69] Thring would have found greater comfort from the Haileybury headmaster's report of the 1886 XI's "gentlemanness" than in their nine-wicket victory.[70]

V

In order to broaden his influence over cricket in the school, Stephenson decided to pay more attention to games on The Middle. If the senior boys would not come to his noon-time nets on The Upper, he would court the next generation on the junior playing field. Then, from 1879, his impact reached the whole school with the publication of the first of a long series of "letters to the editor" in the school magazine. These letters were to build up into a text-book of Uppingham cricket and, indeed, the boys were encouraged to acquire and study the back numbers.[71] All aspects of technique, tactics and play were dealt with in turn, but most attention was devoted to fielding. The offer of a prize "to any one who will by patient practice succeed in becoming a good underhand slow lob bowler" was often repeated but seemingly never claimed.[72]

---

[67] Quoted in Parkin, *Life*, 2:305. It is not dated.
[68] Patterson, *Uppingham Cricket*, 105, 119; Richardson, *Thring*, 233.
[69] Haileybury recorded one win, Uppingham four (six matches were not played, mainly because of illness at Haileybury); Repton won three, Uppingham four, and three draws (one match was not played.) Other matches were against club sides.
[70] Grove diaries, June 16, 1887.
[71] *USM*, April 1886, 125.
[72] *USM*, April, 1885, 112.

The 1880 *Uppingham School Magazine* contains a typical letter:

Sir,

About this time last year you were kind enough to insert in the School Magazine a letter from me on the subject of fielding at cricket. I was very pleased to see that my letter had some effect, and I am induced to ask you for a small amount of space again this year, to remind the cricketers of the School that they are far from being perfect in that department, and to impress on them that they must not to forget the lesson I asked them to learn last year, viz., that they must always keep up a lively feeling, and not be half asleep; and that they must never by any chance wait until the ball comes to them, but must make a rush to meet it; and at the same time collect themselves in such a manner so as to be able to throw the ball either to the bowler or the wicket-keeper without losing time. When at a short distance from the wicket the ball should be thrown straight into the hands of the bowler or wicket-keeper; but if the fielder is a long distance from the wicket, the ball should be made to hit the ground first, so that it reaches the hand as a "long-hop". Especial care must be taken to throw the ball to the *top* of the stumps. *Never*, if it can be avoided, throw the ball to the bottom of the stumps. I make this repetition of my last year's remarks, because I know that there are many here who were not then. There certainly was *some* improvement in the fielding on the Middle Ground last season, and I have no doubt that, if the weather had been fine, it would have been still more noticeable. I mention the Middle Ground because that is our nursery for cricket, and if we can only instil the right form and style *there*, they will find it much easier, when they come to the Upper Ground.

Now I want to say a few words about bowling. I notice in nearly all cases that the first thing that ought to be studied in bowling is the last thing that is even thought of. I mean LENGTH. If a ball is a good *length*, the batsman can't make anything of it, even if it is not straight; and he is very likely to be caught out trying to hit it. Length varies according to the pace of the bowler. If medium pace, the ball must be pitched farther up than is necessary for a fast bowler. A medium-paced bowler must pitch the ball from 4 to 5 yards from the wicket; a fast bowler from 5½ to 6. But a great deal will depend upon the reach of the batsman you are bowling to. If a man has a long reach, it stands to reason that you must pitch your ball shorter than you would to a small man. To bowl a good length you should fix your eyes on something near the spot where you think the ball ought to pitch. There is always a daisy, a blade of grass, or something of the sort, that you can use as a mark. Keep your eye on that spot; try to pitch the ball on it, and your hand and eye are sure to be working together. Be careful not to bowl above your strength; by doing so you will have far greater command over the ball, and you will be able to alter your pace and pitch according to the batsman's play. Keep your *hand and arm* as high as possible.

I seldom see anyone trying to bowl "lobs". There is no bowling more useful in a School Eleven. With fielding, *as School fielding ought to be*, a "lob" bowler is sure to get a great many wickets. I offered, my first year, to give a new bat to anyone who could come out as a good slow "lob" bowler, and I repeat the offer now. I hope it will not be supposed that I have mentioned fielding and bowling as being the only departments at cricket in which the school is deficient. I could mention many other things that ought to be much more studied than they are at present, but I have already taken up a great deal of your space.

I am, Sir, yours, etc.
H.H. STEPHENSON[73]

VI

The steady drift of the rules of Uppingham football towards those of the Association game, which culminated in the match against Shrewsbury during the Borth exodus, caused concern amongst the school's Old Boys and gave rise to much correspondence in the school magazine. An Old Boy up at Oxford hoped that the school would continue with its own code as it equipped boys for both Association Football and Rugby Union: "a good Uppingham player with very little practice can play any rules with success".[74] A second Old Boy supported his colleague, but added that more consideration should be given to playing as a team if a boy wished to succeed at the other codes on leaving school.[75] Other correspondents disagreed, questioning "How long is Uppingham going to labour under the delusion that her rules 'fit a player to a great extent for both Rugby Union and Association'?" Retention of the Uppingham rules only gave rise to the "very shadiest of mediocrity".[76] The contemporary Captain of Football ably defended the home game in an article in the school magazine and the Uppingham game continued unchanged.[77]

Football transferred to The Leicester in 1878 and at some time in that decade jerseys with coloured "trims" were introduced for the hierarchy of XVs. Thring's three daughters were kept busy "ringing the permutations and combinations on the primary colours" as they set about their sewing.[78] School games were nominally compulsory twice a week, although Grove cannot have been the only boy who did not always comply, and house

---

[73] *USM*, April 1880, 123.
[74] *USM*, December 1877, 391.
[75] *USM*, March 1878, 39.
[76] *USM*, July 1879, 189.
[77] *USM*, July 1879, 189.
[78] *USM*, November 1947, 160; Patterson, *Uppingham Cricket*, 119.

games occasionally occupied other days.[79] Umpires gained whistles in 1885 and sixth formers could serve as umpires in house matches.[80] A number of masters regularly joined in games but not in house matches: John Skrine and Philip Fernandez were particularly keen footballers. Six played alongside boys for the 2nd XV against the School XV in 1886.[81] Grove had hoped to be included in the 2nd XV but fell short. He lamented: "I suppose I finish my career as a footballer; my dream of the XV is as smoke."[82] Stephenson coached junior boys in the Lower Club.[83]

Thring's diary records that the "Football Question" came up again in 1887, but on this occasion the boys wanted to adopt the Rugby Union code. During the 1880s the Association game had become increasingly popular in working-class areas in the North of England and in the Midlands, and skilled players were able to supplement their meagre wages from factories and mills with match fees or inflated travel expenses when playing for semi-professional teams. In 1883 The Old Etonians surrendered the Football Association Challenge Cup (today's F A Cup) to Blackburn Rovers and no other public school side ever again reached the final. A number of public schools found their association with the working-class game embarrassing and changed from "soccer" to "rugger". Uppingham was not immune to this pressure. Thring's diary continues:

> The boys mean to go in for that disgusting game Rugby Union, which violates the first principle of every true game to make skill everything and minimise brute force. I don't mean to meddle authoritatively; it is the old old story of rising by goodness and when risen and admitted to be great, imitating the vices of the great. "We will be as the nations, as the families of the countries, in serving wood and stone." But I am vexed at it.[84]

---

[79] *USM*, November 1947, 160. Turner records that boys were compelled to play games five days a week in the late 1880s but he fails to mention that this is after 1887 and Edward Selwyn had succeeded Thring as headmaster. David Turner, *The Old Boys: The Decline and Rise of the Public School* (New Haven: Yale University Press, 2015), 100.

[80] *USM*, October 1885, 277; Grove was asked to umpire in his last year at school. Grove diaries, November 8, 1886.

[81] Grove diaries, October 14, 1886.

[82] Grove diaries, November 27, 1886.

[83] The Rev P. H. Fernandez joined Uppingham from Trinity College, Oxford in 1882. He later became vicar at St Briavel's in Gloucestershire. *USM*, April 1880, 117 and February 1886, 3.

[84] Diary, July 9, 1887. (Ezekiel XX, 32)

That Uppingham retained its own code of football until after the headmaster's death suggests that he did indeed "meddle". There were no more "foreign" matches against other schools at football after the Shrewsbury game; instead, Old Boys would bring scratch sides made up of university friends to play the boys.[85] Uppingham Football lived on until 1910 at Highfield where Charles Cobb, one of Thring's appointments, was housemaster.[86]

---

[85] The Grove diaries list several such teams.
[86] Graham, *Uppingham*, 27.

CHAPTER FIFTEEN

THE IDEAL OF MANLINESS: "THE REGIMENT OF THE BRAVE AND THE TRUE"

I

Physical education at Thring's Uppingham was part of an education in "true manliness". This was Thring's name for his educational ideal. Headmasters and headmistresses of the twenty-first century prefer to call it "wholeness"; educational theorists identity it as "holism".[1] Holistic schooling, whether past or present, is concerned with the development of every pupil's intellectual, emotional, social, physical, artistic, creative and spiritual capabilities and it encourages both personal and collective responsibility. Physical education contributed to several aspects of Thring's true manliness but not to all of them; those were the concern of other ingredients of the curriculum. Some aspects, however, were the sole responsibility of physical education.

True manliness was built on twin foundations, Platonism and Christianity. Virtually all idealistic theories of education can be traced back to Plato: the aim is to produce ideal citizens to play their part in the ideal civic community. Service was the corner-stone: within an ordered society each citizen would disinterestedly concede his own preferment and loyally serve others.[2] Plato was convinced that happiness was the reward of virtue and that the virtuous life was the only pleasant one. It was not the possession of strength, long life, health, or wealth that made men happy but the right use of these gifts that did so.[3] In order to realise this aim, the state's supreme function was education. Most importance was attached to the early years when the soul was pliable, and there was no distinction between the sexes. As Plato believed that the soul assimilated its environment,

---

[1] See, for example, the prospectus or the website of Repton School: http://www.repton.org.uk/Values. The author was a governor from 2006 to 2016.
[2] Frederick Beck, *Greek Education: 450-350 BC* (London: Methuen, 1964), 199. 239.
[3] Walter Pater, *Plato and Platonism* (London: Macmillan, 1912), 239, 241.

it was vital to surround the body with objects worthy of imitation. This was the basis of Plato's educational practice.[4]

In keeping with the Cambridge tradition, Thring was an ardent Platonist. When Charles Rossiter came to decorate the school-room at Uppingham with portraits of the headmaster's heroes, Plato was on the list but there was no place for the Oxonian Aristotle.[5] A favourite pupil of the 1860s, Lewis Nettleship, was inspired to become the leading nineteenth-century authority on Platonic thought. His early death in 1892, whilst climbing on Mont Blanc, left unfinished his major work on the philosopher but an interim essay on "The Theory of Education in the Republic of Plato" was published in *Hellenica* in 1880 and then combined with his other studies by Spenser Leeson in 1935 to produce a book of the same title.[6]

Uppingham owed much to Plato and the ideals set down in the *Republic* became the school's foundation.[7] In Athens of the fifth and fourth centuries BC, Plato had analysed and written on the principles governing human life. He identified three elements to a man's soul: appetitive, spirited, and philosophic. The appetitive element was concerned with the pursuit of bodily desires (food, warmth and so on) and had to be controlled through careful diet and sensible habits. The spirited element was the source of courage and self-confidence, and was realised in ambition and self-assertion. The rational or philosophic element embraced the pursuit of intellect and all learning. The balance of the three elements in the soul was essential in the whole man and this harmony Plato termed *arête*.[8]

The term is hard to define exactly but Harold Nicolson's "balanced achievement" is a fitting interpretation.[9] The three elements of the soul were to aspire to three virtues: truth, courage and self-control. It is from these that Thring's holistic ideal stems so let us use contemporary sources to analyse their meaning. Truth, *aletheia*, implied all honest action, truth to

---

[4] Alfred Taylor, *Platonism and Its Influence* (London: Harrap, 1925), 58, 60, 64, 67; Basil Willey, *The English Moralists* (Cambridge: Cambridge University Press, 1964), 42.

[5] The other portraits are of Homer, Herodotus, Demosthenes, Euclid, Pindar, Cicero, Virgil, Horace, Livy, King David, St John, Aeschylus, Dante, Chaucer, Spenser, Shakespeare, Milton, Corneille, Johnson, Goethe, Scott and Wordsworth.

[6] Lewis Nettleship, *The Theory of Education in Plato's Republic* (Oxford: Clarendon Press, 1935/51). Nettleship was Captain of School for two years, 1863 to 1865, before proceeding to Balliol College, Oxford.

[7] Edward Thring, *Three Letters and Axioms on Education*. 1866. In UA.

[8] Robert Cross and Anthony Woozley *Plato's Republic* (London: St Martin's Press, 1966), 114-115.

[9] Harold Nicolson, *Good Behaviour* (London: Constable, 1955), 54.

oneself and truth to one's loyalties. Courage, *andreia*, had animal bravery as its base but rose to fortitude under affliction and in adversity; it was also the courage of men who are loyal to the principles which had been instilled during their upbringing. Self-control, *enkrateia*, was obedience to authority, whether the authority of a ruler or to one's higher inner-self. Truth, courage and self-control were the axes of a three-dimensional continuum: thus endurance of sorrow, pain, or illness was the meeting point of courage and self-control.

The Greek conception of the education of the whole man is summed up in the term *paideia*. Nettleship defined this as "the education in *arête* from youth onwards, which makes men passionately desire to become perfect citizens, knowing both how to rule and how to be ruled on a basis of justice".[10] The word is derived from *pais*, a child, and originally referred to the education of children, but in Hellenistic times the word came to signify "culture"; thus the means became the end to be achieved. A man's *paideia* is his personal culture, the thing for which he is born, the sum of his intellectual, physical, moral and aesthetic attributes that make him a whole man.

Plato's educational practice to produce the whole man was based on music, *mousikē*, and gymnastic, *gymnastikē*. Music included literature, singing and playing instruments, and the plastic arts; it was central to Plato's philosophy that beauty in nature and art were but an outward sign of goodness. Gymnastic aimed at simplicity of life and diet, and the maintenance of good health without the attention of a doctor. Music and gymnastic did not separately educate the philosophic and the spirited elements of the soul: a good body would not by itself make the soul excellent, but a good soul would render the body as perfect as possible; or, in Nettleship's words:

'music' educates, not the soul merely, but specifically the 'philosophic' part of the soul, through the medium of the eye and the ear, while 'gymnastic', through bodily exercises, not only produces bodily health and strength, but disciplines the psychological element of the 'spirit'.[11]

The correct balance had to be preserved for "the mere athlete is brutal or philistine; the mere intellectual is either unstable or else over-civilised and spiritless". Music and gymnastic thus had to be finely tuned to produce the perfect harmony of the whole man.[12]

---

[10] Nettleship, *Plato*, 95.
[11] Nettleship, *Plato*, 30.
[12] Plato's *Laws* 643e quoted in Edgar Castle *Ancient Education and Today* (London: Penguin, 1961/69), 103; Richard Livingstone, *Plato and Modern Education* (Cambridge: Cambridge University Press, 1944), 10.

II

Christianity was the co-foundation of true manliness. The Protestant line of Platonic humanism reached the nineteenth century through the work of the poet and critic Samuel Coleridge and was disseminated by Frederick Maurice in the 1840s to Thring and his contemporaries studying at the two universities or working in London.[13] "Wholeness" was one essence of Coleridge's thought. A man was a whole man and not an assemblage of parts: he was a living unity rooted in God. In the same way philosophy and theology were a single entity; and, further, religion and politics could not be separated. The main function of the Church as a human institution was the advancement of knowledge, the education of the people, and the civilising of the nation.[14]

It was through *Aids to Reflection* that Coleridge's influence was most directly felt by Thring's generation. These *Aids* aimed to present a rational groundwork for Christianity based on the fusion of reasoned philosophy and spiritual experience. They were prepared "for all, who desirous of building up a manly character in the light of distinct consciousness, are content to study the principles of moral architecture on the grounds of prudence, morality and religion", but they were "especially designed for the studious young at the close of their education or on their first entrance into the duties of manhood and the rights of self-government."[15] The aim was to make the reader manlier; indeed the first edition was titled *Aids to Reflection in the Formation of a Manly Character*. To the Platonic concept of the whole man, Coleridge added Christian moral duties:

> What the duties of morality are, the Apostle instructs the believer in full, comprising them under the two heads of negative and positive; negative, to keep himself pure from the world; and positive, beneficence from loving kindness, that is, love of his fellow men (his kind) as himself.[16]

---

[13] These contemporaries included Daniel and Alexander Macmillan, William Witts and Harvey Goodwin.

[14] Basil Willey, *Nineteenth Century Studies* (London: Chatto & Windus, 1949), 31-32.

[15] Samuel Coleridge, *Aids to Reflection* (London: Taylor and Hessey, 1825/43), xii, xiv.

[16] Coleridge, *Aids*, 6.

This Platonic-Christian manliness was promoted by all parties within the early Victorian Church of England and the imitation of Christ became an all-encompassing ideal for each stage of every man's life.[17]

It is impossible to see the full relevance of Coleridge's teaching without an examination of his relationship with William Wordsworth, Thring's favourite poet. They complemented one another; the expression of Coleridge's ideas was greatly helped by the solvent powers of Wordsworth's poetry. Before their meeting in 1796, Coleridge and Wordsworth had each grown to love the countryside and to hanker after the simplicities of a rustic life.[18] Wordsworth brought to Coleridge the Rousseauian belief that man was by nature good and that civilisation produced the corrupting influence. Modern man could only be saved by *Emile*-like education in which the child should be brought up in the countryside and learn there solely from experience. Both Wordsworth and Coleridge felt that there was a bond between Nature and the soul of man, and that moral impressions were associated with enduring things, especially lakes and mountains:[19]

> Let Nature be your Teacher ....
> One impulse from a vernal wood
> May teach you more of man
> Of moral evil and of good
> Than all the sages can.   (*The Table Turned*, 1798)

Thus the deification of Nature as a means of rehabilitating a man's spirit was passed into the mainstream of Victorian morality, and landscape became an inseparable element of nineteenth-century Englishness.[20] Soon art and craft-work were added as natural aids to learning. It was not necessary actually to live in an area such as the English Lakes, but it should exist as a place to escape to. Its healing power then fitted man with renewed vigour for life's struggle. Many headmasters, including Edward Thring, rented cottages there for their summer holidays. If the Lake

---

[17] William van Reyk, "Christian Ideals of Manliness during the Period of the Evangelical Revival, c.1730-c.1840" (DPhil diss., University of Oxford, 2007), 25, 27, 34.

[18] Herschel Margoliouth, *Wordsworth and Coleridge, 1795-1834* (London: Oxford University Press, 1953), 3-5.

[19] Basil Willey, *The Eighteenth Century Background* (London: Chatto & Windus, 1940), 256; John Purkis, *A Preface to Wordsworth* (London: Longman, 1970), 21; Frederic Myers, *Wordsworth* (New York: Harper & brothers, 1880/1908), 3.

[20] Marion Sherwood, *Tennyson and the Fabrication of Englishness* (Basingstoke: Palgrave Macmillan, 2013), 174, 176.

District was not easily accessible, then any attractive countryside would do: the Bristol poor might go on picnics to the neighbouring downs, the Working Men's College students might ramble in Epping Forest, or Thring's boys might roam the Rutland countryside.

III

Thring fervently believed in the Platonic and Christian principles of manliness that he had met at Cambridge and then he added his own personal stamp. His love for the novels, ballads, poetry and romances of Sir Walter Scott and his delight in Alfred Tennyson's Arthurian tales infused a chivalric spirit. Thring's association of chivalry and manliness was boosted in the 1860s when he read a translation of the French epic poem now known as the *Song of Roland*. It tells of the death of the Lord of the Breton Marches at Roncesvalles in the Pyrenees in 778. The battle portrayed was in fact no more than a skirmish between a detachment of Charlemagne's army and some Basque raiders but the legend embroiders this into a crusade against twelve Saracen chieftains and their huge army. Roland refuses to call for reinforcements to aid his small band, for that would damage his reputation as a knight. Then, before the final overwhelming onslaught, Roland consents to the call. Charlemagne's army arrives, the Saracens flee, and the dying Roland thus claims victory. The moral drawn is that a minor defeat can lead to a resounding victory.

Thring first mentions Roland in a letter to Lewis Nettleship: he wrote that he had composed a poem on the theme. Four Roland poems were eventually included in his *A Wanderer* collection and the legend was to haunt Thring for most of his life. The last verse of *Dream of a Life* embodies the crucial message:

> And so he died and hither came to be
> The king of hopes that live again, the king
> Of battles lost, just in the early spring
> Of a good cause which dies not in the loss,
> But won when summer ripens, and brings on
> The harvest, and the dreams become the life.[21]

Thring explained the message to Nettleship:

> As to the lost battle, it seems to me that all true working life is to the worker of the nature of the lost battle: day by day there is such a pouring

---

[21] Edward Thring, *A Wanderer*. In UA.

out of seemingly wasted blood; and success, as it is called, is such a mockery, that the feeling of the lost battle is always at hand the more one succeeds. Men praise the things one does not fight for, and mock the things one does, and their praise does not please, and their sneers do wound.[22]

Thring's later friendship with the children's author, Juliana Ewing, added to the chivalric theme. In the 1870s the news that a loyal African prince had been killed in a skirmish with Zulus, whilst some accompanying Englishmen had escaped, inspired a story. In the tale Mrs Ewing, the wife of a serving soldier, wanted to promote the military concept of selfless honour that was at odds with civilian indifference. She took as her theme that it was better to die trying to save a stricken comrade than not to risk one's life at all. Thring seems to have heard of the story from its earliest days and was an enthusiastic admirer even before its publication.[23] The story, *Jackanapes*, appeared in *Aunt Judy's Magazine* in 1879 with a frontispiece painting by Randolph Caldecott. In 1883 it was published as a shilling edition by S. P. C. K. and became a best-seller.[24] The story related in simple language how Jackanapes risked his life in battle to save his fallen comrade. As a result of this "heroic example and noble obligation" he is fatally wounded; he dies with pride felt for his "gallantry and devotion". At Jackanapes's funeral, the text taken was "Whosoever will save his life shall lose it, and whosoever shall lose his life for My sake shall find it". Grey Goose, the personification of civilian life, fails to see any point in Jackanapes's brief life.[25]

Thring wrote enthusiastically to Mrs Ewing: "I love Jackanapes, it is perfect." He told her that he was going to lecture to the school on it and that he had insisted that Hawthorn's, the local bookseller, ordered fifty copies for display in his window.[26] To Thring, "Life touches life" in the tale; it was the most direct appeal of heart to heart, exquisite for its simplicity and for its purity of spirit.

---

[22] Letter from Thring to Lewis Nettleship, May 23, 1868; quoted in Parkin, *Life*, 1:278.

[23] Letter from Mrs Ewing to Thring, Christmas 1883, in Thring's casket in UA.

[24] Sales of *Jackanapes* and the other books by Mrs Ewing topped 200,000 copies by the end of the century, a figure similar to the sales of the works of Lewis Carroll.

[25] Juliana Ewing, *Jackanapes* (London: SPCK, 1884/88), passim.

[26] Letter from Thring to Mrs Ewing, October 20, 1883, in Thring's casket; Parkin, *Life*, 2:179-182.

I, for my part, agree with the old General, who is said to have locked himself in his room every Sunday to read Mrs Ewing's story of 'Jackanapes' unseen. I could not trust myself to read it in public.[27]

IV

Thring's experience of schools added concrete practice rather than ideological theory to manliness. The severity of his preparatory school in Ilminster and the anarchy of the Long Chamber at Eton both contributed to his revolutionary plans for the organisation of teaching and welfare at Uppingham. His visits as an examiner to Rugby enabled him to witness at first hand the best and the worst of the legacy of Thomas Arnold. Each headmaster saw his school as a microcosm of the ideal Christian-Platonic society. Once at Uppingham, Thring matched Arnold's decisive leadership and followed his example with the introduction of strong pastoral care, a morally-earnest curriculum, a chapel-centred school life, and regular headmaster sermons. He also invigorated the prefectorial system. Thring's memories of working in the elementary schools in Gloucester and Berkshire convinced him that it was the business of a school to teach and train every child, and not just to offer knowledge to the clever and willing. Uppingham would take boys of all abilities and Thring would rejoice in all their achievements.

John Ruskin's ideals also contributed to Uppingham practice. Although many were fanciful (he would have every public school boy learn to plough) his indirect influence carried great force. Thring actively supported his aim to make "the beautiful in all things that God has made" more universal in the service of education.[28] To this end Ruskin wanted beautiful classrooms, with much decoration, relics of antiquity and engravings of historic sites. He also wanted every boy to learn a manual craft and to take nature study so that the communion with Nature would be the greater.[29] Schools should be situated in the country, both to facilitate these studies and to provide a healthy environment. Natural physical activities such as riding, swimming, running and the like were important: children should be as "active as hares".[30] Everything that Ruskin advocated was implemented at Thring's Uppingham.

[27] Thring, *Addresses*, 153-154.
[28] John Ruskin, *A Joy Forever* (London: George Allen, 1857/1905), para 128; Atwood, *Ruskin*, 4; Edward Cook, *The Life of John Ruskin* (London: George Allen, 1911), 1:132.
[29] Ruskin, *Joy,* paras 104, 105, 106, 128.
[30] Ruskin, *Joy,* letter 16, para 95; Atwood, *Ruskin*, 99, 114.

Cambridge had introduced Thring to Christian Socialism and there he had forged lifelong friendships with some of its greatest supporters, including Daniel and Alexander Macmillan, William Witts and Harvey Goodwin. The man who had inspired them to strive to improve the lives of the poor in such a real and positive way was Frederick Maurice, the Chaplain at Lincoln's Inn in London. To Maurice, man was not composed of two entities, "one called religious, the other secular"; he was an integrated whole. The Church therefore had a role to play in the social and educational advancement of humanity: "the business of the Church was to assert this ground of universal fellowship ... a fellowship in Christ". Maurice saw Christian Socialism as a movement, and not a political party, which would serve as a link between the unsocial Christians and the unchristian Socialists: "Our greatest desire is to Christianise Socialism".[31]

The year 1848 saw the true founding of Christian Socialism. It was the year of revolution in Europe: in Ireland there was famine, and civil strife was only checked by armed force; in February there was revolution in Paris and other continental cities, and the epidemic spread to Britain; in March there were riots in London, Glasgow, Edinburgh and Liverpool, troops were brought into London and a million special constables were enrolled throughout the land. The London disturbances culminated in a Chartist rally on April 10 that year but, in the face of the military, the demonstration collapsed. After the abortive rally, Charles Kingsley and Maurice met and that evening Christian Socialism was born.[32]

The first practical act of Christian Socialism was the formation of a night school in London's Little Ormond Yard in September 1848. This was not just a rebirth of the earlier Utilitarian Mechanics' Institutes but rather an attempt to present a liberal education to the poor. Bible classes under Maurice's tuition and day-trips to Epping Forest soon became vital ingredients.[33] The ideal of a "brotherhood of workers" was then extended with the formation of Working Associations: Kingsley vividly portrayed a tailoring co-operative in his novel on Christian Socialism, *Alton Locke*. But this aspect of Christian Socialism was not a success and by 1854 only the Working Men's College remained as the concrete outgrowth of the movement. This may be the movement's one lasting monument but its creed that charity was an obligation for the well-off had far-reaching

---

[31] Frederick Maurice, *The Life of Frederick Denison Maurice* (London: Macmillan, 1884), 2:35, 41, 258, 269, 277.

[32] Charles Raven, *Christian Socialism, 1848-1854* (London: Macmillan, 1920), 107. Raven was a boy at Uppingham from 1898 to 1904.

[33] Raven, *Christian Socialism*, 128; John Harrison, *A History of the Working Men's College, 1854-1954* (London: Routledge & Paul, 1954), 10.

legacies and, individually, much more was done: John Ludlow and
Friendly Societies; Kingsley and sanitary reform; Maurice and education;
Octavia Hill and housing for the poor. These all owed their inspiration to
Christian Socialism.

Thring met Maurice once, in 1862, when the latter took over a
Leicestershire parish for part of the summer. Thring found him thoughtful-
looking, acute, powerful, but not at all gladiatorial. "He talked pleasantly,
but not very much, gave me the impression of observing men rather than
displaying himself, withal gentle in manner and quiet, a man seemingly
who had rather teach than fight, and rather fight than give way."[34] Thring
was not an ardent disciple of Maurice and, when the FDM Club was
founded in 1882, the original members did include Goodwin and
Alexander Macmillan but Thring was not among them.[35] However, his
practice at Uppingham, culminating in the founding in 1869 of the first
public school mission to the poor at North Woolwich, matched Christian
Socialist ideals.[36] Thring kept his distance because of his distrust of
socialism. In 1886 Canon Edward Girdlestone wrote to seek Thring's
views on Christian Socialism.[37] He replied that he abhorred the ideas
contained in modern socialism but that he was a fervent believer in the
pursuit of Christian brotherhood: "the term Socialism has nothing
Christian in it, ... it has been started and pre-occupied by a devil's parody
of Christian brotherly love, and that it had better be left in the hands of
those who started it."[38]

Thring did however admire Charles Kingsley. He had corresponded
with Mrs Kingsley since 1870 and letters talk of her husband's "strong
feeling for Uppingham and the work here".[39] Thring may have visited the
Kingsleys at the Eversley rectory when he stayed with Edward Benson at
nearby Wellington College in 1872; Benson and Kingsley were close
friends.[40] After Kingsley's death in 1875, his widow sent Thring an
autographed copy of his *Brave Words to Brave Soldiers*: Thring prized it
and in reply wrote : "It cheers me much to find myself, as life goes on,
associated, however far off, with those who have worked for righteousness

---

[34] Diary, September 29, 1863 (Parkin, *Life*, 1:126).
[35] Add. Ms. 7348/4 in Cambridge University Library.
[36] For more on the mission, see Tozer, *Manliness*, 153-160.
[37] The author of *Christian Socialism versus Present-day Unsocialism. A
Description and an Argument*, 1887.
[38] Diary, November 7, 1886; Letter, November 8, 1886, in Thring's casket.
[39] Diary, February 9, 1870 (Parkin, *Life*, 1:218); diary January 18, 1886 (Parkin,
Life, 2:174).
[40] He visited the College in May 1872: Parkin, *Life*, 1:235.

and striven for the good cause, as he did, a real pioneer."[41] Fanny Kingsley was now living in Leamington Spa where, with her daughter Rose, she became closely associated with the High School. In 1886 Thring was invited to the school's Speech Day where he presented the prizes and gave an address.[42]

Thring shared Kingsley's outlook that the clerical function should be never be divorced from everyday life; both were laymen in the guise of clergymen, both abhorred clerical dignity. Thring agreed with Kingsley that Christianity should be alive and happy, and not gloomy or censorious.[43] He matched Kingsley's sense of fun and delight in simple pleasures: staging parties in School House for the children of masters; racing and leaping in the garden with his children; spending two hours building a snow-woman for his daughters; delighting in children dancing at a party at the home of Paul David; or playing charades with the boys at a School House party.[44]

Kingsley's educational aims matched Thring's: "In my eyes the question is not what to teach, but how to educate; how to train not scholars, but men; bold, energetic, methodic; liberal-minded; magnanimous."[45] Kingsley was a keen advocate of natural history and physical education in schools; they were essential elements of the Platonic ideal of manliness. He lectured to the boys at Wellington on flora and fauna and he helped in the founding of a museum. He also instituted a steeplechase, a fine mixture of his rural and sporting aims. In the movement that brought education to the children of the poorer classes, Kingsley was an enthusiast for physical education as well as for hygiene, and girls were not to be neglected.[46] Such activities brought physical and moral health, and educated the whole man. Games brought out virtues that no book could give:

> daring and endurance, but, better still, temper, self-restraint, fairness, honour, unenvious approbation of another's success, and all that 'give and take' of life which stands a man in such good stead when he goes forth in the world, and without which, indeed, his success is always maimed and partial.[47]

---

[41] Letter to Mrs Kingsley, January 1886 (Parkin, *Life*, 2:246).

[42] Diary, October 3, 1886; Thring, *Addresses*, 1887, 83-102.

[43] Guy Kendall, *Charles Kingsley and His Ideas* (London: Hutchinson, 1947), 10.

[44] Haslam diary; Diary, April 14, 1860; March 26, 1861; March 22, 1867; January 22, 1876; and October 23, 1886.

[45] Quoted in Fanny Kingsley, *Life and Letters of Charles Kingsley* (London: Macmillan, 1877), 1:98.

[46] Charles Kingsley, *Health and Education* (London: W. Isbister, 1874), 74.

[47] Kingsley, *Health*, 86.

As David Newsome noted in *Godliness and Good Learning*:

> If Kingsley had been a headmaster, he would have taught his boys to jump
> five-barred gates, to climb trees, to run like hares over difficult country;
> and there would have been nature rambles, a school museum stocked with
> specimens collected by the boys, science lessons and occasional lectures
> on hygiene and drains.[48]

Kingsley never had the opportunity to put all this into practice in a school, but Thring did.

The final ingredient of Thring's true manliness was unique to an English school. It stemmed from his marriage to Marie and their subsequent holidays in Bonn. In the company of her father and her brother-in-law, Friedrich Breusing, he attended the city's *Lese- und Erholungsgesellschaft*, the gentlemen's "reading and recreation club". It is there that he would have heard of the city's holistic schooling that sought to motivate children of all abilities to realise their full potential, an aim close to his heart. Wilhelm von Humboldt, the minister responsible for education, had introduced this innovative curriculum to all the Prussian schools and universities in 1810. Philosophy, literature, science and the arts were taught alongside the traditional subjects, and pupils and students were encouraged to develop their own interests outside the curriculum and beyond the school and university walls. Thring's adoption of Humboldt's theory and practice added music, art, gymnastics, modern languages and science to the Uppingham curriculum and encouraged wide-ranging leisure pursuits. Breusing recruited men from schools in Bonn and other Rhineland towns to teach these new subjects and to broaden the cultural provision.[49]

V

The whole of Thring's efforts were directed towards making each and every boy "manly, earnest and true".[50] The school years were the crucial phase of a boy's life; not a preparation for life, but the most important stage of a life. Each pupil arrived a boy, each left a man, and "nursery milk" was exchanged at Uppingham for "the wine of life".[51] The evolution

---

[48] Newsome, *Godliness*, 211
[49] See Chapter 4 Part VI. For more on Prussian influence on the musical life at the school, see Tozer, "From Prussia with Love".
[50] Thring, *E&S*, 269.
[51] Thring, Index Rerum.

was gradual but the process accelerated for each boy at about the age of fourteen as he prepared to confirm his Christian baptismal vows and assume adult membership of the Church of England. Each would then be ready for service in the "Christian Knighthood". The whole school took part in the annual ceremonies associated with confirmation and, as year succeeded year, so every boy took this rite of passage to manhood. As the manuscript notes held at the back of the first volume of Thring's three-volume Bible state, "Every one must be a communicant".[52]

Each March or April, Thring would inaugurate the confirmation week with a sermon at Sunday's service. Then on successive weekday evenings, at a time when Thring believed that boys were at their most receptive, he would speak to separate groups assembled in the chapel. First he would address the youngest boys about the confirmation process, and then on the next evening he would concentrate on the boys who were that year's confirmation candidates. A visiting bishop, and usually a close friend, led the actual confirmation service on the third day, and on that evening Thring would address all the older boys as communicants. The confirmation week was formally closed on the following Sunday with a second sermon delivered by Thring to the whole school.[53]

Thring's sermon at the beginning of the confirmation week had two purposes: to remind the boys of their membership of a distinctive community and to warn them of the sexual dangers associated with the "mock manliness" of homo-erotic habits. Thring often compared the boys to the Israelites on their flight from Egypt to their new home on the banks of the Jordan; the much-annotated text of *Exodus* in his Bible became "The Architect's Plan" for their moral training. He believed that the rigours and deprivations of the Israelites' captivity had bred a hardiness of character, whilst the rescue at the parting of the Red Sea had inspired a single-mindedness of purity. He urged the boys to identify with the Israelites and to view the confirmation service as the boundary line in their own lives between preparation for battle and eventual victory.[54]

A few evenings after the Sunday sermon, Thring addressed the hundred or so junior boys. He told them that they had outgrown the involuntary demands of mewling childhood and he likened them to the Israelites who had escaped from slavery in Egypt. The crossing of the Red Sea had its parallel in their initiation to the Christian Church at the time of their baptism. They had been freed of original sin and they now walked at

---

[52] Thring, 1885 notes to Confirmation Candidates. All confirmation notes are in UA.

[53] The programme is outlined in Thring's diary, for example March 14, 1887.

[54] Thring, Sermon 238.

liberty as the sons of God. No responsibilities would be placed on them until they had grown in power, purity and manliness, and they should use this interval to learn to become "soldiers of Christ". The boys were encouraged to avoid "mock manliness" by managing their thoughts, avoiding idleness, and keeping busy in their leisure time.[55]

It was the turn of the seventy or so confirmation candidates to be addressed by Thring on the following evening. He developed his Israelite theme, for their lives moved from a childlike baseness to an enlightenment that he associated with adulthood. The dependency of childhood matched the Israelites' call for food in the wilderness and God's answering provision of manna and water. Daily bread was provided for God's people to sustain their power for living and, in return, they would serve God's purpose in the way that they led their lives. The Israelites now stood overlooking their Promised Land, happy to honour the promise they had made to God for their safe deliverance. In the same way, the confirmation candidates were at the boundary between boyhood and manhood, and they should be ready to use all their talents and powers for the good of their fellow men.[56] To do this "true courage" was needed. This was not to be confused with the strength, energy and hardiness of the body, though one could not have "true courage" without those animal qualities. True manliness rose above these by the addition of quiet endurance, righteousness and gentleness, and through a patient willingness to bear reproach, shame, obscurity, pain and misunderstanding. Thring repeated his warning on the consequences of indecency and drew on the happiness of his own marriage, expressing the hope that all boys would in time become happy husbands and fathers.[57]

After the following day's confirmation service, Thring turned his attention in the evening to the one hundred and fifty or so senior boys who were already communicant members of the Church. Here was the opportunity to remind them of their promises. The school was a "regiment for Christ" and anyone found guilty of gross indecency or of corrupting another would leave it at once. The "purity of good women" was recalled and the boys were asked to "reverence it" by keeping their own bodies pure for eventual marriage.[58] He ended with an exhortation: "A great school is an army in the regiment of the brave and the true" where the boys were to live "the high and happy Christian life, the honour and the power of being a Christian, the wisdom, the bravery, the true nobility of

---

[55] Thring, 1886 and 1887 notes to Younger Boys.
[56] Thring, 1880, 1885 and 1887 notes to Confirmees. Grove reports that 72 boys were confirmed at the 1885 service. Grove diaries, June 9, 1885.
[57] Thring, 1885, 1886 and 1887 notes to Confirmees.
[58] Thring, 1886 and 1887 notes to Communicants.

being enrolled in the army of Truth and of Christ".[59] This army would win "victory" on the battlefield of life, and each enlisted soldier would be God's hero:

> God's hero, the man who bears and does all things easily, gently, lovingly – the hero, who may die without glory, but who has been felt to be a perfect pattern of manly power by every living being with the heart of life, whose life has been touched by the life. For life touches life, and passes on in silence, invisible, into other lives, even as rain that falls gently on the earth, and seems to pass away, till the harvest comes, and speaks of a hidden, wonderful spread of unseen goodness.[60]

Thring brought the confirmation week to a close with his sermon to the whole school during the next Sunday's chapel service. After the exhortations and warnings introduced in the previous Sunday's sermon, and developed in the separate evening addresses to the three groups of boys, the second Sunday sermon usually found Thring in cheerful mood. His last confirmation sermon, delivered in March 1887, saw him on particularly happy form. Thring confided that his chief worry as headmaster was that even in a good school sin could gain a toehold:

> Today, once more, I can look on this school, and speak to you as one regiment in the army of Christ, one in Confirmation Week, one on this Commemorative Sunday, one as marching under our Lord, one as having thrown in your lot with life and honour and truth, loyal and faithful soldiers and subjects of Christ your king. It is a glorious feeling to feel we are one body in Christ. I do not mean that evil has gone, or that no traitor is here, but I do mean that we can feel that as one body we are bounded together to do holy service. I do mean that we can feel a happy confidence in the truth and desire to be true of the school as a whole. I do mean that we can feel that we have a common cause and are ready to work together for it. I do mean that the battle against sin in this place is a real battle, and the Holy Spirit of God is dwelling with us here.[61]

Thring's confidence that his boys could lead the "True Life" was high for he believed even the young could be valiant soldiers in that regiment: "The spirit that does right, because it is right, is as strong in the little child as in the old". His closing rallying call saw the promise of "Victory":

---

[59] Thring, Sermons 33 and 66.
[60] Thring, *Sermons Preached*, 2:48.
[61] Thring, Sermon 375.

Brethren, in this Confirmation and Holy Communion, let one spirit breathe
through our ranks. Let us stand today shoulder to shoulder as one regiment
on the battlefield, resolute, with one voice, and one power ....[62]

We know that Thring's message was well received by one sixth-
former, Reginald Grove. Grove had been confirmed at King's College
Choir School before he reached Uppingham. He thus missed Thring's
addresses to new boys and to confirmation candidates but he heard the one
for communicants on four occasions. He recorded in his diary his thoughts
on the last of the four: "Had a very helpful address from Head-master."[63]
Grove had been a regular communicant throughout his school career,
attending this voluntary service on average once every two weeks. He
earned the right to join Thring's "regiment of the brave and the true".

[62] Thring, Sermon 375.
[63] Grove diaries, March 16, 1887.

CHAPTER SIXTEEN

IDEALS REJECTED, 1888-1907:
"NO ENGLISHMAN'S TRAINING IS COMPLETE
BEFORE HE HAS LEARNT TO FACE
AN OPPONENT IN SINGLE COMBAT"

I

Edward Thring died at Uppingham on October 22, 1887 after a week-long illness and was buried in the parish church's cemetery. The school's trustees acted speedily to find his successor: applications were received by December 1 and a fortnight later the appointment was made. Edward Carus Selwyn began his headmastership at the start of the following term.

Selwyn was born on November 25, 1853, two months after Thring began his life's work at Uppingham, at Blackheath in south-east London where his father was principal of the local proprietary school. He was an excellent scholar: at Eton he gained the treasured Newcastle Scholarship, then at King's College, Cambridge he won numerous awards. With the exception of one year's curacy at Jarrow-on-Tyne, the interval between his ordination in 1876 and his appointment to the headmastership of Liverpool College in 1882 was spent as fellow, lecturer and then dean at King's College. Selwyn was a brilliant theologian and he continued his scholarship at Uppingham. He became a doctor of divinity in 1900 and he published a number of texts on the New Testament.[1] Selwyn's connections, as much as his qualifications, must have impressed the Uppingham trustees: on his own side he could list the Bishop of Lichfield, whilst his wife was the grand-daughter of Thomas Arnold. A member of the Alpine Club and an "enthusiastic" fives player, he was keen to have every boy a swimmer.[2]

---

[1] *The Christian Prophets and the Prophetic Apocalypse* (1900), *St Luke the Prophet* (1901) and *The Oracles in the New Testament* (1912).
[2] Graham, *Uppingham*, 116.

A new broom had arrived. Demand to get into Uppingham had long been high but Thring had maintained his limit of 300: now Selwyn relaxed this veto and soon the numbers climbed over the 400 mark. An extra boarding house was acquired, housemasters admitted more boys, and shared studies became common. The curriculum was reformed to match that of most other public schools: compulsory Greek was dropped and special army and engineering classes were introduced for the Sandhurst and Woolwich examinations. With the loss of many of the extra subjects of Thring's time, the curriculum for most boys was dominated by the classics.[3] Selwyn was a respected teacher of the sixth-form but no other boys were taught by him; a gulf grew between headmaster and boys and most regarded him in awe from afar. The emphasis shifted from striving to get the best out of every boy, clever or not, to a concentration on the talented and the scholarly. Henry Bothamley, who never reached the sixth-form, told the school's historian that he hated Selwyn.[4] He was, however, generally popular with the staff, although in the early years men who were especially loyal to Thring's ideals did not readily accept Selwyn's innovations.[5] His relationship with the Thring family was predictably strained: the Thring daughters never liked Selwyn, and his elder son, Gale, recorded that the "changes which upset his father's cherished aims were hard to bear".[6]

Three aspects of school life quickly felt the passing of Thring: school uniform, football, and the cadet corps. School praepostors had worn white straw boaters in Thring's last years; now speckled ones replaced the German-style caps for all other boys.[7] Junior boys dressed in Eton collars and short black jackets, older ones wore striped trousers, and praepostors could wear winged collars with their black tail-coats. The last also gained umbrellas as badges of office. Harold Howitt, later an eminent accountant, recalled that all trouser pockets were sewn up, in part to prevent slouching but also to discourage masturbation.[8] Uppinghamians now looked like all other public school boys.

---

[3] Charles Raven, *A Wanderer's Way* (London: Martin Hopkinson, 1928), 20.

[4] Information received from Bryan Matthews.

[5] Graham, *Uppingham*, 36.

[6] Gale Thring's newspaper obituary (UA).

[7] "One thing I hated more than most was that we had to wear black and white straw hats, Summer and Winter. When it rained the glue used to melt and run down one's neck, and when they dried out they became all out of shape". Cecil Hodson, *Memories*, c1980. (In UA). Hodson was at Uppingham from 1914 to 1918.

[8] Harold Howitt, *Reminiscences*, 1966, 7. (In UA). Sir Harold Howitt, in school from 1901 until 1904, was Chairman of the Trustees when I joined the Uppingham

II

The Uppingham football game was exchanged for Rugby football in July 1889; the acceptance of a national football code was probably both inevitable and sensible.[9] Such a change had nearly happened in 1876, only then it would have been Association football: now the conversion was made to the recognised public school code. Games immediately became compulsory three times a week. The ablest boys played in the various schools XVs, the remainder were occupied on "House Games" with between 20 or 30 a side.[10] New boys had to learn the rules by heart and they were tested on them in the fourth week of term by the Committee of Games.[11] "Hints on Rugby Football" prepared by Old Boys were published in the school magazine.[12] In order to increase "wholesome rivalry", inter-game matches, or "lands", were introduced: the lower XV of third game, for example, played the upper XV of fourth game. The talented were subsequently promoted and the less able demoted.[13] A league system was re-introduced for house matches in 1898 to increase the number of games and to occupy more boys for longer: each house now played eleven games in the autumn term at both Overs and Unders.[14]

The 1st XV adopted modern "rugby football trim" and, from 1891, conventional public school XV caps were awarded: dark blue velvet with a silver tassel, trimmings and a badge.[15] Members of the XV were expected to attend a "daily course of dumbbells in the gymnasium".[16] Old Boys and masters took a keen interest in the coaching of the XV and together they "brought the team on wonderfully".[17] Notable amongst the Old Boys was Harry Alexander, an Oxford Blue in 1897 and 1898, and an England international from 1900 to 1902; he won seven caps as a forward,

---

staff in 1966. The account of his escape from German lines in 1918 was used by John Buchan in his thriller, *Mr Standfast* (1919).
[9] *USM*, July 1889, 237.
[10] *USM*, April 1933, 50.
[11] *USM*, November 1889, 320.
[12] *USM*, October 1889, 255-257.
[13] *USM*, December 1902, 285. Third game comprised the 5th and 6th XVs; fourth game the 7th and 8th XVs.
[14] *USM*, November 1898, 308. Leagues had been abandoned after Borth.
[15] *USM*, December 1891 and November 1898, 297.
[16] *USM*, November 1901, 293.
[17] *USM*, October 1902 and February 1903, 22.

captaining the side on his penultimate appearance.[18] In 1902, Hawthorn, the Uppingham bookseller, published Alexander's *How to Play Rugby Football,* a text prepared primarily for his old school. It was reviewed in the school magazine: "if you want to become useful to the house or the School, you cannot do better than make yourself acquainted with the inside of Alexander's book, where everything you will want is to be found".[19]

Early school matches were, as in the past, against sides led by masters or Old Boys, but from 1889 these were supplemented by Old Boy sides from other schools, including the Old Marlburians and Bedford Rovers.[20] London clubs, including Rosslyn Park and the Harlequins, sent sides to the school every year from 1890; the former built a strong link with the school and many Old Uppinghamians played for the club.[21] Boys and Old Boys called for even more foreign matches and by 1896 there were ten in the autumn term and two in January.[22] The boys' hopes in 1890 for an inter-school match against Haileybury, long-standing cricket opponents, were not realised and their successors had to wait until 1899 for the first public school match. But when it came it was at Rugby, the "Rome" of football.[23] The home side won comfortably; Uppingham had to wait until 1903 for its first victory.[24]

III

Despite the increased status of football, cricket was still the premier game at Uppingham. The 1890s saw the restoration of the London matches and a return to the glories of the 1870s: "over the whole decade", judged Harry Altham, the cricket historian, "few schools can show a record equal to Uppingham's".[25] Of the nineteen inter-school matches played in the

---

[18] Alexander was at Uppingham from 1891 to 1897 and progressed to Corpus Christi. On graduation he taught at Stanmore Park Prep School. He was killed in the Battle of Loos on October 17, 1915, two days after reaching the front line.

[19] *USM*, October 1902, 200-201.

[20] *USM*, November 1889, 326.

[21] 23 of the 108 members of the club who died in the war were educated at Uppingham. Email from Stephen Cooper, October 2, 2014.

[22] *USM*, February 1891, 37 and March 1896, 84.

[23] *USM*, April 1890, 72-76 and October 1899, 236. Haileybury did become the second fixture (1909), followed by Tonbridge School.

[24] The games held before the Great War saw Uppingham win seven and Rugby eight. Each school was dominant for three- or four-year periods.

[25] Altham, *Cricket*, 214.

decade, ten were won, two lost, and seven drawn.[26] Stephenson now had help from an assistant professional, Elijah Bird; he continued to write his "Letters" to the school magazine; and, as he confessed to Edward Lyttelton, the new headmaster of the visiting Haileybury XI, he had gained greater influence:

> 'Well, between you and I,' he said in answer to a question as to the age of a very powerful eleven of boys, 'I tell you what I does. If one of these 'ere parents wants to take one of these boys away, I just writes him a letter and so keep them.'[27]

Stephenson was deeply mourned at his death in 1896. Numerous obituaries and appreciations were recorded, Selwyn preached a thanksgiving sermon, and a brass tablet in the pavilion on The Upper and Stephenson medals became his memorials in the school.[28]

Robert Douglas, who Grace reckoned a "brilliant performer", now became master in charge of cricket, four years after joining Selwyn's staff. Louis Hall of Yorkshire was appointed his professional. When at Selwyn College, Douglas had played in three 'Varsity matches against Oxford, scoring as opening batsman an aggregate of 97 runs in the six innings. Twice he played for the Gentlemen against Players and he represented both Surrey and Middlesex. An all-rounder, he won his Rugby football Blue as a forward in the University rugby match of 1891 and he also played for the Harlequins. Uppingham now had a games master, 38 years after George Dupuis at Eton had become the first.[29]

The organisation of cricket matched that of football with compulsory games, regular "lands" and house leagues. The fixture list for the XI saw the return of the MCC matches, the addition of Malvern and Rugby as school opposition, and visits from the elite travelling club, I Zingari.[30] The whole school travelled to Rugby for the Diamond Jubilee Match in 1897. Douglas was joined by other games masters: William Rashleigh (cricket for Oxford and Kent) in 1889 as the first Blue on the teaching staff, Frank

---

[26] Repton W6 L1 D3; Haileybury W4 L0 D2 and cancelled through illness 4; Malvern D2; Rugby L1. Many other matches were played against sides composed of visiting gentlemen: MCC, Free Foresters, Warwickshire Gentlemen, Quidnuncs, the OUs and more.

[27] Stephenson's rustic vocabulary is unlikely: Lyttelton, *Memories*, 74.

[28] *USM*, February 1897, 3-15 and March 1898, 43.

[29] Roe, *Cricket*, 185; *USM*, October 1895, 218. In 1904 Douglas married Paul David's daughter, Caroline, and in 1910 he was appointed Headmaster of Giggleswick School, a post he held until 1931.

[30] *USM*, March 1896, 76 and June 1898, 115.

Street (cricket for Essex and Association football for Oxford) in 1901, and Douglas Schulze (Rugby football for Scotland) in 1909.[31] Charles Baldwin of Surrey succeeded Hall as professional in 1902 and the ground staff was enlarged to include three bowlers through the generosity of cricketing Old Boys.[32] Despite the increased attention given to the game, cricket at Uppingham after 1896 never reached the standard of Stephenson's time until after the Great War.[33] No master, no professional could replace the incomparable H. H. S., a fact acknowledged by the frequent reprinting in the 1900s of his "Letters" to the school magazine.[34]

IV

Expenditure on games steadily increased as the numbers of boys in the school rose: £450 – 12 – 8½d in 1889, £541 – 8 – 2d in 1897, and £636 – 19 – 7d in 1903.[35] New playing fields were needed to accommodate all the XIs and XVs: Van Diemen's Land was used again from 1889; The Middle was enlarged; The Upper was extended; and The Leicester was levelled. Fives courts were built up against the swimming bath and improvements were made to the pavilion on The Upper.[36] Accounts of all house and school matches were reported in great detail in the school magazine, occasionally needing special supplements.[37] The decoration on football jerseys and cricket blazers blossomed as more trims and colours were devised, allowing the cognoscenti to place every boy in the hierarchy of teams. There was a prolonged debate on whether or not to add house colours to the mix but they were never adopted.[38] Fives, cross-country running and shooting all gained colours at the turn of the century to add to the rainbow collection. In order to maintain their higher status, the cricketers and footballers demanded some form of recognition off the field of play as well as on: badges, caps and hats were suggested as possibilities.[39]

---

[31] Rashleigh took Holy Orders in 1892 and became Rector of St George's, Canterbury. Street relinquished his housemastership of Fircroft in 1914 to enlist and was killed at Ovillers on July 7, 1916. Schulze, later known as Miller, was appointed High Master of Manchester Grammar School in 1924, retiring in 1945.

[32] *USM*, June 1902, 107 and May 1904, 99.

[33] Two wins against Repton and three against Haileybury in fifteen years.

[34] Altham, *Cricket*, 300; for example, *USM,* June 1901, 136.

[35] *USM*, June 1889, 188, February 1898, 35 and April 1904, 61.

[36] *USM*, July 1889, 289; April 1890, 54; November 1896, 359; and 1901, 325.

[37] For example, *USM*, April 1900.

[38] House colours were common at other schools. *USM*, November 1895, 309.

[39] *USM*, December 1895, 355.

Sport in the spring term continued to cause problems. The athletics championships declined in popularity and their results were limited to a short report or just a table of results in the school magazine. Their duration was shortened to two weeks from 1900.[40] The heats of the various events served "to clear out the incompetent" and were disposed of as quickly as possible.[41] Compulsory paperchases were introduced to enliven the "dull" term but were regarded as unimportant without the incentive of a house challenge cup.[42] Keen runners gained races against the Cambridge Hare and Hounds Club in 1897 and their Oxford counterparts in 1905.[43] Their six-mile course is still called the "Long Cambridge". The fives players also gained a foreign match in 1897, against Shrewsbury.[44] "Professor" Frederick Beckwith succeeded Ellingworth as swimming instructor in 1898, and his role in teaching boys to swim gained strong support from Selwyn.

For most boys, the gap between the end of the football season, now in early February, and the start of the cricket season in April was a period of seemingly endless house runs. Another team game was needed. When the purge of the 1860s and disparaging comments of succeeding decades are remembered, it is surprising that, from the list of games under consideration for adoption (Association football, lacrosse and hockey), it was hockey that was chosen. The game had steadily gained in popularity nationally during the 1890s and many Old Uppinghamians played for clubs.[45] Some public schools, notably Marlborough, had already adopted the game. Twenty-four hockey XIs were formed in 1896 and the 1st XI played matches against sides led by masters and by Old Boys. Colours were awarded the same year.[46] Although the ethos of *esprit de corps* was often stressed to boost the new game's standing, it was not until the introduction of "lands", trims and house matches, the last in 1899, that hockey gained any real importance in the boys' eyes. Even then, its status was low compared to that for cricket and football.[47]

---

[40] *USM*, May 1900, 114 and June 1906, 79.

[41] *USM*, April 1901, 101.

[42] *USM*, February 1890, 1 and February 1901, 42,

[43] *USM*, March 1897, 50 and February 1905, 37.

[44] The fives match against Shrewsbury was maintained until the 1990s, and then renewed in 2017. *USM*, March 1897, 81.

[45] The sporting activity of Old Boys was regularly logged in the postscript at the end of each issue of the school magazine.

[46] *USM*, April 1892, 125; March 1896, 86; and April 1896, 90.

[47] *USM*, February 1898, 25; November 1898, 306; April 1899, 118; and March 1900, 58.

The sporting reputation of Old Uppinghamians flourished in the Selwyn years. Alfred Lucas, "one of the finest batsmen" according to *Wisden*, captained England against Australia in 1902 and had been a regular opener with W. G. Grace since 1880.[48] Gregor MacGregor, a wicket-keeper who stood close to the stumps for the fastest bowlers, played many times for England, and Charles Wilson and Tom Taylor both earned glowing praise.[49] In Rugby football, Arthur Rotherham, like his cousin Alan, was an innovative half-back who served as a link between the forwards and the backs, and MacGregor doubled his international representation by playing thirteen times for Scotland.[50] Other Old Boys also won caps in cricket, Rugby football and hockey. The Uppingham Rovers continued to represent the best of Uppingham cricket, although its elitism was challenged in 1900 by the formation of the Incompetent Old Uppinghamian Cricket Club.[51] An Old Uppinghamian Football Club, playing the Rugby code, was formed 1891 and a matching one for hockey in 1907.[52] Unlike the Rovers, both were open to all Old Boys and set low subscription fees. All three clubs organised extensive holiday tours of matches.

V

The cadet corps was formed in April 1889: membership was voluntary, and at the end of its first term the roll numbered a third of the school. Thring had consistently rejected the creation of a cadet corps but he would have found little to oppose whilst William Vale Bagshawe and then Sam Haslam, both loyal and long-serving colleagues, were in command with Georg Beisiegel as lieutenant.[53] A former Royal Marine, Sgt W. Clunies, was appointed as corps sergeant.[54] Activities in the first year were limited

---

[48] Sydney Pardon, *John Wisden's Cricketers' Almanac* (London: Wisden, 1924), 263.

[49] Warner, *Cricket*, 253; Sydney Pardon, *John Wisden's Cricketers' Almanac* (London: Wisden, 1901), 180.

[50] Rotherham was at Uppingham from 1883 to 1888. A two-year Blue at Cambridge, he played five times for England and three times for the British Lions between 1891 and 1899. For Alan Rotherham, see Chapter 10 Part I. MacGregor was at Uppingham from 1884 to 1887. A four-year Blue at Cambridge, captaining the side in 1891, he played in eight Test matches between 1890 and 1893. Taylor, at school from 1892 to 1896, was a three-year Blue at Cambridge, captaining the side in 1900, before playing for Yorkshire.

[51] *USM*, June 1900, 179.

[52] *USM*, February 1891, 2 and October 1907, 248.

[53] Corps roll in *USM*, March 1889, 85-86.

[54] Graham, *Uppingham*, 50.

to drilling, skirmishes in local woods, and Morris Tube practice near Castle Hill, just to the west of the town.[55] A corps band was formed and given its own "Marching Song".[56] In 1894 and 1895 the Uppingham corps took part in field days with Rugby, and then from 1895 joined the annual combined public school field day that was held at Berkhamsted.[57]

In these early years the boys viewed the corps as a games-type activity, but its status was well below that for cricket and football. The games ethos was reinforced with the presentation of a Drill Shield for house competition and the introduction of shooting as a competitive sport but under the aegis of the corps.[58] A thousand-yard rifle range was constructed near Burgess's Pond, two miles west of the town, and was opened with great ceremony in 1890.[59] Copying the style of Queen Victoria's inauguration of the Bisley range in 1865, Mrs Selwyn fired the first shot; the rifle, clamped in a vice, had previously been carefully aimed by Vale Bagshawe and Clunies.[60] Courses and examinations in musketry were introduced, shooting fixtures were organised against other schools, and from 1890 the Shooting VIII travelled to Bisley for the annual public school competitions.[61] The standard of shooting in these early years was high. Although the school had to wait to win the coveted Ashburton Shield for the best team, the prize for the best individual score, the Spencer Cup, was won by an Uppingham cadet in 1892 and 1893. On each occasion the victor was met at Seaton station by the corps band and chaired the two miles to the school by his colleagues in the VIII.[62] The ethos surrounding shooting was similar to that for the early Thring games; there was even a *Bisley Chorus*:

---

[55] A Morris Tube was a device that was inserted in the barrel of a standard rifle to enable it to fire smaller calibre ammunition. *USM*, March 1889, 85-86.

[56] *USM*, April 1890, 69 and October 1890, 248.

[57] *USM*, August 1893, 196 and June 1895, 139.

[58] *USM*, October 1890, 257.

[59] Beisiegel had been commissioned by Selwyn and the masters to "procure the Land": Beisiegel to Monckton, Beisiegel papers.

[60] I owe this point to Simon Pattinson.

[61] Most inter-school matches were shot simultaneously at each school's range, with the results compared using the telegraph. There was an extensive fixture list, including Malvern, Clifton, Glenalmond, Haileybury, Rugby, Sherborne, Rossall and Dulwich. *USM*, October 1890, 251-54 and February 1891, 11.

[62] Such celebrations were less demanding for the carriers from 1894 when the branch line was extended to Uppingham. *USM*, July 1892, 224 and August 1893, 230.

Hands all round,
Let the rifle's praises sound
In this our joyous England's joyful year,
And our own glorious Bisley's round and round.[63]

The "joyful year" was 1897 and the Golden Jubilee of Queen Victoria's accession; ninety Uppingham cadets had paraded in the Windsor Review of public school contingents to honour Her Majesty.[64]

VI

There was an injection of military spirit in the school in 1898 when Selwyn appointed Herbert Jones, aged thirty-three, to teach the Army Class and take over command of the corps. Jones, a professional soldier at heart, was an outstanding commander and under his powerful influence Uppingham leapt to national renown. Jones agreed with Field Marshal Sir Evelyn Wood, Adjutant-General to the Armed Forces, that the country would eventually decide on compulsory military service but that in the interval "the sons of the upper classes should give more time and attention to rendering themselves capable of defending their country in case of need".[65] The Uppingham corps quickly expanded to a battalion and gained additional officers, and from 1899 a detachment attended the newly founded Public Schools Camp at Aldershot.[66]

At the start of the first term of the new century, and in the midst of the Boer War, Selwyn made an announcement that placed Uppingham at the forefront of public school militarism: all boys, whether in the corps or not, were required to pass a shooting test, and no boy would be allowed to take part in any inter-house athletic or sporting contest, nor accept a school prize, until he had passed that test.[67] *The Morris Tube*, a poem published in the school magazine, recorded:

The sovereign lord is he of all house-matches:
His scorners may not touch the cricket ground …
And on the same proficiency depends
Sweet football's joys …[68]

---

[63] *USM*, June 1897, 135.

[64] *USM*, July 1897, 205.

[65] Jones quoted Wood in *USM*, March 1899, 69. He also quoted Lord Wolseley, the Commander-in-Chief of the Forces.

[66] *USM*, August 1898, 170 and October 1899, 226.

[67] *USM*, February 1900, 1-2.

[68] *USM*, April 1905, 54.

Selwyn argued that this "glorious innovation into a Public School curriculum" was based on a lesson learnt from the Boers' tactics, "that any body of men who are not cowards and can shoot straight, even with little or no drill, are an extremely formidable element in the defence of their country".[69] Uppingham was probably the first school to make shooting and instruction in rifle drill a compulsory part of school life.[70]

In February 1900 Jones left for active service in the Boer War as a lieutenant in a volunteer battalion; Selwyn, in his Speech Day address, reckoned that he was probably the only public school master serving at the front.[71] His exploits in South Africa were reported in the school magazine in graphic detail: "We hear that Mr. Jones has killed five Boers single-handed. We congratulate him heartily on the exploit and hope he will dispose of many more." In June 1901 Jones, now a captain, returned to a hero's welcome.[72] James Elroy Flecker, the future poet, who was at the school at this time, recorded the scene in a letter to his parents:

> On Saturday the conquering hero, Captain Jones, came. By a stretch of unparalleled generosity we were let off an hour school and a half on Monday. The Rifle Corps parade in vast solemnity down to the station; our drummer looks resplendent in his leopard skin. ... The masters assemble on the green in the quad. The chief robes himself in a great hood like a red ensign fluttering in the wind. ... Sedgwick bawls forth his peroration ... Captain Jones also bawls forth some soldierly words apropos of the corps, and there are more cheers ... and the solemn and impressive ceremony ends.[73]

Jones's "soldierly words" predicted "great days, and greater days still in store for Public School Corps". Back in harness as a schoolmaster, Jones

---

[69] *USM*, February 1900, 1-2 and February 1919, 13; Graham, *Uppingham*, 15.

[70] Newspaper cutting in Scrap-book of Archdeacon Johnson's School, Uppingham, 1874-1906.

[71] *USM*, February 1900, 53 and August 1900, 265.

[72] *USM*, September 1900, 265. This entry caused quite a stir for the editors of the next issue apologised and placed all blame on the magazine's publishers. Then the issue with the retraction was withdrawn from circulation "by orders received from Headquarters". I have been unable to discover whether Headquarters referred to Selwyn or to the military. *USM*, November 1900, 313 and June 1901, 125.

[73] Quoted in Geraldine Hodgson, *The Life of James Elroy Flecker* (Oxford: Blackwell, 1925), 52. Leonard Sedgwick was Captain of School from 1900 to 1902. He won a scholarship to Pembroke College, Cambridge and joined the Indian Civil Service. See *USM*, June 1901, 126.

kept the school informed of progress in the war, told of his own experiences, and reviewed military novels for the school magazine.[74]

Selwyn usually invited senior soldiers to present the prizes at the annual Speech Day; in 1906 this duty fell to General Sir Charles Brunt, a family friend. Brunt had served as British attaché to the Japanese army during the Russo-Japanese campaign of the previous year.[75] His speech to the assembled boys and their parents was recorded in full in the school magazine: his theme was "Patriotism".

> The burning question of the moment is, Is this Empire of ours going to last …? The answer to that question, I submit, rests with the rising generation, with their fathers, with their mothers, and with their instructors. … Play by all manner of means; enjoy yourselves certainly …; but in the midst of all your amusements remember the duty you owe to your King, to your country, and to yourselves. … If there is one thing more certain than another, it is that the nation with the biggest reserves will win the next big war, and the question is, where are we to get these reserves from? … I think I see the dawn of a national army which will give us all the reserves we want if it is only properly carried out, and surely it is a far higher and a far nobler ideal to see the citizens of a great country of their own free will preparing themselves to defend their rights, and the rights of their country, as opposed to any system founded on compulsion. (Hear, hear.) In this respect, Uppingham School has set a noble example, and I am quite convinced that when history comes to be written, not only will the fact not be overlooked, but I am sure it will meet with favourable comment. (Loud continued applause.)

Selwyn responded that the "words would sink into their hearts, into the parents' hearts, the boys' hearts, and the masters' hearts, and that they would bring forth fruit in due season. (Applause)."[76]

In the early years of the new century about half the school was in the corps and by 1905 over a thousand cadets had passed the Uppingham "Recruit Drill and Fire Exercise". To Selwyn the corps was "one of the glories of the school"; to the visiting Lord Roberts, Uppingham's lead was an example to all public schools. Speaking in 1905 at the opening of Uppingham's South African War Memorial, a combined gymnasium and

---

[74] *USM*, July 1901, 154 and December 1901, 325. After the Boer War, Jones played a significant role in the transformation of the Cadet Corps to the Officer Training Corps. He later served with distinction in the Great War: see Timothy Halstead, *A School in Arms: Uppingham and the Great War* (Solihull: Helion, 2017), 138-139.

[75] February 8, 1904 to September 5, 1905.

[76] *USM*, August 1906, 139-145.

concert hall, Roberts congratulated the school on its "very satisfactory results" in the war; 222 Old Uppinghamians fought in South Africa, nine lost their lives. Roberts hoped that other schools would follow Uppingham's lead in making shooting compulsory. Rear-Admiral W. F. S. Mann of the National Service League echoed this praise in the same year when he presented the school with the League's medal for patriotic service.[77]

VII

In the early Selwyn years gymnastics continued much as in the past: the gymnastic classes were still held, and a high standard of work was maintained, but a gradual loss of status saw the end of reports in the *Uppingham School Magazine*.[78] From 1890 just the first three positions in the gymnastic competition were listed in the table for the Athletics Championships.[79] The possibility of building a new gymnasium as a memorial to Robert Hodgkinson was aired in 1890 but nothing materialised.[80] Beisiegel, aged sixty in 1896, did however gain an assistant. W. M. Vardon of the National Society of Physical Education held the post for seven years before leaving to become Director of the St Bride's Gymnasium in London; he was succeeded by R. T. White also of the Society.[81] Beisiegel was closely associated with this professional organisation, becoming its president on three occasions at the turn of the century.[82] It was founded in 1897 with the aim of modifying the German system of gymnastics, as used at Uppingham, to create a British system, partly for patriotic reasons and partly to adopt aspects of the Swedish tradition of free-standing exercises without apparatus that were becoming popular with women and girls.[83] These had been developed by Pehr Henrik Ling in the early nineteenth century.[84]

Jones's appointment as commander of the corps in 1898 led to the immediate introduction of punishment drills for minor offences including

---

[77] *USM*, April 1905, 41-51 and July 1905, 128.
[78] *USM*, June 1888, 180.
[79] *USM*, May 1890, 86.
[80] *USM*, May 1890, 117.
[81] Beisiegel paid the salaries of both assistants: Beisiegel to Monckton, Beisiegel papers.
[82] "Extract from the "Gymnasium", "Men of the Day", etc. – G. H. C. Beisiegel, C. C.", 1902 in the Beisiegel papers.
[83] McIntosh, *Physical Education*, 163.
[84] McIntosh, *Physical Education*, 97-99.

lateness, untidiness, or forgetting books. They were held between first and second schools, and often meant that offenders had to miss breakfast.[85] It is probable that Beisiegel was asked to supervise these drills, and that he refused on the grounds that gymnastics should not be used as a punishment.[86] This stand, and perhaps other disagreements, led Selwyn in May 1902 to dismiss Beisiegel from the teaching staff.[87] Sgt Clunies took over the drills in the short term but, on Beisiegel's departure, they were passed back to his successor. Gymnastics had already lost status in 1900 when it was removed from its coveted position in the scoring system for the athletics championship. Instead, a house "gymnasium competition" was inaugurated and, as the editor to the school magazine noted, gymnastics was "at last … reduced to its proper level".[88] There is no record of the format of this house competition, only the rank order of the top houses.[89]

Selwyn ensured that Beisiegel's *vale* in the school magazine was brief, even insulting:

> Mr Beisiegel has been here 42 years, and during that time, alike in the Music-room and in the Gymnasium, he has done useful work, and been a valued friend to many boys.[90]

The pioneer physical education teacher at an English school, the director of the first school gymnasium, the President of the National Society of Physical Education, and the second-in-command to Paul David in music for thirty-seven years was dismissed in a few words for doing "useful work". The trustees of the school partially atoned for Selwyn's action by awarding Beisiegel an annual pension of £100, and 113 Old Boys added their names to an illuminated testimonial that was presented to Beisiegel in

---

[85] John Gibson, *Reminiscences of a Railwayman* (London: Frederick Books, 1968), 8. Gibson was at Uppingham from 1901 to 1904.

[86] *USM*, October 1898, 263.

[87] Selwyn's decision was made without consulting the trustees. They expressed their dismay in correspondence to Beisiegel but, because he was not a housemaster, they had no authority to challenge the headmaster. Copy of a letter from Beisiegel to Selwyn, May 21, 1902; a copy of Selwyn's reply, May 22, 1902; letters from trustees to Beisiegel, June 1902. Beisiegel papers.

[88] *USM*, February 1900, 3.

[89] For example, *USM*, May 1901, 107.

[90] *USM*, August 1902, 45. Thring had always held Beisiegel in high esteem, as seven letters from Thring to Beisiegel, dated from 1860 to 1886, show: Beisiegel papers. On the headmaster's death in 1887, Marie gave Beisiegel Thring's academic gown as a memento. It is now in UA.

June 1903.[91]

Georg Beisiegel died the following year: the obituary in the *Uppingham School Magazine* by one of his colleagues was generous:

> We regret to announce the death of Mr. G. H. C. Beisiegel, which occurred at his residence on Monday, March 21st, after a short illness. Mr. Beisiegel was at Uppingham for over 40 years, and knew the School when it was far different from what it is now,— knew it when 28 years ago it passed through the great crisis of its history, and took his share in that anxious time. In the public work of town and county he played an unusually active part; while much friendly feeling continued between him and many generations of Old Boys, who will ever hold his name in affectionate remembrance. He was buried in Uppingham Churchyard, on Friday, March 25th, the coffin being carried by those masters who were his colleagues in the School for many years.[92]

VIII

On Beisiegel's departure, Jones, the commanding officer of the corps, assumed the role of "director of the Gymnasium", and a military approach to what was now termed "physical training" began.[93] The military link was strengthened when Staff Sergeant F. A. Wallace was appointed "School Gymnastic Instructor". This was a post common in most public schools. Wallace had been a regular soldier in the Argyll and Sutherland Highlanders since the age of fourteen. After several years of service as a bugler and piper, he transferred to the "Head Quarter Gymnasium" at Aldershot where he attended courses under Colonel Malcolm Fox. Wallace was on the Aldershot staff for eight years, and an instructor with the Lanarkshire Regiment for four more, before arriving at Uppingham.[94] As a non-commissioned officer, Wallace did not have the status of a master: he was an instructor or a "non-commissioned master". For the next sixty years, gymnastics and swimming in the school were taught by ex-service instructors, whilst the management of the instructors, gymnasium and swimming bath was directed by a master with no physical education qualifications and no experience of teaching the subject.

---

[91] Equivalent to £11,000 in 2018. A copy of the testimonial is in the Beisiegel papers.

[92] *USM,* April 1904, 94. The "public work" refers to his role as one of the town's elected representatives on Rutland County Council. This aspect of his life received warm praise in his obituary in the *Grantham Journal*, March 26, 1904.

[93] *USM*, October 1902, 223.

[94] The information comes from Wallace's *vale* in 1912. *USM*, October 1912, 188.

Wallace's appointment coincided with national developments in physical education. Colonel Fox had relinquished his position at Aldershot to join the Board of Education as Inspector of Physical Training. His brief was to implement the new *Model Course of Physical Training 1902*, to encourage the introduction of military drill as detailed in *Infantry Training 1902*, a handbook prepared by the War Office, and to appoint men who had been trained by him at Aldershot to do the work in schools. Peter McIntosh judged that the army's influence on physical education was unfortunate in several respects:

> In the first place the training of instructors in the Army was entirely restricted to N.C.O.s. ... N.C.O.s in those days were ill-educated and when they were projected into schools 'drill' came to be regarded as well beneath the dignity of the trained school teacher. ... Colonel Fox's instructors, once appointed, persisted in their work, even into the nineteen-twenties. ... They were faithful servants ... but were so lacking in intelligence that not even further courses could equip them adequately for physical education in schools.
>
> Another unfortunate result of army influence in schools was in the nature of the drill imposed. Whilst the London School Board and other authorities [including girls' public schools] had fostered and developed the Swedish system, the Army was still using barrack square drill and a haphazard collection of exercises without order or system ... The introduction, therefore, of the model course of 1902 was for many schools a retrograde step.[95]

IX

Following the proposal of Stanley Christopherson at the Old Boys' Dinner in 1903, the school's trustees decided that the proposed South African War Memorial would be a dual-use building, the Paul David Memorial Concert Room and a new Gymnasium.[96] The building was opened with military pomp and ceremony by Field Marshal Earl Roberts on March 30, 1905.[97] The new gymnasium, just to the east of the swimming bath, was vastly different from its predecessor. The former fixed German/MacLaren apparatus was replaced with portable pieces so that the large floor area could be cleared for marching, drilling, free-standing exercises and

---

[95] McIntosh, *Physical Education*, 148-150. It should be noted that McIntosh was also the Senior Inspector of Physical Education in London.
[96] *USM*, February 1903, 4.
[97] *USM*, April, 1905, 41ff.

concerts.[98] The inter-house gymnastic competition, soon to gain the Whitehead Cup, was based on squad drilling and "Free Gymnastics", callisthenic exercises performed in unison.[99] In Jones's words, the supreme aim of gymnastics was the "learning to obey a word of command, moving smartly and accurately the instant the word is given".[100] "In", "Out", "Up", "Down", "Steady" would be the only sounds as Wallace led forty or fifty boys dressed in spotless flannels through their "different military evolutions".[101] Gymnastics was now a team sport and, like football and cricket, would inspire *esprit de corps*. Wallace also taught boxing, never permitted at Thring's school: "No Englishman's training", wrote Jones, "is complete before he has learnt to face an opponent in single combat."[102]

---

[98] On the completion of the new Sports Centre in 1970, the building was converted to a theatre.
[99] *USM*, March 1906, 45-46.
[100] *USM*, March 1906, 56.
[101] *USM*, April 1904, 83.
[102] *USM*, April 1907, 69.

CHAPTER SEVENTEEN

THE ATHLETOCRACY RULES: "CONFORM OR BE KICKED"

I

Uppingham's trustees eventually came to regret giving Selwyn unlimited power to propel Uppingham to the top table of public schools, but it was the mass of boys below the athletocracy who suffered the consequences of that rush for fame. The *vale* on Selwyn's retirement in 1907 recorded: "We [Uppingham] were still very much in the rough, and to him fell the task of smoothing out that roughness".[1] If this meant that he had turned Thring's unique school into a conventional and conservative public school, then Selwyn did indeed smooth out that roughness. No matter what criterion was applied, Uppingham was now on that elite list. But the price paid was high: Charles Paget Wade, later a renowned architect, labelled the school the "Tiny World of Limited Vision".[2] Athleticism swelled, militarism flourished, morality slipped, and the Thringian ideal of manliness became the Selwyn goal "to fear God, to speak the truth, and to shoot straight".[3] The rapid growth of the school was a prime cause of the change in ethos, reaching a peak of 440 after 1900, and the type of boy changed too. No longer were most parents from professional backgrounds, attracted to the school by Thring's reputation, but many were "the newly rich from Yorkshire and Lancashire" who sought any public school education for their sons.[4]

The relationship between boys and masters became more formal. Paget Wade noted it: "An impossible icy gulf was placed between the Masters and the Boys and no speech passed between them outside the

---

[1] *USM*, December 1907, 289.
[2] Paget Wade was at Uppingham from 1897 to December 1900. See Michael Jessop, *Days Far Away: Memories of Charles Paget Wade* (Tewksbury: National Trust, 1996), 68.
[3] Rome, Uppingham, 99.
[4] Christopher Nevinson, *Paint and Prejudice* (London: Methuen, 1937), 10.

classroom".[5] The housemasters had changed too: where once housemasters' families had several young children adding to the domesticity, now there were few and the old homeliness had gone.[6] The Sunday liberty, so vital to Thring's philosophy, was replaced with chapel morning and afternoon, and "Sunday Questions" for the spare moments.[7] Christopher Nevinson, later the celebrated war artist, was a boy in the school immediately after the Boer War; he "attended endless divine services; listened to strange sermons by doctors of divinity in which Englishmen were confused with God, Nelson with Jesus Christ, Lady Hamilton with the Virgin Mary".[8] The habit of roaming the countryside disappeared on what James Flecker termed "about the busiest day in the whole week." [9]

The cult of athleticism joined forces with the new militarism, and the virtues of Tom Brown were extolled to the boys alongside those of Lords Roberts and Kitchener. Nevinson recalled that "the main object of the boys … undoubtedly was cricket and perhaps rugby football", and he witnessed the school bathed in "appalling jingoism".[10] Boys in their house XI or XV were excused fagging, and only rarely did other than the talented games player reach the rank of praepostor. The Captain of Games became the post of real authority and even masters were seen to judge a boy's ability solely on his athletic prowess.[11] Charles Raven, later an eminent Cambridge theologian, recalled how moral goodness was equated exactly with games prowess, that Christianity was at a low ebb, and "good form" became the all-pervading ethos.[12] Flecker looked back on his Uppingham experiences in *The Grecians: A Dialogue on Education*. He noted that games' coaching was limited to the star players while the "athletic dullards" like himself played out interminable games without

---

[5] Jessop, *Paget Wade*, 66.

[6] The census returns for 1891 and 1901 show 1 and 3 bachelor housemasters, 7 and 6 in Holy Orders, and 14 and 9 children under 7. The figures were 0, 10 and 22 in 1871.

[7] Sunday Questions were divinity work set by Selwyn; biblical research lasting two hours was needed to answer the five to seven questions. A notebook belonging to William Gibson, in school 1890 to 1892, lists many of the questions (UA); *USM*, March 1898, 70.

[8] Nevinson was at Uppingham from 1903 to 1907. Selwyn was a doctor of divinity! Nevinson, *Paint*, 7.

[9] Hodgson, *Flecker*, 46.

[10] Nevinson, *Paint*, 7-8.

[11] *USM*, July 1895, 190 and 1933, 50; Hodgson, *Flecker*, 54, 59.

[12] Raven was at the school from 1898 to 1904: Raven, *Wanderer*, 9, 16.

guidance merely as occupation, or spent whole afternoons watching school matches by compulsion. Physical education had been "perverted".[13]

Selwyn showed no interest in his pastoral responsibilities, nor did he seek to influence the policy in the houses. The baize-covered door between the private side and the boys' side in each of the boarding houses was closed and the reign of the "swell" began.[14] Harold Howitt recalled "I arrived at Uppingham [1901] at a period of very low morality".[15] Paget Wade had similar memories: "I was imprisoned in LORNE HOUSE ... a loathsome murder-hole atmosphere hung about it".[16] It still had the reputation of being the unruliest house a decade later.[17] Praepostors would beat boys for not cheering at football matches; and from their bicycles would whip dawdlers on house runs. Boys were bullied, coerced and tortured for the diversion of the swells. Nevinson, next door in the headmaster's house, was "kicked, hounded, caned, flogged, hairbrushed, morning, noon and night".[18] If two boys of unequal ages and different houses were seen speaking, immorality was taken for granted; sexuality was driven underground, passion became distorted, and there grew a "dirty delight in illicit acts".[19]

The inscription over the Tudor school-room at Uppingham reads, in a translation of the Latin, "let no foul word or sight approach a house which holds a boy". Henry Bothamley, a historian of the school, believed that this sentence "ought to have been in front of the H-M and his staff in blazing letters".[20] Bothamley was at Uppingham from 1897 to 1902, the same period as Flecker, Nevinson, Howitt, Paget Wade and Raven. Harry Lyon, John Gibson, Frank Savery and William King were also at the

---

[13] James Flecker, *The Grecians: A Dialogue on Education* (London: J. M. Dent, 1910), 54, 57, 59.

[14] A school poet offered this advice to new boys: "The title 'Blood', I'll first of all explain, / Is won by excellence at any game; / For ev'ry new boy must at once be taught / To hold all work as but a thing of naught. / 'Tis games alone can win the schoolboy fame / And make his comrades all revere his name. / And so one purpose fills the minds of all, / But to excel at cricket or football." (And so on for another thirty-two lines.) *USM*, July 1907, 135-136.

[15] Quoted in Matthews, *By God's Grace,* 130.

[16] Jessop, *Paget Wade*, 66.

[17] From the biography of Eric Dorman-Smith, the future general: Lavinia Greacen, *Chink: A Biography* (London: Macmillan, 1989), 17.

[18] Nevinson, *Paint*, 7-9.

[19] Raven, *Wanderer*, 28.

[20] Letter from Henry Bothamley to William Westray, November 4, 1948 (UA). See Bothamley, *Some Notes*.

school at this time and their observations match those already cited.[21] Paget Wade thought that the school's motto should have been "Boys are the lowest form of animal life".[22] These ten Old Boys span six houses and sixteen years, so the laxity in discipline was not restricted to "a bad house in a bad time". A rot had set in and soon numbers in the school began to fall. From 1899 onwards the trustees and Selwyn were increasingly at loggerheads: breaking point was reached in March 1906 when the trustees were appalled at the nature of Selwyn's punishment of a boy and incensed by his desire to withhold the facts. His resignation was demanded; in 1907 Selwyn retired to Hindhead to follow his theological studies.[23]

II

Games now played an enormous part in the life of all public school boys, and the chief ambition for many was distinction in sport. Boys felt that "the swiftest and surest way to eminence is through athletics". The most prominent games player was in practice head of school and his position was "more absolute than the Pope's". The veneration with which boys regarded their heroes was such that George Lyttelton, nephew of the Haileybury headmaster, could write:

> [the] body of the school are far more interested in the prowess of the school eleven than in playing the game themselves. For days before the principal school match, excitement is at fever heat; during the match itself all other games are left off, the whole school assemble round the protagonists to yell themselves hoarse with delight or dismay, and the excitement takes some time to settle down.[24]

Manliness for many was now acquired second-hand and by association.

The games master was both a product of the system and a prime factor in its continuance. The legend that a cricket Blue, on completing his century in the 'Varsity match at Lord's, received five telegrams from headmasters offering him posts, may not have been true, but it was

---

[21] See letter to Henry Bothamley from Harry Lyon, August 1, 1949 (UA); Gibson, *Railwayman*, 8; for Savery, see John Sherwood, *No Golden Journey* (London: Heinemann, 1973), 15; for King see Halstead, *Great War*, 46.
[22] Jessop, *Paget Wade*, 66.
[23] *Trustees Minute Book*: March 1899; April 1899; March 1900; March 1906; and October 1906 (UA). See also Matthews, *By God's Grace*, 120ff.
[24] Schoolmasters, *Public Schools*, 192, 195; Arthur Benson, *The Schoolmaster* (London: John Murray, 1902), 97. Both Lyttelton and Benson were Eton masters.

believable. Parents too not only supported the games ethos and lobbied headmasters for more matches and London tours, but also worshipped the games player. Arthur Gilkes, the headmaster of Dulwich College, recalled dining with a parent

> who after dinner said to me, with some feeling in his tone, that he had that day taken his son for the first time to ---, naming a great school, and that he had taken the opportunity given him by the parting to offer the boy the best advice in his power. I said that the occasion was well chosen ... for then his heart was soft and open, and thus he would receive and remember what was said. The father agreed with me, and said that the advice which he had given his boy was to take up bowling rather than batting as likely really to be of more service to him.[25]

Parents, staff and boys were agreed that games were a vital and central feature of school life. Edward Mack's conclusion is apt: "the religion of athletics seems the perfect expression of a Philistine age".[26]

The increase of the athletic ethos at the public schools in the 1890s and 1900s, and at Uppingham in particular, took place against a growing national obsession for competitive sport. Games were now part of the culture for both the gentleman and the working-man. Special papers were published for the separate sports; the respected reviews contained summaries of the sporting seasons; and most men and boys immediately turned to the sports pages of their newspapers. A cult of participation was becoming a cult of the spectator. Sport even began to displace other news on the front page, as Arthur Benson, an Eton housemaster, noted:

> It is apt to disconcert the philosophical mind to find a leading evening paper displacing the war news (1900) for a column, introduced by prodigious headlines, recording the performance of an English team of cricketers in Australia.[27]

III

Many of Thring's cherished aims were abandoned during his successor's tenure at Uppingham and in those first years of the new century Thring would have found little to connect the Uppingham of the so-called Golden

---

[25] Arthur Gilkes, "The Worship of Athletics," *National Review*, September 1897, 77.

[26] Mack, *Public Schools*, 338.

[27] Arthur Benson, *The Schoolmaster* (London: John Murray, 1902), 96.

Age of public schools with the school he had created fifty years before.[28]
But is it fair to denigrate Selwyn when perhaps all he did was conform to
the standards of his time? Thring came to Uppingham in a period ripe for
educational innovation, and in mid-Victorian England a headmaster as
strong as Thring could, and did, set his own course without much
reference to the accepted public schools. In that isolated market town in
the heart of the Rutland countryside, it was perhaps relatively easy for
Thring to fashion his own school, and then to set and attain his own ideal
of manliness.

Selwyn had to face problems in late Victorian and Edwardian England
that Thring would have been glad to have been spared. The country was
now brash, noisy and materialistic. With 30,000 boys in the public schools
of 1900, there were more boys than ever but headmasters had to be more
business-like in their operation to compete for them. The rise or fall in
numbers did much to reflect parental popularity and a sharp drop in
numbers, as Selwyn found, could settle the fate of an ailing headmaster.
The competition may have made a headmaster's position more precarious
but the boom brought the schools comparative collective immunity from
outside criticism. They were confident in their purpose and of their ability
to realise it, and this confidence was not shaken until the later Edwardian
years when the economic depression after the Boer War and the impact of
the new industrial strength of Germany brought about a liberal onslaught
on these conservative bastions of privilege. But before these factors took
their toll, this was the greatest time for public schools; so, in an age of
crushing conformity, perhaps Selwyn did no more than conform.[29]

Certainly Selwyn conformed to the accepted pattern of the public
school headmaster, a pattern seen both in fiction and in reality. In *Good-
bye Mr Chips*, Ralston, the new young headmaster, is efficient, ruthless
and ambitious; as he glides around the school in his rustling silk gown, a
sartorial necessity for headmasters, he exudes confidence with a pontifical
air.[30] Herbert James was headmaster at Rugby at the turn of the century,
and regarded by a boy of the period as "outwardly an impressive figure in
the fashion of his time". James's punishments were remembered as "quite

---

[28] The earliest use that I have found of the term Golden Age to refer to public
schools in the late Victorian and Edwardian period is in Thomas Worsley,
Barbarians and Philistines (London: Robert Hale, 1940), 85.
[29] "There is no doubting the collective corporate conformism of Imperial Harrow":
Tyerman, *Harrow*, 397.
[30] James Hilton, *Good-bye Mr Chips* (London: Hodder & Stoughton, 1934), 65, 70.
Hilton was a boy at The Leys, Cambridge, c1911-c1918.

primitive".[31] James Welldon, headmaster of Harrow from 1885 to 1898, flogged an average of a hundred boys each year.[32] Bertram Pollock, headmaster of Wellington, was worshipped by his sixth-form but feared by the rest of the school, and perhaps by the staff. To the smaller boys, Harold Nicolson remembered, he appeared as a distant and majestic figure; robed in silk, it was said, to make a visible distinction between himself and his subordinates. Punishments were severe, and years later Pollock could still recall with sadistic pleasure what he had set for a boy who misbehaved at the end of a term:

> A boy would be sent for to see me after breakfast and I would then tell him I was busy for the morning and he would come back before lunch. The other boys had left at 7 a. m., and he had a very dull and desolate morning.[33]

If the headmasters had changed since mid-Victorian times, so too had the boys and their parents. From about 1900 boys from homes of the *nouveaux riches* arrived in droves to make fashionable friends and to become gentlemen. Compared to his predecessor, the public school boy of 1900 was pampered in terms of food and clothing, furniture and fittings, and, above all, in pocket money. Dressiness and an over-appreciation of sartorial splendour became commonplace in the schools.[34]

The growing regimentation of school life and the attendant erosion of a boy's individuality, factors noted in the late Victorian public school, continued in the new century. Still more time was given to studies, to games, and to other organised activities, and less time was available for a boy's own disposal. At Rugby, the whole town was out of bounds, including places of worship, and mid-afternoon call-overs ensured that no boy could wander too far. Sunday afternoon chapel prevented long country walks, and for some its retention was a bastion of morality. As housemasters relinquished the pastoral role that had been the norm in the past, and now rarely penetrated the boys' part of the house beyond the dining hall, so the general running of the school fell on the prefects.[35] New boys at Harrow were forced to box to amuse their elders; pretty boys were

---

[31] James Simpson, *Schoolmaster's Harvest* (London: Faber & Faber, 1954), 76.

[32] Tyerman, *Harrow*, 365.

[33] David Newsome, *A History of Wellington College* (London: John Murray, 1959), 253-257.

[34] Arthur Ponsonby, *The Decline of the Aristocracy* (London: T. F. Unwin, 1912), 205-206. John Galsworthy labelled the schools "caste factories": quoted in Tyerman, *Harrow*, 356.

[35] Simpson, *Harvest*, 61, 63, 67.

in high demand as fags; and violent initiation rites were rife.[36] In many schools this prefectorial power evolved into an absolute monarchy with, as at Harrow and Wellington, positive encouragement from the headmaster: the rule of the bloods was in earnest. The individual average boy, as Nicolson recalled, nearly sank without trace:

> At Wellington ... one ceased to be an individual, to have any but a corporate identity, that the question scarcely arose whether one might or might not be odd. One was just a name, or rather a number on the list. The authorities in their desire to deprive us of all occasion for illicit intercourse deprived us of all occasion for any intercourse at all. We were not allowed to consort with boys not in our own house: a house consisted of thirty boys of whom ten at least were too old and ten too young for friendship; and thus during those four years my training in human relationships was confined to the ten boys who happened more or less to be my contemporaries. In addition, one was deprived of all initiative of action or occupation. The masters took pride in feeling that not only did they know what any given boy should be doing at that particular moment, but that they knew exactly what the said boy would be doing at 3.30 p.m. six weeks hence. We thus had no privacy and no leisure, there was never open to us the choice between two possible alternatives.[37]

IV

Games continued to be an important part of the process of occupation and regimentation. As the new century progressed, so more time was given to games and matters athletic dominated schoolboy thought, as Robert Bruce Lockhart remembered: "Everyone *still* talked sport; in fact, talked more sport than ever".[38] Little had changed in the purpose of school sport: in 1885 Lord Harris wrote of the qualities of command and leadership that games instilled; fifteen years later, and now President of the MCC, he expounded in the same manner at a Dulwich speech day. In Harris's view, the public school had two aims: first, to make a boy a good citizen so that he might maintain England's honour and uphold the dignity of the British

---

[36] Tyerman, *Harrow*, 369.

[37] Harold Nicolson, *Some People* (London: Constable, 1927), 31; Tyerman, *Harrow*, 373.

[38] The emphasis is in the original: Robert Bruce Lockhart, *Your England* (London: Putnam, 1955), 42. Bruce Lockhart was at Fettes College, Edinburgh, c1898-c1905.

flag; secondly, to ensure that each boy got as much exercise as possible.[39] In this period of relative immunity from criticism, games as an institution went untroubled. Kipling's outburst in *The Islanders* on "muddied oafs" and "flannelled fools" had not been universally well-received, for it was read as an affront to values which were widely shared, but one cannot but smile at Harold Nicolson's picture of such a hero:

> A tall figure, he seemed, in his black and orange jersey striped as a wasp. Upon his carefully oiled hair was stuck a little velvet cap with a gold tassel; he would walk away from the field, his large red hands pendant, a little mud upon his large red knees. He would pause for a moment and speak to a group of lower boys. 'Yes, Marstock, – no, Marstock', they would answer, and then he would smile democratically, and walk on – a slight lilt in his gait betraying that he was not unconscious of how much he was observed.

> How clean he was, how straight, how manly! How proud we were of him, how modest he was about himself. And then those eyes – those frank and honest eyes. 'One can see,' my tutor said, 'that Marstock has never had a mean or nasty thought' ... It took me six years to realise that Marstock, although stuffed with opinions, had never had a thought at all.[40]

Edmond Warre's call in 1900 to the Headmasters' Conference to establish cadet corps in all public schools was answered swiftly. In the late 1890s only twelve per cent of all public school boys were in the corps, but soon it was to grow to more than a half.[41] Many advocated that all boys should be taught the rudiments of weapon training and should learn how to shoot, and in quick succession Harrow, Rossall, Glenalmond, Repton, Dover and Wellington followed Uppingham's universal call to arms.[42] At first the corps rated poorly when compared to games but gradually the corps gained status and time, and by 1905 it rated as highly as any game. The Boer War helped to change attitudes but much of the credit was due to the skilful propaganda of the advocates, headmasters such as Warre at

---

[39] *Contemporary Review*, July 1885, 121; *The Alleynian*, November 1900, 262, quoted in John Mallea, "The Boys' Endowed Grammar Schools in Victorian England: The Educational Use of Sport" (PhD diss., Columbia University, 1971), 171.

[40] Nicolson, *People*, 33, 44.

[41] At Clifton in 1901 more than half the boys were in the corps, three years before the peak. Charles Cornish, "A Chance for the Public Schools", *National Review,* March 1900, 82; Christie, *Clifton*, 246.

[42] Schoolmasters, *Public Schools*, 214; Newsome, *Wellington*, 249.

Eton, Cyril Norwood at Bristol Grammar School (and later Marlborough
and Harrow) and John Way at Rossall, all of whom had actually
commanded school corps. The cries of militarism were stifled with strong
protestations of peaceful intent and of service to the community; more
importantly, the corps was offered to the boys and parents in the manner
that Kipling advocated, as if it were a game. Character-training overtones
that had earlier been the preserve of games were readily attached to corps
activities.[43] It comes as no surprise to find the term "manly" attached to
them:

> The voluntary submission to a sound military training, as a duty,
> for the good of their country, and the defence of those near and
> dear, may indeed be said to lay a sound foundation for the finest
> type of Christian manliness.[44]

In the conservative public school world, where there is no house like the
house, and no school like the school, the narrow, local patriotism of *esprit
de corps* was easily extended to the corps.

The first years of the new century saw the public schools at the peak of
their popularity. They were full; they were respected; they educated
royalty as never before; they were relatively free of criticism. Their speech
days were magnificent, their ceremonials were grand. They were the very
picture of conservative, imperialist, Edwardian England. But, as David
Newsome found when writing on the Pollock period at Wellington,
appearances were deceptive: the life of the average boy was not as
glowing as painted; and the gloss and glamour hid the true health of the
school. The Golden Age was less solid gold and more a thin film.
Newsome's predicament over Pollock can legitimately be extended to
many headmasters. The Edwardian headmaster may have given his school
a bit of polish and a grace of manner, the *gravitas* of a leisured gentleman
and the *dignitas* in outward appearance to match it, but beneath the surface
all was not well. "Conform or be kicked", as Arnold Lunn declared in *The
Harrovians*, was the command that should have been written over the
portals of every public school.[45] These years saw the destruction of the
individual boy and his absorption into the group type; the acceptance of

---

[43] Cyril Norwood and Arthur Hope, *Higher Education of Boys in England*
(London: John Murray, 1909), 446; Cornish, "Public Schools," 82.
[44] Schoolmasters, *Public Schools*, 210.
[45] Arnold Lunn, *The Harrovians* (London: Methuen, 1913), 70. Tyerman, the Harrow
historian, reckoned that "conformity was athleticism's triumph": Tyerman,
Harrow, 340.

the materialism and snobbery of the *nouveaux riches*; the peak in athleticism; and the noisy rattle of militaristic imperialism.

Selwyn and Uppingham were perhaps no more than a typical headmaster and a typical school; but the contrast with the Thring years is stark.[46]

---

[46] Bryan Matthews, in his history of Uppingham, gives the chapter on the Selwyn years the title, "Following the Fashion": Matthews, *By God's Grace*, 117.

CHAPTER EIGHTEEN

EARLY LEGACY, 1889-1930:
"WE NOW RECOGNISE MORE CLEARLY THAT EDUCATION IS CONCERNED WITH THE WHOLE HUMAN-BEING"

I

The Schools Inquiry Commission of the late 1860s, led by Lord Taunton, examined all the secondary schools that lay between the great public schools and those which educated children from the labouring classes. The Endowed Schools Act of August 1869 that resulted from the Taunton Commission's recommendations was then applied to all schools that were wholly or partly maintained by means of any endowment, except for the Clarendon Nine. Many headmasters of the new public schools were outraged that the older foundations were receiving special treatment and their agitation led to the foundation of the Headmasters' Conference. Twelve of the thirty-seven headmasters invited by Thring assembled for its first meeting at Uppingham in December that year. No invitations had been sent to the headmasters of the Clarendon Nine.[1]

Thring explained his stance in a letter to Hugo Harper, the headmaster of Sherborne:

> For my part I desire to separate my lot entirely from the fashionable schools, and to cast it in, come weal come woe, with the earnest working men, and smaller schools, which one may hope to see doing honest work.[2]

The exclusion of the Nine was raised at the Uppingham conference. Thring's diary records:

---

[1] For more on Thring's role in the founding of the Headmasters' Conference, see Richardson, *Thring*, 108-115.

[2] Letter from Thring to Harper, January 18, 1869. Quoted in Parkin, *Life*, 1:171.

Dr. _____ wished to make concession to try and bring in the great
schools, and tack us on to them. I laid down plainly that I thought it was
simple death to do so; we rested on our vitality and work, they on their
prestige and false glory: if they would meet us on common ground, well
and good; if not, not.[3]

The minutes of the meeting identify Steuart Pears of Repton as the Doctor
and they record more on Thring's objections:

Our schools depend entirely on the vitality of progressive work; ... Eton ...
has wonderful powers of a certain kind and earnest men using that power;
but [in] progressive work, we stand better than they; more alive to the
necessity of it; comparatively unfettered in carrying out our discoveries,
and we do carry them out more effectively.[4]

Pears did not press the point and the matter was dropped.[5]

Thring's commitment to progressive schooling continued for the
remainder of his life and in the 1880s he was called upon to expand on his
ideas and methods to trainee teachers, practising teachers and teacher
trainers: he addressed conferences, wrote articles and produced a
celebrated book, *Theory and Practice of Teaching*. Then, in 1885, he
invited the Association of Headmistresses to hold its 1887 gathering at
Uppingham. The ladies came, but not before Thring had issued a challenge
to Frances Buss and Dorothea Beale, headmistresses of North London
Collegiate School and Cheltenham Ladies' College respectively, to "do
something to reform our wretched Education (so called)".[6]

It is surely more than mere coincidence that the birth of what came to
be called "the progressive school movement" occurred in the late 1880s,
and almost in Thring's lifetime. Abbotsholme, the first progressive school,
was founded in 1889, less than two years after Thring's death. Like
Uppingham in the early Thring years, Abbotsholme and its direct and
indirect successors, were innovative schools, created to counter the

---

[3] Diary, December 18, 1869 (Parkin, *Life*, 1:207).
[4] Quoted in Alicia Percival, *The Origins of the Headmasters' Conference* (London:
John Murray, 1969), 40-41.
[5] The headmasters of Winchester and Shrewsbury asked to attend the second
conference at Sherborne in 1870, Eton joined in 1871, and the remainder of the
Nine followed over the course of the decade. Diary, January 10, 1871 (Parkin, *Life*,
1:208).
[6] Diary, May 8, 1887. For more on these themes, see Richardson, *Thring*, 254-261,
305-307.

conformity of the traditional public schools. They provided a lifeline for Thring's theory and practice in physical education.

II

Cecil Reddie, the founder of Abbotsholme, was the first of a new generation of educational radicals. There are many similarities between Reddie and Thring. Both had a deep belief in the Platonic whole-man concept of education, both admired Ruskin, and both were much influenced by German educational thought. After schooling at Fettes College and graduation from Edinburgh University in 1878, Reddie gained a doctorate in chemistry at Göttingen University six years later. Both were autocrats, both had battles with their masters and their governing bodies (or partners in Reddie's case), and both tolerated no outside influence. Like Thring, Reddie hated sophisticated luxury, loathed a slovenly posture, and enjoyed long rambles in the countryside. He was seen by one biographer as the embodiment of *mens sana in corpore sano*.[7]

The New School at Abbotsholme was founded as a protest against what Reddie viewed as the rapid degeneration of England; the remedy was to lie in the abandoning of all that was cramping and conformist in the public school curriculum that he had encountered when teaching back at Fettes and later at Clifton, and the adoption of all that could be individualistic and aesthetic.[8] Compulsory games were an immediate target: they would be limited to two afternoons a week, compulsory watching of matches was denounced, and other interests were brought in to destroy athletic "shop" as the only talk between boys.[9] The other interests reflected the strong influence of Ruskin's thought on Reddie's practice. Building, hay-making and general estate work were afternoon activities and much time in the curriculum was devoted to craft-work. Further evidence of Ruskin's and Thring's belief in an aesthetic education is seen in the importance Reddie attached to a freedom to roam the surrounding Derbyshire countryside and on the care he bestowed on the architecture of school buildings and on the decoration of the chapel and classrooms.[10] His concern for physical health and hygiene was even

---

[7] Johannes Giesber, *Cecil Reddie and Abbotsholme* (Nijmegen: Centrale Drukkerij N.V., 1970), 49.

[8] The New School title was dropped after the first year. Bernard Ward, *Reddie of Abbotsholme* (London: Allen & Unwin, 1934), 176.

[9] Ward, *Reddie*, 116; William Stewart, *Progressives and Radicals in English Education 1750-1970* (London: Macmillan, 1972), 146.

[10] Stewart, *Progressives*, 147; Ward, *Reddie*, 60, 67-68, 152-153.

stronger than Thring's and owed more to the influence of Almond: a wholesome diet, a ban on tuck, and the adoption of "sensible" clothing all show the Loretto trade-mark. Hygiene was taught in class; there was a carefully conceived physical education programme in which every boy's weight and height were logged; and the encouragement of positive health rather than just responding to illness and injury prevailed.[11]

<h1 style="text-align:center">III</h1>

One of Reddie's first appointments to the staff of Abbotsholme was John Badley. He had been a boy at Rugby in the 1880s and there felt the full brunt of its philistine education. After graduating in 1889 with a first in classics from Trinity College, Cambridge, Badley determined to do his best to remedy the traditional public school educational malaise, and Abbotsholme seemed to be the best means. He was in sympathy with almost all Reddie's philosophy, and he worked hard for the success of the new school, but there was one marked disagreement: the female sex. Badley wished to get married, Reddie could not abide women; the engaged couple wanted the school to become co-educational, Reddie would not tolerate the arrival of girls. The result was that Badley left Abbotsholme in 1892 and the following year opened his own school, Bedales, in Sussex with just three boys. Two more of Reddie's masters followed in 1902.[12]

At first Bedales just took boys but in 1898 it admitted girls and thus became one of the first co-educational boarding schools in Britain. By 1900 the school had grown to 240 and this necessitated a move to new premises in Petersfield in Hampshire to allow for further expansion. Bedales was true to Abbotsholme's fundamental principles, and Badley added to them ingredients taken from the educational theories of Maria Montessori and Friedrich Froebel, and also from the practice of Robert Baden-Powell's Boy Scouts.[13] In addition, through the early appointment of Oswald Powell to his staff, Badley gained direct contact with Thring's Uppingham; Powell had been a boy in Thring's last years, 1881 to 1886. After Cambridge and a spell of teaching at Manchester Grammar School, Powell had "cast about to find some school that might be putting into practice the ideas Thring had in mind when he founded Uppingham without being frustrated, as he was, by the medieval layout and traditions

---

[11] Ward, *Reddie*, 27, 66, 208, 211.

[12] John Badley, *A Schoolmaster's Testament* (Oxford: Blackwell, 1937), 60-62; Stewart, *Progressives*, 151.

[13] John Badley, *Memories and Reflections* (London: G. Allen & Unwin, 1955), 165.

of the Public School".[14] Powell's eye fell on Bedales and together as headmaster and second-master, Badley and Powell served their lives' work at the school.[15]

Bedales was firmly founded on the whole-man philosophy:

> Scholarship, good breeding, and leadership no longer form the whole of our educational idea. We now recognise more clearly that education is concerned with the whole human-being, on every side of his nature, and cannot neglect any of his activities and needs.[16]

The Ruskin influences were there: many of the school's facilities were built by the pupils and estate work was tackled by all. Craft-work, art, music and drama all flourished as part of the curriculum and not just as extra-curricular activities: here Badley cited Thring's influence.[17] Rambling in the countryside was encouraged and camps modelled on Baden-Powell's practice were introduced in the early 1900s to facilitate this union with nature. Badley was one of the first headmasters to bring the wider possibilities of outdoor activities into the regular curriculum.[18]

Badley visited Loretto and on his return to Bedales adopted several of Almond's principles: the introduction of a wholesome diet; a ban on tuck; and the wearing of "sensible" forms of dress. He recognised that games were not enjoyed by all and so a variety of physical activities was introduced together with many non-sporting alternatives. Games were held on two afternoons a week, with two more given to outdoor manual work.[19] Gymnastics was to have an important role and, through the appointment of Reginald Roper in 1913, Badley made the greatest contribution to curricular physical education since Thring's appointment of Georg Beisiegel in 1860.[20] Roper had spent two years at the Royal Central Gymnastic Institute in Stockholm where he fully absorbed the Swedish gymnastic tradition. On his return to England in 1910 he taught at Edward Lyttelton's Eton for three years; then, a year before the outbreak of the

---

[14] Quoted in Gyles Brandeth and Sally Henry, *John Haden Badley* (Bournemouth: Bedales Society, 1967), 22.

[15] Pupils at Bedales called Powell "Oz Boz".

[16] Badley, *Testament*, 30.

[17] Badley, *Testament*, 49, 55, 60; Brandeth and Henry, *Badley*, 11, 37.

[18] Badley, *Testament*, 145; Brandeth and Henry, *Badley*, 12, 29.

[19] Badley, *Testament*, 80.

[20] Swedish gymnastics, performed in the open air, was included in Badley's 1900 prospectus. John Badley, *Bedales School: Outline of its Aims and System* (Cambridge: Cambridge University Press, 1900), 39.

Great War, he arrived at Bedales.[21] With Badley's encouragement, Roper put into practice the philosophy that physical education was not just games and gymnastics but also all those aspects that would later be known as health education. Diet, clothing and hours of rest all came under Roper's supervision. Weights and measures were regularly logged, checks were made on posture and feet, and remedial exercises were prescribed for those in need. Roper was convinced that Platonic "gymnastic" was one of the two ingredients of life, a view expounded in his 1915 publication *Physical Education in Relation to School Life.*[22]

Thus the ingredients of Thring's ideal of manliness and his commitment to a sane and balanced physical education entered the twentieth century under the banner of The New School Movement. Though it is highly unlikely that Thring would ever have contemplated admitting girls to Uppingham, he would have been pleased that their education at Bedales matched that of the boys and that they too experienced an education of the whole man.[23] What the old public schools no longer valued, the new progressive schools adopted wholeheartedly.

IV

A second direct line from Thring's Uppingham can be traced to Gresham's School at Holt in Norfolk. George Howson, who taught chemistry and physics to the Uppingham schoolboy diarist, Reginald Grove, joined the school in 1886 specifically to be under Thring but he was granted just one year before the headmaster's death. He stayed on under Selwyn, finding as time elapsed that his position became increasingly uncomfortable. He felt very much the odd man out: the only Oxonian in a Common Room dominated by Cambridge men; a scientist in a non-scientific atmosphere; and a poor games player in a school where such prowess now meant so much.[24] Life at Uppingham brought Howson no pleasure: he disliked the sharp boundary that had developed between boys and masters, he feared the growth of athleticism, and he felt that boys were left far too much to

---

[21] PEA, *Nine Pioneers in Physical Education* (London: Physical Education Association, 1964), 37-38.
[22] Badley, *Testament*, 34, 63; Reginald Roper, *Physical Education in Relation to School Life* (London: George Allen and Unwin, 1915), passim.
[23] In the last year of his life, 1887, Thring was an ardent supporter of Uppingham High School for Girls, an initiative of the daughters of Georg Beisiegel. It opened in January 1888. See Malcolm Tozer, "Thring's 'favourite wish'," 363-372.
[24] Grove judged him a poor cricketer; Grove diaries, May 26, 1887. Later Grove sent his own son to Gresham's.

their own devices in the boarding houses. When the Gresham's headmastership became vacant in 1900, he left to make a fresh start in a school that had no adverse traditions to hamper him.

Howson's move to Gresham's was fortunate. Like Uppingham, the school was an Elizabethan grammar school and on his arrival it still occupied the original buildings and had no more pupils than at its foundation in 1555. Three years later, after the trustees had negotiated vastly increased income from the renewal of farm leases, the school moved to purpose-built accommodation on the outskirts of Holt and pupil numbers began to rise. In 1900 there were 44 boys and four staff; three years later the boys numbered 103; and by the time of Howson's death in 1919 the figure had reached 240. Howson was also fortunate in the geographical location of the school: not only was there ample countryside and bracing air on the east coast of Norfolk but, more importantly, the school was remote from the influences of other public schools; indeed Uppingham, seventy miles to the west, was his nearest traditional neighbour. In this setting Howson was able to start a school from scratch, just as Thring, Almond, Reddie and Badley had done in their turn.

Many of Thring's best principles and practices went with Howson to Gresham's. Both shared the belief that "a school chapel is the heart of a school"; Gresham's got its heart when the newly built chapel was consecrated in 1916.[25] Pupil numbers were kept low enough so that the headmaster would know every boy and, against the pattern of many schools, Howson made himself a housemaster so that School House would be the model for others to emulate. Boys had individual studies as at Uppingham; the barriers that existed between the boys' side and the private side in the boarding houses were largely destroyed; the relationship between boys and masters became less formal and more friendly; Howson invited boys to join him on holiday fishing trips in Wharfedale; and facilities and expert teaching were available across a broad curriculum, though with the notable absence of Greek.[26] Intellectual training was important but Howson gave most attention to moral education; here his belief that "in comparison with moral worth, intellectual excellence counted for little" coincides exactly with Thring's judgement.[27] Howson knew that his methods were a departure from the public school norm and that their standards were not Gresham's standards, but he was careful not to align himself with the New School Movement. Gresham's aimed to be a

---

[25] The quotation comes from Howson's address at the 1908 Speech Day. Sue Smart, *When Heroes Die* (Derby: Bredon Book Publishing Co. Ltd, 2001), 15.

[26] Simpson, *Harvest*, 84, 96; Smart, *Heroes,* 74.

[27] Simpson, *Harvest* , 90; Smart, *Heroes,* 13.

public school and so had to avoid being labelled cranky. "This is not the kind of school where, if a boy is not good at arithmetic, he is allowed to keep rabbits instead", Howson once told his biographer, James Simpson.[28]

Howson set out at Gresham's to create the conditions necessary to foster the moral aims he sought; in this, as in all respects, the life of the school was centred on his own personality. "Fresh Air and Morality" could well have been Gresham's motto.[29] The attractive site of the school gave easy access to the surrounding countryside and no locked doors, barred windows or unreasonable limits to the bounds curtailed the boys' liberty to roam. There were no printed school rules and the freedom of the Sunday afternoon was restored. Hobbies and the arts flourished and each boy was encouraged to develop his own particular interests. Gresham's was one of the first public schools to form a scout troop on the Baden-Powell model.[30] All boys were expected to be hardy, active and free of minor ailments, as Howson was. Fussiness over such matters was regarded as almost criminal.[31] Howson was also a bitter foe of athleticism: games were regarded as healthy and agreeable exercise that promoted proper moral behaviour, and nothing more. Howson's biographer recalled a discussion:

> I remember being asked, with some of my colleagues, to meet at dinner a rather distinguished visitor to the School House. "Bad news from Australia, isn't it?" had begun the latter in a harmless attempt to make conversation, when he was brought up short by Howson's blank expression. It would be difficult to say which was the more surprised, the guest at finding a public schoolmaster who did not know that a Test Match was in progress, or his host at the idea of anyone of intelligence sparing a thought for so trivial a matter.[32]

Games at Gresham's were played keenly and well but with a non-devotional attitude. Any factors that smacked of professionalism were banned: there were no cups, no school matches, no scrum caps or starter's pistol, and spectators could clap but not cheer at matches. The result was that athletic idolatry dropped, prowess as a games player counted little in the appointment of prefects, and the less athletic boys and masters felt that they too could join in and enjoy games without receiving the impression that their efforts were absurd.[33] Howson's impact on these matters was so

---

[28] Simpson, *Harvest*, 80, 82.
[29] Simpson, *Harvest*, 84.
[30] Smith, *Stretching*, 52.
[31] Simpson, *Harvest*, 86, 87, 95.
[32] Quoted in Smart, *Heroes*, 10-11.
[33] Simpson, *Harvest*, 85, 91, 92; Smart, *Heroes*, 10.

strong that even after his death these policies were maintained by his successors and it was not until the 1930s that Gresham's met another school at sport: a hockey match with Kurt Hahn's Schule Schloss Salem. The Germans came to play at Gresham's in 1930 and then the English school returned the visit in 1933. When regular school matches were adopted in the late 1930s, Hahn's Gordonstoun was on the fixture list.[34] In this same period a comprehensive programme of physical education had been introduced by Philip Smithells, who as a boy at Bedales had been strongly influenced by Reginald Roper.[35] Smithells was provided with a purpose-built gymnasium and open and covered swimming baths.[36] All boys attended timetabled lessons, Smithells logged their progress through a series of postural measurements, and remedial and rehabilitation gymnastics were provided for those in need of correction or recovery. Smithells later presented a paper to other physical education masters on the value of compiling physical data to reveal personal variation and group trends.[37]

V

Thring's support for the education of girls began a few years before he invited the Association of Headmistresses to bring their annual conference to Uppingham in 1887.[38] The few schools for girls that existed before 1850 deliberately neglected academic subjects and physical exercise in favour of stylish accomplishments; by the 1860s, however, many middle-class parents wanted to do better by their daughters. They were supported by the findings of the 1868 Taunton Commission: in a side effect of the examination of endowed grammar schools for boys, the commissioners were highly critical of girls' education. The result was that new day schools for girls were founded to provide a rigorous academic education, beginning in London and then extending to most major cities. The first was North London Collegiate School, founded in 1850 by Frances Mary Buss; the term "collegiate" was used to distinguish the schooling from that provided by "home-based" governesses. The first girls' boarding school,

---

[34] David Smith, "A Study of the Provision of Physical Education in the Schools of the Nineteenth and Twentieth Centuries: An Examination of Changing Views" (MPhil diss.; University of East Anglia, 1971), 469, 471.
[35] Smith, "Provision," 470.
[36] Smith, *Stretching*, 52.
[37] McIntosh, *Physical Education*, 303.
[38] For more on Thring's support for female education see Tozer, "High School," passim.

Cheltenham Ladies' College, followed three years later; Dorothea Beale became its principal in 1858. Miss Buss and Miss Beale had studied under Frederick Maurice, the inspiration for Christian Socialism, at Queen's College in London and whilst there they were greatly influenced by the example of Charles Kingsley.[39]

A select few women were able to receive a university education, if not university degrees, with the foundation of Girton and Newnham Colleges at Cambridge (1869 and 1871) and Lady Margaret Hall and Somerville College at Oxford (1878 and 1879). In 1878 the University of London was the first to accept women on equal terms with men and to award degrees to female students. Teaching was one of the few professions open to women, though their status was much lower than that for their male counterparts, and in the following decades the new girls' public schools and high schools appointed young mistresses from the universities, many of whom had enjoyed sports. These "Lady Blues" carried their love of learning and enthusiasm for games with them, and shared them with the next generation of girls. The girls' schools emulated much that was happening in boys' schools but they avoided imperial jingoism, and athleticism never became a cult. Sport was primarily used for health and moral education purposes but it was also associated with freedom and thus played its part in the push for women's progress in education and in society.

Following the lead of Thring, who maintained close friendships with Miss Buss and Miss Beale, the girls' schools adopted a comprehensive physical education programme well before the majority of games-mad boys' schools. Gymnastics, swimming and games were all on the curriculum: North London Collegiate School built a gymnasium in 1879; taught swimming in the 1880s; and acquired playing-fields in 1885. Physical education and games at Cheltenham Ladies' College were taught solely by a team of specialist teachers, the start of a female tradition that was not to be rivalled by the men until the 1940s. Newly adapted or imported female-only games such as rounders, netball and lacrosse were adopted to avoid taints of masculinity. The 30-plus high schools of the Girls' Public Day School Company maintained this progress with a physical education specialist in every school and an overall inspector for the subject. The boarding schools at St Leonards and Roedean placed even more emphasis on physical education: the former introducing Swedish gymnastics in 1891, the latter appointing three graduates of what was to become the Bergman-Österberg Physical Training College. This, the first of a string of women's colleges founded in the 1890s, espoused the

---

[39] McIntosh, *Physical Education*, 128.

Swedish tradition whilst the rival Chelsea College, as it was later known, looked to Germany for its gymnastics. Together they created a new career path for girls from middle-class families.[40]

VI

Charlotte Mason also worked in the years immediately after Thring's death to spread ideas and methods associated with his theory and practice. In her case it was to teachers of younger boys and girls at independent preparatory schools, to those working in local education authority elementary schools and, above all, through the network of "home schools" supported by the organisation she created, the Parents' National Educational Union (PNEU). The daughter of a Liverpool merchant, Miss Mason was born in 1842 and received her education at home. On the early deaths of both parents whilst she was still in her teens, she entered the Home and Colonial School Society in London where she trained as a teacher of young children in the methods advocated by the Swiss educationalist, Johann Pestalozzi. She then taught at the Davison School in Sussex for ten years from 1861, first with infants of both sexes and later with older girls. In 1874 she was appointed Mistress of Method at Bishop Otter College in Chichester, a former college for elementary schoolmasters that now trained women only. There she lectured on the educational practice needed to teach infants up to the age of seven.[41]

After two long bouts of illness, Mason realised that her health was insufficiently robust to permit a full-time career in lecturing or teaching. She decided instead to turn to writing and lecturing to spread her message: first through a series of text-books for young children and, later, in talks to audiences of parents, teachers, governesses and educationalists who were keen to hear her ideas on infant education.[42] These lectures were published in 1886 as *Home Education* and they broadcast across Britain her belief that the well-rounded education of children began in the home:

> ... my object is to show that the chief function of the child – his business in the world during the first six or seven years of life – is to find out all he can, about whatever comes under his notice, by means of his five senses; that he has an insatiable appetite for knowledge got in this way; and that,

---

[40] Malcolm Tozer, *Physical Education and Sport in Independent Schools* (Woodbridge: John Catt, 2012), 33-34.
[41] Essex Cholmondeley, *The Story of Charlotte Mason* (London: Parents' National Educational Union, 1960), 6-12.
[42] Cholmondeley, *Mason*, 14-15.

therefore, the endeavour of his parents should be to put him in the way of making acquaintance freely with Nature and natural objects; that, in fact, the intellectual education of the young child should lie in the free exercise of perceptive power, because the first stages of mental effort are marked by the extreme activity of this power; and the wisdom of the educator is to follow the lead of Nature in the evolution of the complete human being.[43]

The next step came in 1887 when Mason and an enthusiastic devotee, Emeline Steinthal, formed the Parents' Educational Union to provide support, advice and teaching materials to enable parents to turn her ideas into practice.[44] Further PEU branches quickly sprung up across the country, prompting the word National to be added to the Union's title from 1892.

Mason had by this time already started a monthly periodical for the PEU, *The Parents' Review*, and a home correspondence course for potential teachers, and she was preparing to create her own women's teacher training college. This, the House of Education, opened in 1892 with a class of twenty-one in the village of Ambleside at the heart of Wordsworth's Lake District; two years later it moved to a permanent home at Scale How, the estate of the poet's cousin, Dorothy Harrison. A model Parents' Union School for children of subscribers to *The Parents' Review* was attached to the training college. For the next thirty years, until her death in Ambleside in 1923, Charlotte Mason continued her work with the training college, its teaching practice school, a series of publications, and the network of PNEU schools across the country.[45]

Mason's methods were in sympathy with all that Thring had developed thirty years earlier at Uppingham, even though she did not always acknowledge or appreciate the debts that she owed. The adaptations for younger pupils, of course, were hers. Several of her supporters drew the parallels with Thring's work in articles that they contributed to the teaching materials published in the monthly issues of *The Parents' Review*.[46] Two of Thring's Old Boys, the brothers Willingham and

<hr>

[43] Charlotte Mason, *Home Education* (Bradford: Kegan Paul, Trench & Co, 1886), 96-97.
[44] Mrs Steinthal, c1856-1921, was a sculptor and painter. Her works include *A British Maid* and *The End of a Long Life*.
[45] The House of Education was renamed Charlotte Mason College in 1923. It is now the Ambleside campus of the University of Cumbria.
[46] Philip Bagenal, a schools' inspector, in 1901 used George Parkin's recently published biography to emphasise the similarity of Thring's theory and practice to Mason's methods in a long essay on "Thring as an Educationalist". Two years later, M. MacEachern contributed a pair of essays that contrasted the exciting educational practice found at Thring's Uppingham thirty years earlier with the

Hardwicke Rawnsley, were enthusiastic supporters of Mason's work and they saw many links between Uppingham and the PNEU.[47] Willingham, the elder brother, lived in Ambleside and so was able not only to assess Mason's work at first hand but also, as a PNEU historian recorded, to sing her praises: "Mr Willingham Rawnsley, an ever welcome visitor in the schools of Yorkshire, Gloucestershire and elsewhere, who has served us … by means of many addresses and articles in the press".[48] In his biography of his own headmaster he wrote of Mason as "that great educationist" who felt like Thring "that children should be dealt with as individuals and not in masses".[49] Hardwicke was already busy encouraging the education of young children from his parish at Crosthwaite when Mason arrived in 1892 as a near neighbour and for the next twenty-eight years, until his death in 1920, he was an active supporter of the PNEU.[50] Both brothers provided a steady stream of essays for *The Parents' Review*, including the very Thringian topic of "Educational Value of Observing Nature" by Hardwicke in 1904. Willingham contributed to *In Memoriam Charlotte M. Mason* in 1928: he had no doubts at all that Mason was a true guardian of Thring's theory and practice of teaching, and that she had extended his reach to include children aged up to seven years, whether educated in PNEU homes and schools or at the elementary schools in several English counties.[51]

The physical education recommended by the PNEU for under-sevens was based on singing games and rhythmic dances for the youngest pupils, and on Swedish gymnastics for the oldest. Half-an-hour on alternate days was allocated for the work. When Muriel Spalding, Mistress of Physical Education at London County Council's physical training college at Avery Hill, and Laura Collett, Senior Gymnastics Mistress at Blackheath High School, published *The Swedish Drill Teacher* in 1910, its use was

---

dullness of the Edwardian public school under headings that included "Public Schools Teach Conformity", "School Boys Indifferent to the Wonders of Nature", "School Boys Don't Know Their Own Language", and "Schools Dull Eager Minds".

[47] For more on Hardwicke Rawnsley, a co-founder of the National Trust, see Tozer, *Manliness*, 182-192.

[48] Cholmondeley, *Mason*, 174.

[49] Willingham Rawnsley, *Edward Thring: Maker of Uppingham School* (London: Kegan Paul, Trench, Trubner & Co, 1926), 84.

[50] Cholmondeley, *Mason*, 126.

[51] Willingham Rawnsley in PNEU, *In Memoriam Charlotte M. Mason* (Keighley: PNEU, 1928), 33-38.

recommended for all PNEU schools.[52] Charlotte Mason's methods were
now widely adopted by teachers at preparatory and elementary schools,
often without due credit, enabling many of England's youngest children to
have access to a planned physical education.

---

[52] Muriel Spalding and Laura Collett, *The Swedish Drill Teacher* (London: J.
Curwen and Sons, 1910). Spalding had trained under Rhoda Anstey, Collett under
Martina Bergman-Österberg.

Uppingham Rugby Football XV, 1890

Uppingham Shooting VIII, 1893

Uppingham Hockey XI, 1896

Athletics Sports at Uppingham, 1904

Uppingham School Gymnasium, 1905

Uppingham Rovers XI, 1908 © Uppingham Rovers

Cecil Reddie of Abbotsholme
© **Abbotsholme School**

John Badley of Bedales
© Bedales School

George Howson of Gresham's
© Gresham's School

Charlotte Mason of the PNEU
(public domain)

Maurice Jacks of Mill Hill
© Mill Hill School

Thorold Coade of Bryanston
© Bryanston School

Kurt Hahn of Gordonstoun
© Gordonstoun

John Royds of Uppingham

Squash in the Uppingham School Sports Centre, 2010

Badminton in the Sports Hall, 2010

Cricket on The Upper, 2014

Hike in Iceland, 2014

Swimming in the Sports Centre, 2014

Rugby football on The Leicester, 2014

CHAPTER NINETEEN

FROM PT TO PE, 1870-1930: "PHYSICAL EDUCATION INCLUDES ALL ACTIVITIES LIKELY TO MINISTER TO PHYSICAL HEALTH"

I

Physical training made steady progress in schools provided by or supported by the state in the period between William Forster's Elementary Education Act of 1870 and Herbert Fisher's 1918 Secondary Education Act. The introduction of military drill for boys, but not for girls, may have been for mixed motives, but a start had been made: the government wanted strong discipline; the schools welcomed the enhanced financial grant. Girls got their turn in 1878 when schools administered by the London School Board adopted Swedish gymnastics, an initiative led by Martina Österberg, and gradually this system was approved for girls in most schools across Britain.[1] The Cross Commission on Elementary Education of 1886 recommended that both military drill and Swedish gymnastics should be provided for all pupils up to the age of eleven, but it also acknowledged that there was a shortage of qualified teachers, especially for boys. By 1893 physical training was officially recognised as a subject of instruction and it was on the curriculum of all elementary schools. The government still wanted firm discipline but it had broadened its aims to include instruction in personal hygiene, the development of sound posture, and the encouragement of good health.[2]

The high rejection rate of men needed to fight in the Boer War added physical fitness to the list of expected outcomes from elementary school physical training. This change promoted a therapeutic system of physical exercise above military drill as the best means to achieve the new ends and led to physical training becoming part of the remit of the medical

---

[1] Martina Bergman-Österberg on her marriage in 1886.
[2] For more on this period, see: Knaggs, "Physical Education," 211-27; McIntosh, *Physical Education*, 107-124; Smith, *Stretching*, 88-105.

department of the Board of Education, an innovation that continued until 1944. The Board issued a syllabus of physical training in 1904 based on Swedish gymnastics.[3] From this time until the start of the Great War, the sound development, good health and physical fitness of the nation's children remained major concerns of government; thus regular medical inspections, school lunches and daily gymnastics lessons were introduced in all elementary schools. The Swedish system of gymnastics was also officially recognised by the armed forces and was adopted in all teacher training colleges as well, whether for class teachers in elementary school receiving limited training or women at the specialist colleges preparing to teach older children. Commander Francis Grenfell, R.N., was appointed His Majesty's Inspector of Physical Training in 1909, and in the same year the 1904 syllabus was modified to add recreational activities and games to the staple diet of gymnastics, if only to relieve the monotony.[4] Arthur Balfour's Secondary Education Act of 1902 had led to the expansion of education for children up to the age of twelve and by 1911 they too were receiving lessons in Swedish gymnastics. The Fisher Act would later raise the age to fourteen.[5]

Despite the more pressing concerns for a nation at war, the concept of physical education broadened during and immediately after the Great War. In 1914 the Chief Medical Officer at the Board of Education, Sir George Newman, highlighted "the need for an expansion and improvement of physical training throughout the country in both elementary and secondary schools".[6] Newman had been educated at two progressive schools run on Quaker principles, Sidcot School in Somerset and Bootham School in York.[7] Swedish gymnastics continued as the basis of physical education but was happily supplemented with dance, games, swimming, camping and open-air education; and swimming now included learning to swim in place of mere bathing.[8] There was a ready supply of qualified teachers for

---

[3] Board of Education, *Syllabus of Physical Exercises for use in Public Elementary Schools* (London: HMSO, 1904).

[4] Board of Education, *Syllabus of Physical Exercises for Schools* (London: HMSO, 1909).

[5] For more on this period, see: Knaggs, "Physical Education," 302-329; McIntosh, *Physical Education*, 143-169; Smith, *Stretching*, 106-122.

[6] *Annual Report of the Chief Medical Officer of the Board of Education,* 1914, 187. Quoted in Knaggs, "Physical Education," 356. Newman was knighted in 1911.

[7] A gymnasium for German gymnastics was opened at Bootham School in 1880; Newman would have attended classes in it when he was at the school from 1885 to 1887. Information from Elaine Phillips, school archivist, October 1, 2018.

[8] See *CMO Reports* for 1912, 297; 1914, 197; and 1917, 120; Knaggs, "Physical Education," 357.

girls from the specialist physical training colleges for women, but a lack of equivalent colleges for men left their physical training in the hands of former military or naval NCOs or class teachers supervising playground games. The official encouragement for swimming lessons in elementary and secondary schools was also hampered by a lack of suitable instructors.[9]

The new physical training syllabus of 1919 promoted this broader concept of physical education in all elementary schools and for pupils up to the age of fourteen at secondary schools; the syllabus for older pupils eventually arrived in 1927.[10] The change coincided with Newman's promotion to Chief Medical Officer at the Ministry of Health. His Introduction to the 1919 syllabus signalled that physical training, or Swedish gymnastics, was now regarded as just one element in a comprehensive physical education:

> The object of Physical Education and Training is to help in the production and maintenance of health in body and mind.
>
> Physical Education includes all activities likely to minister to physical health, not only gymnastics, games, swimming, and dancing, but sports, walking tours, school journeys, camps, and all forms of occupation and exercise likely to create a love of open air and a healthy way of living. The syllabus does not pretend to deal with Physical Education in its widest sense, and it should be recognised that Physical Training given at, or in connection with, the school, is only a part, though a very important part, of the whole subject.[11]

Newman echoes Edward Thring's theory and practice of physical education of sixty years earlier.[12]

---

[9] Board of Education, *The Health of the School Child* (London: HMSO, 1923), 114.

[10] Board of Education, *Syllabus of Physical Training for Schools* (London: HMSO, 1919); Board of Education, *Syllabus of Physical Training for Schools, Supplement for Older Girls* (London: HMSO, 1927); Board of Education, *Reference Book of Gymnastic Training for Boys* (London: HMSO, 1927).

[11] Board of Education, *Syllabus of Physical Training for Schools* (London: HMSO, 1919), 6.

[12] For more on this period, see: Knaggs, "Physical Education," 356-406; McIntosh, *Physical Education*, 180-215; Smith, *Stretching*, 125-137.

II

In the wake of Newman's instruction from the Board of Education in 1911 that all secondary schools must provide lessons in Swedish gymnastics, a request was made to the Headmasters' Conference that all public schools should be asked to fall in line to show fraternal support for their fellow head teachers. The response was half-hearted: many schools ignored the request; some made the change but reverted to military drill after a few years; only Eton made a serious attempt at it adoption.[13] Newman repeated the request in 1914. He deplored the poor provision of physical education in the public schools, arguing that games were "not in themselves sufficient physical training", that "something more was needed to improve carriage, and to correct faults of development", and that Swedish gymnastics "will make the pupils more fit for their games".[14] But his call was in vain, especially when the revival of military drill in the years before the Great War was seen by the schools as a patriotic necessity. Newman's insistence seemed to have paid off eventually when, in 1924, the Headmasters' Conference issued a sixty-page physical education syllabus for public schools, *The Practice of Health*.[15] However, it was largely ignored by the schools, although some of the prescribed exercises were used to improve the fitness of sports teams.[16]

Edward Lyttelton was the sole public school headmaster to support the Chief Medical Officer whole-heartedly. He had been appointed from his headmastership at Haileybury to lead Eton in 1905. He immediately checked the craze in games and he reduced the aura of militarism. Games were important to Lyttelton but he regarded the education they provided, both morally and physically, as lopsided.[17] Games did nothing to feed the minds: "Bowen of Harrow", Lyttelton wrote, "stated boldly that games furnish the boys' minds with something to think about. So they do, but it is thin fare, and if the mental anaemia is combined with a full-blooded physique, complications set in."[18] Nor did games fully develop the body: in 1907 he introduced classes in gymnastics for the youngest boys and in

---

[13] Knaggs, "Physical Education," 321, 329.

[14] *Annual Report of the Chief Medical Officer of the Board of Education,* 1914, 198; Knaggs, "Physical Education," 322, 324.

[15] Headmasters' Conference, *The Practice of Health* (Winchester: Warren and Sons, 1924).

[16] Knaggs, "Physical Education," 408.

[17] Lyttelton had captained Cambridge at cricket and played Association football for England.

[18] Lyttelton, *Memories*, 158, 167, 280.

1910 he built a gymnasium on the Swedish pattern. Attendance at gymnastics classes was compulsory and masters trained in "scientific physical education" were appointed. One new master, Reginald Roper, we have met in the chapter on progressive schools. Lyttelton and Roper argued that drill and games taught by untrained instructors and games masters provided a poor physical education; military drill was replaced by three half-hour physical education classes every week. These lessons included compensatory exercises to counter the debilitating effects of boys sitting at their desks for up to eight hours each day.[19] Many of Lyttelton's and Roper's innovations were abandoned during the Great War and they departed with the two men. In the spring of 1915 Lyttelton, perhaps unwisely, preached at St Margaret's Church, Westminster on the moral aspects of war; in the frenzied atmosphere of the first year of hostilities, his comments that the whole German nation should not be condemned were vilified by the press. As a consequence, and "in deference to a view of his patriotism entirely inconceivable to anyone who knows him", Lyttelton tendered his resignation. Roper, a pacifist, had already left for Bedales.[20]

III

Harry McKenzie succeeded Selwyn as headmaster of Uppingham in 1908. He came with a reputation for good management: within a year the pupil numbers reached the 400 mark again, and by 1911 they were back to the earlier pattern of 440. Uppingham's position in the public school world was re-established and when The Public Schools Club was founded in 1909, the school was one of just twenty-six on the list.[21] Ernest Hornung, the popular novelist and poet, celebrated with the *Old Boy's Song*.[22]

> Eton may rest on her Field and her River.
> Harrow has songs that she knows how to sing.
> Winchester slang makes the sensitive shiver.
> Rugby had Arnold, but never had Thring!
> Repton can put up as good an Eleven.

---

[19] Lyttelton, *Memories*, 169.

[20] Lyttelton, *Memories*, 185-186; Cyril Alington, *Things Ancient and Modern* (London: Longmans, Green, 1936), 158; Cyril Alington, *Edward Lyttelton: An Appreciation* (London: John Murray, 1943), 1.

[21] *USM*, June 1909, 110.

[22] First published in *USM*, April 1913, in part to celebrate the golden anniversary of the school magazine. This is the sixth and final verse.

Marlborough men are the fear of the foe.
All that I wish to remark is thank Heaven
I was at Uppingham ages ago!

Known as "the Man", and a "resolute, sure muscular Christian", McKenzie absorbed into the prefectorial body the talented athletes who had run amok in the last Selwyn years, and the brutal self-appointed privileges of the swell and the hearty ceased.[23] The reign of terror came to an end, as did the horrific accounts from Old Boys of bullying and worse. Life was still hard, but now it was largely fair. Ronald Browne recalled that his house captain's strong arm kept the house in such good order that the appearance of the housemaster in the boys' studies and dormitories was resented.[24]

Although McKenzie did curtail the excesses of athleticism, there was little change in the games organisation or the athletic outlook; more than three-quarters of school magazine content was devoted to match reports. Brian Horrocks, the future general, felt he was typical of many boys of the period: "I was a games addict, and did as little work as possible – my whole life was devoted to sport."[25] Company Sergeant Major Robertson of the Army Gymnastic Staff had succeeded Sgt Wallace in the gymnasium; more school matches were introduced in this period, and some second-team matches were added; and a large increase in the playing area on The Middle became one of the material legacies of the McKenzie years. The corps continued to flourish and the number of boys choosing the Army as a career doubled to an average of thirteen a year.[26] Jones was now a major and soon a lieutenant-colonel.[27] McKenzie supported his efforts keenly, telling the boys that such service taught discipline, submission and eventually command. It made, in McKenzie's words, a boy "manly".[28] He would have given headmasterly approval to the publication in the school magazine of July 1912 of Lord Roberts's "Message To Boys Leaving School":

As you know, some of our fellow-countryman across the seas have already adopted the principle that it is the duty of every man to be trained in the use of arms; believe me, boys, you can give no greater service to your

[23] Graham, *Uppingham,* 121-122.
[24] Memories of Ronald Browne, in school 1914 to 1918. (UA).
[25] Brian Horrocks, *A Full Life* (London: Collins, 1960), 13-14.
[26] Halstead, *Great War*, 50.
[27] *USM*, August 1909, 157.
[28] Speech Day, 1909: *USM*, August 1909, 157.

country than by doing your utmost to procure the adoption of the same noble principle in the Motherland.[29]

Vera Brittain, author of the acclaimed *Testament of Youth*, came to Uppingham for her brother's last Speech Day in the idyllic summer of 1914. She liked this stern man, almost an intimidating figure, for he knew his boys well and always recognised their parents. She remembered too the closing words of McKenzie's speech that day: "If a man cannot be useful to his country, he is better dead."[30]

IV

When McKenzie retired early through ill health in December 1915, the Uppingham trustees opted for youth over experience in their appointment of twenty-eight-year-old Reginald Owen as his successor. He did not have an easy start. In a period when women presented white feathers to men who might be shirking their patriotic duty, many boys and masters felt that a former Oxford rowing Blue, able to play Rugby football and cricket with the XV and XI, should not limit his military service to the school's cadet corps. Owen never explained, and he was judged a coward. Owen then compounded matters in 1917 by taking Holy Orders, at a time when several bishops refused to ordain men of military age.[31] Many young masters were now in the armed forces: their replacements were often elderly, some in their eighties; others already on the staff had been persuaded to delay retirement; discipline began to slip. Boys reckoned that three long-serving housemasters were incompetent and it was known that a fourth housemaster had agreed to keep to the private side if the boys behaved.[32] It took Owen four years to impose order.

The author Adrian Bell was at the school from 1915 to 1919; it was "not in good shape". He had been given a copy of *Tom Brown's Schooldays* by an aunt to prepare him for his new life and he found many similarities to Rugby of the 1820s. Life in his house was barbaric and

---

[29] *USM*, July 1912, 111-112. The "fellow-countrymen" were Australians.

[30] *USM*, August 1914, 166-167. McKenzie came to regret these words; see Tozer, *Manliness*, Prologue.

[31] Bryan Matthews, the school's historian, found that the Ministry of Defence had no evidence that Owen had been passed unfit for service overseas, and that many OUs were still highly critical sixty-five years later: Matthews, *By God's Grace*, 144-145, 265.

[32] Matthews, *By God's Grace*, 145-146; Memories of Stephen Ballard, at the school from 1917 to 1920. (UA).

"self-preservation was our chief preoccupation": bullying was rife, youngsters ran the nightly gauntlet of knotted wet towels, and senior boys were periodically expelled. Praepostors, always the games hearties, "flogged hard and often", so too did his housemaster, and so did Owen. Bell was beaten for shirking, having a "bum-slit" in his jacket, and for walking on the wrong side of the street. House beatings were carried out on Saturday evenings after prayers when the praepostors caught up on the week's wrong-doers. Punishment continued even on twelve-mile cross-country runs as junior boys were whipped by seniors wielding hunting crops. Bell labelled his housemaster a "dreamer": when a boy complained to him about the bullying, he replied that he would not interfere for that would only make matters worse. In Bell's opinion, Uppingham was a "totalitarian police state". He did not know it, but the school had reverted to the days of Selwyn ten years earlier.[33]

Owen got Uppingham under control a year after the end of the war. Bell noticed the improved "tone" and there was now "daylight at the end of the tunnel".[34] The appointment of new housemasters to seven of the thirteen houses helped, so too did the retirement of four masters and the return of five after war service.[35] In addition, fifteen new masters were appointed between 1919 and 1922 to accommodate the increased pupil numbers: 418 boys in 1918 rose to 501 in 1926. Owen believed that the school was resting too firmly on the reputation of a once great past; now he sought to increase the boys' endeavours in both work and games. Owen was tireless and his whole energy was devoted to the school. He was never absent overnight in term-time, he taught a hefty timetable, he regularly played games with the boys, and through weekly meetings with the praepostors he had a firm hand on the pulse of the school. Derek Patmore, the playwright, met little bullying when he arrived in 1922.[36]

Owen reputedly knew the name of every boy but personal relationships, whether between headmaster and masters, or both and the boys, were not to be encouraged. Young boys could not address their seniors unless they were spoken to first; few boys managed friendships outside the narrow

---

[33] Adrian Bell, *My Own Master* (London: Faber & Faber, 1961), 62, 64, 65, 66, 67, 68, 69.

[34] Bell, *Master*, 68.

[35] Owen instituted the scheme whereby the school bought the houses from the housemasters; this gave headmasters greater control over housemasters, including shorter tenures. The scheme began in 1919 and was completed in 1966.

[36] Derek Patmore, *Private History* (London: Jonathan Cape, 1960), 41. He was the great-grandson of the poet Coventry Patmore.

circle of their house contemporaries.[37] Old Boys remembered Owen arousing more fear than affection, even in the praepostors who might have expected "something warmer than an official relationship". His edict to the masters was clear: "However friendly the relations between master and boy, and they ought to be friendly – it is not healthy for the element of fear to be absent entirely."[38] Owen was a stern disciplinarian and could look incredibly severe. An Old Boy remembered: "If a boy strayed from the straight and narrow, punishment was merciless and administered personally, and on busy sessions reported to be as painful to the recipient at the tail of the queue as it had been to the first victim." A dilapidated straw hat, a hair-style without a parting, and irregularities of dress were not "tolerated".[39] Owen's grip extended to the masters and their wives; any laxity in appearance or smoking in the wrong place would produce a written reprimand.[40] Praepostors matched the headmaster's methods, maintaining house discipline through corporal punishment.[41] In a play on Owen's Christian name, the boys declared that they were "reggiemented".[42]

There were some on the staff who feared that such rigid rule might restrict the full development of the individual boy but to Owen the aim was the subordination of self to the needs of the community. "Service" was Owen's call but his version could be realised in just two ways, the corps and games; his insistence on the school's insularity prevented exploration of other options.[43] Jones was still commander of the Uppingham corps; he was the only master Owen could not dominate.[44] The corps was not compulsory but in the words of Uppingham's annual entry in the *Public Schools Year Book*, "almost all boys were in it".[45] The

---

[37] Arthur Farmiloe, *A Tarnished Silver Spoon* (Harlow: privately published, 2010), 28, 29, 34. Like Patmore, Farmiloe met little bullying.

[38] Penelope Jessel, *Owen of Uppingham* (London: A. R. Mowbray, 1965), 21, 34-35, 44, 45, 95, 97.

[39] "R. H. O. 1916-34" in *USM*, 1961, 93. This is Owen's obituary. See also Brian Belk, "RHO: a memorial sermon", 1961, in UA.

[40] One master was said to have a drawer full of reproofs, mainly for smoking. Another was asked to wear a more *sub fusc* jacket: Matthews, *By God's Grace*, 163.

[41] Farmiloe, *Spoon*, 31.

[42] Matthews, *By God's Grace*, 146.

[43] Jessel, *Owen*, 40; *USM*, 1939, 142.

[44] Information from Bryan Matthews.

[45] Farmiloe reported that boys felt obliged to join: Farmiloe, *Spoon*, 36. Bell relates how two boys who wished to resign from the corps were subjected to a tirade by Jones in front of the whole school: on duty, shirking, patriotism and honour. Bell, *Master*, 72-73.

compulsory shooting test that Selwyn had instituted in 1900 was maintained until at least 1932: only in 1935, when Wolfenden had succeeded Owen, did it no longer figure in the book's entry.[46] A few boys joined a scout troop on its founding in 1932 but the innovation was never popular.[47] Company Sergeant Major Bacovitch was appointed gymnasium instructor in 1919 and he served in this capacity until 1952. Bacovitch also supervised "breathers": summoned by a bugle call, the whole school assembled in the quadrangles at morning break, removed their jackets, and performed free-standing exercises under the command of praepostors and the CSM's watchful eye.[48]

Games "were a fetish", recalled Derek Patmore.[49] Uppingham XIs and XVs played them extremely well whereas the less talented endured interminable house league games with little or no instruction.[50] As a near-haiku in the 1928 school magazine recorded: "Dreams / Mere puff and bluff! / 'Tis teams / Both rough and tough / The School esteems / Enough."[51] The cricket under Frank Gilligan and the Rugby football under Alastair Smallwood were in the highest rank of public school sport and no school won more Blues in the latter during this period.[52] Owen intended his school to be narrow in outlook, insulated from the outside influences, and philistine, and that is what he made. The arts, he decided, "were a dangerous waste of time".[53]

V

Uppingham was not alone in seeing pupil numbers surge during and after the Great War. Many public schools had benefited from a rapid rise in numbers after 1917 when the War Office ordered that boys who were likely to make efficient army officers should remain at school until eighteen and a half. Eton, Harrow, Repton and Oundle all increased; Lancing doubled in size in the decade after the war; and Durham outdid that. Several new schools were founded to meet the demand for places,

---

[46] *Public Schools Year Book*, 1918 to 1932 and 1935. The 1933 and 1934 editions are not in the London Library.
[47] *USM*, 1932, 69.
[48] Matthews, *By God's Grace*, 184.
[49] Patmore, *History*, 42.
[50] Farmiloe, *Spoon*, 30.
[51] *USM*, 1928, 69.
[52] *USM*, 1952, 181.
[53] Only music flourished, still directed by Robert Sterndale Bennett: Matthews, *By God's Grace*, 161; *USM*, 1952, 182.

including Canford School and Stowe School in 1923 and Bryanston School in 1928. As Cyril Norwood, headmaster at Harrow from 1926 until 1934, proclaimed: "The boarding-schools of the country are at the present time enjoying a period of unexampled prosperity".[54]

Reforms that seemed ready for implementation in the public schools before the war were dropped; policies that were politically safe were adopted; and all that was conventional and conservative was re-discovered and re-emphasised. The liberal reformers had made great advances in the years before 1914, the war swung the debate their way, and then a shift in the economic climate brought about total rejection. A decade of activity was wasted, a real chance was lost, and no second chance was to come for another fifteen years. So entrenched and so conservative did the public schools now become that to criticise them was seen as unpatriotic. The twentieth century had lost its spring with a vengeance and it was all too easy to point to the public school statistics of the war and make propaganda out of the dead.[55] The return to Edwardian ways at Harrow was seen as a corporate tribute to the fallen.[56]

The public schools of the 1920s and early 1930s exuded an air of conventionalism and conservatism. Life may not have been as exotic as in Edwardian days but the fundamental principles were much the same.[57] Each school became a small conservative world, protecting its charges from the bustle of the surrounding turmoil. *The Times* and *Punch* formed the staple reading for the boys; there were no radios or gramophones; sermons of the "Cross and Union Jack" variety were delivered regularly from chapel pulpits; and Navy League lecturers once more flew the banner of military imperialism.[58] Despite the passing of compulsory Greek at Oxford and Cambridge, all schools still based their curriculum firmly on

---

[54] Tyerman, *Harrow*, 410; Turner, *Old Boys*, 179.

[55] Lord Dartmouth's reminder (of the 384 public school boys who had shot for the Ashburton Shield at Bisley in 1914, 66 were dead and 29 were wounded) was just one example of such figures being used to support the schools and to resist all calls for change. Quoted in *The English Review*, March 1919, 229.

[56] Tyerman, *Harrow*, 408.

[57] See, for example, Guy Kendall, *A Headmaster Remembers* (London: Victor Gollancz, 1933); Albert David, *Life and the Public Schools* (London: A. MacLehose, 1932); Bernard Darwin, *The English Public School*, (London: Longman, 1929); Cyril Norwood, *The English Tradition of Education* (London: John Murray, 1929); Cyril Alington, *Things Ancient and Modern* (London: Longmans, Green, 1936); and *The Head Master Speaks*, by various headmasters (London: Kegan Paul, Trench, Trubner & Co, 1936).

[58] Reginald Snell (L. B. Pekin pseud.), *Public Schools: their Failure and their Reform* (London: Hogarth, 1932), 101.

the classical languages whereas the inclusion of "material" and "commercial" subjects was resisted strongly. A public school education was to be a training of the mind was the oft-heard cry and all attempts to broaden the curriculum or to let boys specialise in modern subjects were seen as undermining this principle.[59] Art and music were now more commonly taught in these schools, and handicrafts were starting to come in, but in general they were regarded as extra-curricular, voluntary, and of little importance. The belief that such aesthetic training could have a moral value was viewed with great suspicion.[60]

Games were once again compulsory and still reflected the status of a school: a "rugger" school was decidedly one up on a "soccer" one, Harrow was one of several schools that changed codes, and to be classed a "Lord's school" was the supreme epithet.[61] At most schools, as at Repton, it was the long-standing housemasters who "were the high priests of the cult of athletics".[62] The time given to games, the compulsion, and the values derived from their play were exactly as in pre-war schools. Games inculcated courage, endurance, self-control, public spirit, a sense of fair play, leadership, discipline, and unselfish team spirit; all virtues attested to by the example of those who had fought in Flanders and Gallipoli.[63] Rugby football, rowing and cricket were still the major games, major in terms of their character-training facilities, whereas hockey and soccer were acceptable merely as a change, and running was good for the "stick to it" attitude. On the other hand, golf, tennis and racquets were hardly fit to be school games for "they were not painful enough".[64] If the character-training effects were to work on all boys, games had to be compulsory and, in like manner, the compulsory watching of school matches encouraged *esprit de corps*.[65] Swedish gymnastics had been rejected and no more appointments were made to match Roper's at Eton in 1911; the physical education revolution had been thwarted. Military drill and

---

[59] *Contemporary Review*, May 1920, 673, 681; *Nineteenth Century*, February 1926, 168; *The Head Master Speaks*, 63.

[60] *Edinburgh Review*, October 1919, 355; *The Head Master Speaks*, 57, 58, 190.

[61] Ian Hay, *Housemaster* (London: Hodder & Stoughton, 1936), 37; Tyerman, *Harrow*, 352.

[62] John Plowright, *Repton to the End* (London: Third Millennium, 2007), 33.

[63] *The Head Master Speaks*, 127, 212.

[64] Arthur Benson, *Cambridge Essays on Education* (Cambridge: Cambridge University Press, 1917), 153-154; Norwood, *Education*, 103-106. Tennis was derided as 'woolly ball' when the author arrived at Uppingham in 1966.

[65] *The Head Master Speaks*, 127; John Bradstreet, *Repton Sketches* (London: Ernest Benn, 1928), 62.

boxing, "a fine instrument of education", were back in the hands of ex-service instructors or, as at Uppingham, had never been removed from them.[66]

The games were as competitive as ever; school magazines were filled with sporting exploits; the national press was keenly interested in the progress of school matches; and *The Times* still published portraits of the Eton and Harrow XIs on the eve of their match at Lord's. The cult of athleticism continued unabated but with two new aspects that were not present before the war. First, it was now the masters and the parents, as much as the boys, who encouraged the playing of games; and secondly, there was no underlying ideal to be promoted through their play. Games were now used to "occupy" boys, a popular term of the period, as well as to keep them from mischief and to send them to bed too tired for sexual irregularities.[67] The talented games players continued to rule over other boys: members of the Philathletic Club at Harrow had the right to wear distinctive grey waistcoats and bow-ties, and to walk arm-in-arm down the middle of the road; the last survived until motor cars became popular![68]

The cadet corps was compulsory too, if not by actual headmasterly statement then with the assistance of prefectorial and peer pressures. Every school with public school ambitions had its own corps; at Harrow it became the central feature of school life and all masters were expected to join.[69] Apologists maintained that the cadet corps did not encourage militarism but merely encouraged the military virtues; nonetheless, officials at the War Office reckoned they were getting value for money.[70] A corps' training was seen by most headmasters as a means to prepare boys for the needs of their country by awakening a patriotism that was greater than narrow school loyalty. Alec Ashcroft, the headmaster of Fettes, was unusual when he voiced the opinion, more often heard in private than in public, that service in the corps was a preparation for national defence and that this formed an integral part of a public school education. In Ashcroft's opinion, this was religion in a most practical form.[71]

---

[66] Benson, *Education*, 153-154; Joanna Bourke, *Dismembering the Male: Men's Bodies, Britain and the Great War* (London: Reaktion Books, 1999), 188.

[67] Benson, *Education*, 161; Norwood, *Education*, 135; James Simpson, *Sane Schooling* (London: Faber & Faber, 1936), 228.

[68] Tyerman, *Harrow*, 472.

[69] Tyerman, *Harrow*, 446.

[70] Alington, *Things*, 121; *Edinburgh Review*, October 1919, 345; Snell (Pekin), *Public Schools,* 109.

[71] *The Head Master Speaks*, 93.

At first glance, there is little to distinguish a public school of the 1920s and early 1930s from a school of the Golden Age beyond a slight tightening of the economic belt. The Edwardian school, however, looked forward, buoyed by its confidence in Imperial Christianity. The post-war school looked back at the past, found support in the substance of the pre-war school but could not believe in its Christianity, nor in its ideal of manliness. Religion now taught safe civic virtues and chaplains, more pastoral leaders than schoolmaster-priests, found it difficult to encourage inner spiritual life.[72] It had been hard to distinguish between sham and idealism in the Edwardian school but at least there was some idealism; now the post-war school was in danger of becoming a means without an end. Headmasters recognised that there was a need to reassert the old manliness in a new guise, one fit for a society undergoing rapid change.[73] To fill that vacuum, "public school spirit" was raised as the ideal.[74] The search for "That Something" occupied headmasters and Old Boys from 1924 to 1928 with articles and correspondence filling the reviews. Eventually the components of public school spirit were agreed: total trust, cheerful obedience, ability to get on with others, honour, and service to one's country. It was *esprit de corps* in new clothing. Life in the boarding houses and games on the playing-fields were seen as the formative influences, but how short this falls of earlier ideals. "Good form" was a poor substitute for Christianity; "play the game" was a weak maxim for a hero; to be a "sport" was hardly a fitting life's ambition.[75] Manliness had become chappishness.[76] Yet in the post-war public school world, life was indeed a game: games were the main form of school service; athletic goals provided the ultimate ambitions; fair play was the rule of life.[77] A British plot to assassinate Hitler during the 1930s was turned down as "not cricket", the very words used by the government of the day.[78]

---

[72] Tyerman, *Harrow*, 455, 457.

[73] Bourke, *Men's Bodies*, 14, 19.

[74] Tyerman, *Harrow*, 453.

[75] Fettes in this period had special hymns to be sung before and after matches with rival schools: Turner, *Old Boys*, 103.

[76] I owe some of these points to Gerald Murray. See also Worsley, *Barbarians*, passim; Thomas Worsley, *Flannelled Fool* (London: Alan Ross, 1967), 93.

[77] Cyril Alington, *English Review*, April 1924, 460ff; Stephen Foot, *Nineteenth Century*, February 1926, 169ff; James Welldon, *Contemporary Review*, November 1927, 612ff; C. H. P. Mayo, *Quarterly Review*, October 1928, 205ff; Norwood, *Education*, 140; Darwin, *Public School*, xiv, 21-28.

[78] Norman Dixon, *On the Psychology of Military Incompetence* (London: Futura, 1976), 292.

VI

The progress of physical education in most boys' schools may have ground to a halt after the Great War, or even gone into reverse, but for girls in secondary schools, whether privately owned or supported by the state, the movement was decidedly forward. Young women galore were studying at the new physical training colleges before moving on with missionary zeal to spread the ideas of Pehr Henrik Ling, the practice of Swedish gymnastics, and their love of games and dance. They were well received by headmistresses, girls and parents, and well provided with gymnasia, swimming pools, playing fields, and more. Martina Bergman-Österberg's physical training college had moved from Hampstead to the open spaces of Dartford in 1895; one of her pupils, Rhoda Anstey, in 1897 founded in Halesowen the college that later bore her name, then moved it to Birmingham in 1907; and Dorette Wilke, a German immigrant, opened the Chelsea College in London in 1898. The first years of the new century witnessed the expansion of the system from three to six: Irene Marsh founded her college in Liverpool in 1900; another of Bergman-Österberg's pupils, Margaret Stansfield, opened Bedford Physical Training College in 1903; and in 1905, Flora Ogston, a pupil of Wilke at Chelsea, was appointed the first principal of the Dunfermline College of Hygiene and Physical Training.[79] There was a healthy rivalry between the colleges, and strong links developed between schools and colleges: a Dartford-trained head of department at a school would probably appoint Dartford-trained assistants; Bedford had a close association with the schools of the Girls' Public Day School Company.[80]

Former students were prominent in the development of sport and dance for girls and women: Mary Hankinson and hockey, Edith Clarke in lacrosse, Ethel Adair Impey with netball, and Jean Milligan for Scottish country dancing are just four examples.[81] Hankinson was also the initiator of the first association for physical education teachers. In 1899 she brought together thirty former pupils of Bergman-Österberg and formed The Association of Swedish Physical Educationists, soon to be renamed the Ling Association. Initially membership was limited to "Madame's girls"

---

[79] Webb, *Physical Education*, 1-7. Marsh's college was called the I. M. Marsh College of Physical Training. Nonington became the seventh college in 1938, Lady Mabel the eighth in 1949, and Ulster the ninth in 1953.
[80] Sheila Fletcher, *Women First: the Female Tradition in English Physical Education 1880-1980* (London: The Athlone Press, 1984), 62-63.
[81] Jonathan May, "The Bergman-Österberg Physical Training College", in McIntosh, *Physical Education*, 293.

and anyone trained at the Royal Central Gymnastic Institute in Stockholm but gradually former students from the other five physical training colleges were admitted.[82] Reginald Roper joined in 1911.[83] Over the course of the next century the Ling Association evolved to become the Physical Education Association (PEA) and then the Association for Physical Education (afPE).

---

[82] Webb, *Physical Education*, 3.
[83] Steve Bailey and Wray Vamplew. *One Hundred Years of Physical Education 1899-1999* (London: Physical Education Association, 1999), 12.

CHAPTER TWENTY

LATER LEGACY, 1930-1970:
"TOTAL EDUCATION"

I

Despite the return to conservative values at the traditional public schools, the Thringian legacy of physical education continued to extend into the inter-war years. Reginald Roper served at Bedales from 1913 until 1923, teaching physical education, remedial gymnastics and Latin, and his former pupil, Philip Smithells, worked at Gresham's until 1937. After graduating from Clare College, Cambridge in 1932 with a degree in English and economics, Smithells had studied gymnastics privately with Roper before taking up his post at Gresham's as master in charge of physical education and teacher of English. There he developed his lasting commitment, imbibed from Roper, to remedial work for pupils with poor physical skills.[1]

The whole-man philosophy of education was brought to light once more in the late 1920s and early 1930s through the widely received views of Lawrence Jacks, professor of philosophy and theology at Manchester College, Oxford.[2] In various journals and newspapers, at schoolmasters' conferences, and in two books (*The Education of the Whole Man* and *Education through Recreation*) Jacks expressed his plea for a new spirit in education.

> The training of the whole man in the skilful achievement of excellence within the bounds of a socially valuable vocation – such is the general formula of education when viewed in the social perspective. .... Much emphasis will be laid on the *whole man*. To achieve his education in the

---

[1] In 1937 Smithells was appointed lecturer in charge of physical education at the University College of the South-West of England in Exeter, and in 1939 he moved to New Zealand, eventually becoming Professor of Physical Education at the University of Otago.

[2] He also served as Principal from 1915 until his retirement in 1931.

wholeness of his personality, the conception of man as a patchwork partnership of mind and body, in which the mind alone, as the celestial partner, falls within the province of education, while the body, as the terrestrial, is left to hygienists and medical practitioners – an evil inheritance from the past which still dominates our educational methods ... – will have to be abandoned. In place of it our plans must be laid for a vigorous co-education of mind and body regarded as an inseparable unity in every stage of their development.[3]

Jacks mistrusted the fragmentary nature of a traditional public school education in which the mind was "educated" by teachers in the classroom, the body was "trained" by instructors in the gymnasium, and the soul was the province of the chaplain in the chapel. Such schools either produced narrow scholars or efficient games-playing barbarians; in both true Christianity was missing. Jacks sought to combine the two extremes and then infuse them with a Christianity that was not restricted to the chapel but went with the boy to playgrounds, the classrooms and the workshops.[4] Jacks felt that the current imbalance of the whole-man ideal was primarily at the physical extreme of the spectrum; he thus devoted most attention to what he termed "the wider possibilities of physical culture". Here, using colourful phrases to illustrate his points, Jacks asserted that "man is a skill hungry animal" yet a majority of the population were "physical illiterates".

> I regard a trained body – trained to be master of its movements as a whole and not in fragments – as the necessary foundation for all kinds of creative activity, just as reading and writing are the necessary foundation for the acquisition of knowledge.[5]

Thus, in this most Thringian of concepts, Jacks asserted that physical education was the core of all creative activity or what other educationalists would term aesthetic education or simply leisure. To realise his aim, physical education needed to be given due importance in schools and its teaching had to be by men and women who were as well qualified as the other members of the teaching staff.

---

[3] The stress is in the original. Lawrence Jacks, *The Education of the Whole Man* (London: University of London Press, 1931), 41-42.
[4] Jacks, *Whole Man*, 163; Lawrence Jacks, *Education Through Recreation* (London: University of London Press, 1932), 3, 9.
[5] Lawrence Jacks, "The Wider Possibilities of Physical Culture," in *Education Today*, ed. Edward Laborde (Cambridge: Cambridge University Press, 1935), 49.

II

Jacks knew of such a school and he was able to report that with good modern physical education the composition of Latin prose had improved; a sentiment close to Thring's heart.[6] The school was Mill Hill, and its young headmaster was his son, Maurice Jacks. Not only was Jacks the active propagator of his father's theories but he was also a keen disciple of Thring. One of his staff, Gerald Murray, related to the author how frequently Jacks mentioned Thring's pioneering work and his books contain many Thring quotations.[7] Jacks referred to the whole-man ideal of education as *Total Education*, the title of the book that expounded his views in detail, seeing it as the synthesis of all aspects of schooling.[8]

On his appointment as headmaster in 1922 at the age of twenty-eight, Jacks was encouraged by the governors to reform and develop the school. Jacks sought to build a Christian-Platonic community in which service to one's fellows was implicit in every aspect of its life. Personal experience of the rigours of pre-war public school athleticism at Harrow, together with his later efforts as a junior officer to provide meaningful recreation for his soldiers when in rest billets, had convinced him that curriculum change was needed. Education should be nothing less than an apprenticeship for citizenship; this would later be seen in active involvement by Old Boys in local politics, charities, youth organisations and the like.[9] Following his Ruskinian beliefs, Jacks gave much time in the curriculum to leisure activities and he put his father's ideals for physical education into practice. Health was seen as a positive sense of well-being and not merely the absence of disease. Jacks believed that the athletic balance and outlook were all wrong at the traditional public schools, with too much emphasis placed on team games and on the talented players.[10] To remedy this situation, Jacks appointed Gerald Hedley to his staff as "director of physical education" with the brief "to cover promotion of the physical development of every boy in the school, especially the less skilful, the weak and the unstable, and liaison with the school doctor, the form

---

[6] Jacks, "Physical Culture", 45, 51. Thring believed that many of the best readers were to be found among the gymnastic pupils.

[7] Conversation with Gerald Murray at Marlborough, c1976. For Thring quotations see: Maurice Jacks, *Education as a Social Factor* (London: Kegan Paul, Trench, Trubner, 1937), 6; Maurice Jacks, *Trends in Education Modern* (London: Andrew Melrose, 1950), 40, 70, 114.

[8] Maurice Jacks, *Total Education* (London: Kegan Paul, Trench, Trubner, 1946).

[9] Jacks, *Social Factor*, 9, 14, 123, 197.

[10] Jacks, *Social Factor*, 137, 139.

masters and the house masters."[11] Hedley was an ex-army officer, an Oxford graduate, and he had attended various physical education courses.

Hedley began work in 1929 with his new title and the freedom to appoint his own team. The governors provided a gymnasium that was well equipped with apparatus in the Swedish style. Lessons were timetabled as "Educational Gymnastics" and comprised much from the Board of Education's syllabus, elements of Danish rhythmic work derived from Niels Bukh, vaulting and agility of the German tradition, and simple indoor games. Outdoor afternoon activities included swimming, life-saving, cross-country running, and athletics. Each boy was provided with a Health Book which logged termly changes in physical measurements, health records, and comments from the school doctor and from Hedley.[12]

III

Queen Elizabeth's Boys' Grammar School in Barnet, not far from Mill Hill, was one of a number of grammar schools that adopted a similar stance regarding physical education. Gerald Murray was its Director of Physical Education from 1932 and in 1937 he would succeed Hedley at Mill Hill. Both Hedley and Murray were ardent disciples of Reginald Roper. Two PE periods each week for every boy were augmented by two afternoons of games, primarily Rugby football, athletics and cricket. These sessions were not just nurseries for the talented but were an integral part of the physical education programme, and each boy's progress was logged alongside his gymnasium record. At any one time about 50 of the 320 boys in the school would be receiving remedial or rehabilitation gymnastics to cure developmental defects or to aid recovery after injury or illness.[13]

Hedley and Murray, together with Smithells of Gresham's, were instrumental in the development of the Secondary Schoolmasters' Physical Education Association which, through its conferences at Mill Hill from 1934 and by means of various publications, disseminated these modern ideas on physical education to all who would listen. The association had been formed in the early 1920s to cater for men who were excluded from the Ling Association and, working in partnership with the Board of Education, had awarded appropriate professional certification through its holiday courses. Lawrence Jacks was the association's president and the

---

[11] Gerald Hedley and Gerald Murray, "Physical Education at Mill Hill School, 1929-1939", in McIntosh, *Physical Education*, 299.

[12] Hedley and Murray, "Mill Hill", 299-300.

[13] Kenneth Woodland, "Physical Education for All: First Principles and Practice", in McIntosh, *Physical Education*, 306-312.

two vice-presidents were Maurice Jacks and Cyril Norwood, headmaster at Harrow.[14]

Maurice Jacks publicised his support for physical education with a letter to *The Times* in 1931:

> The fundamental need appears to me to be the substitution of the wider conception of "physical education" for the rather limited physical training to which we have been accustomed. This involves the creation of a "Physical Education Department" ... on a level with the other educational departments ... into which school life is naturally divided. The director of this should be a member of the Masters' Common Room, with a University degree [... and fully qualified ...] for his highly specialized duties by post-graduate study ...
>
> The director's duties would be not only to supervise and to carry out physical training [that is, Swedish gymnastics] ... but also to keep an eye on a boy's physical development and to guide it throughout his school life.
>
> ... [I]n this department the exercises and the work should all be so devised as to employ the mind all the time, to develop mental alertness, and, through team-work, practice in leadership, and so forth, to strengthen the character; a boy should come out from a period in the gymnasium better in mind and character, as well as fitter in body.[15]

A week later, in a subsequent letter to the newspaper, the Secretary of the Secondary Schoolmasters' Physical Education Association took the professionalisation of physical education for men a step further:

> Much good has been accomplished by the special courses organized by the Board of Education for masters in secondary schools during the last eight years, but there is no doubt that we have been greatly handicapped by the lack of a special training centre similar to the women's colleges. ...
>
> It is, therefore, with very great pleasure that I have read that a Carnegie Hall of Physical Education is to be opened in connexion with the Leeds Training College for Teachers. ...
>
> In our opinion the physical training master should be one who has been first trained as a teacher in a university or training college, and has then received one year's special training in this subject. ... On behalf of this association, I would ask headmasters of public and secondary schools and Directors of Education to help in making the Carnegie Hall a success. There is much hope for the future.[16]

---

[14] McIntosh, *Physical Education*, 216-217.

[15] *The Times*, November 7, 1931, 11.

[16] F. H. Jenner of the Grammar School, Eastbourne, in *The Times*, November 12, 1931, 15.

Carnegie College of Physical Education opened in 1933 and provided one-year courses for men who already possessed a university degree or who had completed a general teacher training course. The men's course differed in two respects from the long-standing women's courses: its students would be qualified to teach a classroom subject as well as physical education, whereas the women were full-time physical education specialists; and students at Carnegie could be funded by the Board of Education, whereas all the women's colleges were privately owned and charged fees.[17] The Board of Education also published a new *Syllabus of Physical Training for Schools* in 1933 to guide the teaching of children aged five to eleven.[18]

When similar courses were started at Loughborough College in 1935 and Goldsmiths' College in London in 1937, not only were men given the chance of catching up with women but a new group of well-qualified and technically aware physical education teachers joined with the women to raise the standard of their subject and to boost the status of those who taught it. Loughborough took professionalisation a step further in 1937 by creating a three-year course for first-time students in "Athletics, Games and Physical Education".[19]

In 1937 Jacks left Mill Hill to become director of the Department of Education at Oxford University; there he continued to argue the case for every school to have a physical education department whose status, and that of its director, should be on par with every other subject area.[20]

IV

One of the outlets of Lawrence Jacks's philosophy of education was the Harrow Conferences for Young Schoolmasters, and these same gatherings heard papers on physical education delivered by Smithells and Murray.[21]

---

[17] McIntosh, *Physical Education*, 236.

[18] Board of Education, *Syllabus of Physical Training for Schools* (London: HMSO, 1933).

[19] McIntosh, *Physical Education*, 237.

[20] Jacks, *Total Education*, 64.

[21] Gerald Murray, "Physical Education in the Curriculum", in Edward Laborde, *Problems in Modern Education* (Cambridge: Cambridge University Press, 1939), 137-147; Thorold Coade, *Harrow Lectures on Education* (Cambridge: Cambridge University Press, 1931), passim; Philip Smithells, "Physical Education"; Thorold Coade, *Manhood in the Making* (London: P. Davis, 1939), 3-19; Gerald Murray and Thomas Hunter, *Physical Education and Health* (London: Heinemann, 1966), passim.

These conferences were founded in 1931 by a Harrow schoolmaster, Thorold Coade, and after the Second World War were reconstituted by him as the Oxford Conference for Schoolmasters. When, in 1932, the headmastership of Bryanston, the new Dorset public school, surprisingly became vacant only four years after its foundation, Coade was appointed its headmaster and remained there until his retirement in 1959. Bryanston's first headmaster was an Australian graduate of Melbourne and Oxford, Jeffrey Jeffreys, who set out to create a school based on two principles that were departures from general public school practice. First he brought with him the Dalton Plan of learning in which the boys worked on an organised system of personal study guided by one or more tutors and, secondly, he advocated an Almond-like code of health. Life at Bryanston was to be simple: no servants would wait on the boys, the school uniform was to be of the shorts and open-necked shirts variety, and all corporal punishment was banned.[22] When Coade arrived, he thus found a new, lively and receptive school, one in which he could put into operation his own germinating educational plans.

Thorold Coade was born in 1896, the son of a clergyman. At his preparatory school in Norfolk, where he was shocked by the innate cruelty of under-supervised small boys, and at Harrow, where he experienced all the limitations of such a school at the turn of the century, his simple faith received a bruising. His disillusionment with the public school system was reinforced by what he saw when he went to Sandhurst in 1915. Here the cream of public school youth appeared smart and orderly on the parade ground but off-duty all was chaos and licence; and no-one in authority seemed to mind. Coade was horrified at the naked barbarism and the stark philistinism of the behaviour of his fellow cadets and he vowed that, if he survived the war, he would endeavour to remedy that situation.[23]

Coade had a fundamental belief in the public school system of education but he felt that it was now anachronistic in terms of its curriculum, its attitude and, above all, its imperial-sahib type of product. He set out to build a school that was a balance between the old-fashioned Victorian autocracy and the ultra-modern liberal school; a school at the progressive end of the public school spectrum. Individuality and not selfish individualism was to be the aim; friendliness and service to others would be the all-pervading atmosphere. Bryanston was to be "the place of the Individual in the Community".[24] Coade aimed at strong teacher-parent liaison and he sought to develop a relationship between master and boy

---

[22] Stewart, *Progressives*, 308.
[23] Thorold Coade, *The Burning Bow* (London: Allen & Unwin, 1966), 29, 30, 31.
[24] Coade, *Burning Bow*, 21, 51, 52.

built on mutual education and mutual respect, and to do this through common interests. He had a Thringian mistrust of examinations and prizes; he regarded Maurice Jacks's *Total Education* as a teaching philosophy of great significance; and he became a close friend of the German educationalist, Kurt Hahn.[25] Their friendship began in 1929: some boys from Bryanston exchanged with boys from the Schule Schloss Salem for some weeks in 1932; and when Hahn was exiled to Britain in 1933, Bryanston was his first resting-place.[26] Coade greatly appreciated Hahn's notion of the *grande passion*, every boy must do something well was Thring's equivalent, and his stress on physical achievement other than through team games.[27]

Coade placed great emphasis on what other schools labelled "extra-curricular activities", providing more than fifty clubs and societies for the boys to choose from.[28] He felt that too many schools were satisfied with just the occupation of the boys' leisure-time and accepted low involvement provided the boys were amused and kept out of mischief. To Coade these activities were "when most of our significant and creative thinking takes place", thus they should be of vital importance to educators and should be brought into the mainstream of the curriculum. He did not believe that this would reduce the level of academic or sporting success for, if the proportions were right, the general enrichment of life would be reflected in higher standards at everything. The corporate activity came through various forms of community service; these also formed a significant part of Coade's conception of a school. The Pioneers were instituted in 1933 as a liberal alternative to the cadet corps; here Bryanston blazed the trail of community action that many schools were to adopt in the 1960s and which led indirectly to the founding of Community Service Volunteers (CSV) and Voluntary Service Overseas (VSO). Group projects could be hut building, outdoor manual work and the building of an open-air theatre, whilst pioneer holidays included exploration expeditions and visits to Outward Bound Schools. The adventure activities associated with the Sea Cadets were added in 1946 as another means of community service.[29]

All aspects of physical education fitted into the framework of creative and corporate activity. Games were encouraged, and there was a broad spectrum of choice, but compulsion was limited to a boy's first three

---

[25] Coade, *Burning Bow*, 24, 28, 33, 101.

[26] Coade, *Burning Bow*, 24; William Stewart, *The Educational Innovators* (London: Macmillan, 1968), 173.

[27] Coade to Harry Armytage, quoted in Stewart, *Progressives*, 307.

[28] Stewart, *Progressives*, 313.

[29] Stewart, *Progressives*, 312.

years. Individual sports such as canoeing and climbing were keenly followed.[30] As David Smith remarked, "in its breadth of approach and variety of activities Bryanston anticipated by many years what has since become standard physical education practice".[31]

The philosophy and practice of Christian-Platonism stood out from every aspect of the curriculum at Bryanston. "Religion is Education and Education is Religion" was Coade's guideline. By religion he meant a relationship with God, and education was the process by which each individual became aware of it. Education was not just moral, intellectual and physical but also spiritual; and spiritual education could only be realised in the Platonic manner through music, arts, crafts and literature. The object was the awakening of the whole personality and harnessing that energy to the purposes of God; the aim was the "wholeness of man" or, its Coade equivalent, "the holiness of spirit".[32] Here indeed is Thring's ideal of manliness.

V

Coade put his ideals into practice at Bryanston quietly and with very little publicity. His friend Kurt Hahn ran his school at Gordonstoun in Morayshire on many of the same principles, including the Dalton Plan, but here Hahn's undoubted gifts as a publicist brought the work to world-wide attention and his efforts were to contribute much to developments in various sectors of British education. Hahn was born in Germany in 1886 of Jewish parents. He was educated first in Berlin and then from 1904 at Christ Church, Oxford. By this time he was an avid Platonist; his years at Oxford made him an admirer of Thomas Arnold and brought about an abiding affection for Britain.[33] He was introduced to Reddie's ideas and methods when he met a party of Abbotsholme boys on an expedition in the Alps.[34]

In the years immediately after the Great War Hahn served as private secretary to Prince Maximilian of Baden, the last Imperial Chancellor of Germany. Prince Max settled on education as the most likely means of restoring the nation's confidence and, in 1920, he founded Schule Schloss

---

[30] Stewart, *Progressives*, 313.

[31] Smith, *Stretching*, 65.

[32] Coade, *Burning Bow*, 23, 26, 34, 41, 43, 142; Stewart, *Innovators*, 152.

[33] Lodewijk van Oord, "Kurt Hahn's Moral Equivalent of War," *Oxford Review of Education* 36, no. 2 (June 2010): 254; David Sutcliffe, *Kurt Hahn and the United World Colleges* (Cambridge: Gordonstoun Schools, 2013), 53.

[34] Information from Mary Byatt.

Salem in Bavaria, a boarding school for boys and girls aged ten to eighteen. Hahn was appointed headmaster. At Salem Hahn was particularly concerned with physical fitness and moral independence, and powerful emphasis was placed on the character-training qualities that appropriately chosen physical activities could inculcate. As Hahn admitted, nothing at Salem was original: ideas were borrowed from Plato, Arnold's Rugby, Eton, Abbotsholme and a host more schools and educationalists; and other features were rejected, including the public school shortcomings of arrogance, privilege, entitlement and games-worship.[35] It was the mixture that was unique. The school was already internationally famous when Hahn's denunciation of the Nazis led to his imprisonment and then, in July 1933, his exile to Britain. With the help of powerful supporters, Hahn secured Gordonstoun as the setting for his British continuation of the Salem scheme.[36] The first boys arrived in 1934, mainly the sons of German refugees known to Hahn and attracted by his philosophies; others were the misfits and failures from British public schools. Numbers climbed to 135 by 1939 but Salem's practice of admitting girls had to wait until 1972.[37]

There were many Platonic parallels at Gordonstoun: the terms "Guardian" and "Helper" were adopted for school officers; *paideia*, defined by Hahn as the development of energetic participation, became the central ideal; and the morally responsible person, not the scholar, artist or games player, became the educational exemplar of the school. To cut down on nationalism and to harness all energies in the cause of peace, Hahn sought for "a moral equivalent of war"; here community service, sports and arduous training activities were to play their part.[38]

The plan at Gordonstoun was precise. Each boy was responsible for his own physical fitness and had to tick off his daily routine on a chart: this was the basis of the school's "Trust System". School uniform included

---

[35] Stewart, *Innovators*, 191; Gary McCulloch, *Philosophers and Kings: Education for Leadership in Modern England* (Cambridge: Cambridge University Press, 1991), 25; Sutcliffe, *Hahn*, 57.

[36] Including Geoffrey Winthrop-Young, William Arnold-Forster, Archbishop William Temple, Sir George Trevelyan and John Buchan, later Lord Tweedsmuir.

[37] As Gordonstoun was within a military area, the school was evacuated to Plas Dinam in Wales; numbers slipped to 50. Once back in Scotland, numbers climbed to 400. When girls did arrive in 1972, admission was for all ages and not just sixth-formers. Information from Mary Byatt; Martin Flavin, *Kurt Hahn's Schools and Legacy* (Wilmington, Delaware: Middle Atlantic Press, 1996), 27, 28.

[38] van Oord, "Moral Equivalent," 256-257. The term "a moral equivalent of war" was coined in 1910 by William James, an American psychologist and philosopher.

shorts and sweater; the day started with a run and a cold bath; a mid-morning athletic break was designed to sharpen the senses; and no tuck was allowed.[39] The physical education programme was based on individual skills; running, jumping, throwing, and the like. Team games were played, and were both keenly contested and successfully performed, but they were not allowed to dominate the programme. A broad spectrum of art and craft activities was introduced and compulsorily followed by all boys: here the aim was to find one activity for each boy that would be his *grande passion*.[40] Hahn insisted, like Thring, that "Every boy could do something well and that it was the task of the schoolmaster to find out what that was". [41]

Vigorous and arduous outdoor activities, such as sailing, climbing and canoeing were included for the hazards they presented to boys in order that they would learn to triumph over defeat. Service to the community was encouraged through activities including life-saving, manning a coastguard station, running the local fire-service, practical estate work, and mountain rescue patrols: here a reality of useful service was the keynote.[42] Underlying the whole was a belief that everything should be done in the service of God.

Encouraged by his undeniable success at Gordonstoun, Hahn set out to extend his influence. He inaugurated the Gordonstoun Badge in 1936 so that boys in the surrounding area could benefit from some of Gordonstoun's principles; the badge was earned through fitness tests, life-saving drills and cross-country expeditions.[43] During Gordonstoun's wartime evacuation to North Wales, Hahn in 1940 set up a summer school to demonstrate his methods and the following year the Outward Bound Sea School was founded at Aberdovey. Here was Hahn's "war equivalent" in action. In his address at the launching ceremony for the school's schooner *Garibaldi*, Sir George Trevelyan voiced the Hahn creed: "If ever youth loses the thirst for

---

[39] Information from Mary Byatt.

[40] Arts and crafts worked better at Salem, outdoor activities were preferred at Gordonstoun: Flavin, *Kurt Hahn*, 26.

[41] Quoted in Sutcliffe, *Hahn*, 128.

[42] The fire-service was inaugurated during the school's wartime evacuation to Wales; information from Mary Byatt.

[43] The Gordonstoun Badge was quickly renamed the Moray Badge and became the Moray County Badge in 1938; information from Mary Byatt. See also Flavin, *Kurt Hahn*, 27.

adventure, any civilisation, however enlightened, and any state, however well ordered, must wither and dry up".[44]

Within a decade this first Outward Bound School was followed by five more in Britain, and a score were established across the world. It is through Hahn's work that outdoor activities soon formed an integral part of the physical education programmes at public and state schools, and his Outward Bound Schools spawned countless outdoor activity centres where, if only for a limited period, the benefits of a boarding school life, together with those of an arduous training programme of activities, were experienced by the nation's youth. In 1956 the Duke of Edinburgh Award Scheme was launched as a nationwide successor to the Gordonstoun Badge: at first it was for boys only but soon the scheme was widened to include girls. Under the vigorous sponsorship of the Duke of Edinburgh, who had been a boy under Hahn at both Salem and Gordonstoun, thousands of youngsters were attracted to a scheme built on physical fitness, community service, outdoor pursuits and expedition training. The declared aim to promote useful citizenship ensured that the scheme was widely adopted by schools and youth organisations and in industry.

Hahn's main contribution to the practice that physical education is a vital ingredient of holistic schooling was as the publicist *par excellence.* Coade may have been truer to Thring's original concept but Hahn drew the nation's attention to its benefits. Since his early days as Prince Max's private secretary, Hahn had the knack of getting influential people on his side. These men all saw the value of Hahn's passion and inspiration, and they were able to temper his innovations to meet British needs. By the 1950s and 1960s, most public and state secondary schools had assimilated many of Hahn's ideas, even if they took only those that they regarded as acceptable or those that could be fashioned into their own traditional mould.

---

[44] Quoted in Hermann Rohrs, *Kurt Hahn* (London: Routledge and Kegan Paul, 1970), 126.

CHAPTER TWENTY-ONE

FULL CIRCLE, 1930-1970:
"GIGANTIC CHANGES ARE AFOOT"

I

Cyril Norwood, headmaster at Harrow, boasted in 1929 that the public schools were enjoying a period of great prosperity:

> Applicants crowd to their doors, and parents sue humbly for the admission of their sons. They house themselves in buildings of increasing convenience and splendour, and lay out playing-fields with an elaboration which would astonish our immediate forerunners.[1]

It did not last long. The world economies plunged into the Great Depression as Norwood wrote these words and its effects were to last a decade. The incomes of the rich plummeted and school fees were out of reach for many. Pupil rolls for some schools in the north of England fell to forty per cent of capacity. Repton, in the Midlands, closed a boarding house, made several masters redundant, and reduced the salaries of the remainder. Even Harrow, in wealthy London, closed a house.[2]

There were other hard facts to be faced. As the century had progressed so the state provision of secondary education had improved. Through the innovation of the School Certificate examinations in 1917 and the introduction of State Scholarships to universities in 1920, a steadily increasing stream of grammar school boys and girls was gaining graduate status for entry to the professions, traditionally the preserve of the public schools. These grammar schools were closely modelled on public school practice, though usually they were a shade more progressive, and now they were seen to produce a rival product at little or no cost. The effect was immediate: the public schools had to work harder on academic attainment, and harder work meant less time for games.

---

[1] Norwood, *Education*, 129.
[2] Bernard Thomas, *Repton, 1557-1957* (London: Batsford, 1957), 127-129; Tyerman, *Harrow*, 410.

That change had to come was obvious to all public school headmasters
but the process of bringing it about was sporadic, seemingly radiating out
from London and the Home Counties at so many miles a year. But for the
intervention of the Second World War, it is probable that reform would
have reached all schools by the 1940s. A change in the attitude to games
also cast doubt on the value of "team spirit" and the role games played in
its inculcation.[3] Calls were made for the inclusion of individual sports such
as golf and tennis to supplement the traditional diet.[4] In addition, games
alone were seen as insufficient for the whole physical well-being of a boy
and the Roperian view of physical education gained wider acceptance
through the efforts of Smithells, Hedley and Murray.

The desire for better practice, however, was hampered by the shortage
of qualified male physical education teachers. Relief eventually came with
the founding of Leeds Carnegie and Loughborough but the reforms that
many headmasters wanted could not be achieved until these teachers were
available. Instead the schools encouraged their ex-service instructors to
cope with the new approach and success was not universal. Nonetheless,
the intention that public schools should adopt a broad approach to physical
education had been signalled and in 1942 the Headmasters' Conference
recommended that all schools should appoint a qualified director of
physical education.[5] The weakening of the over-riding belief in the values
of athleticism and team spirit had begun. The movement was not
consistent, with some schools attaining in the 1970s what others had
accepted in the 1930s, but the momentum had been generated; it could be
resisted but not checked.

II

Owen retired from Uppingham at Easter 1934 and was later appointed
Archbishop of New Zealand. He was succeeded by the twenty-seven-year-
old John Wolfenden; he would also find fame in later life as vice-chancellor
of Reading University and chairman of two influential government reports.[6]

---

[3] Guy Kendall, *A Headmaster Reflects* (Edinburgh: William Hodge & Co, 1937),
134.
[4] Kendall, *Reflects*, 135.
[5] James Mangan, "Athleticism: A Comparative Study of the Emergence and
Consolidation of an Education Ideology" (PhD diss., University of Glasgow,
1976), 347.
[6] The reports were *Sport in the Community* (1960) and *Homosexual Offences and
Prostitution* (1963). Wolfenden was knighted in 1956 and created Baron
Wolfenden in 1974.

The Uppingham trustees had made a brave appointment, and not just because of the headmaster's youth. The first day of the summer term was a multiple first for Wolfenden: at a public school, at a boarding school, as a housemaster and as a schoolmaster. His lack of pedigree was dwarfed by his achievements: a first in *Literae Humaniores* and hockey goal-keeper for both Oxford University and England.

Wolfenden had only five years to implement changes at Uppingham before the declaration of the Second World War checked his efforts but they were five years of reform.[7] He questioned the amount of time and energy that were devoted to games in a memorandum to housemasters:

> In comparison with other schools in our class we are, on the whole, better at games than they are; but are we as much better than they are at games as they are better than we are at other things? What are we sacrificing for our athletic success? Do we encourage our boys to think too highly of athletic success to the exclusion of some other things? Is it not our job as Housemasters to correct anything that is wrong in our values?[8]

Wolfenden then set out to raise academic attainment, telling the ablest boys to work hard for the School Certificate, "a necessary qualification without which you have little chance of entering a university".[9] An indication that he had hoped to give Uppingham a broader cultural outlook, a balanced curriculum, a stronger sense of community and a commitment to holistic ideals can be found in the address that he delivered on his return to the school in 1953 at the time of the Thring centenary celebrations. In this most succinct summary of his predecessor's theory and practice, Wolfenden drew out the three strands that made Thring a revolutionary. Two were principles, the third was a method, and all three had relevance for the modern public school. They were that individual attention should be given to every pupil; that teaching should be directed to the education of the whole man; and that every school should create a system to ensure that the two principles were realised.[10] The accident of war had denied Wolfenden the realisation of his ambitions.

---

[7] From December 1940 Wolfenden did war service at the Air Ministry in London as Director of Pre-Entry Air Training for the RAF.

[8] Quoted in Matthews, *By God's Grace*, 167.

[9] Matthews, *By God's Grace*, 167-168.

[10] *USM*, 1953, 16-20.

III

Reforms at Uppingham and in other schools may have stalled in 1939 but the pressure for change was now even greater. Pupil numbers were in free-fall; in part, and contrary to experience in the Great War, because boys were leaving school early in order to serve in the armed forces.[11] There had been 510 boys in the school when Wolfenden arrived in 1934; now in 1942 the total had dropped sharply to 406. It was a similar story across the public school system. The governors at both Mill Hill and Liverpool College debated the chances of survival after the war; numbers at Repton fell from 393 in 1937 to 276 five years later, necessitating the shutting of a second house. Cyril Norwood, now President of St John's College, Oxford, told the Board of Education of the public schools' difficulties and that, in exchange for training the nation's leaders, they should receive some government funding. His proposal that ten per cent of places at public schools should go to pupils from elementary schools was incorporated in the *Norwood Report on Secondary School Education* in 1943 and again a year later in the *Fleming Report on The Public Schools and the General Educational System*.[12] The public schools had embraced the principle of equality of opportunity, if only to survive.

But the wartime desire for social equity and national unity did not persist. By the time of the publication of the *Fleming Report*, and to the amazement of public school headmasters, the demand for fee-paying places had risen sharply and the schools were now financially secure. There was no need to trade independence for cash. In addition, the election of the Labour Party to government in 1945 ensured that Norwood's other proposal that state secondary schools should adopt the ethos of public schools had become unattractive, if not incendiary, and that Fleming's recommendations were never revived.[13] One element of equality of opportunity did survive, however, when the Butler Education Act of 1944 granted 179 grammar schools a degree of state funding in exchange for accepting a quarter of their pupils from state primary schools; these were soon known as direct grant schools.

The pressures on the public schools had been relieved but not eliminated. The academic demands were greater than ever because, as Ralph Moore, the new headmaster of Harrow, complained: "the age of assumed and assured privilege is over" now that the "subsidised and

---

[11] Plowright, *Repton*, 35.

[12] McCulloch, *Philosophers*, 31-32; Tyerman, *Harrow*, 412-413; Turner, *Old Boys*, 191.

[13] McCulloch, *Philosophers*, 37, 39, 65; Turner, *Old Boys*, 191-192.

specialised second rate" from the grammar schools was squeezing out the public school boy in the chase for university places.[14] The competition attending state secondary schools had doubled between 1944 and 1955, and throughout the 1960s examination results of public school leavers were below the national average.[15] Team games thus began to lose some of their stranglehold on a boy's time, energy and interest as the new physical education departments at Marlborough in 1938, at Worksop from 1947, and elsewhere thereafter introduced more individual sports. The liberal revolution did not always move purposefully but rather leapt randomly when new headmaster succeeded old headmaster. As James Mangan discovered, Harrovians only began to challenge compulsory team games in the 1970s when Marlburians had won that battle before the war.[16] As late as 1966, Eton had just one physical education teacher for the thousand or so boys in the school, compared to the thirty-two masters needed to teach classics.[17]

IV

With the prospect of men from Carnegie, Loughborough and Goldsmiths' joining, if not working alongside, the women from Dartford, Anstey, Chelsea, I. M. Marsh, Bedford and Dunfermline to teach physical education in the nation's schools, Newman's successor as Chief Medical Officer at the Board of Education, Arthur MacNalty, was able to claim in 1939 that

> Physical education ... is now an established part of the curriculum of all the schools within the purview of the Board. Every child in these schools, unless medically exempt, receives regular instruction in gymnastics and in one or more branches of physical education ... which, in scope and quality, need not fear comparison with that which can be produced in any other country.[18]

But for boys the optimism was short-lived. The Second World War saw the closure of the men's colleges, the conscription of men already at work in schools, and the decision of many not to return to teaching when peace resumed in 1945. Not until the mid-1950s were most boys' schools staffed

---

[14] Quoted in Mangan, *Athleticism*, 212.
[15] Turner, *Old Boys*, 194, 196, 241.
[16] Mangan, "Athleticism," 354.
[17] *The Public Schools Yearbook*, 1967, 192-194.
[18] Quoted in Smith, *Stretching*, 145-146.

with qualified physical education teachers and, even then, the majority did not have graduate status and so were excluded from the masters' common room.[19] Only the men and women who had studied together at the University of Birmingham from 1946 had degrees in physical education, albeit in combination with an arts subject; other male graduates had followed the Jacks route, attending a post-graduate course in physical education at Carnegie, Loughborough or Goldsmiths', or at one of the new specialist colleges in Cardiff, Cheltenham, Exeter or York.[20] Gymnastics formed the core of the two PE periods on the weekly school timetable; these were supplemented with a games afternoon where the specialist teacher received assistance from other members of staff. The games afternoons of the Victorian public schools were now the norm at all secondary schools, state and independent. Innovations in curriculum content came from Marlborough, where Murray had moved before the war, and from Worksop, with John Coghlan as director of physical education from 1952. Murray and Tommy Hunter, the school doctor, used circuit training in their programmes of developmental, remedial and rehabilitation gymnastics; Coghlan broadened provision to include individual sports such as badminton and tennis, and moved athletics from the spring to the summer term.[21] Other teachers added expressive and creative ingredients to lessons in the gymnasium: dance came from Lisa Ullman's Art of Movement Studio in Manchester and educational gymnastics through Ruth Morrison's work at I. M. Marsh.[22]

The responsibility for the inspection of physical education in schools had transferred in 1945 from the office of the Chief Medical Officer to His Majesty's Inspectors within the Board of Education. This change signalled a decline in official interest in the therapeutic and developmental roles for physical education and a greater interest in the actual physical activities on the curriculum and how they were taught; this adjustment has persisted to this day.[23] The programme offered at most schools expanded far beyond gymnastics, three team games, and perhaps some athletics and swimming to a spectrum of thirty or more sports. Inter-school matches and multi-

---

[19] Three colleagues of my generation who taught in grammar schools in the mid-1960s were "below the line" on staff lists and were not admitted to the staff room; the graduates were "above the line".

[20] McIntosh, *Physical Education*, 253, 254.

[21] Coghlan was Deputy Director of the Sports Council in the 1970s, Secretary General of the International Council of Sport Science and Physical Education from 1976 until 1982, and its Vice-President from 1982.

[22] McIntosh, *Physical Education*, 262, 270, 273.

[23] McIntosh, *Physical Education*, 252.

school competitions flourished and most grammar schools included local public schools in their fixture lists.[24]

The general acceptance in the 1960s of physical education as a subject worthy of degree status encouraged post-graduate study in scientific aspects of human movement and in teaching methodology. The former led at many schools to the inclusion of termly measurements of pupils' height and weight, and the introduction of periodic tests of strength, speed, agility and endurance to map pupils' progress; the latter applied psychological research in skill acquisition to techniques and tactics in sport. Other researchers went further: physical education "through the body" was judged to be as valuable as physical education "of the body", and pupils' social, moral, spiritual and cultural education was deemed to benefit as much as their physical development and skill acquisition. The claims were hard to prove but, like Thring a century earlier, many teachers were convinced by the double benefit argument.[25] Enquiries by the newly founded Schools Council revealed that pupils, school leavers and parents agreed that school physical education had a vital role to play and there was general acceptance that sound physical development and fitness were the best foundations for pupils' future health and well-being.[26]

The most far-reaching change for physical education, as Peter McIntosh noted, came in 1969 when the ablest students on three-year courses at the specialist physical education colleges, now rebranded as colleges of education, could add a fourth year to gain a Bachelor of Education (BEd) degree, with the courses covering both academic study and professional training. Post-graduate degrees and professorships followed over the next decade. Physical education in schools now had the same status as every other subject, and the opportunity for promotion to senior management and headships was open to all.[27]

---

[24] When I was a sixth-former in Plymouth in the early 1960s, there were "Public and Grammar School" competitions in most sports and county teams had mixed membership; as I began teaching at Uppingham at the end of the decade, some of the strongest sporting opposition came from King's School in Peterborough, Northampton Grammar School and Wyggeston School in Leicester, all state schools.

[25] Smith, *Stretching*, 161.

[26] *Schools Council Enquiry 1: Young School* Leavers (1968) and *Schools Council Sixth Form Enquiry* (1970): Smith, *Stretching*, 161-162.

[27] McIntosh, *Physical Education*, 278.

V

John Wolfenden left Uppingham in 1944 to become headmaster of Shrewsbury and was succeeded by Martin Lloyd. Educated at Marlborough and with a first in modern languages from Gonville and Caius College, Cambridge, Lloyd had taught at Rugby before the war. On arrival at Uppingham he instituted the practice, already common at many schools, of limiting an incoming housemaster's tenure to fifteen years. This opened promotion prospects for young men and curtailed the athletic influence of housemasters who had presided for thirty years or more. Nonetheless, team games continued to "occupy" a boy's time five afternoons a week, even though the new General Certificate of Education (GCE) examinations at Ordinary and Advanced levels had raised the importance of academic attainment.[28] Some of the two-day cricket matches had been abandoned in 1945 but boys still might be let out of lessons early to attend batting practice in the nets.[29]

In 1948 there was a call from some boys for more individual sports such as tennis, athletics and swimming but an apologia on the virtues of *esprit de corps* by the captain of games signalled that the time was not yet ripe. A team from His Majesty's Inspectorate who visited the school in 1949 were impressed by the pleasant buildings and the life in the boarding houses but not by what they found in the classrooms: academic standards were "not as high as the reputation of the School would lead one to expect". All might have been well with parents and Old Boys if the school's traditional prowess at Rugby football and cricket had remained high but standards there were falling.[30] Old Boys were dismayed, the school's trustees were concerned, and Lloyd was ordered to prepare a report on the lack of success and to propose remedies. He concluded that talented boys were going to rival schools, few masters were expert coaches, and not enough attention was given to boys in the lower teams and to younger boys. Changes were needed.

Some were already underway. The PTI appointed by Owen in 1919 retired in 1952 and his successor, John Hall, had gained PT periods with the younger boys. With his encouragement the athletic sports were enlarged to include throwing events, clubs for fencing and badminton were added in 1958, and inter-school matches in athletics and tennis were

---

[28] These were introduced in 1951.

[29] *USM*, 1945, 4.

[30] In the five-year period from 1955, just two-fifths of matches for the XV and one-fifth for the XI resulted in Uppingham victories. The XI won just six inter-school matches in the period 1950 to 1962, and lost twenty-one.

introduced in 1960 and 1961 respectively.[31] 1959 witnessed a turning point when an editorial in the school magazine was permitted to voice objection to the dominance of school life by compulsory games and to the authority of the Committee of Games to enforce attendance, with a beating if necessary. The editor noted that to be in the XV meant instant popularity and that few praepostors were other than games players. Clever boys were dismissed as "weeds" and "the swots" whilst "rugger chaps" were the real heroes. The appeal for a broader sporting programme and more recreational activities was objectively stated.[32] Compulsory team games lasted a few more years but "breathers" and boxing soon went.[33]

When Lloyd retired in March 1965, his *vale* recalled the liberal innovations he had made: an increased freedom on Sundays, a reduction in personal fagging, and the broadening of the games programme were the three examples cited. But that was not enough and pupil numbers had begun to slide: 591 boys in 1962 but only 550 were promised for 1965.[34] All public schools were now faced with the problem of restless teenagers wanting greater say in their appearance and dress, in the music they listened to and the films and television programmes they watched, in how they spent their leisure time, and how they could secure a reduction in the number of activities they were required to attend, especially compulsory team games. Revolution reached Uppingham when the praepostors decided unilaterally that they would no longer beat miscreants.[35]

VI

The post-war public schools had enjoyed fifteen years of prosperity and complacency, and suffered five years of discomfort; now they were to be threatened from without and challenged from within. They were subject to compulsory inspections from 1957 and in 1965 the Labour government signalled its intent to integrate them within the state system by appointing a Public Schools Commission chaired by Sir John Newsom; its main recommendations, however, were never implemented. Five years later a second commission, headed by Professor David Donnison, led to the demise of the direct grant schools. Parents now demanded better teaching

---

[31] *USM*, 1952, 137; 1953, 105; 1956, 101; 1957, 144; and 1958, 3.

[32] *USM*, 1959, 157-158.

[33] Science teaching moved to new buildings in 1956. These were a five-minute walk from the centre of the school and made break-time assembly for "breathers" difficult. *USM*, 1964, 2 and 1965, 10.

[34] *USM*, 1965, 3; Matthews, *By God's Grace*, 196.

[35] Some housemasters followed the praepostors' lead.

to fend off state school competitors in the race for higher education places. Boys and girls needed to work harder and so they rebelled against compulsion and conformity, restrictions and rules, conventions and corporal punishment.[36] A different and better product was required: modernisation was signalled with the sector's rebranding as "independent schools". John Dancy, Master of Marlborough, was quickest off the mark:

> The public schools of Great Britain will only survive if they cater for the whole man: his intellectual, cultural, technological, physical, emotional, and spiritual growth and understanding.[37]

Girls' schools were less alert, with many still devoting more time to social accomplishments than to academic attainment, and several boys' schools tempted their brightest and best to join their sixth forms. Marlborough led the way in 1968, quickly followed by Wellington and Charterhouse, and then a rush of many more in the 1970s. The presence of the girls boosted A-level results, raised the importance of the arts, and softened much of the athletic heartiness. The all-pervading masculinity of the boys' schools was further diluted with more women on the staff and married couples with young children running boarding houses. Co-education brought the ideal of the family into the classroom and domestic ties were strengthened with the introduction of weekend exeats and half-term breaks, and through the encouragement of regular visits by parents for concerts, plays, matches and the innovation of parent-teacher meetings.[38]

VII

It fell to John Royds to bring about change at Uppingham, not least because Oakham School, just six miles to the north, was shedding its direct-grant status and beginning its evolution to Britain's largest independent co-educational day and boarding school. His life before Uppingham had been rich and varied; he was not afraid of change and innovation. Born on September 23, 1920, he was the third son of a clergyman-schoolmaster at Liverpool College. He attended Monkton Combe School in Bath, where he was head prefect and captain of cricket, before going up to Queens' College, Cambridge in 1939 to read history.

---

[36] For more on these changes see Turner, *Old Boys*, 193-219.

[37] John Dancy, *The Public Schools in the Future* (London: Faber, 1966), 40, 55. Also quoted in Tyerman, *Harrow*, 547.

[38] John Rae, *Public School Revolution* (London: Faber, 1981), 129, 132, 141; Turner, *Old Boys*, 208-210, 212, 216; Tyerman, *Harrow,* 480.

When war intervened he enlisted in the ranks of the Royal Artillery before transferring to the Indian Army, serving in the Far East and attaining the rank of major. He was captured by the Japanese and incarcerated as a prisoner-of-war. On repatriation he resumed his studies, graduated with an upper-second in 1947, and joined the teaching staff at Bryanston. There he served as head of history, master-in-charge of cricket and housemaster. In 1961 Royds was appointed headmaster of the General Wingate School in Ethiopia. His ability to raise funds to enable talented boys from poor homes to receive the same education as sons of the country's elite brought him both gratitude and renown.

The Uppingham trustees recognised that Royds was a visionary. His unconventional career brought unconventional ideas and methods to Uppingham; or, rather, brought them back to Uppingham. Twelve years as a master under Coade at Bryanston had given Royds an apprenticeship at the school where the theory and practice in every aspect of the curriculum most closely represented the legacy of Thring's ideal of manliness. The wheel had turned full circle. That everything Royds initiated in his ten-year headmastership quickly became commonplace in all schools bears testament to the clarity of his vision and his determination to bring it to reality.

Change began at the end of Royds's first year with the appointment of fifteen new members of staff, nearly a third of the total. Seven of the fifteen had graduated from universities other than Oxford and Cambridge and several had attended state schools. One taught physical education, the first master to do so since Beisiegel retired in 1902, and his qualifications matched those recommended by Maurice Jacks in 1931: a university degree, a post-graduate diploma from Loughborough, and eligible to join the masters' Common Room.[39] Physical education needed better facilities so Royds set about appealing to Old Boys and other friends of the school to build a sports centre that would incorporate the 1883 swimming pool alongside a gymnasium and sports hall; the 1902 gymnasium became a theatre. The Bryanston-inspired Pioneers were established some thirty years after the original to offer outdoor manual labour and estate work as an arduous alternative to the cadet corps. When volunteer numbers in the corps stabilised, the Pioneers gave way to Community Service, whether service to the school or to the town and county. The greatest change came

---

[39] Royds ended the master-instructor distinction in 1966. John Hall, the PTI appointed by Lloyd in 1952, and his colleagues teaching metalwork and woodwork could now enter the Common Room. They no longer appeared "under the line" on school lists.

in 1973 when the first girl was admitted to the sixth form; there were fifty three years later.

Many of the young men and women appointed by Royds were talented coaches and the results for the school's traditional sports steadily improved. The decade from 1966 saw the Rugby football XV under the leadership of Malcolm Bussey and Michael Gavins hold its own against other schools, as did the cricket XI when Garth Wheatley gained assistance from Maurice Hallam. Peter Colville's hockey XI won the majority of its matches.[40] New or upgraded sports did even better: tennis, cross-country and athletics, led by Ashley Dawe, Michael Tolkien and Malcolm Tozer respectively, won most of their matches whilst the shooters coached by Simon Pattinson took the school to national renown, winning the Ashburton Shield five times in thirteen years.[41] Good coaching was not the whole story. Royds had introduced timetabled lessons in physical education for all in the first two years, appointed a team of five specialist teachers who also taught another subject up to sixth-form level, and initiated both remedial and rehabilitation gymnastics. Boys in their first year played Rugby football and hockey out of step with the rest of the school so that they could be taught by the best coaches and, when a year older, many were permitted to opt instead for activities in the sports centre. This allowed teams in badminton, basketball, fencing, squash, swimming and water polo to flourish, and soccer became a popular Sunday recreation. Canoeing, climbing, life-saving and sailing broadened the choice still further. Only Thring's beloved Eton fives languished.[42]

Attention to the individual child was once more stressed; academic standards rose; music, art and drama were no longer viewed as purely effeminate activities; the cadet corps was voluntary; community service and charitable support were important; choice of leisure-time activities was permitted; team games no longer served merely to occupy time; athleticism had mellowed. A balance returned, both to the total educational experience and to its physical education content. Thring would have been pleased to see PE lessons on the timetable and qualified staff to teach them. He would also have liked the broad programme of games and sports,

---

[40] Rugby football 1966-75, won 42, lost 50; cricket 1966-75, won 9 lost 10 (and lots of draws); hockey, 1966-75 won 24, lost 17.

[41] Tennis 1966-75, won 33, lost 12; cross-county, won about 60%; athletics 1966-75, won 62, lost 25; shooting, Ashburton Shield winners in 1969, 1976, 1978, 1981 and 1982. Most athletics matches were triangular fixtures, hence the high number of results.

[42] Fives colours were not awarded after 1992.

the enthusiasm of those who ran them, and the excellence of the new facilities. The increased provision of recreational opportunities and the attention given to remedial gymnastics were both sympathetic to his principles. The weekend and holiday expeditions in outdoor activities were merely a modern extension of Thring's rambles in the Rutland countryside. Seventy years had been lost but not Thring's "True-life".

The novelist Ernest Hornung remembered Thring best for his sermons in chapel; Nigel Richardson, when preparing his address for Royds's memorial service, found that many of his former pupils recalled how powerfully their headmaster commanded the pulpit, whether challenging them to think about the existence of God or to spell out how the stronger members of the community had a duty to protect the weak and eccentric. Royds told them how fortunate they were and how they must capitalise on that good fortune:

> Rotten boarding schools are the rottenest of schools, but the best ones offer unrivalled opportunities for co-operation – for doing things together; games and good music, arts and crafts, the visiting of handicapped and old people; adventurous training and field studies in term-time and holidays.[43]

> Go out to meet life. On your first day at Uppingham, I urged you to make the most of the great opportunities here. Now I say it again. Don't come to the end of your life wishing you had been more adventurous, or had made better use of your opportunities. Always volunteer; always be ready to chance your arm, to accept responsibility. Your privilege lies in actually being able (more or less) to choose your work in life. Most of your fellow human beings have no such choice. Remember the other 99% and be generous in giving yourself to others.[44]

Bryan Matthews, his Second Master and an Old Boy of the school, appreciated that Royds shared Thring's belief in the value of "True Life" and he recalled these words from Royds's final sermon, delivered shortly before he left to take Holy Orders: "True life is to be found in true worth, where the common wealth, the common weal, the common good are the concern of all."[45] In one of his first sermons at the school, Royds had warned parents and staff in the congregation:

---

[43] Royds had been bullied as a young boy: Nigel Richardson, *Memorial Address for John Royds,* 2011, 1.
[44] Both quotations from Richardson, *Memorial*, 2, 3.
[45] Quoted in Matthews, *By God's Grace*, 207.

> Gigantic changes are afoot ... we need special wisdom in helping young
> people steer a course between dangerous extremes ... individuality is
> precious, but so is unselfish service to the community.[46]

Royds had that special wisdom; from 1965 to 1974 he guided
Uppingham through the turbulent years of political and social unrest,
outrage at home and abroad, student rebellions and public school
demonstrations, long hair and loud music, and brought it safely to the
calmer decades ahead.[47] He had managed more change in ten years than
his predecessors had in thirty, or perhaps even seventy, and he brought the
school full circle to rediscover its Thringian inheritance.[48]

---

[46] Quoted in Richardson, *Memorial*, 2.

[47] Take 1968, for example: the Black Power movement for civil rights in America;
worldwide condemnation of America's role in the Vietnam War; the Soviet
invasion of Czechoslovakia; the assassination of Martin Luther King; Enoch
Powell's "Rivers of Blood" speech; and the beginning of The Troubles in Northern
Ireland.

[48] Royds was ordained in 1975 and served in Northamptonshire, with the Church
Missionary Society in Pakistan, and in Salisbury until his death, aged 90, in 2011.

CHAPTER TWENTY-TWO

FROM PE TO PESS, 1970+: "PHYSICAL EDUCATION IS THE ONLY SUBJECT WHICH CONTRIBUTES TO ALL ASPECTS OF THE EDUCATION OF YOUNG PEOPLE"

I

Brian Ashley called the first Public (later Independent) Schools' Physical Education Conference (ISPEC) at Marlborough in 1970; this successor to the Secondary Schoolmasters' Physical Education Association of the 1930s still thrives today. As the men's tradition had more or less caught up with the women's, women were happy to join the Conference three years later. Differences remained, however. Women had responsibility for all physical education and sport in girls' schools, whereas men working in boys' schools were keen to maintain the involvement in games coaching of their colleagues who taught other subjects. The men also usually taught a classroom subject alongside their physical education. As many schools became co-educational, so the traditions merged: the teacher in charge of girls' tennis, for example, was likely to be a female physical education teacher or male geographer, but rarely a female mathematician.

Sports centres comprising a whole range of indoor facilities including gymnasia, sports halls, swimming pools, squash courts and much more became the urgent priority for every ambitious independent school. Winchester, where Geoff Dyson, the former national coach for athletics, was the director of physical education, led the way in 1968. Millfield School developed as the first centre of sporting excellence from the late 1950s, awarding scholarships to outstanding candidates. Preparatory schools for children aged three to thirteen felt the change too: broadening their games provision, sending teachers on in-service courses on the new physical education that were organised by ISPEC, and eventually appointing specialist staff who had been trained for the younger age-group. In 1972 a committee chaired by Mike Gover, co-headmaster of The

Dragon School in Oxford, published the first physical education curriculum for preparatory schools: it comprised gymnastics, creative movement, swimming, games, athletics and adventure activities.[1]

John Kane's 1971 survey on *Physical Education in Secondary Schools* contained an appendix by Brian Ashley, then chairman of ISPEC, which compared provision in state and boys' independent schools.[2] The time allocated to PE periods and games of over seven hours was four times that of state schools; organic development was the preferred objective rather than training in leisure; but both ranked enjoyment of physical activity as the most desired pupil effect. Independent school teachers, usually grammar school educated and a quarter with degrees, generally taught a second subject; all sought equal status with their classroom colleagues, a concern that no longer worried those who taught in state schools. The position had changed considerably by 1985 when ISPEC commissioned Nick Aplin of Loughborough University to re-examine independent school provision. Now half the teachers were former pupils of independent schools and the same number were graduates. Most men taught a second subject; most women did not. The time allocation in boys' and co-educational schools stayed steady at over seven hours; in girls' schools it was six hours. Organic development remained the major objective; enjoyment continued as the most desired pupil effect. Women teachers felt totally secure in their schools, whereas some men still worried that their subject's place on the timetable was not guaranteed.

Many public school Old Boys and Old Girls from the Victorian era onwards had continued to play sport at a high level on leaving school, representing clubs, counties, and the four home countries, as well as competing for Britain in the four-yearly Olympic Games, but they always did so as amateurs. In 1963, however, the Marylebone Cricket Club abolished the distinction between Gentlemen and Players and this made it socially acceptable for public school alumni to become professionals in all sports that drew crowds and television revenue large enough to meet the costs.[3] Golf, Rugby football and tennis matched cricket's initiative, and many more sports followed their lead over the next decade. Independent schools adapted accordingly: no longer were all former pupils destined for

---

[1] Common Entrance Board, *Curriculum for the Preparatory Schools* (London: HMC & IAPS, 1972), M1-M5.

[2] John Kane, *Physical Education in Secondary Schools* (London: Macmillan, 1974), 111-118.

[3] W. G. Grace cannot be the only amateur sportsman or sportswoman to have ignored the convention.

the traditional professions now that sport (as well as music, drama, art, film, television and more) could provide both fame and financial security.

II

Kane's survey of physical education in state secondary schools in the early 1970s reported favourably on the teachers and their teaching. Teachers were "dedicated (averaging an additional eight hours of unpaid extra-curricular service each week), have a broad educational commitment ... and an enlightened capacity for sustained hard work".[4] Most were young, with an average age of twenty-six, few were graduates, and over half taught a second subject. In response to the predicted forthcoming "Leisure Age", the highest ranking teaching objectives were skill acquisition, self-realisation and recreation, and teachers wanted their pupils to enjoy involvement in physical activities and to achieve success.[5] Games therefore dominated the curriculum for both boys and girls, and at all age groups.

The move from selective to comprehensive secondary schooling in the 1970s and 1980s had little effect on physical education other than a reduction in inter-school matches. In part this was because three or more schools were combined to produce one large one, often with rolls of over a thousand pupils, and in part because some local education authorities discouraged competition in all areas of school life. Thus Peter McIntosh's report on physical education and school sports in London at the end of the 1980s was equally praising of teachers' performance but he also suspected that a twenty-year period when physical education was most pupils' favourite subject was coming to an end.[6] McIntosh was a former Senior Inspector of Physical Education in London; he had been educated at Mill Hill School when Maurice Jacks was headmaster and Gerald Hedley was director of physical education.[7]

---

[4] Kane, *Physical Education,* 62.

[5] Many people believed that the rise of automation, robotics, computers, atomic energy, communications, and efficiency would improve productivity so drastically that technology would eliminate almost all human labour. The main problem would be how to prevent boredom.

[6] Peter McIntosh, *'My Favourite Subject'* (London: ILEA, 1988), 93-94.

[7] He read classics at Oxford University, taught geography and physical education at Malvern College (1939-1942) and lectured at the University of Birmingham (1946-1959) before his move to London (1959-1974). He succeeded Philip Smithells as Professor of Physical Education at Otago University, New Zealand (1975-1978).

McIntosh found that the average time allocation to physical education was 30 minutes daily in primary schools and four periods of the 40-period week in secondary schools. Almost all secondary schools had a gymnasium and a hard-surface outdoor sports area but few had on-site playing fields or their own swimming pool but had to use off-site facilities. Lessons comprised, in descending time allocation: games, gymnastics, swimming, dance, athletics and outdoor pursuits. The recent introduction of an extended school day enabled almost all secondary schools to provide extra-curricular sport to all-comers in both competitive and non-competitive activities. Fitness training, football, badminton and dance were the most popular options. Most schools fielded school teams for football, athletics, cricket and netball; these competed after school or at the weekends. London-wide sports competitions thrived.

One consequence of the exclusivity of the Ling Association was the founding of additional organisations to represent those working in physical education as organisers, lecturers and inspectors.[8] This fracturing of the profession, with each group protecting its own interests, led to a weakening of the leadership of physical education, governments deciding on physical education policy and practice without due consultation, and the profession being left to pick up the pieces. Eventually, in response to the establishment in 1970 of a Committee of Inquiry into Teacher Training led by Lord James, the former High Master of Manchester Grammar School, four associations and representatives of the specialist colleges agreed to work together to provide joint evidence.[9] This collaboration, however, failed to save the specialist colleges, with most from the mid-1970s becoming schools of physical education within polytechnics or universities. Students intending to teach now studied an academic course related to physical education for three years, followed by a year of professional training. The model proposed by Maurice Jacks forty years earlier was at last adopted.

But a lesson had been learned: strong leadership of physical education was needed. In 1973 the four associations were joined by the Independent Schools' Physical Education Conference to form the British Council of Physical Education to provide "an overarching body able to represent the views of the profession to the government and other organisations". The

---

[8] The Ling Association became the Physical Education Association in 1956 and the Physical Education Association of the United Kingdom in 1992.
[9] The Physical Education Association, the British Association of Organisers (Advisers from 1975) and Lecturers in Physical Education, the Association of Teachers in Colleges and Departments of Education, and the Universities Physical Education Association.

call to unify the profession was strong but twenty-one years of deliberation, including two weekend seminars at Uppingham, achieved nothing of consequence. Agreement on major matters was rare, association self-interest prevailed, and the government and other organisations continued to ignore the profession. The BCPE disbanded in 1994.[10]

III

Following a decade of cuts in education budgets, Margaret Thatcher's Conservative government planned in 1985 to restructure teachers' salaries and to change their conditions of service. After a series of unproductive meetings with the government, the teachers' trade unions withdrew from the negotiations and instituted a ban on meetings, lunchtime supervision and extra-curricular activities as well as selective strike action. Most programmes of after-school sport and Saturday matches were terminated at a stroke and secondary school children quickly became accustomed to going home at 3.30pm. Once the dispute was settled, a teacher's year was specified as 1265 hours spread over 195 working days, or 33 hours a week of "contact time" with pupils. As this did not include time spent preparing lessons, marking pupils' work and other such tasks, a compromise was agreed that teachers were no longer required to supervise after-school activities. Thereafter headteachers had to use their best diplomatic skills to persuade colleagues to offer even a skeleton programme, and many soon gave up trying. McIntosh's fears were realised.

The year of McIntosh's London report, 1988, also witnessed the Seoul Olympic Games. Sportsmen and sportswomen educated at state schools won the lion's share of Britain's twenty-four medals.[11] Eight of the twelve newly capped players in that year's England team for Rugby football came from state schools, as did nine of the ten new caps in England's cricket team. It was a similar story in other sports. In short, former pupils from maintained schools, ninety-four per cent of the school population, rightly dominated international sport in 1988, most of them had attended comprehensive schools, and national teams were performing well. But it was a different story in 1996, the year of the Atlanta Olympic Games, when Matthew Pinsent and Steve Redgrave won Britain's sole gold medal, and the demise of state school sport was held largely to blame.[12]

---

[10] The author represented ISPEC on the BCPE for all twenty-one years. See Bailey, *One Hundred Years*, 103.

[11] Only 10 of the 48 medal winners had been educated privately; all competitors in team sports received a medal.

[12] In rowing, Men's Coxless Pair.

The Education Reform Act of 1988 led to the introduction of a National Curriculum for schools and it was with a mixture of joy and relief that, three years later, teachers and organisations welcomed the inclusion of physical education as a foundation subject. John Major had succeeded Thatcher as prime minister and both he and Kenneth Clarke, the Secretary of State for Education and Science, were determined that sport, and team games in particular, should be at the core of the National Curriculum. It thus needed dogged resistance by the National Curriculum Working Group on Physical Education to guarantee that the eventual published curriculum was both broad and balanced. Ian Beer, chairman and Head Master of Harrow School, and his two lieutenants, Elizabeth Murdoch and Margaret Talbot,[13] ensured that the programmes of study covered "games activities, dance forms, gymnastic activities, athletic activities, swimming and water based activities, and outdoor education and adventure activities" but they were unable to specify a weekly time allocation for physical education: that was left for each school to decide.[14] But the purpose was clear: "Physical Education is the only subject which, through the use and knowledge of the body and its movement, contributes to all aspects of the education of young people."[15]

Beer's working group regarded extra-curricular sport as a valuable extension to timetabled lessons but it could do no more than encourage its reinstatement. Few schools responded positively but John Beckwith, an Old Harrovian businessman, did.[16] In 1994 he founded a charity, the Youth Sport Trust, to provide more opportunities in sport for children and young adults, both in school and in the community. Under the dynamic leadership of Sue Campbell, a former physical education teacher, the trust managed to retrieve some of the lost extra-curricular provision through a range of initiatives.[17] With the several physical education associations still in mute disarray, Campbell took the lead in articulating to government agencies the potential for physical education and school sport to help bring about whole school improvement. Her efforts were rewarded when Tony

---

[13] Miss Murdoch was Head of Chelsea School of Human Movement at Brighton Polytechnic; Mrs Talbot was Carnegie Professor of Physical Education at Leeds Polytechnic.

[14] Ian Beer, National Curriculum Working Group on Physical Education: Interim Report, December 21, 1990, 61.

[15] Beer, Interim Report, 5.

[16] He was knighted for his service to youth sports in 2002.

[17] These included the TOPs programme resource cards for teachers in 1995 and the creation of eleven Sports Colleges in 1997 (there were 550 in 2010). Email from Alison Oliver, August 14, 2018.

Blair's Labour government came to power in 1997 and saw the creation in 2000 of the School Sport Co-ordinator Programme to ensure that all children spent a minimum of two hours each week engaged in physical education and sport.[18]

Two years later the Blair government issued its Physical Education, School Sport and Club Links Strategy with the three-fold purpose to boost whole school improvement, improve fitness levels, and raise the standard of elite sport. Foremost amongst the initiatives was the rebranding of some schools as Specialist Sports Colleges and the creation of School Sport Coordinator Partnerships to link them to a family of secondary and primary schools. Physical education and school sport were now officially recognised as parallel but distinct means to realise the government's social, health and sporting aims; one during the school day, the other after school. The launch of *School Sport Magazine* in 2004 confirmed the separation; it is now published five times a year and its list of subscribers has grown steadily.[19]

IV

Physical education continued to secure its place in the curriculum of independent schools during the decades either side of the new century: timetabled periods, afternoon games, recreational activities, inter-house and inter-school matches and competitions, and outdoor pursuits and adventure activities at the weekends and in the holidays. State schools only rarely provided match opposition but the gaps in the fixture lists were filled by travelling to more distant schools and through the creation of national competitions in athletics, cricket, Rugby football and more, but the real explosion came in individual sports. The Independent Association of Prep Schools (IAPS) organised similar events for younger pupils. The importance to a school of a strong reputation for sport, particularly in the major teams games (cricket, hockey and Rugby football for boys; hockey, lacrosse and netball for girls), combined with the overriding holistic aim to make the most of every pupil's talent (in diving, golf, swimming, tennis and other individual sports), led to most schools offering all-rounder and sports scholarships to pupils with observed potential.

The need to staff such broad provision led to the increased appointment in schools of peripatetic professional coaches to teach specific activities during games afternoons. These visiting coaches were usually managed by

---

[18] Renamed the School Sport Partnerships Programme in 2004.
[19] 4000 in 2018. Email from Julie Penrose, August 21, 2018.

a director of sport who also assumed responsibility for roles formerly undertaken by the teacher in charge of games: providing in-service training for teachers helping with sport, supervising the grounds staff, co-ordinating fixture lists, organising transport and the like. The director of sport, usually a qualified physical education teacher and often a retired professional sportsman or sportswoman, worked alongside the director of physical education; the latter concentrated on the timetabled lessons. The introduction of the Children Act in 1989, which had increased the commitment of all teachers to ensure that pupils were safeguarded at all times, and the ever-increasing pressure to improve examination results at GCSE and GCE A-level, in part through the publication in national newspapers of academic league tables, saw the gradual withdrawal of classroom teachers from helping with the afternoon games programme.[20] They were replaced by additional PE teachers or sports coaches and, to make optimum use of their time, many games lessons moved into the academic timetable.

Several independent schools from the 1970s promoted classroom studies in physical education as part of integrated science, general studies or health-related fitness programmes and these contributed to the introduction in the 1990s of GCSE and A-level examinations in both physical education and sports studies. Courses directed at these examinations became popular and many physical education teachers now devoted all their time to their specialist subject, whether in the sports centre or in the classroom.

By the end of the century the quality of physical education provision and the standard of sporting achievement were high in most independent schools, and particularly so in the major senior schools, whether single-sex or co-educational, day or boarding. One measure of their success was the healthy life-style of pupils; another was their high involvement in competitive and recreational sports; a third was the contribution independent schools made to national sporting success. More than 500 former pupils who had attended independent schools since 1970 gained senior international representative honours in 50 different sports for Team GB or one of the four home countries in the period 2000 to 2012, and 40 won medals in the Olympic Games of 2000 (Sydney), 2004 (Athens) and 2008 (Beijing).[21]

---

[20] The first General Certificate for Secondary Education, or GCSE, examinations were taken in 1988. John Clare published the first academic league tables in *The Daily Telegraph* in 1990.

[21] For more information see Tozer, *Physical Education and Sport*, 275-299.

V

Much happened between 2004 and 2019 to form the modern history of physical education in Britain but the close proximity of these events to the present day prevents an objective assessment. Five developments in these fifteen years, however, would seem to stand out from the many and each has had a direct bearing on the current state of physical education.

First, the amalgamation in 2006 of the Physical Education Association of the United Kingdom and the British Association of Advisers and Lecturers in Physical Education to form the Association for Physical Education at last gave the profession a unified voice. Under the energetic leadership of Margaret Talbot (2006 to 2009) and Sue Wilkinson (2009 onwards), school physical education gained advocates who could match the promotional skills of Sue Campbell and the Youth Sport Trust.[22] When working in constructive partnership, much can be achieved.

Secondly, the medal haul of Team GB at the Olympic Games in London in 2012 and Rio de Janeiro in 2016 was a remarkable triumph after the ignominy of 1996 and was seized upon by government and governing bodies of sport as evidence that financial investment could bring about change. Britain came third in the medal table in London and second at Rio. The latter was the first occasion when a host nation had improved its tally at the subsequent Olympiad.[23] Former pupils of independent schools were well represented, forming seventeen per cent of Team GB in London and twenty-three per cent in Rio.[24]

Thirdly, David Cameron's Conservative government that had succeeded Labour in 2010 introduced the PE and Sport Premium in 2013 to improve the provision of physical education and school sport in primary schools across England.[25] Schools could use the extra funding in various

---

[22] Each was honoured: Mrs Talbot was appointed OBE in 1993; Mrs Wilkinson MBE in 2016; and Ms Campbell MBE in 1991, CBE in 2003, and created Baroness Campbell of Loughborough in 2008.

[23] 65 medals in 2012 (29 gold, 17 silver, 19 bronze); 67 medals in 2016 (27 gold, 23 silver, 17 bronze).

[24] Six sports comprising 139 competitors were dropped from Team GB for Rio, and the team was more highly selective than its London predecessor. These changes had little effect on independent school numbers but severely reduced state school participation, thus increasing the independent school percentage.

[25] The Conservatives led a coalition government with the Liberal Democrats from 2010; it was succeeded by a Conservative government in 2015. In 2010 the Specialist Sports Colleges were scrapped and the School Sport Coordinator Partnerships were replaced by the School Games (from intra-school competition to national finals) and a network of School Games Organisers (who also introduced

ways including sharing the cost of a specialist teacher with three or four other schools, providing training for staff to teach PE more effectively, and hiring coaches to work alongside teachers. The programme has received warm support from the Association for Physical Education and the Youth Sport Trust.

Fourthly, the much publicised legacy of the London Olympic Games for the improvement of the nation's health and well-being has still to be realised. The fit may well be fitter but most adults take little or no part in physical activity, with nearly eighty per cent failing to meet the government's target of half-an-hour of moderate exercise twelve times a month. Exercise for many has become a fashion style rather than a life-enhancing habit.[26] Fitness levels in children are also falling: research by Gavin Sandercock's team at Essex University found that muscle strength of ten-year-old boys and girls had decreased by twenty per cent between 1998 and 2014, and muscle endurance by thirty per cent, and that the rate of decline of both was accelerating. Obesity in children is another major concern: in 2017 the National Health Service classified ten per cent of children entering primary school and twenty per cent of primary school leavers as obese.[27]

And fifthly, physical education is being squeezed out of the timetable in state secondary schools despite being rated by pupils as their third most enjoyable subject.[28] Research by the Youth Sport Trust in 2017 reported that more than a third of schools had reduced timetable provision for pupils aged fourteen to sixteen since 2012, and a quarter had done so in the previous year. Many pupils receive no physical education in the years when they sit examinations at GCSE and A-level.[29]

---

activity clubs in primary schools for the least active children). Email from Alison Oliver, August 14, 2018.

[26] The style is is known as 'athleisure'. Sports shoes comprise three-quarters of footwear sales. *The Times*, February 24, 2019.

[27] National Health Service, *Statistics on Obesity, Physical Activity and Diet - England*, 2018; Gavin Sandercock and Daniel Cohen, "Temporal trends in muscular fitness of English 10-year-olds 1998–2014: An allometric approach," *Journal of Science and Medicine in Sport* (August 2018), https://www.jsams.org/article/S1440-2440(18)30438-9/fulltext, accessed September 26, 2018.

[28] After art and computing: https://yougov.co.uk/news/2018/09/04/which-school-subjects-do-boys-and-girls-enjoy-more/, accessed September 15, 2018.

[29] *Physical Education Matters*, Summer 2018, 90. Analysis by *Tes* (formerly the *Times Education Supplement*) revealed that between 2011 and 2017 the time allocated to PE in state-funded secondary schools fell by five per cent for pupils aged 11 to 14 and by twenty-one per cent for those aged 15 to 16: *Tes*, August 31, 2018.

VI

The commitment to holistic education in all schools in membership of the Independent Schools Council has cemented physical education's place in the timetable and sport's role in the co-curricular programme regardless of the ever-increasing academic pressures and the never-ending parental demand for value for money.[30] Governors, headmasters and headmistresses give keen support for both and readily explain why they do so.[31] Schools are well staffed with physical education teachers and sports coaches, often with postgraduate degrees; promotion opportunities see many progress to school leadership teams and headships. The provision of on-site sports centres, swimming pools, courts and playing fields is generous, and liberal funding permits extensive fixture lists for countless teams in an alphabet of sports and also gives pupils access to a range of off-site adventure activities. Ample opportunities are provided for recreation and play, especially in boarding schools.

A survey of 169 senior independent schools undertaken by the Headmasters' and Headmistresses' Conference in 2015 showed that more than five hours were allocated to physical education and sport each week, and that the figure was consistent for all age groups, for boarding schools and day schools, and for single-sex and co-educational schools. Participation in sport was dominated by each school's major games (usually cricket, hockey, netball and Rugby football) with up to ninety per cent of each age group playing, but many more sports were provided. Forty-three sports were offered to girls, thirty-eight to boys, with inter-school and inter-house matches in most. Nearly 7000 pupils in the 169 schools had represented their county in sport and 1400 their country; there were national representatives in forty different sports.

Each school on average employed six teachers of physical education and sport together with nine visiting specialist coaches, and they enjoyed the support of thirty teachers of other subjects. In response to four

---

[30] Schools now prefer to use the term co-curricular rather than extra-curricular to confirm that sport, drama, music and the arts are an integral part of the total curriculum and not a voluntary add-on. In 2018 529,164 pupils attended 1,326 ISC schools.

[31] See the essays by a chairman of governors, seven headmasters and headmistresses, and the chief executives of two schools' association in Tozer, *Physical Education and Sport,* 59-66, 83-90, 95-100, 113-116, 191-198, 199-206, 221-228, 237-244, and 261-274; as well as articles by two headmasters and two headmistresses in recent editions of *Physical Education Matters*, the journal of the Association for Physical Education.

questions, the schools reported that it was becoming more difficult to recruit teachers of other subjects to help with sport; that fixture lists remained extensive in the two winter terms but were harder to maintain in the examination-dominated summer term; that there was no pressure from academic subjects to reduce the timetable allocation for physical education; and that the increase in the number of national competitions that extended over more than one term was leading to unwanted early specialisation by the talented all-rounder.[32]

A sampling survey carried out by the author of twenty-eight day and boarding senior independent schools (*SIS 2018*), all in membership of the Headmasters' and Headmistresses' Conference or the Girls' Schools Association, ranked the pupil benefits and desired outcomes for physical education in the following order: enjoyment of participation; physical development and health; self-realisation and self-confidence; perseverance and co-operation; stress release and mindfulness; skilfulness and co-ordination; social contacts and friendships; discipline and good behaviour; and academic improvement. The top three almost match the order reported by Brian Ashley in 1971 in a survey of forty-three schools in membership of the Independent Schools' Physical Education Conference (*ISPEC 1971*) to reveal consistency across half a century.[33]

Rank order of pupil benefits and desired outcomes	SIS 2018	ISPEC 1971
Enjoyment of participation	1	1
Physical development and health	2	3
Self-realisation and self-confidence	3	2
Perseverance and co-operation	4	>6
Stress release and mindfulness	5	4
Skilfulness and co-ordination	6	5
Social contacts and friendships	7	>6
Discipline and good behaviour	8	>6
Academic improvement	9	-

There is, however, some variation between boys' schools, girls' schools and co-educational schools, as shown by the average rank order for each type of school. Enjoyment of participation and physical development and health clearly lead in all types, with discipline and good behaviour and academic improvement consistently bottom, whereas the

---

[32] *HMC Sports Survey*, March 2015.
[33] Ashley's published list had just six items: Kane, *Physical Education*, 113.

average rank orders for the five remaining benefits are similar and often overlap.[34]

Average rank order in SIS 2018	Boys' schools	Girls' schools	Co-ed schools
Enjoyment of participation	3.1	1.6	2.1
Physical development and health	2.3	3.6	4.0
Self-realisation and self-confidence	4.2	3.7	4.1
Perseverance and co-operation	4.0	4.3	4.3
Stress release and mindfulness	5.9	4.7	4.8
Skilfulness and co-ordination	5.5	4.9	6.7
Social contacts and friendships	6.2	6.0	5.8
Discipline and good behaviour	6.9	7.0	6.6
Academic improvement	6.8	8.0	6.8

In response to Lord Coe's call that one legacy of the London Olympic Games should be the improvement of the nation's health and well-being, the Independent Schools Council in 2015 revived the dormant Independent/State Schools Partnership Forum. Under the chairmanship of Deborah Leek-Bailey, and with financial support from the Department for Education, Schools Together has created nearly 600 partnerships in physical education and sport between independent and state schools. Most partnerships involve the sharing of teachers, teacher training and facilities; many see pupils from the partnership schools playing sport together.[35]

---

[34] The author thanks the correspondents at the twenty-eight schools who responded to his survey.

[35] See https://www.schoolstogether.org/projects/?category=Sporting

CHAPTER TWENTY-THREE

MODERN LEGACY, 1970+: "THE POTENTIAL TO STIMULATE SIGNIFICANT HEALTH AND EDUCATIONAL ATTAINMENT BENEFITS"

I

The teaching of physical education in state schools and academies has been guided since 1992 by a National Curriculum with its associated programmes of study and attainment targets. Most independent schools have also accepted this guidance, usually amplified to meet their own needs. Edward Thring would have resisted all external meddling on what was taught in his school, and how it was to be taught, but he was happy to publicise what he believed to be the purpose of physical education and how that purpose should be achieved. *Sermons Delivered at Uppingham School* (1858) and *Education and School* (1864) were the mid-Victorian equivalents of a printed prospectus or an online website for his school, and together they tell the reader much about physical education at Uppingham. The evidence that Thring provided to the Schools Inquiry Commissioners in 1865 adds facts to support his opinions; his talks to the boys after the annual athletic sports provide much down-to-earth encouragement and advice; the later sermons often include explanations on the benefits and pitfalls of playing sport; his *Theory and Practice of Teaching* (1883) expands on the views expressed in the earlier book; and the addresses that he made in his last years, when famous, look back on the battles that he fought to maintain the purity of his original ideals.

Thus it is possible to analyse the purpose of physical education at Thring's Uppingham; to discover its aims and objectives; to examine its staffing, curriculum content, timetabling, and provision of facilities; and to compare them with modern examples in order to discover whether or not Thring's legacy has had any influence in schools of the twenty-first century. The modern examples selected for that comparison span nearly fifty years from 1971 to 2018. They are:

John Kane's 1971 survey for the Schools Council that was published in 1974 as *Physical Education in Secondary Schools* (*Kane 1971*);

Brian Ashley's appendix to Kane's survey on independent schools for boys (*Ashley 1971*);

Peter McIntosh's 1988 report for the Inner London Education Authority, published as *"My Favourite Subject"* (*McIntosh 1988*);

The first National Curriculum for Physical Education, 1992. (*NC 1992*);

The latest National Curriculum for Physical Education, 2014. (*NC 2014*); and

The 2018 report on "The Case for Physical Education becoming a Core Subject in the National Curriculum" by Jo Harris, published in *Physical Education Matters* (*Harris 2018*).

II

The purpose of physical education at Thring's Uppingham was to contribute its part to the ideal of manliness, the Christian-Platonic concept of the whole man. The equivalent terminology in 2018 would be holism or wholeness:

> Holistic schooling, whether past or present, is concerned with the development of every pupil's intellectual, emotional, social, physical, artistic, creative and spiritual capabilities and it encourages both personal and collective responsibility. Physical education contributed to several aspects of Thring's true manliness but not to all of them; those were the concern of other ingredients of the curriculum. Some aspects, however, were the sole responsibility of physical education.[1]

Thring declared his commitment to holistic schooling in *Education and School*, his 1864 prospectus for Uppingham:

> Health of body, health of intellect, health of heart, all uniting to form the true man, and being the common object of teacher and taught.[2]

---

[1] See Chapter 15 Part I.
[2] Thring, *E&S*, 32.

How does this holism compare with modern purposes?

Neither *Kane 1971* nor *Ashley 1971* asked the question. *McIntosh 1988* did and was disappointed to discover that "participation as a basis for competent function and learning" was second in rank order to "social behaviour", a throwback to the late nineteenth century.[3] The first National Curriculum, *NC 1992*, saw an overarching purpose for physical education: "general and specific skills are acquired, knowledge and understanding developed, and positive attitudes and personal and social attributes encouraged".[4] The most recent National Curriculum, *NC 2014*, placed great emphasis on the purpose of physical education as preparation for sport:

> A high-quality physical education curriculum inspires all pupils to succeed and excel in competitive sport and other physically demanding activities. It should provide opportunities for pupils to become physically confident in a way which supports their health and fitness. Opportunities to compete in sport and other activities build character and help to embed values such as fairness and respect.[5]

III

Thring's aims for physical education were in sympathy with Ruskin's statement that "The body must be made as beautiful and perfect in its youth as it can be, wholly irrespective of the ulterior purpose".[6] In *Education and School* Thring wrote:

> ... the one pre-eminent mark of the highbred man is the simple play of the limbs that move with perfect ease, and, as they move, throw off a sense of liberty, and grace, and unconstrained command of strength, able at any moment to do anything that courage may demand of activity, or duty impose on endurance.[7]

Twenty-three years later, he repeated:

---

[3] McIntosh, *'Favourite'*, 34.

[4] Beer, Interim Report, 5; Department of Education and Science, *Physical Education from 5 to 16* (London: HMSO, 1989), 1.

[5] Department for Education, *National Curriculum in England: Physical Education Programmes of Study* (London: HMSO, 2013).

[6] Ruskin, *Time and Tide*, letter 16, para. 95.

[7] Thring, *E&S*, 132.

The life builds the body. A bad life builds an ugly, unhealthy body; and a good life builds a good and healthy body, and in a short time prints the character on the body, as much as if a label was put round a man's neck, to ticket him as a scamp or an able man.[8]

And throughout his headmastership, Thring commended the "joy of strength and movement".[9] These are Platonic aims.

Kane 1971 and *Ashley 1971* did not include the aims of physical education in their remit, but *McIntosh 1988* did and his findings were in sympathy with Thring's:

… to lay the foundations for a physically literate population, cultured in the sense of both having an understanding of physical activity and experiencing enjoyment in it.[10]

The first National Curriculum for Physical Education (*NC 1992*) had a straightforward aim that was also similar to Thring's: "Physical education in schools aims to develop control, co-ordination and mastery of the body."[11] The latest National Curriculum, *NC 2014*, expanded the number of aims to four but was more prosaic:

to ensure that all pupils … develop competence to excel in a broad range of physical activities, are physically active for sustained periods of time, engage in competitive sports and activities, [and] lead healthy, active lives.[12]

IV

Early in 1860 Thring appointed a gymnastics master, Georg Beisiegel, the first at a British school. It seems that he originally considered giving the role to a military non-commissioned officer; this man would have had no specialist qualifications for it was not until later in 1860 that the Army sent its first dozen NCOs to train under Archibald MacLaren at the Oxford Gymnasium. Whether on the advice of his wife, Marie, or that of Gerold Benguerel, Thring chose a civilian candidate with a specialist qualification from a Prussian school of gymnastics, probably Berlin. It was fifty years

---

[8] Thring, *Addresses*, 119.
[9] Thring, Sermons 32, 70 and 373.
[10] McIntosh, *'Favourite'*, 17.
[11] DES, *Physical Education*, 1.
[12] Department for Education, *National Curriculum in England: Physical Education Programmes of Study* (London: HMSO, 2013).

before a similar appointment was made at another boys' school: Reginald Roper at Eton in 1910.

All physical education teachers in *Kane 1971* had specialist qualifications but fifteen per cent of those teaching in independent schools (*Ashley 1971*) were ex-service NCOs.[13]

Thring joined the boys in their games until he reached fifty, and he encouraged all his masters to follow his example. There are ample records of those who did and none of those who chose not to. Even the Swiss Benguerel and the unathletic Howson took part. Specialist and non-specialist could each play a role in physical education, as teacher or participant.

The contribution of teachers of other subjects to the teaching of athletics, games, and outdoor pursuits was acknowledged by *Ashley 1971* but not by *Kane 1971*. *McIntosh 1988* warmly welcomed their role in London's schools and commended the practice whereby many physical education teachers also taught another subject.[14] The first National Curriculum, *NC 1992*, assumed that all physical education would be taught by teachers with specialist qualifications as did it most recent successor, *NC 2014*.

V

The content of the physical education curriculum at Thring's Uppingham was five-fold: gymnastics (including fencing), games (team and individual), athletics (track, field and cross-country), swimming (including life-saving), and country pursuits (both summer and winter). These were the Uppingham equivalent of today's programmes of study.

A century later, *Kane 1971* found the same five activities in school physical education programmes but now with the addition of dance. *McIntosh 1988* reported the same six at the end of the following decade, as did the first National Curriculum (*NC 1992*). Games were given highest priority in the most recent National Curriculum, *NC 2014,* followed by dance and outdoor pursuits; athletics, gymnastics and swimming were optional additions.

---

[13] Few PE teachers at this time were graduates; the first BEd students graduated in 1968.

[14] This practice meant more teachers and a greater range of expertise. McIntosh, *'Favourite'*, 34.

VI

Thring had advertised in 1864 that he planned to equip his school with "a School Library, Museum, Workshop, Gymnasiums, Swimming Baths, Fives Courts, or any other pursuits that conduce to a healthy life."[15] The gymnasium had been built five years earlier; the provision of playing fields increased steadily throughout his headmastership from the solitary cricket field on The Upper to additional large expanses on The Middle and The Leicester, as well as short-term access to rented fields; the Tectum served as an indoor games hall in the early years until it became the first of many under-cover Eton fives courts; swimming was taught in pools excavated in rivers and tar-pits, or in the sea at Borth, until the construction of the indoor heated pool in 1883; and outdoor pursuits took place across the Rutland or Welsh countryside, or on the skating rink beside the swimming pool.

Kane 1971 reported that most schools had on-site facilities for gymnastics, dance, athletics and games, and access to swimming and outdoor pursuits off-site. This was echoed by *McIntosh 1988*. The first National Curriculum, *NC 1988*, assumed that all secondary schools would have access to all these facilities, as did *NC 2014*.

VII

As Thring reported to the Schools Inquiry Commissioners in 1865, the school day was designed in part to accommodate physical education.[16] Gymnastics was taught on weekdays at noon or in the evening; two hours were free for sport during the afternoon on the four whole school days each week; and all afternoon on the two half holidays each week was set aside for sport, recreation or country pursuits. Sunday allowed time for long-distance rambling or skating and sledging. It is likely that the average boy had an hour a day of physical education, seven hours a week.

This is more than the two hours in *Kane 1971* but about the same for the boys' independent schools in *Ashley 1971*. *McIntosh 1988* found that about ten per cent of the school week was allocated to physical education (excluding extra-curricular activities), or two and a half hours. The first National Curriculum (*NC 1992*) made no recommendations about timetable allocation as it was not on the working party's remit, but research by the Department for Education reported that it was 107 minutes

---

[15] Thring, *E&S*, 179.

[16] See page 46. *Schools Inquiry Commission.* V, 97.

in 2004. The most recent National Curriculum, *NC 2014*, recommends that schools should provide a minimum of two hours physical education each week but research by the Youth Sport Trust has shown that many pupils receive much less.[17]

VIII

All ingredients of Thring's physical education programme had distinct objectives and they worked together to achieve the desired outcomes.

Gymnastics

> [is] the only representative we have of pure exercise of the natural body, combining strength and skill, and stands quite apart in its character from either the races or the games.[18] (1)

Athletics

> produce the manly spirit of competition, and the love of training the body, for training's sake.[19] (2)

Games

> represent the right actions of bodily life, and all right action is pleasure. But the very games they play are full of pain, possible disagreeables, blows, defeat, disappointment, mortified pride, trials of temper, trials of courage, trials of honesty.[20] (3)

> One could ... escape [from the classroom] to a thorough good game, and restore the balance of human nature by a hearty game on both sides [boys and masters].[21] (4)

Swimming

> ... provision ought to be made for a ... Swimming Baths ...[22] (5)

---

[17] "Youth Sport Trust," *Physical Education Matters*, Summer 2018, 90.

[18] *USM*, June 1864, 195.

[19] *USM*, March 1866, 2.

[20] Thring, *Addresses*, 121.

[21] Thring, *E&S*, 248.

[22] Thring, *E&S*, 179.

Outdoor pursuits

> A good walk in the country can do more in some ways for a boy with eyes than twenty games of cricket or football.[23] (6)

Health

> The first object of a man, then, would be to train the body to be strong.[24] (7)

> We do not seek to avoid colds by wrapping boys up in furs, but by making them strong.[25] (8)

Hardiness

> If we train ourselves to be perfectly ready, to bear hunger and cold then we have got rid of the main temptation. If we are able to have the hardy elastic feeling of not caring for hardship then is our own spirit strong within us, then are we beginning to be free indeed. Food and warmth and vanity soon pass into laziness and lust and a hatred of active life.[26] (9)

School-work

> Many of the best readers in the school were to be found among the gymnastic pupils.[27] (10)

Wholeness

> If I wanted to train a soldier, I should not take a child and drill him every day and put him through the regimental movements; I should teach him to race, to climb, to swim, to be a gymnast, to play games, to make his body as strong, as active, as enduring as possible. It will be quite time enough to narrow this, and teach him the goose step, when he enlists.[28] (11)

Thring's objectives for physical education incorporate the nine identified by *Kane 1971* in this rank order of importance: organic development and health (1, 2, 7, 8, 9, 11), motor skills (1, 5, 11), self-realisation (2, 11),

---

[23] Rawnsley, *Early Days*, 114.
[24] Thring, *E&S*, 33.
[25] Diary, June 4, 1879 (Parkin, *Life*, 2:90).
[26] Thring, Sermon 134c.
[27] *USM*, June 1864, 195.
[28] Quoted in Parkin, *Life*, 2:201.

leisure (4, 6), social competence (2, 4, 6), moral development (2, 3, 4, 6, 9), emotional stability (2, 4, 6, 9), cognitive development (6, 10) and aesthetic appreciation (6).

IX

Kane 1971 recorded motor skills, self-realisation and leisure as the highest ranked objective, whereas organic development and health was seventh. *Ashley 1971* reported a different order, with organic development and health, motor skills and self-realisation at the top to match Thring.

McIntosh 1988 listed eight objectives which, when combined, covered seven on Kane's list but omitted cognitive development and aesthetic appreciation. There was no rank order. The first National Curriculum for Physical Education (*NC 1992*) did have one, with organic development and health and motor skills top and all but one of Thring's objectives covered in its list of eleven; cognitive development was absent.[29] The latest National Curriculum for Physical Education, *NC 2014*, matched its prosaic aims with generalised objectives:

> [Pupils] should develop the confidence and interest to get involved in exercise, sports and activities out of school and in later life, and understand and apply the long-term health benefits of physical activity.[30]

Perhaps in response to the blandness of *NC 2014* and the reduction of physical education's time allocation in many schools, Jo Harris and her colleagues on the Physical Education Expert Group (*Harris 2018*)[31], published a list of objectives or expected outcomes for physical education from their review of research literature to argue the case for physical education as a core subject in the National Curriculum.[32] Using the earlier

---

[29] Although it was present on the interim report that was submitted to Kenneth Clarke, the Secretary of State for Education and Science.

[30] DfE, *Physical Education*.

[31] Lorraine Cale (Loughborough University), Roger Davies (The Football Association), Steph Doehler (Sports Leaders UK), Jo Harris (Loughborough University), David Johnson (King Alfred's Academy), Laura Mitton (Loreto High School), Anita Richardson (Claremont Primary School), Christine Sprowell (Tennis Foundation), Will Swaithes (Youth Sport Trust), Sue Trotman (Dance Desk), Hannah Vecchione (St John's Roman Catholic Primary School), Rosalind Whitworth (Frederick Bird Primary School) and Sue Wilkinson (Association for Physical Education).

[32] Jo Harris, "The Case for Physical Education becoming a Core Subject in the National Curriculum", *Physical Education Matters*, Summer 2018, 9-12. Core

headings, they were: organic development and health, motor skills, aesthetic appreciation, moral development, social competence, emotional stability, cognitive development, self-realisation, and leisure. No rank order was intended, but the early listing of organic development and health and motor skills matches Thring's priorities.

The Physical Education Expert Group (*Harris 2018*) shared Thring's purpose for physical education in the curriculum: its contribution to holistic schooling.

> Making physical education a core subject in the National Curriculum has the potential to stimulate significant health and educational attainment benefits and ensure greater connectivity between physical education and other curriculum subjects, resulting in whole school improvements and an effective school-wide approach to children's personal development, behaviour and welfare …[33]

X

A second sampling survey carried out by the author of the twenty-eight day and boarding senior independent schools (*SIS 2018*) ranked the *Kane 1971* objectives for physical education as follows: organic development and health, motor skills, self-realisation, emotional stability, moral development, social competence, cognitive development, leisure, and aesthetic appreciation.[34] The top three match the order reported by *Ashley 1971* to indicate consistency in these schools over nearly half a century. Seven of the nine *SIS 2018* objectives correlate closely with Thring's rank order, with only emotional stability and leisure regarded with different emphasis.

---

subjects (currently English, mathematics and science) have higher status than non-core subjects and their place in the timetable is protected.

[33] Harris, "Case," 12.

[34] See Kane, *Physical Education*, 35. The author added health to organic development.

Rank order of objectives	SIS 2018	Thring
Organic development and health	1	1
Motor skills	2	2
Self-realisation	3	3
Emotional stability	4	7
Moral development	5	6
Social competence	6	5
Cognitive development	7	8
Leisure	8	4
Aesthetic appreciation	9	9

There is, however, some variation between boys' schools, girls' schools and co-educational schools, as shown by the average rank order for each type of school. Organic development and health clearly lead in all types, with leisure and aesthetic appreciation consistently bottom, whereas the average rank orders for the six remaining objectives are similar and often overlap.

Average rank order of objectives in SIS 2018	Boys' schools	Girls' schools	Co-ed schools
Organic development and health	1.9	2.0	1.8
Motor skills	4.3	3.6	3.8
Self-realisation	4.0	2.9	5.4
Emotional stability	4.5	3.4	4.8
Moral development	4.0	5.0	5.1
Social competence	5.7	4.6	4.1
Cognitive development	5.9	4.9	4.1
Leisure	6.0	7.8	7.6
Aesthetic appreciation	8.8	8.6	8.3

This comparison of the objectives for physical education at mid-Victorian Uppingham School and a small sample of its twenty-first-century successors suggests that Thring's legacy continues to be influential within the independent sector.[35]

---

[35] The author renews his thanks to the correspondents at the twenty-eight schools who responded to the survey.

XI

Beyond the independent sector, Thring's legacy to modern physical education found its fullest realisation in the initial National Curriculum for Physical Education (*NC 1992*). Its purpose had holistic intent; its straightforward aim to develop control, co-ordination and mastery of the body would have won Thring's approval; as would the employment of well-qualified teachers. Curriculum content was balanced and the working party wanted adequate time allocation. The rank order of objectives, although compiled over a century apart, was very similar; only cognitive development was absent from the modern list.[36]

In comparison, the most recent National Curriculum for Physical Education (*NC 2014*), with its emphasis on sport and its lack of holistic purpose, would seem to be a legacy of the athleticism of all the other Victorian public schools and not of Thring's Uppingham. Are the Spartans ousting the Athenians? Jo Harris and her colleagues (*Harris 2018*), in response, seek to restore the holistic purpose, broad aims and balanced programmes of study. This will, they believe, secure physical education's place in the school curriculum to the benefit of all children and to the nation's health, fitness and well-being.

---

[36] The Chairman of the Physical Education Working Group that created the initial National Curriculum was Ian Beer, Head Master of Harrow School from 1981 to 1991. Christopher Tyerman, the author of the most recent history of the school, judged that Beer subscribed to the whole-man ethos: at Harrow he "refashioned the ideals of Christian manliness" through "his enthusiasm for holistic education". Beer insisted that Harrow "must be seen to be producing from the School pupils … who are motivated by the power of the spirit to go out into the world to work for the service of others". Tyerman, *Harrow*, 407, 558, 561.

CHAPTER TWENTY-FOUR

EPILOGUE

I

James Mangan was the first to classify the Victorian cult of games as an educational ideology and in the text of three books he identified the components of his model of athleticism. These can be grouped under three headings: motives, machinery and myopia.[1] Motives refers to the purpose of athleticism; machinery to the means that translated theory into practice; myopia to the unforeseen consequences of the ideology.

The rank order of the five motives for athleticism was clearly signposted by Mangan: social engineering (cohesion and control), moral education (the Christian gentleman), patriotic leadership (obedience and command), imperial preparation (both civil and military) and physical training (physical development and health).

The machinery of athleticism identified by Mangan had ten ingredients: team games, playing facilities, the role of masters, compulsion to play, occupation of leisure time, boarding house patriotism, the support of Old Boys and parents, rituals and symbols, school literature, and Homeric heroes and chapel sermons.

The myopic shortcomings became evident as athleticism took hold in the schools: loss of liberty, lack of leisure activities, uncontrolled boy government, philistinism, and militarism.[2]

II

The creation of the rank order of five motives was perceptive; short enough to be recalled easily but each item had sufficient breadth to cover

---

[1] The three books are *Athleticism in the Victorian and Edwardian Public School* (Cambridge: Cambridge University Press, 1981); *The Games Ethic and Imperialism* (London: Viking, 1985); and *'Manufactured' Masculinity: Making Imperial Manliness, Morality and Militarism* (London: Routledge, 2011).
[2] For more detail, see Malcolm Tozer, *'Fashionable Idolatries': Thring, Uppingham and the Mangan Model of Athleticism* (Truro: Sunnyrest Books, 2017).

variations. Social engineering at one school could impose hard disciple whereas another might favour caring cohesion; moral education stretches from the Platonic virtues to the code of the warrior; training in leadership spans civilian management across military command to administration of the Empire; imperial service links mid-Victorian support for a commercial and cultural federation of the white dominions to later military imposition of colonial rule on much of Africa and South-east Asia; and the combination of physical development and good health allows for the various fitness regimes that came and went over time.

The ten well-defined cogs of the machinery of athleticism were not in a rank order; they worked in unison to propel the ideology. Headmasters chose which to use, their choice expanded as the nineteenth century progressed, and eventually all were deemed essential. The three that are most closely tied to the five motives are the first: what forms of exercise are imposed to achieve the desired effects; the fourth: what ideal is promoted to legitimise compulsory participation; and the last: how religious worship and the classical curriculum give theological and intellectual support for athleticism. These three reveal what each headmaster thought he would gain through harnessing play as an educational tool.

The gains were anticipated; the losses were not. The myopic concentration on the means of athleticism persuaded many headmasters to lose sight of the intended ends, and the gulf widened as the ideology's hold grew stronger. Should they have foreseen that herding teenage boys together in under-supervised boarding houses and granting the best footballers and cricketers the right to inflict corporal punishment on their juniors might demean scholarship and culture, enforce dulling conformity, and undermine moral standards? Perhaps. The concentration on social engineering, the first motive of athleticism, was the ruin of the second, moral education. And the damage was self-inflicted.

Mangan's model of the ideology of athleticism is an original and effective tool, his exploration of the games-playing cult is accurate and wide ranging, and the analytical method that he created is both precise and flexible. Together they represent Mangan's most important and most enduring contribution to the histories of education, sport and culture. But does the Mangan model work for Uppingham?

III

The Selwyn and McKenzie years, 1888 to 1915, match it perfectly. Uppingham was a conventional public school that deliberately followed the fashion set by Eton, Harrow and Rugby. And if we wind the clock forward, the model continues to apply until the appointment of John Royds in 1965, bar a five-year interlude from 1935 until 1940 when John Wolfenden strove to break the hold of team games.

But Thring's school does not wholly conform to the model. That the cult of athleticism never fully took hold during his headmastership was primarily due to his early recognition of the ideology's limitations and shortcomings. Thring was far-sighted when most headmasters were myopic. He strove to maintain the boys' liberty to roam, never curtailing it. The broad curriculum and strong cultural provision acted as a barrier to the intrusion of philistinism. Moral courage was consistently valued more highly than physical bravery, and all attempts to import militarism were defeated. The individual boy was all-important, thus conformity, *esprit de corps*, and rule by muscle were denied a role. And, bar one quickly remedied mistake, no games-mad master ever joined his staff.

Thring introduced physical education to his school with clear motives but they were in a different order to the Mangan model. Physical development and good health came top, followed by moral education, leadership training and imperialism, with social engineering last. Mangan's machinery of athleticism was applied at Uppingham and, except for the middle third of his reign, Thring kept firm control of all ten ingredients. Only between 1863 and 1876 did his grasp weaken but it was regained on the school's return from Borth.

So why was Thring's Uppingham different? Thring had three advantages over every other Victorian and Edwardian public school headmaster. First, he inherited a very small school with no long-standing traditions. This meant that as the number of boys rose from 25 to 300, so the headmaster was allowed to learn on the job; Thring had an idea for a school on his appointment but not a detailed plan. Secondly, he was open to fresh ideas and new methods, and he heeded the opinions of thoughtful and experienced colleagues; means that proved their worth were readily applied to the running of the school. And thirdly, he arrived at Uppingham engaged to be married to Marie Koch, whom he had met in Rome the previous year. This union encouraged him to look to Prussia for well-proven ingredients of educational theory that were foreign to current English practice, and to import them. These included continental notions of nurturing children; a broad curriculum of music, art, gymnastics, modern languages and science; and men to apply the first and to teach the second.

IV

What lessons does a physical education at Thring's Uppingham have for schools of today?

First, physical education is not worthy of its place on the curriculum unless it has a clear purpose, a credible aim, and relevant objectives.

Secondly, the purpose of physical education is to play its part to promote holistic schooling; it is the only subject that can contribute to all aspects.

Thirdly, the aim of physical education should be to realise the physical potential of every pupil and to foster a healthy life-style.

Fourthly, objectives that are unique to physical education should rank higher than those shared with other subjects.

And finally, what Thring termed "fashionable idolatries", the fads and fallacies that regularly afflict physical education, should be viewed with caution. It was sound advice in the 1870s, it remains sound advice today.

V

Sarah Singlehurst and Chris Dossett, respectively Director of Physical Education and Director of Sport at Uppingham, are best placed to report on Thring's physical education legacy at the school in 2019. It is proper that they should have the final word.

Physical education and sport at Uppingham in 2019 are central to both the curriculum and the co-curriculum and are of great significance to all pupils. Many sports field up to fifteen teams each Saturday and the talents that are nurtured and the social, emotional and physical qualities that are developed are of equal importance to all pupils, whether in the School's 1st XI or the Under-14s F side. The breadth of sports experience has multiplied enormously since Thring's time, not least through the provision of impressive facilities, and this permits his legacy that each pupil's talents should be discovered and developed to be more readily realised.

The PE Department delivers timetabled lessons to all pupils in the Fourth Form (Year 9). The breadth of this programme ensures that the skills required for participation in sport are in place, that the importance of physical exercise has been imbedded, and that the seeds have been sown for life-long enjoyment of physical activity. As in Thring's time, the curriculum comprises gymnastics, athletics, swimming, a range of games, and adventure activities. The emphasis on body management and skill acquisition ensures that education through the physical is both evident and valued. Timetabled lessons in physical education for older pupils are elective and lead towards GCSE and A-level examinations in PE or the

BTEC in Sport. These courses open up the many and varied opportunities for careers within and around sport.

Up to five hours a week of sport form part of the co-curricular programme. Sessions for each age group operate at different times through the day and across the week to make the best use of facilities and specialist teachers. The broad programme includes some legacy sports – athletics, cross-country running, cricket and Eton fives – but now adds other activities such as badminton, basketball, cycling, dance, sailing, squash and tennis as well as the traditional team sports of hockey, netball and Rugby football. Thring's foresight in investing in facilities and teachers has been reinforced several times over in Uppingham's history but most especially in the last decade. The Uppingham School Sports Centre is a flagship facility, combining school and community use, and a team of specialist PE teachers delivers the curricular and co-curricular programme. The PE department comprises seven teachers (including the Director of PE and the Director of Sport), specialist directors of cricket, Rugby football and tennis, and four sports graduate assistants.

Thring's insistence that each pupil's every talent should be nurtured is our guiding principle. His mid-Victorian aims and objectives are still relevant in 2019 as we prepare the next generation for the twenty-first century world of work and leisure through a purposeful curriculum that delivers physical, social and emotional intelligence and thus promotes health, happiness and general well-being.

PRIMARY SOURCES

A. Uppingham Archives (UA)

1. Edward Thring

A Wanderer
An Address delivered before the Education Society. 1885
Boarding Schools, a manuscript
Diary of his European tour. 1852
Diary: 1853 to March 1862
Diary: October 1886 to October 1887
Euripedes Autoclyus, a manuscript
Index Rerum: a collection of jottings
Letters: numerous
Little jotting book
Notes to communicants and confirmation candidates
Photographs and photograph albums
School Delusions. 1860
Sermons: 388 manuscripts
Three Letters and Axioms on Education. 1866
Uppingham School: The Statement of the Rev Edward Thring, Head Master, respecting the Organisation of the School: and the Decree of the Governors. 1859
White note book: begun in 1847

2. Other sources

Ballard, S., *Memories.* c1990
Beisiegel papers belonging to Miss Lillian M. Beisiegel and Mrs Camilla English
Belk, T. B., Fives at Uppingham, manuscript notes
Belk, T. B., A copy of the rules of Uppingham Football, 1857, manuscript notes
Belk, T. B., Sources for School History from the *Uppingham School Magazine*, typescript
Belk, T. B., *RHO:* a memorial sermon. 1961
Borth scrap-book. 1877
Bothamley, H. W., *Some Notes on the History of Uppingham School.* 1951
Box containing various medals and cups
Browne, R. B., *Memories.* 1979
Committee of Games Rules. 1877 onwards
David, Paul; a collection of papers

Donnelly, Ann, *Bisham Abbey Village School; Uppingham School; Bedales School; A Family Connection.* 1974

Endowed Schools Commission, a bound volume of manuscript and printed material

Essays and Translations, a manuscript volume of work by boys, 1854-1864

Founder's Day. 1882

Grove, W. R., copy of diaries, 1883-1887 (original in the possession of Peter Flower, OU)

Guide Book, 1869

Haslam, S. L. E., diary. 1870-1873

Hodson, C. G., *Memories.* c1980

Holden, Henry, a bound collection of printed material

Howitt, H. G., *Reminiscences.* 1966

James, W. P.*, Thring and Uppingham*

Minute Book and scrap-books of the Uppingham Rovers Cricket Club. 1863 onwards

Miscellaneous letters, papers etc in folders

Parkin correspondence: copies of extracts of letters from Marie, Sarah, Margaret and Grace Thring to George Parkin. 1871 onwards

Photograph albums

Reimers, Christian. *The Uppingham Cricket and Fives Songs.* 1857

Report of the Meeting of Head Masters of Schools. Winchester. 1873

Richardson, Nigel, *Memorial Address for John Royds.* 2011

Rome, R.C., Uppingham: The Story of a School – 1584-1948. Typescript. 1948

School Rules. 1869 and 1877.

Schools Inquiry Commission. V, Minutes of Evidence taken before the Commissioners, part ii. 1868

Schools Inquiry Commission. XVI, North Midlands Division. Special Reports of the Assistant Commissioners. 1869

Scrap-book of Archdeacon Johnson's School, Uppingham. 1874-1906

Scrap-books of the Uppingham and District Cricket Club. 1857-1922

Stephenson Papers belonging to Mr L. S. Oakley

The Hospitaler. February 1851 to June 1853

Thring, Gale, newspaper obituary. 1920

Thring, Margaret, *Memories*

Trustees' Minute Books

Uppingham Football Rules, 1857; a manuscript copy

Uppingham School – Christmas Examination. 1859, 1863 etc.

Uppingham School Library Catalogue. 1867

Uppingham School Magazine (USM). April 1863 onwards

Uppingham School Roll. 1885, 1894, 1906, 1914, 1922, 1932, 1948, 1962, 1974, 1987 & 1997

Uppingham School: Thring Centenary 1853-1953. 1953

Uppingham Tercentenary, 1884

Wilson, H. F., Scrapbook of Memorials to Edward Thring. 1887

Wooden box (carved by Thring) containing various letters and papers

B. Other Archives

1. Cambridge University Library

Add. Ms. 7348/4 'F.D.M.' Club. 1882

2. British Library

Add. Ms. 55171 Letters from Thring to the Macmillans

3. De Montfort University Library

Notes written by Gerald Murray (donated by Malcolm Tozer)

4. Stadtarchivs, Bundesstadt Bonn

Adressbuch der Universität-Stadt Bonn. 1859/60
Bonner Bürger-Buch. 1858
Bonner Kalender. 1834, 1841, 1846, 1847, 1848, 1850, 1855
Bürgermeister-Amtes, registration book for Dr Friedrich Breusing's Knabeninstitut.
    1856

5. University of Southampton Library

Beer, Ian (chairman), National Curriculum Working Group on Physical Education:
    Interim Report. 21 December 1990

C. Early Journals, Periodicals, Magazines, Newspapers & Reference Books

Contemporary Review. December 1866 to November 1927
Cornhill Magazine. May 1860
Dublin Review. July 1865
Edinburgh Review. August 1810 to October 1919
English Review. April 1918 to May 1933
Illustrated Sporting and Dramatic News. November 15, 1935
Musical Times. July 1, 1906
National Review. November 1864 to August 1911
Nineteenth Century. January 1880 to January 1927
Public School Magazine. March 1875
Quarterly Review. October 1860 to October 1928
Saturday Review. August 8 & October 3, 1857
The Century Magazine. September 1888
The Ludgate Illustrated Magazine. May 1894
The Parents' Review. 1901 & 1903
The Public Schools Yearbook. 1899, 1905, 1907, 1913 & 1967
The Times. April 14, 1876; April, 23, 1877; July 26, 1884; September 14, 1912;
    March 19, 1913; & April 27, 1914

BIBLIOGRAPHY

Alcock, Charles. *The Football Annual.* London: Lillywhite, 1870.

Alington, Cyril. *Things Ancient and Modern.* London: Longmans, Green, 1936.

Alington, Cyril. *Edward Lyttelton: An Appreciation.* London: John Murray, 1943.

Allen, Dennis. "Young England: Muscular Christianity and the Politics of the Body in Tom Brown's Schooldays." In *Muscular Christianity: Embodying the Victorian Age* edited by Donald Hall, 114-132. Cambridge: Cambridge University Press, 2006.

Altham, Harry. *A History of Cricket.* London: George Allen & Unwin, 1926.

Annan, Noel. *Leslie Stephen.* London: Weidenfeld & Nicholson, 1951.

Annan, Noel. *Leslie Stephen: The Godless Victorian.* London: Weidenfeld & Nicholson, 1984.

Arnold, Matthew. *Higher Schools and Universities in Germany.* London: Macmillan, 1874.

Ashley-Cooper, Frederick. *W. G. Grace – Cricketer.* London: Wisden, 1916.

Atwood, Sara. *Ruskin's Educational Ideals.* Farnham: Ashgate, 2011.

Badley, John. *Bedales School: Outline of its Aims and System.* Cambridge: Cambridge University Press, 1900.

Badley, John. *A Schoolmaster's Testament.* Oxford: Blackwell, 1937.

Badley, John. *Memories and Reflections.* London: G. Allen & Unwin, 1955.

Bailey, Richard *et al.* "The educational benefits claimed for physical education and school sport: an academic review," *Research Papers in Education* 24, no. 1 (March 2009): 1–27.

Bailey, Steve, and Wray Vamplew. *One Hundred Years of Physical Education 1899-1999.* London: Physical Education Association, 1999.

Barnard, Howard. *A History of English Education from 1760.* London: University of London Press, 1947/64.

Beck, Frederick. *Greek Education: 450-350 BC.* London: Methuen, 1964.

Bell, Adrian. *My Own Master.* London: Faber & Faber, 1961.

Benson, Arthur. *The Schoolmaster.* London: John Murray, 1902.

Benson, Arthur. Introduction. In William Cory, *Ionica.* London: George Allen & Unwin, 1905.

Benson, Arthur. *Cambridge Essays on Education.* Cambridge: Cambridge University Press, 1917

Best, Geoffrey. *Mid-Victorian Britain.* London: Weidenfeld & Nicolson, 1971.

Bettesworth, Walter. *Chats on the Cricket Field.* London: Merritt & Hatcher, 1910.

Blackman, Paul. *Christian Reimers – A Spirited Performer.* Campbelltown, South Australia: Blackman, 2016.

Blyth, William. *In Memoriam: Ernest Henry Blyth.* Norwich: privately published, 1866.

Board of Education. *Syllabus of Physical Exercises for use in Public Elementary Schools*. London: HMSO, 1904.

Board of Education. *Syllabus of Physical Exercises for Schools*. London: HMSO, 1909.

Board of Education. *Syllabus of Physical Training for Schools*. London: HMSO, 1919.

Board of Education. *The Health of the School Child*. London: HMSO, 1923.

Board of Education. *Syllabus of Physical Training for Schools, Supplement for Older Girls*. London: HMSO, 1927.

Board of Education. *Reference Book of Gymnastic Training for Boys*. London: HMSO, 1927.

Board of Education. *Syllabus of Physical Training for Schools*. London: HMSO, 1933.

Board of Education. *The Public Schools and the General Education System*. London: HMSO, 1942.

Bonney, Thomas. *Memories of a Long Life*. Cambridge: Metcalfe, 1921.

Bourke, Joanna. *Dismembering the Male: Men's Bodies, Britain and the Great War*. London: Reaktion Books, 1999.

Bowen, William. *Edward Bowen*. London: Longmans, 1902.

Bradley, Arthur, Arthur Champneys and John Baines. *A History of Marlborough College*. London: John Murray, 1893.

Bradstreet, John. *Repton Sketches*. London: Ernest Benn, 1928.

Brandeth, Gyles, and Sally Henry. *John Haden Badley*. Bournemouth: Bedales Society, 1967.

Briggs, Asa. *Victorian People*. London: Odhams, 1954/70.

Bruce Lockhart, Robert. *Your England*. London: Putnam, 1955.

Bryce, James. *Studies in Contemporary Literature*. London: Macmillan, 1903/20.

Burn, William. *The Age of Equipoise*. London: Allen and Unwin, 1964.

Castle, Edgar. *Moral Education in Christian Times*. London: Allen & Unwin, 1958.

Castle, Edgar. *Ancient Education and Today*. London: Penguin, 1961/69.

Chandler, Timothy. "Emergent Athleticism: Games in Two English Public Schools." *The International Journal of the History of Sport* 5, no. 3 (1988): 312-330.

Chandler, Timothy. "Games at Oxbridge and the Public Schools, 1830-80: The Diffusion of an Innovation." *The International Journal of the History of Sport* 8 no. 2 (1991):171-204.

Chichester, Shane. *E. W. Hornung and His Young Guard*. Wellington: College Press, 1941.

Cholmondeley, Essex. *The Story of Charlotte Mason*. London: Parents' National Educational Union, 1960.

Christie, Octavius. *A History of Clifton College, 1860-1934*. Bristol: Arrowsmith, 1935.

Clarendon, Lord. *Public Schools Commission*. London: HMSO, 1864.

Clias, Per. *An Elementary Course of Gymnastic Exercises*. London: Sherwood, 1825.

Coade, Thorold. *Harrow Lectures on Education.* Cambridge: Cambridge University Press, 1931.

Coade, Thorold. *Manhood in the Making.* London: P. Davis, 1939.

Coade, Thorold. *The Burning Bow.* London: Allen & Unwin, 1966.

Coleridge, Gilbert. *Eton in the 'Seventies.* London: Smith, Elder, 1912.

Coleridge, Samuel. *Aids to Reflection.* London: Taylor and Hessey, 1825/43.

Common Entrance Board. *Curriculum for the Preparatory Schools.* London: HMC & IAPS, 1972.

Compton Mackenzie, Faith. *William Cory.* London: Constable, 1950.

Cook, Edward. *The Life of John Ruskin.* London: George Allen, 1911.

Cornish, Francis. *Extracts from the Letters and Journals of William Cory.* Oxford: privately published, 1897.

Cory, William. *Ionica.* London: George Allen & Unwin, 1905.

Cotterill, Charles. *Suggested Reforms in Public Schools.* Edinburgh: Blackwood, 1889.

Cotton Minchin, James. *Old Harrow Days.* London: Methuen, 1898.

Cox, Gordon, and Robin Stevens. *The Origins and Foundations of Music Education: Cross-Cultural Historical Studies of Music in Compulsory Schooling.* London: Continuum, 2011.

Cross, Robert, and Anthony Woozley. *Plato's Republic.* London: St Martin's Press, 1966.

Crunden, Colin. "The effect of formal and informal influences upon physical education in England between 1870 and 1920." MEd diss., University of Manchester, 1971.

Curry, Graham "Football: a Study in Diffusion." PhD diss., University of Leicester, 2001.

Dancy, John. *The Public Schools in the Future.* London: Faber, 1966.

Darwin, Bernard. *The English Public School.* London: Longman, 1929.

David, Albert. *Life and the Public Schools.* London: A. MacLehose, 1932.

Davies, John, and David Vaughan. *The Republic of Plato.* London: Macmillan, 1852/1902.

Department of Education and Science. *Physical Education from 5 to 16.* London: HMSO, 1989.

Department for Education. *National Curriculum in England: Physical Education Programmes of Study.* London: HMSO, 2013.

Deslandes, Paul. *Oxbridge Men: British Masculinity and the Undergraduate Experience, 1850-1920.* Bloomington: Indiana University Press, 2005.

Dickinson, William. *A Glossary of the Words and Phrases of Cumberland: Supplement.* Whitehaven: Callander and Dixon, 1867.

Dixon, Norman. *On the Psychology of Military Incompetence.* London: Futura, 1976.

Dukes, Clement. *Health at School.* London: Cassell, 1884/94.

Endowed Schools Act. *Report.* London: HMSO, 1869.

Ensor, Robert. *England 1870-1914*, Oxford: Clarendon Press, 1964.

Erdozain, Dominic. *The Problem of Pleasure: Sport, Recreation and the Crisis of Victorian Religion.* Woodbridge: Boydell Press, 2010.

Ewing, Juliana. *Jackanapes.* London: SPCK, 1884/88.

Farmiloe, Arthur. *A Tarnished Silver Spoon.* Harlow: privately published, 2010.

Farrar, Frederic. *Eric, or Little by Little.* London: A. & C. Black, 1858/1915.

Fisher, George. *Annals of Shrewsbury School.* London: Methuen, 1899.

Flavin, Martin. *Kurt Hahn's Schools and Legacy.* Wilmington, Delaware: Middle Atlantic Press, 1996.

Flecker, James. *The Grecians: A Dialogue on Education.* London: J. M. Dent, 1910.

Fletcher, Charles. *Edmond Warre.* London: John Murray, 1922.

Fletcher, Sheila. *Women First: the Female Tradition in English Physical Education 1880-1980.* London: The Athlone Press, 1984.

Foster, Joseph. *Alumni Oxonienses: the Members of the University of Oxford, 1715-1886.* Oxford: James Parker & Co, 1891.

Gibson, John. *Reminiscences of a Railwayman.* London: Frederick Books, 1968.

Giesber, Johannes. *Cecil Reddie and Abbotsholme.* Nijmegen: Centrale Drukkerij N.V., 1970.

Grace, William. *Cricket.* Bristol: J.W. Arrowsmith and Simpkin, Marshall, Hamilton, Kent & Co, 1891.

Graham, John. *Forty Years of Uppingham.* London: Macmillan, 1932.

Greacen, Lavinia. *Chink: A Biography.* London: Macmillan, 1989.

Hall, Donald. *Muscular Christianity: Embodying the Victorian Age.* Cambridge: Cambridge University Press, 2006.

Halstead, Timothy. *A School in Arms: Uppingham and the Great War.* Solihull: Helion, 2017.

Harris, Jo. "The Case for Physical Education becoming a Core Subject in the National Curriculum", *Physical Education Matters* 13, no. 2 (Summer 2018): 9-12.

Harrison, John. *A History of the Working Men's College, 1854-1954.* London: Routledge & Paul, 1954.

Hay, Ian. *Housemaster.* London: Hodder & Stoughton, 1936.

Haygarth, Arthur. *Cricket Scores and Biographies: 1855-1875.* London: Lillywhite, 1878.

Headmasters. *The Head Master Speaks.* London: Kegan Paul, Trench, Trubner & Co, 1936.

Headmasters' Conference. *The Practice of Health.* Winchester: Warren and Sons, 1924.

Hilton, James. *Good-bye Mr Chips.* London: Hodder & Stoughton, 1934.

Hodgson, Geraldine. *The Life of James Elroy Flecker.* Oxford: Blackwell, 1925.

Honey, John. *Tom Brown's Universe.* London: Millington, 1977.

Hornung, Ernest. *Raffles.* London: Hamish Hamilton, 1889.

Hornung, Ernest. *Fathers of Men.* London: Smith, Elder & Co, 1912/19.

Horrocks, Brian. *A Full Life.* London: Collins, 1960.

Howard, John. *Gymnastic Exercises.* London: Longman, Green, Longman and Roberts, 1860.

Howson, Edmund, and George Warner. *Harrow School.* London: Arnold, 1898.

Hoyland, Geoffrey. *The Man Who Made a School.* London: S.C.M. Press, 1946.

Hughes, Thomas. *Tom Brown's Schooldays.* London: Macmillan, 1857/1919.

Hughes, Thomas. *Tom Brown at Oxford.* London: Macmillan, 1862/80.

Hughes, Thomas. *Memoir of Daniel Macmillan.* London: Macmillan, 1882.

Hunter, Andrew. *Cheltenham College Register, 1841-1889.* London: George Bell, 1890.

Jacks, Lawrence. *The Education of the Whole Man.* London: University of London Press, 1931.

Jacks, Lawrence. *Education Through Recreation.* London: University of London Press, 1932.

Jacks, Maurice. *Education as a Social Factor.* London: Kegan Paul, Trench, Trubner, 1937.

Jacks, Maurice. *Total Education.* London: Kegan Paul, Trench, Trubner, 1946.

Jacks, Maurice. *Modern Trends in Education.* London: Andrew Melrose, 1950.

Jessel, Penelope. *Owen of Uppingham.* London: A. R. Mowbray, 1965.

Jessop, Michael. *Days Far Away: Memories of Charles Paget Wade.* Tewkesbury: National Trust, 1996.

Jones, Peter. *The Christian Socialist Revival, 1877-1914.* Princeton: Princeton University Press, 1968.

Kane, John. *Physical Education in Secondary Schools.* London: Macmillan, 1974

Kendall, Guy. *A Headmaster Remembers.* London: Victor Gollancz, 1933.

Kendall, Guy. *A Headmaster Reflects.* Edinburgh: William Hodge & Co, 1937.

Kendall, Guy. *Charles Kingsley and His Ideas.* London: Hutchinson, 1947.

Kingsley, Charles. *Health and Education.* London: W. Isbister, 1874.

Kingsley, Charles. *True Words for Brave Men.* London: Macmillan, 1878.

Kingsley, Fanny. *Life and Letters of Charles Kingsley.* London: Macmillan, 1877.

Kirk, David. *Physical Education Futures*. London: Routledge, 2011.

Kirk, David, Doune Macdonald and Mary O'Sullivan. *The Handbook of Physical Education.* Thousand Oaks, CA: Sage, 2013.

Kitson Clark, George. *The Making of Victorian England.* London: Methuen, 1962.

Knaggs, George. "A Study of the Historical Development of Physical Education in English Schools to 1945." DEd diss., University of Houston, 1957.

Kühn, Dieter, *Clara Schumann, Klavier: Ein Lebensbuch.* Düsseldorf: Fischer, 1996.

Laborde, Edward. *Education Today.* Cambridge: Cambridge University Press, 1935.

Laborde, Edward. *Problems in Modern Education.* Cambridge: Cambridge University Press, 1939.

Leonard, Fred, and George Affleck. *A Guide to the History of Physical Education.* Philadelphia: Lea and Febiger, 1947.

Livingstone, Richard. *Plato and Modern Education.* Cambridge: Cambridge University Press, 1944.

Lubbock, Percy. *Shades of Eton.* London: Jonathan Cape, 1929.

Lunn, Arnold. *The Harrovians.* London: Methuen, 1913.

Lyttelton, Edward. *Memories and Hopes.* London: Murray, 1925.

Mack, Edward. *Public Schools and British Opinion, 1780-1860.* London: Methuen, 1938.

Mack, Edward. *Public Schools and British Opinion since 1860.* New York: Columbia University Press, 1941.

Mack, Edward, and Harry Armytage. *Thomas Hughes.* London: Benn, 1952.

Mackenzie, Robert. *Almond of Loretto.* London: Archibald Constable & Co, 1905.

MacLaren, Archibald. *Training in Theory and Practice.* London: Macmillan, 1866.

MacLaren, Archibald. *A System of Physical Education.* Oxford: Clarendon Press, 1869.

MacLaren, Wallace. *A System of Physical Education.* Oxford: Oxford University Press, 1895.

Maitland, Frederic. *The Life and Letters of Leslie Stephen.* London: Duckworth, 1906.

Mallea, John. "The Boys' Endowed Grammar Schools in Victorian England: The Educational Use of Sport." PhD diss., Columbia University, 1971.

Mangan, James. "Athleticism: A Case Study of the Evolution of an Educational Ideology." In *The Victorian Public School*, edited by Brian Simon and Ian Bradley, 147-167. Dublin: McGill, 1975.

Mangan, James. "Athleticism: A Comparative Study of the Emergence and Consolidation of an Education Ideology." PhD diss., University of Glasgow, 1976.

Mangan, James. *Athleticism in the Victorian and Edwardian Public School.* Cambridge: Cambridge University Press, 1981.

Mangan, James. *The Games Ethic and Imperialism.* London: Viking, 1985.

Mangan, James. *"Manufactured" Masculinity: Making Imperial Manliness, Morality and Militarism.* Abingdon: Routledge, 2012.

Margoliouth, Herschel. *Wordsworth and Coleridge, 1795-1834.* London: Oxford University Press, 1953.

Marples, Morris. *A History of Football.* London: Secker & Warburg, 1954.

Martin, Maureen. "'Boys who will be Men': Desire in 'Tom Brown's Schooldays'." *Victorian Literature and Culture* 30, no. 2 (2002): 483-502.

Marylebone Cricket Club. *Cricket Scores and Biographies from 1855-1875.* London: Lillywhite, 1877.

Mason, Charlotte. *Home Education.* Bradford: Kegan Paul, Trench & Co, 1886.

Matthews, Bryan. *By God's Grace: A History of Uppingham School.* Maidstone: Whitehall Press, 1984.

Maurice, Frederick. *The Life of Frederick Denison Maurice.* London: Macmillan, 1884.

Maxwell Lyte, Henry. *A History of Eton College.* London: Macmillan, 1899.

May, Jonathan. *Madame Bergman-Österberg.* London: Harrap, 1969.

McCulloch, Gary. *Philosophers and Kings: Education for Leadership in Modern England.* Cambridge: Cambridge University Press, 1991.

McIntosh, Peter. *Physical Education in England since 1800.* London: Bell, 1952/68.

McIntosh, Peter. *Landmarks in the History of Physical Education.* London: Routledge, 1957/65/2013.

McIntosh, Peter. *'My Favourite Subject'.* London: ILEA, 1988.

McNair, David. "The Development of Physical Education in Scotland before 1914." MEd diss., University of Manchester, 1961.

Murray, Gerald, and Thomas Hunter. *Physical Education and Health.* London: Heinemann, 1966.

Myers, Frederic. *Wordsworth.* New York: Harper & brothers, 1880/1908.

Nettleship, Lewis. *The Theory of Education in Plato's Republic.* Oxford: Clarendon Press, 1935/51.

Nevinson, Christopher. *Paint and Prejudice.* London: Methuen, 1937.

Newsome, David. *A History of Wellington College.* London: John Murray, 1959.

Newsome, David. *Godliness and Good Learning.* London: John Murray, 1961.

Nicolson, Harold. *Some People.* London: Constable, 1927.

Nicolson, Harold. *Good Behaviour.* London: Constable, 1955.

Norwood, Cyril. *The English Tradition of Education.* London: John Murray, 1929.

Norwood, Cyril, and Arthur Hope. *Higher Education of Boys in England.* London: John Murray, 1909.

Oldham, Basil. *History of Shrewsbury School.* Oxford: Blackwell, 1952.

Pardon, Sydney. *John Wisden's Cricketers' Almanac.* London: Wisden, 1901 & 1924.

Parker, Eric. *Eton in the 'Eighties.* London: Smith, Elder, 1914.

Parker, Eric. *Playing Fields.* London: Philip Allan & Co, 1922.

Parkin, George. *Life and Letters of Edward Thring.* London: Macmillan, 1898.

Patmore, Derek. *Private History.* London: Jonathan Cape, 1960.

Patterson, William. *Sixty Years of Uppingham Cricket.* London: Longmans, 1909.

PEA. *Nine Pioneers in Physical Education.* London: Physical Education Association, 1964.

Pelmear, Kenneth. *Rugby Football: an Anthology.* London: George Allen and Unwin, 1958.

Percival, Alicia. *The Origins of the Headmasters' Conference.* London: John Murray, 1969.

Percival, Alicia. *Very Superior Men.* London: Charles Knight, 1973.

Phillips, Murray, and Alexander Roper. "History of Physical Education." In *The Handbook of Physical Education*, edited by David Kirk, Doune Macdonald and Mary O'Sullivan, 123-140. Thousand Oaks, CA: Sage, 2013.

Pitcairn, Robert. *Uppingham School.* London: Charles Drake, 1870.

Plowright, John. *Repton to the End.* London: Third Millennium, 2007.

PNEU. *In Memoriam Charlotte M. Mason.* Keighley: PNEU, 1928.

Polley, Martin. *The History of Sport in Britain, 1880-1914.* London: Routledge, 2003.

Ponsonby, Arthur. *The Decline of the Aristocracy.* London: T. F. Unwin, 1912.

Purkis, John. *A Preface to Wordsworth.* London: Longman, 1970.

Rae, John. *Public School Revolution.* London: Faber, 1981.

Raven, Charles. *Christian Socialism, 1848-1854.* London: Macmillan, 1920.

Raven, Charles. *A Wanderer's Way.* London: Martin Hopkinson, 1928.

Rawnsley, Eleanor. *Canon Rawnsley.* Glasgow: Maclehose, Jackson, 1923.

Rawnsley, Hardwicke. *Edward Thring: Teacher and Poet.* London: T. F. Unwin, 1889.

Rawnsley, Hardwicke. *Harvey Goodwin.* London: Macmillan, 1896.

Rawnsley, Willingham. *Early Days at Uppingham under Edward Thring.* London: Macmillan, 1904.

Rawnsley, Willingham. *Edward Thring: Maker of Uppingham School.* London: Kegan Paul, Trench, Trubner & Co, 1926.

Reich, Nancy. *Clara Schumann: The Artist and the Woman.* Ithaca: Cornell University Press, 2001.

Richardson, Nigel. *Typhoid in Uppingham: Analysis of a Victorian Town and School in Crisis.* London: Routledge, 2008.

Richardson, Nigel. *Thring of Uppingham: Victorian Educator.* Buckingham: University of Buckingham Press, 2014.

Rigby, Cormac. "The Life and Influence of Edward Thring." DPhil diss., University of Oxford, 1968.

Rigby, Cormac. *Edward Thring: The Teachers' Teacher.* Truro: Sunnyrest Books, 2017.

Roe, William. *Public Schools Cricket 1901-1950.* London: Max Parrish, 1951.

Rohrs, Hermann. *Kurt Hahn.* London: Routledge and Kegan Paul, 1970.

Roper, Reginald. *Physical Education in Relation to School Life.* London: George Allen and Unwin, 1915.

Ruskin, John. *A Joy Forever.* London: George Allen, 1857/1905.

Ruskin, John. *Time and Tide.* London: George Allen, 1867/1905.

Schoolmasters. *The Public Schools from Within.* London: Leopold, 1906.

Shearman, Montague. *Athletics and Football: Badminton Library.* London: Longmans Green and Co, 1889.

Sherwood, John. *No Golden Journey.* London: Heinemann, 1973.

Sherwood, Marion. *Tennyson and the Fabrication of Englishness.* Basingstoke: Palgrave Macmillan, 2013.

Simon, Brian, and Ian Bradley. *The Victorian Public School.* Dublin: Gill and Macmillan, 1975.

Simpson, James. *Sane Schooling.* London: Faber & Faber, 1936.

Simpson, James. *Schoolmaster's Harvest.* London: Faber & Faber, 1954.

Sinclair, Archibald, and William Henry. *Swimming: Badminton Library.* London: Longmans Green and Co, 1903.

Skrine, John. *Uppingham-by-the-Sea.* London: Macmillan, 1878.

Skrine, John. *A Memory of Edward Thring.* London: Macmillan, 1890.

Smart, Sue. *When Heroes Die.* Derby: Bredon Book Publishing Co. Ltd, 2001.

Smith, David. "*A Study of the Provision of Physical Education in the Schools of the Nineteenth and Twentieth Centuries: An Examination of Changing Views.*" MPhil diss.; University of East Anglia, 1971.

Smith, David. *Stretching Their Bodies.* Newton Abbot: David & Charles, 1974.

Snell, Reginald (L. B. Pekin, pseud.) *Public Schools: their Failure and their Reform.* London: Hogarth, 1932.

Spalding, Muriel, and Laura Collett. *The Swedish Drill Teacher.* London: J. Curwen and Sons, 1910.

Spencer, Herbert. *Education: Intellectual, Moral and Physical.* London: Williams & Norgate, 1861/91.

Stanley, Arthur. *The Life and Correspondence of Thomas Arnold.* London: Murray, 1844/52.

Stephen, Leslie. *Sketches from Cambridge.* London: Smith Elder, 1863.

Stephenson, Roy. *H. H. Stephenson: A Cricketing Journey.* Uppingham: Uppingham Local History Study Group, 2009.

Stewart, William. *The Educational Innovators.* London: Macmillan, 1968.

Stewart, William. *Progressives and Radicals in English Education 1750-1970.* London: Macmillan, 1972.

Sutcliffe, David. *Kurt Hahn and the United World Colleges.* Cambridge: Gordonstoun Schools, 2013.

Taylor, Alfred. *Platonism and Its Influence.* London: Harrap, 1925.

Thomas, Bernard. *Repton, 1557-1957.* London: Batsford, 1957.

Thring, Charles. *The Winter Game: Rules of Football.* Uppingham: Hawthorn, 1862.

Thring, Edward. *School Songs.* Cambridge: Macmillan, 1855 & 1858.

Thring, Edward. *Sermons Delivered at Uppingham School.* Cambridge: Macmillan, 1858.

Thring, Edward. *Education and School.* London: Macmillan, 1864 & 1867.

Thring, Edward. *Borth Lyrics.* Uppingham: Hawthorn, 1881.

Thring, Edward. *Songs of Uppingham School.* London: E. Stanford, 1881.

Thring, Edward. *Theory and Practice of Teaching.* Cambridge: Cambridge University Press, 1883 & 1885.

Thring, Edward. *Sermons Preached at Uppingham School.* London: Deighton, Bell and Co, 1886.

Thring, Edward. *Addresses.* London: T. Fisher Unwin, 1887.

Thring, Edward. *Poems and Translations.* London: T. Fisher Unwin, 1887.

Todd, Larry. *Mendelssohn: A Life in Music.* Oxford: Oxford University Press, 2005.

Tosh, John. *A Man's Place: Masculinity and the Middle-class Home in Victorian England.* New Haven: Yale University Press, 1999.

Tosh, John. *Manliness and Masculinities in Nineteenth-century Britain: Essays on Gender, Family and Empire.* Harlow: Pearson Longman, 2005.

Tozer, Malcolm. *Physical Education at Thring's Uppingham.* Uppingham: Uppingham School, 1976.

Tozer, Malcolm. "In the Beginning." In *Physical Education and Sport in Independent Schools*, edited by Malcolm Tozer, 31-37. Woodbridge: John Catt, 2012.

Tozer, Malcolm. *Physical Education and Sport in Independent Schools.* Woodbridge: John Catt, 2012.

Tozer, Malcolm. "'One of the worst statistics in British sport, and wholly unacceptable': The contribution of privately-educated members of Team GB to the summer Olympic Games, 2000-2012." *The International Journal of the History of Sport* 30, no. 12 (August 2013): 1436-1454.

Tozer, Malcolm. *The Ideal of Manliness: the Legacy of Thring's Uppingham.* Truro: Sunnyrest Books, 2015.

Tozer, Malcolm. "Going the extra mile: The contribution of privately educated members of Team GB to the summer Olympic Games of 2016." In *Physical Education and Sport in Independent Schools*, edited by Malcolm Tozer, 318-338. Woodbridge: John Catt, 2016.

Tozer, Malcolm. *Education in Manliness: the Legacy of Thring's Uppingham.* London: Routledge, 2018.

Tozer, Malcolm. "Thring's 'favourite wish': Uppingham High School for Girls, 1888-1893". *Rutland Record* 38, (2018): 363-372.

Tozer, Malcolm. "From Prussia with love: music at Uppingham School, 1853-1908." *Journal of Historical Research in Music Education*, forthcoming.

Tristram, Henry. *Loretto School.* London: T. Fisher Unwin, 1911.

Turner, David. *The Old Boys: The Decline and Rise of the Public School.* New Haven: Yale University Press, 2015.

Turner, George. *Unorthodox Reminiscences.* London: Murray, 1931.

Tyerman, Christopher. *A History of Harrow School.* Oxford: Oxford University Press, 2000.

van Oord, Lodewijk. "Kurt Hahn's Moral Equivalent of War." *Oxford Review of Education* 36, no. 2 (June 2010): 253-265.

van Reyk, William. "Christian Ideals of Manliness during the Period of the Evangelical Revival, c.1730-c.1840." DPhil diss., University of Oxford, 2007.

Vargas, Dale, and Peter Knowles, *A History of Eton Fives.* London: Quiller Press, 2012.

various. *Great Public Schools.* London: Edward Arnold, 1893.

Ward, Bernard. *Reddie of Abbotsholme.* London: Allen & Unwin, 1934.

Warner, Pelham. *Cricket: Badminton Library.* London: Longmans, Green and Co, 1920.

Webb, Ida. "The history of Chelsea College of Physical Education with special reference to curriculum development, 1898-1973." MEd diss., University of Leicester, 1977.

Webb, Ida. *The Challenge of Change in Physical Education.* London: Routledge, 1999.

Willey, Basil. *The Eighteenth Century Background.* London: Chatto & Windus, 1940.

Willey, Basil. *Nineteenth Century Studies.* London: Chatto & Windus, 1949.

Willey, Basil. *The English Moralists.* Cambridge: Cambridge University Press, 1964.

Worsley, Thomas. *Barbarians and Philistines.* London: Robert Hale, 1940.

Worsley, Thomas. *Flannelled Fool.* London: Alan Ross, 1967.

Wymer, Norman. *Dr Arnold of Rugby.* London: Robert Hale, 1953.

Yonge, Charlotte. *Life of Patteson.* London: Macmillan,1873.

Young, George. *Victorian England: A Portrait of an Age.* London: Oxford University Press, 1936/69.

Young, Percy. *A History of British Football.* London: Methuen, 1968.

INDEX